Braided Relations, Entwined Lives

CYNTHIA M. KENNEDY

Braided Relations, Entwined Lives

The Women of Charleston's Urban Slave Society

INDIANA UNIVERSITY PRESS
Bloomington and Indianapolis

Publication of this book is made possible in part with the assistance of a Challenge Grant from the National Endowment for the Humanities, a federal agency that supports research, education, and public programming in the humanities.

This book is a publication of

Indiana University Press
601 North Morton Street
Bloomington, IN 47404-3797 USA

http://iupress.indiana.edu

Telephone orders   800-842-6796
Fax orders   812-855-7931
Orders by e-mail   iuporder@indiana.edu

The paper used in this publication meets the minimum requirements of American National Standard for Information Sciences—Permanence of Paper for Printed Library Materials, ANSI Z39.48-1984.

Manufactured in the United States of America

Library of Congress Cataloging-in-Publication Data

Kennedy, Cynthia M.
   Braided relations, entwined lives: the women of Charleston's urban slave society / Cynthia M. Kennedy.
      p. cm.
   Includes bibliographical references and index.
   ISBN 0-253-34615-0 (cloth : alk. paper)
   1. Women—South Carolina—Charleston—History. 2. Women—South Carolina—Charleston—Social conditions. 3. African American women—South Carolina—Charleston—Social conditions. 4. Charleston (S. C.)—Race relations—History. I. Title.
   HQ1439.C42K46 2005
   305.4′09757′915—dc22
                                                                    2005011535

1 2 3 4 5   10 09 08 07 06 05

For Ellie, Jerry, and Deborah Kennedy

If you're going to hold someone down you're going to have to hold onto the other end of the chain. You are confined by your own system of repression.

Toni Morrison, in Brian Lanker, *I Dream a World* (1989)

It is not really difference the oppressor fears so much as similarity.

Cherríe Moraga, "La Guëra," in Cherríe Moraga and Gloria Anzaldúa, eds., *This Bridge Called My Back* (1983)

Contents

Acknowledgments

As in most projects of this sort, many people and institutions provided assistance and I am happy for this opportunity to offer special thanks. The University of Maryland at College Park, the Albert J. Beveridge Fund of the American Historical Association, the Institute for Southern Studies at the University of South Carolina, and Clarion University of Pennsylvania all contributed to research funding.

Archivists, historians, and librarians offered insights and help: Stephen Hoffius, Peter Wilkerson, and their coworkers at the South Carolina Historical Society; Charles H. Lesser and others at the South Carolina Department of Archives and History; Henry Fulmer, Laura Costello, and their colleagues at the South Caroliniana Library; Oliver Smalls in Special Collections at the College of Charleston; Susan L. King at the Charleston City Archives; Robert Leach at the Nathaniel Russell House; Sharon Bennett at the Charleston Museum; Elizabeth Young Newsom at the Waring Historical Library; and the fine archivists and librarians at the Avery Research Center for African American History and Culture, Charleston County Library, Charleston Library Society, Duke University Special Collections, the Southern Historical Collection, the National Archives, and the Library of Congress.

Friends and colleagues aided the project in various ways. Edward (Ted) Pearson and Michael Tadman, fellow researchers on the road, generously shared ideas from their own works in progress. While working in Columbia, Constance and Carl Schulz opened their home to me, providing a welcome respite from dormitory lodgings. Sistie and Franklin Wells and Deb and Rob McNeill likewise temporarily folded me into their families on two different research trips, thereby confirming that southern hospitality is not a myth.

Several people contributed to this work by reading all or part of the manuscript. Ira Berlin read many early drafts and furnished a combination of encouragement and honest criticism. For that, and for the insights and example of his scholarship, I will always be grateful. Gay Gullickson offered congenial support and good advice. E. Susan Barber and Marie Jenkins Schwartz provided thoughtful criticism on parts of the work at early stages in addition to camaraderie on research trips and stimulating discussion within the context of their own work. Steven L. Piott took time off from his own book to read the manuscript in its entirety. His observations and suggestions precipitated invaluable constructive changes. An anonymous reader for the Indiana University Press commented and encouraged in equal measure and that interest in the project refueled my own. I also greatly appreciate the astute work of copy editor Karen Kodner.

For conference collaborations, comments on working papers, and productive suggestions, I would also like to recognize E. Susan Barber, Peter Bardaglio, Catherine Clinton, Lois E. Horton, James O. Horton, Charles Ritter, Leslie Rowland, Frank Towers, and LeeAnn Whites.

I am grateful for permission to publish material that appeared in different form as "'Nocturnal Adventures in Mulatto Alley': Sex in Charleston, South Carolina," in *Searching for Their Places: Women in the South across Four Centuries,* ed. Thomas H. Appleton, Jr. and Angela Boswell (University of Missouri Press, 2003), and "'Moral Marriage': A Mixed-Race Relationship in Nineteenth-Century Charleston, South Carolina," in the July 1996 issue of the *South Carolina Historical Magazine.*

Friends and family beyond academia have also encouraged and aided me in this enterprise. Linda E. Mosakowski read beginning drafts of most chapters, which are the better for her keen legal mind. Deborah Kennedy read the entire manuscript early on and her common sense and aptitude in asking just the right questions provided enormous help. Her love and support, as well as that of our parents, Ellie and Jerry Kennedy, and her daughter, Erin Elizabeth Scott, remain sublime gifts.

Braided Relations, Entwined Lives

Introduction

Early in 1820, Charleston, South Carolina, municipal authorities captured Lavinia and John Fisher, leaders of the infamous "Six Mile House Gang." Two men claimed that "lovely Lavinia" lured travelers into the Six Mile House—an inn situated six miles outside the city—poisoned their food, and pushed their bodies into a cellar. No mere myrmidon, Lavinia allegedly plotted and orchestrated a series of grizzly murders by capitalizing on her physical beauty. City guardsmen found several human skeletons on the grounds of the Six Mile House, giving credence to these sensational accusations. The court quickly convicted Lavinia and her husband and sentenced them to hang. In response, several "amiable ladies" of the master class rallied behind Lavinia. They publicly declared "distasteful" the very thought of a white woman being hung. Such an act, they proclaimed, "would reflect badly on all women." The ladies petitioned Governor John Geddes for a pardon, incorporating into their plea notions of the ideal woman and arguing the necessity of protecting this image and assuring proper treatment of white women. The images they elaborated were, of course, wholly antithetical to Lavinia Fisher's conduct. This genteel cabal failed to save Lavinia's life. In February during the city's high social season, a huge crowd assembled to watch her and John swing from the gallows. Unrepentant and unladylike to the bitter end, Lavinia shouted to them, "if you have a message you want to send to hell, give it to me—I'll carry it!"[1]

Despite their inability to save Lavinia Fisher, these Charleston ladies revealed the complicity of southern white women in constructing both gender and race. They explicitly demarcated women whom they judged to be above public punishment (white women) and implicitly identified those who were not so privileged (women of color). Lavinia Fisher threatened these women of the master class because she did not act white and because she was white but no lady. They responded to this quandary by publicly defending a convicted murderess and, more precisely, by reiterating and defending the place of white women in slave society. In the process, members of this "amiable" cabal of 1820 engaged in the ongoing work of patrolling social boundaries and weaving the power relations of urban slave society.

This study explores women's lives in one of the antebellum South's most fascinating cities. In doing so, it also elaborates the roles of women and gender, as well as race, condition (slave or free), and class, in conveying and replicating power in slave society. It builds on the work of scholars who have reassessed the complexity of these overlaid and interrelated social categories—gender, race, color, condition, and class—in creating and upholding racial slavery in the American South. It extends their analyses of what it meant to be a woman in a world where these historically specific social classifications determined destiny and where people of color and white people mingled frequently. In particular, it builds on Kathleen Brown's study of the uses of "patriarchal forms" in forging early American culture and extends Brown's analysis of the ways people used gender to construct racial categories and legitimate authority. It investigates these processes and their effects on women of African and European descent in the urban South during the American Revolution and continuing until the decade before the American Civil War. It reveals southern women as complicit in producing and reproducing the pyramid of power relations in slave society.[2]

This study of the women of Charleston, South Carolina, also reveals a simple but formative reality of southern slave society: women knew who they were precisely because they mingled daily in explosive intimacy and observed constantly who they were not. Southerners of all social groups entwined women inextricably (the subordination of all women was imperative to slave society) yet separated them relentlessly based upon race, color, condition, and wealth. Their relationships were like a braid, a metaphor that informs this work and conveys the intricacies of human relationships and the processes and functions of identity formation. The metaphor is not intended to represent a united community of women or to diminish the continual power struggles among women. Disparate types of Charleston women—wealthy white mistresses, slaves, laboring free women of color, white women of the laboring classes, women of the brown elite—encountered different realities and possibilities. Their lives were driven or constrained by different practices and aspirations. These distinctions simultaneously defined, separated, and connected women. Just as important, the contingent definitions of "woman" were, in turn, crucial to the maintenance of power by wealthy white people—the master class—who remained a numerical minority in Charleston during the period covered.

There are several reasons for focusing on the women of an urban society rather than the more typical rural South. While it is true that the southern population was more homogenous than the northern population, southern cities were home to Germans, Scots, Irish, French, and Huguenots, as well as Caribbean émigrés of all colors and—while the international slave trade flourished—Africans as well as African Americans. Population diversity in the urban milieu permits greater elaboration of the mercurial alliances and enmities among different groups of women and between women and men. These dynamic, shifting relations of power were constructed, contested, and reconstructed in mundane social exchanges as well as during times of personal and citywide upheaval. People encode meaning and power in language, and the city affords ample opportunity to eavesdrop. I have listened carefully to what Charleston women and men said in their personal correspondence, journals, reminiscences, novels, wills, meeting minutes, laws, legal testimony, court reports, medical theses, and newspapers. This analysis of words and deeds in private and public arenas discloses women's centrality to the task of building and patrolling social boundaries so crucial to urban slave society.

Work and labor relations also differ in cities. Studying women in a southern city provides greater prospects of analyzing the skilled and unskilled work of women, slave and free, black, brown, and white. The urban environment also serves as a window on slave hiring, one of the best examples of the malleability of slavery as a labor system and of the prevalence of women in the city's economic transactions. This contested yet common practice afforded constraints and opportunities to all parties involved: those hiring out their slaves, those hiring the labor, and the laborers themselves, some of whom negotiated their own terms of service. White women of the laboring classes also found greater opportunities in the cities. Their experiences add complexity to our understanding of the American South and the labor relations of slavery. The work of enslaved and free market women, as well as sole traders of all colors, reveals the vital roles women played in the city economy. Their economic independence, however, was contested. White sole traders, in particular, violated southern domestic ideology mandating their economic dependence. Consequently, the courts increasingly constrained their privileges. Statute and case law bolstered not only the power of owners over slaves, white over color, and the better sorts of people over the lower sorts but also of men over women. Judges distinguished between worthy and unworthy women they wielded gender as a judicial tool in upholding patriarchal authority—and in this way courts protected a white man's dominion over his household, an institution that represented slave society in miniature.[3]

Many qualifications make Charleston, South Carolina, an excellent place to study women of the urban South. In 1776 Charleston, with approximately 12,000 residents, ranked second only (in mainland North America) to New York in population. The city had established itself as a vital commercial center of the British Empire, with three to four hundred commercial trading vessels clearing Charleston's harbor annually, carrying cargo to England, Holland, the Mediterranean, Portugal, the West Indies, and the northern colonies. In the eighteenth and early nineteenth centuries it was the port of entry for tens of thousands of enslaved Africans as well as thousands of free white immigrants. Hordes of transient sailors, businessmen, and travelers passed in and out of the city. A surveyor general for the southern colonies described Charleston in 1773 as "the most imminent and by far the richest city in the southern district of North America." Mainland North America's wealthiest residents called Charleston home on the eve of the American Revolution. In sharp contrast, nearly two-thirds of those living in the city were white people or slaves without property of their own. Enslaved people of African descent consistently comprised at least half of the city's population from the Revolution until the final decade before the Civil War.[4]

Another reality commends Charleston as a fitting place for this analysis. Its environs became a locus of bloody and tenacious guerilla warfare during the Revolution. In one of the greatest victories of the war, the British occupied the city for two-and-a-half years beginning in May 1780. Consequently, Charleston is a laboratory in which to examine how women encountered the chaos and violence of war. They shared the experiences of terror, privation, grief, loss, and a determination to survive the turmoil. While adversity potentially nourished female solidarity, unbridgeable chasms of race, condition, wealth, and political allegiance eroded that unity and precluded the formation of any collective women's identity or women's culture forged in the fires of the Revolution. Precisely because this study opens during the American Revolution, it enters the ongoing debate on the extent to which white women participated in forging a new nation, the nature of that involvement, and the effect of the war on the status of women. As such it joins several historians who have revealed women as agents in the creation of a new nation rather than as passive participants whose lives were little changed by the war.[5]

The postwar period—the first reconstruction in American history—underscores the interconnectedness of white freedom and hegemony and black bondage and subjugation. Women figure prominently in this saga of resisting, rebuilding, and accommodating. Charleston ladies and gentlemen wielded antithetical images of lady and wench—stereotypes reified during the war—to reconfigure and revitalize slavery and patriarchy. After American patriots ousted the British from Charleston in December 1782, the lives of African Americans and European Americans quite literally intertwined in mutual definition when patriots of the master class rebuilt their lives, in part, by restraining the lives of people of color. Their experiences provide a southern perspective, complicated by racial slavery, on women's transition from the colonial period to the nineteenth century.

In addition, wealthy white residents fashioned themselves exemplars of southern society and gentility. The city remained South Carolina's social, economic, and political center even after Columbia supplanted Charleston as the state capital in 1786. Its leadership role in the nullification crisis of the early 1830s and in the secession movement of the 1850s solidified Charleston's position as the standard bearer for the southern way of life. Social activities loomed as essential to this southern order, and members of the master class worked exceedingly hard at playing. The city gained a reputation for seasonal debauchery. But these amusements were more than mere frolic. Leisure for the rich—enabled by slave labor—provided forums for exhibiting wealth, status, and power. A slave woman's hard work and the recreation of her mistress were two sides of the same coin. Master-class mothers and daughters took center stage in ritualized social activities, as did women of the brown elite at their separate but similar affairs. Every ball and picnic hosted by women in these distinct social groups served to reenact and reinforce the social boundaries of slave society.

This is a study of women in the urban South, and Charleston acquits itself well on this count also. At the time of the first census in 1790, white women and women of color presided over 18 percent of Charleston's 1,900 households, and together they owned more than 1,300 slaves. Over the next seventy years, slave women, free women of color, and white women consistently made up well over half the inhabitants of the city, which grew from 16,000 in 1790 to nearly 43,000 people at mid-century (see table 1). Slave women outnumbered every other group, female and male, and constituted from 25 to 28 percent of all city residents (see table 2). Because of sheer numbers and women's prominence in the

Table 1. City Population by Condition, Race, and Sex.

City Population by Condition, Race, and Sex, 1790–1810

	1790	1800	1810
Slaves	7,684	9,819	11,671
As a % of city population	47	49	47
FPOC*	586	1,024	1,472
As a % of city population	4	5	6
White females	3,718	4,599	5,705
As a % of city population	23	23	23
White males	4,371	5,031	5,863
As a % of city population	27	25	24
Total city population	16,359	20,473	24,711

Percentage increases in population 1790–1810		Avg. percentage of the total city population 1790–1810	
Slaves	52%	Slaves	48%
FPOC*	151%	FPOC*	5%
White females	53%	Slaves & FPOC*	52%
White males	34%	White people	48%
All whites	43%		

Continued on the next page

city's social and economic life, Charleston is an ideal location for an investigation of women's lives and roles and the work of gender in perpetuating racial slavery.[6]

A major goal of this study is to build on the work of scholars who, beginning in the decade after 1980, rejected the notion of a singular "slave experience" and argued that sex, gender, and class, as well as race, fundamentally determined the lives of both slaves and mistresses. Continuing into the next two decades, these analyses have focused on topics as diverse as interracial sexual relations, political culture, slave childhood, and slave healers. They have roamed from the slave quarters and the big house to the state house. Scholars of the American South and the Caribbean have examined plantation slaves and mistresses, women of the yeomen class, and urban slave women. These works share the fundamental premise that a true understanding of slavery as both a labor system and a social structure requires thorough examination of women's roles and their status. I

Table 1. *Continued*
City Population by Condition, Race, and Sex, 1820–1860

	1820	1830	1840	1850	1860
Slave women	6,957	8,577	8,339	10,901	7,346
As a % of city population	27	28	29	25	18
Slave men	5,695	6,777	6,334	8,631	6,563
As a % of city population	23	22	22	20	16
FWOC*	852	1,293	975	2,086	1,990
As a % of city population	3	4	3	5	5
FMOC*	623	814	583	1,355	1,247
As a % of city population	2.5	3	2	3	3
White women	5,330	6,502	6,203	9,774	11,662
As a % of city population	21	21	21	23	29
White men	5,899	6,326	6,827	10,238	11,712
As a % of city population	23	21	23	24	29
Total city population	25,356	30,289	29,261	42,985	40,522

*Abbreviations: FPOC = free people of color; FWOC = free women of color; FMOC = free men of color.

Note: Slave women, FWOC, and white women averaged 53% of the total city population, 1820–1860. Slave women averaged over 55% of all city slaves, just over 48% of all city women, and over 25% of the total city population, 1820–1860. FWOC averaged nearly 61% of all free people of color, 1820–1860. White women averaged over 49% of all white people, 1820–1860.

Source: U.S. Bureau of the Census, First through Eighth Censuses (Washington, D.C.: 1790, 1801, 1811, 1821, 1832, 1841, 1853, 1864).

Table 2. Slave Women as a Percentage of Charleston's Population.

	City Population	Slave Population	Slave Women	Percentage of City	Percentage of Slaves
1820	25,356	12,652	6,957	27	55
1830	30,289	15,354	8,577	28	56
1840	29,261	14,673	8,339	29	57
1850	42,985	19,532	10,901	25	56
1860	40,522	13,909	7,346	18	53

Source: U.S. Bureau of the Census, Fourth through Eighth Censuses (Washington, D.C.: 1821, 1832, 1841, 1854, 1864).

build on this proposition by analyzing not one or two types of women, but all groups—slaves, free women of African descent, white women of the laboring classes, and women of the master class—in juxtaposition. Differences both defined women and reinforced social chasms between them. Notwithstanding urban propinquity, the intimacy of many women's connections, and the ability of race and racism to forge potent links, there were few easy alliances. Brawling Irish and Jewish women of the laboring classes led vastly different lives than did genteel inhabitants of the great mansions overlooking Charleston Harbor. Likewise, the most affluent women among the free brown elite identified more closely with the city's white ladies than with many laboring free black women. Men and women of all groups daily wove a world of patriarchy and paternalism. They did so, in part, by contrasting wenches, women, and ladies. The city's people deployed and altered shifting notions of "woman" in common discourse and routine activities to empower men over women or one group of women over different groups of women. Slavery magnified gender as a social category, slave owners used gender to rationalize and fortify slavery, and the social project of creating gender was fueled with entwined, interdependent images of women. It is impossible fully to comprehend slavery without understanding this dialectic and the enmeshed lives, statuses, and roles of the women in slave society.[7]

A specific understanding of race, class, and gender infuses this work. These classifications are linked and overlaid social categories that should not be pitted against each other for "analytical supremacy." All three are historically specific. Notions of each alter over time and space. Gender comprises the language, social roles, status, and identities attached to and defining sexual difference. Likewise, notions of racial difference vary. Race constitutes "social meanings attached to physical appearance." Both gender and race are often wielded as tools for building and maintaining social, political, and economic power. Class is similarly constructed but also "includes the power deriving from material inequalities [and] the systemic maintenance of those inequities by dominant social groups." People produce all three of these defining social categories in relationships; none has any meaning absent this relativity. None is universal or fixed except in the minds of those who create and perpetuate them.[8]

Charleston's residents and visitors left myriad clues that reveal their thoughts and aid in understanding their actions. I draw upon traditional manuscript sources such as letters, diaries, journals, and daybooks. I also mine other evidence that constitutes the stock-in-trade of historians: census statistics, city directories, court records, local and state laws, municipal reports, newspapers, organizational and church records, petitions to the general assembly, travelers' accounts, and the Works Progress Administration (WPA) interviews with former slaves. In addition, I utilize contemporary literary evidence. Charleston was home to many talented women, some of whom wrote fiction and poetry. This literature provides rich sources of information on women's self-perceptions and their attitudes about women's place in southern society. All these sources help to reveal women's daily experiences and, specifically, the ways in which women's lives entwined to reinforce their social status and images.

American Revolution pension records provide yet another window on Charleston women. While historians of the Civil War and Reconstruction have excavated and interpreted pension records from that conflict, petitions to the federal government following the American Revolution (Revolutionary War Pension and Bounty-Land-Warrant applications) have not attracted as much attention. As is true of Civil War records, post-Revolution depositions shed light on the war experiences and material conditions of wives and widows as well as petitioners' notions of their roles and rights (see appendix 1).

South Carolina court reports also yield invaluable and fascinating data on the intersections of gender and slavery. Women of the master class and white women of the laboring classes turned to the courts when patriarchy malfunctioned and they sought to realize the ideal of paternalism. Accounts of these legal battles—marital disputes, bastardy cases, criminal cases, conflicts over dower and other property—involving slaves, free people of color, and white women of all classes bring alive women's realities. A close reading of these case documents and court reports also reveals multiple and conflicting images of southern women, notions instrumental to the perpetuation of slave society (see appendix 2).

Two final stylistic notes seem in order. First, I refer to people (in second and subsequent references) by their given names rather than by their surnames. Documents often exclude slave surnames or assign the owner's surname that a slave may or may not have accepted. A similar situation pertains to free women of color. The sources preclude using surnames for all women. Accordingly, I treat all women and men equally through the use of given names. Adopting this general editorial policy has the added merit of resolving yet another quandary. Many white Charlestonians intermarried with first cousins. Consequently, using surnames obscures more than it enlightens because many different people had the same last name. Referring to people by their given names affords quick and sure identification of the participants. Second, I have adopted the eighteenth-century and nineteenth-century Charleston nomenclature "free people of color," rather than "free blacks," because it was the terminology contemporaries used and because it is a more precise referent for people whose skin color ranged from nearly white to black.

Part One.   *The Place, the War,*
the First
Reconstruction

1 The Place and the People

From the American Revolution to the Civil War, Charleston, South Carolina, was a city divided by a great disparity of wealth, and it was ill at ease with its black and brown majority. Charleston's gaping social divisions and fundamental inquietude originated in its geographical situation and its founders' goals, as well as the city's development as a crossroads of trade and a self-styled exemplar of the southern way of life, which was built upon the extensive and oppressive institution of slavery. Ultimately indigo, rice, and cotton would drive the city's economy and virtually every aspect of women's lives in Charleston. Rice and cotton early on became inextricably linked with slave labor, and slavery drove Carolina's politics, social institutions, legal system, cultural forms, and everyday social intercourse. The path of Charleston's early development constitutes the foundation for comprehending women's braided relations and contested lives.

Geographically situated two-thirds of the way down the South Carolina coast, Charleston sits on a narrow peninsula of low, tidal land at the convergence of the Ashley and Cooper rivers, which merge to form Charleston Harbor. Carolina comprises six landform regions: coastal zone, outer coastal plain, inner coastal plain, sandhills, piedmont, and blue ridge. One of these, the coastal zone, stretches 185 miles between the borders of what ultimately became North Carolina and Georgia, and extends approximately ten miles inland, forming a total land mass of over 1.2 million acres. This coastal zone is further divided into three sections, one of which is the 100-mile Sea Island complex. Located just off the coast of Charleston, this area encompasses over fifteen diverse islands. This coastal zone is the Carolina low country, a regional denomination with colonial roots. Charleston is the centerpiece of the low country. It was here that English and Barbadian settlers carved out a new society. Charleston's merchants and traders turned to plantation agriculture, amassed their fortunes, and fashioned themselves into a wealthy master class.[1]

Climatically classified as humid subtropical, the low country's weather is hot and humid, a meteorological reality fraught with economic and social consequences. "The heat and moisture of the climate," observed more than one traveler to Charleston, "give to the buildings the hue of age, so as to leave nothing of the American air of spruceness in the aspect of the place." Climate altered the population's health and lifestyles as well as their buildings. Visitors may not have known much about Charleston, but they seemed to be experts on the sicknesses bred by pestilential marshes surrounding the city. Architect, traveler, and social observer Frederick Law Olmsted declared Charleston to have "the worst climate for unacclimated whites of any town in the United States."[2]

The low country's weather encouraged a peripatetic lifestyle among the master class. Those who could afford to do so fled Carolina each summer. They traveled to northern states and Europe and, by the 1820s and 1830s, to mineral springs and mountain resorts in the hilly midlands of South Carolina, North Carolina, and Virginia. If they could not afford to migrate farther afield, low-country planters and their families relocated to Charleston, where they sought refuge in the city's late afternoon and evening sea breezes. Occasional trips to Sullivan's Island, just off the coast, ameliorated hot, humid summers as well.[3]

In addition to weather, South Carolina topography determined Charleston's destiny. The rich, loamy, alluvial soil and abundant freshwater marshes and river floodplains of the low country supported cultivation of indigo and rice. The Sea Islands off Carolina's coast proved conducive to the production of fine, long-staple cotton. Sea Island cotton differed from upland cotton, which was cultivated abundantly in west-central South Carolina. The difference lay in the length of the fibers of the cotton bolls and, consequently, in the refinement of the spun cloth. Oyster beds dotted the inundated salt marshes, providing another commercial product and food source for coastal residents. But mosquito larvae, unwelcome beneficiaries of this climate and topography, also thrived and contributed to Charleston's devastating epidemics. The "diabolic multitude of mosquitoes . . . exceed[ed] all exaggeration," carrying malaria and yellow fever.[4]

Charleston's geography and climate made the city an exotic anomaly, so it quickly became a customary stop on tours of North America. The city's milieu precipitated comment from a host of foreign and domestic travelers, who, in the eighteenth and nineteenth centuries, vividly described Charleston's vistas. In 1769 a British sea captain drew upon his personal experiences in Charleston and penned this now-famous, yet unflattering description of the port:

> Black and white all mix'd [sic] together / Inconstant, strange, unhealthful weather . . . / Boisterous winds and heavy rains / Fevers and rhumatic [sic] pains / Agues plenty without doubt / Sores, boils, the prickling heat and gout / Musquitos [sic] on the skin make blotches / Centipedes and large cock-roaches . . . / Houses built on barren land / No lamps or lights, but streets of sand . . . / Water bad, past all drinking / Men and women without thinking / Every thing at a high price / But rum, hominy and rice / Many a widow not unwilling / Many a beau not worth a shilling / Many a bargain, if you strike it / This is Charles-town, how do you like it.[5]

Visitors also recorded more complimentary impressions of the city. Many marveled at its compact urban estates with their characteristic "Charleston single houses," each with a veranda or piazza adorned with foliage and flowers. The single house, an architectural form original to this city, turned sideways to fit on long, narrow lots in both the lower city and the northern suburb known as Charleston Neck, and was situated to catch sea breezes. One room wide and two rooms deep, the single house included a central hall and stairway. A false door faced the street. Open porches or piazzas extended along one side and overlooked an elaborate garden. The urban compound comprised a single residence and a yard with separate slave quarters and outbuildings: a kitchen, stables, sheds for livestock, a well, a cistern, and privies at the extreme rear of the yard. A fence or brick wall enclosed the entire compound. A typical brick kitchen, measuring twenty by forty feet, was home to some urban slaves. They inhabited the second floor, which was divided into separate rooms opening onto a common corridor. The Aiken-Rhett House, for example, included a similar kitchen and matching carriage house situated in a yard approximately 100 feet wide and 175 feet deep. Several travelers likened the overall impression of such distinctive architecture and gardens to that of a "Mediterranean," "tropical," "equatorial," or "southern European" city. Upon entering Charleston early one February morning in 1820, Englishman Adam Hodgson declared, "we seemed to be transported into a garden." Nearly everyone took pleasure in the private yards overflowing with lush, fragrant orange and peach trees, roses, and magnolias. They commented as well on the wide avenues lined with palmetto palm trees.[6]

However wide the avenues, visitors also confronted and railed at Charleston's inconveniences. The abominable state of most city thoroughfares caught people's attention, as well as feet and carriage wheels. French botanist François André Michaux complained, "every time your foot slips from a kind of brick pavement before the doors, you are immerged [sic] nearly ankle-deep in sand." By 1825 smaller city streets were paved, but because of the expense of importing paving stone from the North, completion of this municipal improvement took decades. Residents of Charleston Neck constructed log causeways in some streets. Intrepid traveler and author Harriet Martineau reported optimistically in 1838 that "the inhabitants hope[d] soon to be able to walk about the city in all weathers, without danger of being lost in crossing the streets." However, two years later there was "very little pavement yet," and the fine, sandy soil turned into "a most deceptive mud" after each rainfall, making pedestrian travel a decidedly messy and hazardous undertaking. Moreover, at low tide, great expanses "of reeking slime" lay exposed on all sides of the city, "over which large flocks of buzzards [were] incessantly hovering." Odiferous, oozing mud and buzzards that "stalk[ed] about here and there" and perched on stakes in the Ashley and Cooper rivers (and also on the roof of the city market, like gargoyles) generated an olfactory and visual spectacle that drew most visitors' notice. Another "noisome smell" occasionally emanated from adjacent wetlands, and it bespoke Charleston's position as mainland British America's largest slave entrepot. Nearly one-quarter of all Africans brought to mainland North America entered through Charleston Harbor. Those who died before disembarking in Charleston were "cast without ceremony into the harbor." In June 1769, instead of washing out to sea, a "large number of dead negroes" was swept by the tide up the Cooper River and into surrounding marshes where "their putrefaction" posed a stench and a danger "to the health of the inhabitants" of the city.[7]

Charleston women "occupied a large space in the public eye," observed one traveler in 1857. This wry remark rang just as true seventy years earlier. During his 1783 visit, Caracas-born adventurer Francisco de Miranda observed that "the number of this sex [was] very large compared to that of the men [and] there [was] no lack of those who ma[d]e the computation of five to one." Francisco especially admired groups of young white women riding on horseback through city avenues, "the favorite diversion of the ladies in this region." Charleston was the place to come, he concluded, if one sought a wife, for the city was filled with Revolutionary War widows.[8]

Charleston's people of color also excited lengthy commentary from city guests, who perceived them as a bizarre oddity. Visitors remarked that the "negroes swarm[ed] in the streets," and travelers particularly noted the plethora in this southern port of "fat negro and mulatto women" with "turbaned heads surmounted with water-pots and baskets of fruit." Many observers described, in detail, slave women and slave men stretched on the whipping rack or pacing ceaselessly on the prison's two treadmills. Other onlookers attended public slave auctions and painted verbal pictures of slave women "exposed for sale" in the street, describing their health, their demeanor, their clothing, and the bidding process.[9]

From the early national period until the Civil War, women and girls of African and European descent together regularly represented 52 to 54 percent of all city residents (see table 3). Whether they were peddling foodstuffs in the Charleston market, sewing or vending articles of clothing, selling their bodies, languishing in the Poor House, visiting sick and destitute women and children, or hosting lavish dinners and balls, Charleston women constituted an enormous presence in the city. Their sheer numbers suggest that women played essential and varied roles in slave society. Moreover, women and girls composed over 50 percent of all city slaves and made up a greater percentage of city residents than did their counterparts in other southern cities, like New Orleans, Savannah, Richmond, and Baltimore. Because all slave women worked, their large numbers suggest that they formed an integral part of Charleston's economy.[10]

Most Charleston women labored in the city's work force. Although slave women constituted, by far, the bulk of that group, most free women of color worked for wages, as did a growing number of white women. During five sample years from 1790 to 1802, women represented an average of 5.3 percent of free residents listed with their professions in city directories. These directories routinely undercounted Charleston's laboring women (often listing only their husbands' professions), and increasing numbers of Irish and German immigrant women also augmented the ranks. Nevertheless, since slave women and free women of color constituted approximately 56 percent of all Charleston women, if only 5 percent of the city's white women worked for wages, then more than 60 percent of Charleston's women labored in the city's work force.[11]

Clustered in consumer service industries, women keenly felt the effects of Charleston's economic upturns and downswings in the early national years and throughout the antebellum period. The devastating effects of the United States's 1812–1815 embargo, national panics and depressions that began in 1819 and

Table 3. Women as a Percentage of Charleston's Population.

	1820[1]	1830	1840	1850[2]	1860[3]
Number of slave women	6,957	8,577	8,339	10,901	7,346
% of city population	27.4	28.3	28.5	25.4	18.1
Number of white women	5,330	6,502	6,203	9,774	11,662
% of city population	21.0	21.5	21.2	22.7	28.
Number of FWOC*	852	1,293	975	2,086	1.990
% of city population	3.4	4.3	3.3	4.9	4.9
Total women	13,139	16,372	15,517	22,761	20,998
% of city population	51.8	54.1	53.0	53.0	51.8

*Abbreviations: FWOC = free women of color.
Notes:
1. Not until 1820 did the census enumerate people of color by sex and by age.
2. In December 1849, Charleston extended the city limits north to include the Neck, which explains substantial population increases in this census year.
3. Population decreases reflect substantial statewide southwest migration of South Carolina planters in search of new fertile cotton lands in Georgia, Alabama, and Mississippi.
Source: U.S. Bureau of the Census, Fourth through Eighth Censuses (Washington, D.C.: 1821, 1832, 1841, 1854, 1864).

1837, and the cotton boom of the 1850s affected women's lives as well as city revenues. Overproduction of cotton led to a global collapse of prices in spring 1819. The depression lasted four years. In addition, increasing use of waterways to ship cotton from upland South Carolina down to the city resulted in a sharp drop-off in the number of wagoners who had formerly hauled cotton to Charleston and patronized the shops on King Street. White women and women of color who sewed clothing, kept shops, or taught school acutely experienced the effects when women and men of the master class curtailed spending during tight times. Keepers of respectable boardinghouses also suffered when one of the many epidemics raged in Charleston, because rumors and reports of people dying discouraged the wanderlust of northerners and Europeans.[12]

Even when the city's economy surged briefly, as during the 1840s, Charleston's laboring women struggled to sustain themselves and their families. When large numbers of Irish and German immigrants migrated to Charleston from New York in the late 1830s and 1840s, the men worked on railroad or canal projects. Irish women, however, found it difficult to procure positions as children's nurses or housekeepers, because wealthy residents had long accustomed themselves to relying on slave women. Slavery limited economic opportunities for the city's free but poor women. Moreover, there was no manufacturing base in the city, so women could not look to factory jobs to support themselves. Thus, Charleston's scant opportunities for white laboring women in particular resulted in more immigrant children in the Orphan House as well as more foreign-born inmates in the Poor House, in Shirras's Dispensary, and in Roper Hospital. After 1839 Irish people outnumbered South Carolina natives in the city's Poor House and women outnumbered men in that institution's lunatic ward. This dearth of jobs also produced more prostitutes. Sailors provided a steady clientele for destitute women who worked in brothels along French Alley (between Meeting and Anson streets) and who also plied their trade in sailors' boarding houses.[13]

In addition to laboring in this chronic struggle to subsist, Charleston's women of the working classes of all colors were also kept busy bearing and rearing children, as were their wealthy counterparts. Not only did women outnumber men, and people of African descent outnumber white people (until 1860), but also children represented a significant portion of the total city population. More than 41 percent of white people were under age fifteen in 1800 and 1810 (see table 4). In 1820 children younger than fourteen or fifteen constituted the largest group among Charleston slaves, free people of color, and white people (see table 5); they made up over 35 percent of all city residents. Although the Charleston population was not as young twenty years later, children composed a substantial number of inhabitants throughout the antebellum period. In 1840 over 35 percent of white people were under fifteen. New census age categories ("under ten" and "ten to twenty-three") for slaves and free people of color render it impossible to compute exactly how many children of color were under fifteen. However, over 38 percent of free people of color and 27 percent of slaves were younger than age ten. In addition, 24 percent of white people were in this same age category. In excess of 26 percent of all city residents were under age ten in 1840. These consistently sizable numbers of children indicate that mothers and slave nurses had their hands full, literally and figuratively. Much of their time was devoted to caring for Charleston's children.[14]

Charleston women inhabited a world characterized by an elemental vexation of spirit. Visitors often commented on this undercurrent of tension in describing the city's stark emotional and physical contrasts. Writing just before 1840, English social critic Harriet Martineau commented on the "want of repose," the result, she concluded, of "two classes" living in "mortal dread of each other." She characterized Charleston as "a place of great . . . gaiety, [but] without much ease and pleasure." Her assessment hit the mark, for the city bristled with anxiety produced by the fundamental inequality that so fragmented its inhabitants. Charleston was "grand" and "aristocratic," but its buildings and some of its people appeared "shabby." The city boasted immense wealth, yet manifested utter poverty; economic and racial inequality was its hallmark. Although wealthy Charlestonians prided themselves on the city's gracious reputation, more than one nineteenth-century visitor encountered an "apparent coldness of character and cordiality." Doors to the best homes were opened wide to visitors who boasted proper social credentials, but "of such hospitality, the traveler . . . [found] nothing [unless] his rank or character g[a]ve an éclat to his entertainers."[15]

Table 4. White Population:
Percentages by Age and Sex in 1800 and 1810.

	<10	10–15	16–25	26–44	45+
1800[1]					
% of city total	28	14	18	31	9
% of women	29	15	19	28	10
% of men	26	14	18	34	9
1810					
% of city total	26	15	21	25	14
% of women	30	17	15	24	15
% of men	22	14	26	26	12

Note:

1. The first U.S. census did not enumerate by age categories, and the first three censuses did not enumerate people of African descent by age.
Source: U.S. Bureau of the Census, Second and Third Censuses (Washington, D.C.: 1801 and 1811).

Table 5. 1820 Population: Percentages by Age, Race, Sex, and Status.

Years of Age	<10	<14	10–15	14–26	16–25	26–44	45+
% of white population	25		13		25	22	15
% of white women	26		16		21	22	16
% of white men	24		11		29	22	14
% of slave population		33		31		25	8
% of slave women		30		32		25	12
% of slave men		36		28		25	11
% of FPOC*		38		20		23	19
% of FWOC*		35		20		25	20
% of FMOC*		43		20		19	18

*Abbreviations: FPOC = free people of color; FWOC = free women of color; FMOC = free men of color.
Source: U.S. Bureau of the Census, Fourth Census (Washington, D.C.: 1821).

Another striking and, indeed, defining characteristic of this southern port was its practice of interracial sex, a custom that persisted throughout the eighteenth and nineteenth centuries and produced substantial numbers of women and men of mixed descent. It elicited comment from travelers and new residents alike. In the 1730s, Swiss immigrant Samuel Dyssli and another minister condemned the slave women who "live[d] in Whoredome" and "those white Sodomites who commit[ted] fornication with their black slave women." Charleston newspapers alternately made light of sexual mixing and censured it. One writer labeled the customary practice "an Evil . . . spreading itself among us [like a] dreaded . . . epidemical Disease." But still another correspondent wrote, "Kiss black or white, why need it trouble you? Of all things that makes us truly blest, Is not that dear variety the best?" Most of the sexual mingling in Charleston occurred between white men and women of color, slave and free. Although white women—primarily but not exclusively of the laboring classes—also had sex with enslaved and free men of color, no catchy rhymes celebrated this form of sexual mixing.[16]

Consequently, many of Charleston's free people of color were descended from a mother or grandmother who arrived in Charleston a slave, and who achieved freedom when a former owner and sexual partner manumitted her. Light-skinned women of color particularly drew the attention of city visitors. On the eve of the American Revolution, geographer-historian Ebenezer Hazard expressed curiosity about "mulatto women" who "dress[ed] elegantly . . . [had] no small acquaintance with polite behavior," and who hosted balls "to which they invite[d] the white gentlemen." Another observer remarked that "the enjoyment of a negro or mulatto woman [was] spoken of as quite a common thing," and that it was routine "to see a gentleman at dinner, and his reputed offspring a slave to the master of the table."[17]

The women of Charleston were separated by great divides of color, condition, and wealth, yet their daily lives and their destinies entwined tightly in this patriarchal, urban slave society. A key that unlocks the apparent contradiction of segregated but braided lives lies in the story of Charleston's founding and its evolution.

In 1670 an English expedition of 150 colonists arrived in this semitropical locale from Barbados. Eight Englishmen financed this expedition but worked in close collaboration with leading merchants and planters of the British colony of Barbados. These eight "True and Absolute Lords Proprietors of Carolina" held a charter from the King of England granting them all land from present-day North Carolina south to Spanish Florida and west to the Pacific Ocean, and they retained for themselves title to two-fifths of that land after colonization. The Proprietors proposed for the new colony an oligarchic government ruled by a governor and an elected "Grand Council" modeled after the English House of Commons. Besieged by Indians and pirates, fearful of the Spanish to their south, and resentful of the Proprietors' meddling in their political and economic affairs, Carolina colonists petitioned for the Crown's protection in 1709. The

Lords Proprietors retained control until 1719, when Carolina became, on paper, a royal colony. The change became effective in 1728, and the first royal governor arrived two years later. During the royal period (1720 to 1775), South Carolina experienced slow but steady growth. By mid-century Charleston equaled New York and Boston as a social and cultural center.[18]

Early settlers had established themselves at Albermarle Point on the western bank of the Ashley River. Among the original group were sixty-three white indentured female and male servants, at least one black slave, and twenty-nine landowning men, only one of whom brought a wife on the voyage. Almost immediately, several colonists relocated across the river to Oyster Point, the peninsula between the Ashley and Cooper rivers and the site of present-day Charleston. By 1680 this new location was the seat of government. Creeks and marshes divided and indented the site into a number of low-lying peninsulas with little high ground. Town expansion and development required constant land reclamation, so servants and slaves were put to work draining marshes and filling in creeks and ponds. Charleston's low elevation continued to influence its maturation and contributed to its distinctive disease environment throughout the eighteenth and nineteenth centuries.

Colonial Charleston absorbed subsequent white immigrants who sought riches through commerce and plantation agriculture, and together they constituted the low country's nascent master class. A substantial number of French Protestants, or Huguenots, fled their country in the 1670s and 1680s. By 1723 French inhabitants composed approximately one-fifth of the city's population. Direct emigration from Ireland continued unabated from at least the 1730s, when a Carolina royal bounty enticed settlers, and persisted after officials abolished the bounty in 1768. In late 1772, a city newspaper reported the arrival of four ships from Ireland in four days filled with over 1,000 women, men, and children. A number of Sephardic Jews from the Iberian Peninsula emigrated to Charleston, but the city's first Jewish residents may have arrived from Barbados where, in late-seventeenth-century Bridgetown, fifty-four of some four hundred households were Jewish. The first mention of a Jewish person in Charleston occurred in 1695. By 1749 the Jewish community had established its religious congregation in the city, and by 1800 Charleston's Jewish population of more than four hundred exceeded that of all other American cities. Other early inhabitants entering Charleston harbor included Dutch, Swiss, German, and Scottish immigrants as well as Acadiens, or French people from Nova Scotia. This motley group of immigrants shared several behavioral patterns. They Anglicized their names, intermarried, and entered virtually all arenas of the city's economic, social, legal, and political life. By the time of the American Revolution, descendants of these early immigrants numbered among Charleston's most prominent families.[19]

These white residents also shared a determination to exploit the province's rich resources, so they and the British Crown profited from trade with the area's native peoples throughout Carolina's first forty years. By the end of the seventeenth century, merchants were shipping 50,000 deerskins annually to England.

Naval stores (pitch, tar, rosin, and turpentine extracted from coastal plain pine-wood) slowly augmented Carolina's trade, as did the shipment of wood products to the West Indies. By the second decade of the eighteenth century, Charleston merchants had extended this provision trade to include Dutch settlements in South America. All the colony's trade passed through Charleston.

It was rice, however, that brought extraordinary wealth to Charleston merchants, inextricably linking Charleston to staple-crop agriculture. As merchants acquired capital, they invested in land and slaves, turning planter as well as trader. A labor-intensive crop, rice required many hands for successful cultivation. Carolinians appropriated the labor of slaves—Indians first, then people of African descent—from the time they stepped on shore. As a consequence, before the mid-seventeenth century, slave traders imported increasing numbers of West Africans at the rate of about one hundred annually. By the end of that century the annual figure had risen to "hundreds." Accounts differ on the arrival of the slaves. Some claim that at least one servant of African descent arrived on the first ship in 1670. Another narrative sets the date two years later, when Englishman and future governor Sir John Yeamans arrived from Barbados with an undetermined number of slaves. Within thirty-eight years of its founding, Carolina residents included over 4,000 negro slaves, 1,400 Indian slaves, approximately 120 white servants, and about 6,000 white colonists, most of whom lived in the stockaded town. As early as 1696 Carolina had passed its first comprehensive slave law. As the next decade opened, Charleston residents numbered nearly 3,500 people.[20]

Between 1715 and the 1730s, annual shipments of rice jumped from 8,000 to 40,000 barrels, the market value of rice nearly doubled in just six years, and Charlestonians formulated agricultural and commercial innovations to capitalize on this "white gold." As income from their cash crop increased, Charleston exporters expanded their import trade to satisfy a growing demand not only for slaves, wine, and rum but also for English-made consumer goods. Drawing on the knowledge and expertise of African slaves, low-country rice planters adopted a new technology by mid-eighteenth century, changing from inland swamp cultivation to tidal culture, which used the ebb and flow of river tides to irrigate and drain rice fields in floodplain swamps. Tidal culture required enormous amounts of labor, both during the growing season and in the off-season when ditches, dikes, canals, and trunks required maintenance, so Charleston merchants increased their trade in human property. The city established itself as a major slave trading center. During the decade of the 1730s, Charleston traders imported nearly twenty thousand slaves, most of them from Angola. The city boundaries expanded to accommodate its growing population during this same period. From 1729 to 1739, Charleston nearly doubled its original size of approximately eighty acres.[21]

In 1739 and 1740, three incidents rocked Charleston and presaged an intensified, fundamental disquiet that had quickly characterized the city's social relations, tensions that originated in enormous racial inequality. In early September 1739, at Stono River Bridge just south of Charleston, a group of about twenty slaves looted and burned a store, then marched from house to house, plundering, setting homes on fire, and killing white people. The insurgents enlarged their ranks as they marched south to claim freedom in Spanish Florida. Later the same day, armed and mounted planters tracked them down and exacted quick and violent retribution. All told, more than sixty people died in the Stono Rebellion.

The following year, rumors spread that slaves in Goose Creek Parish, just a few miles north of Charleston, planned to seize the city. Municipal officials tried sixty-seven alleged conspirators, hanged some, and branded, whipped, and mutilated others. It is no coincidence that the South Carolina assembly, in May of the same year (1740), enacted its new and comprehensive "Act for the Better Ordering and Governing Negroes and Other Slaves in This Province." This black code drew upon the colony's earlier "negro laws" and remained in effect with but few modifications until the Civil War. Stono and Goose Creek heightened virtually all white people's anxiety about the low country's "black majority," including large slaveholders whose prosperity was predicated on that racial imbalance and, specifically, on slavery. Acting on this fear and on the belief that "new negroes," or slaves newly arrived from Africa, were more likely to foment rebellion, assemblymen also placed prohibitive duties on slave imports for the next three years to limit the number of African slaves in the state. One historian has argued that Stono fundamentally altered slave demography in the low country by slowing slave imports. By 1750 the number of native-born black people was substantial enough to "create a reproducing slave population despite the high levels of African immigration during the late colonial period."[22]

Finally, six months later, Charleston's most destructive fire, fanned by a strong sea breeze, burned for four hours and demolished some three hundred houses in addition to stores, wharves, and enormous quantities of goods. No evidence emerged to prove a suspected act of arson by slaves. Nevertheless, many city residents considered this fact almost immaterial, convinced as they were that slaves had set the fire. Stono, Goose Creek, and the fire of 1740 quickened in many white Charlestonians a conviction that they were surrounded by "Enemies very near."[23]

Notwithstanding these ominous formative events of 1739 and 1740, Charleston women performed integral functions in the process of urban social construction. Women—in this case, white women—were central to the city's maturation from a crude outpost to a thriving city center of the Atlantic trade. They were crucial, also, to the ascension of a master class that built its fortunes on the backs of slave women and men, consolidated its power, and assimilated various ethnic groups. First and foremost, marriages augmented and secured the burgeoning fortunes and power of both merchants and planters. Slave traders, for example, wed the daughters of successful planters and, thus, acquired further wealth. Lawyers, politicians, and merchants likewise married into the great planter families and substantially increased their wealth and cachet in Charleston society.

In the formation of the master class, white women played a second role, which was decorative as well as functional. Conspicuous consumption served as an effective tool of an evolving master class as it elevated itself above all other Charleston residents; its personal possessions reinforced its prosperity and high status. Husbands and fathers built great mansions, purchased elaborate carriages, and clothed their slaves in liveries. They also displayed their bejeweled and elaborately attired wives and daughters as visual proof of high social rank. Numerically outnumbered by the city's poor and by its people of color, wealthy slave owners constantly reinforced their hegemony, not only with a whip but also with the glitter of gold on their ladies' wrists. In these ways, white women played both active and symbolic roles in establishing and patrolling social boundaries, borders that ensconced them near the top of Charleston's social pyramid. Theirs was an inherently contradictory role—they were both handmaidens of the master class and members of that ruling coterie. Moreover, slave women were made unwilling foils in this enterprise, for women and men of the master class purposefully contrasted slave wenches and white ladies.

Thus, to tell the story of early Charleston and women's role in its evolution is to relate how a motley group of ambitious, acquisitive white men and women survived a devastating disease environment, acquired enormous wealth—through trade, staple-crop agriculture, and the exploitation of African slave labor—and consolidated themselves into a powerful ruling class. Mid-eighteenth-century Charleston was a city bursting with energy, its economy thriving and a harbor full of slavers and other trading vessels. By 1742 Charleston's commerce with English cities exceeded that of Boston and New York. On the eve of the American Revolution, Charleston had transformed into one of mainland North America's four principal cities and a trade nexus of the Atlantic economy. This urban jewel in the British imperial crown flourished in the years preceding the Revolution, but not all shared in the prosperity. Charleston was dominated by a self-ordained, slave-owning aristocratic gentry comprising planters, slave traders, other merchants-turned-planters, and their female kin. They bought hegemony by investing in land and slaves, they secured it through intermarriage, and they brandished and reinforced it through public displays of their wealth. The master class exercised power far greater than its numbers. These affluent women and men formed a minority in a city where over one-half the inhabitants were slaves of African descent, and where impoverished white residents and transients, together with slaves, made up fully three-quarters of the city's population. Because racial mingling as well as economic inequality characterized Charleston's first century and continued to exemplify the city throughout the antebellum era, most city residents were also brown or black (and numerous nuances of color) instead of white.[24]

In the decades leading up to the American Revolution, Charleston women lived in a heterogeneous society rent by deeply rooted aversions. City residents trenchantly divided along overlapping fault lines of white and color, rich and poor, slaveholder and non-slaveholder, planter and merchant, native Carolinian and British emigrant, Carolina assemblyman and English placeman. Slave women, master-class ladies, free brown elite women, and white, brown, and black women of the laboring classes inhabited different but intersecting worlds on the eve of the American Revolution.

South Carolina households were larger than the colonial mainland North American average of five to seven persons, so many Revolutionary-era Charleston women lived in close, urban quarters with several family members, apprenticed or bound-out white children, and slaves. However, in this city of extremes, most Charlestonians could not afford to own slaves on the eve of the American Revolution.[25]

At mid-eighteenth century, nearly 11,000 people lived in Charleston, well over 60 percent of them enslaved and free people of African descent. Average annual importations of 3,000 or 4,000 slaves twenty years later, and nearly ten thousand each in 1772 and 1773, as well as a harbor full of slavers, created the impression that "about 30,000 black Negro slaves" overran the city. This inflated estimate aside, slave women no doubt constituted an imposing urban presence—twelve for every male slave—and Africa's influence was evident in "country marks" and filed teeth.[26]

Whether from Angola, "the Guinea country," or "this country born," slave women also formed an economic force in pre-Revolutionary Charleston. They "acted as agents in an intricate economic network" linking the hinterlands, the city, and beyond. In city markets and along the streets, female slaves sold a variety of foods, dry goods, and handcrafted items. Charleston markets truly were "black markets" because women of color dominated them. In 1763 city commissioners complained that "Negroes and other slaves . . . [had] raised the price of almost every necessity of life beyond anything heretofore known." Market women not only set the prices but were also said to be "insolent," "abusive," "notorious," and "impudent." In fall 1772, other white city residents protested that market women "possessed . . . large sums of money," and they were "contemptuous" of the government. White Charlestonians persisted in their complaints, and they were simultaneously suspicious and jealous of market women's independent economic activity, but the city's black markets endured nonetheless. Market women's economic and social impact exceeded their numbers.[27]

Notwithstanding slavery's earmarks—extraction of labor, physical and psychological abuse—slave women's economic activities facilitated a symbiotic relationship with their mistresses that entwined their lives all the more tightly. "The widow Brown's old Negro wench, named Lizette, [attended] the lower market and frequently [had] things to dispose of there." Lizette and her widowed owner, like many Charleston slave women and mistresses, benefited financially from these market transactions. Because the practice of slave hiring was already well entrenched, some women applied their "labours and industry" toward the purchase of their freedom, sometimes from white men with whom they had a sexual relationship. Other slave women obtained their freedom in the pre-Revolution years by dint of their husband's hard work in addition to their own. However, unlike the plethora of foodstuffs and handcrafted goods these women sold, manumissions were hard to come by in Charleston.[28]

Relative autonomy in city markets and in "negro washing-houses," as well as the customary practices of slave hiring and self-hire, cultivated the "proud bearing" of Charleston slave women and their fondness for "dressing well," sometimes to the point of "extravagance." In 1772 an anonymous editorialist complained that there was "scarce a new mode" of fashion that "favourite [sic] black and mulatto women slaves [were] not immediately enabled to adopt."[29]

The numerical predominance of slave women, coupled with unique urban work environments, drew runaways to the city. Liberty carried different meanings for different people, so while some slave women ran away from their city owners, others headed *toward* Charleston, children in tow, seeking their own form of liberation. Slave women appeared in some 225 slave runaway advertisements placed in three Charleston newspapers during the period 1759 to 1775.[30] The sticks and carrots of urban slavery effectively prevented most slave women from running away. The former—the "sticks"—comprised municipal restrictions on mobility and assembly, as well as city patrols, quick resort to the lash and other forms of torture, and slave quarters just steps away from the owners' residences. But slavery's carrots also inhibited escape. Slave women (and men) cultivated networks of friends and family, mothers looked to their children's well-being, and they exploited all economic and social openings afforded by an urban environment. Thus, family, friends, economic opportunity, and the chance to melt into Charleston's brown and black majority drew slave women from the country to the city. A "slender made wench" named Miley was said to be recognizable not only by her "yellow complexion" and "her country marks in her face," but also because she was pregnant when she ran. Twenty-year-old Fanny was similarly "very big with child," and both Charlotte and Jubee ran with "sucking male child[ren]" at their breasts. A "Guinea Country negro" named Patt, for example, was determined to be reunited with her husband, whose owner lived in Charleston.[31]

Slave women who sought freedom in the city were familiar with and, indeed, said to be "well known in Charles-Town" and likely "to be harboured" (sic) by enslaved or free relatives. Runaway slave advertisements disclose slave women's large presence in the city, their centrality to the city economy, and their ties to Charleston's free people of color. Sukey had been "lately employed in selling Milk" in the city, and Juda had "been hired out for some years past to different people, to wash and iron." The "very black" Betty, a Charleston-born seamstress lately sold away from the city, and a slave woman named Banaba were said to be lurking in town, the latter allegedly being "harboured by some Jamaica negroes" in the port. Urban work and distinctive labor relations provided plausible alibis for runaways like Betty, who likely "hire[d] herself out at needle-work . . . under pretence of having [her owner's] permission."[32]

Charleston's growing population of free people of color also afforded a perfect cover for escapees. A young woman named Mary supported herself with her needlework and "past [sic] herself for free," while "pretty black [and] very sensible" Amey sold "things about the streets, pretending to be a free woman." Similarly, a "Mestizoe woman named Elsey" probably changed her name to

Sally, "said she was free," and worked either as a seamstress, cook, or washer and ironer, all of which she was "very good" at. In the company of her sister, Hannah had "passed in Charles-Town for a free negro near three months," so she tried it again, much to her owner's annoyance.[33]

While many of these women seized freedom and evaded capture by mingling with the city's free people of color, other runaways defined liberty in different terms; they hoped to quit Charleston entirely. Chloe had been absent "about 3 months," but her owner doggedly alerted city residents to watch for her on the wharves, because someone had "seen [her] on board his majesty's ship Mercury." Likewise, Sarah absconded to the city "with a design to get on board a vessel bound for some of the islands." Charleston slave women constituted a majority within a motley population of enslaved people, free people, nominally free people (legally slaves but living on their own), and some whose status depended upon their success at evading capture. If they were lucky, a parent or parents, husbands, and other kin also resided in the city. If they were not so favored, slave women strove to reunite their families, doing so at great personal risk.[34]

Precisely because of Charleston's status as the principal southern port, Revolution-era slave women inhabited a fluctuating and fragmented world of "new Negroes" from Africa, assimilated slaves and Carolina-born people, transient and permanent enslaved residents, rural and urban slaves. While some knew "but a little broken English," other slave women had mastered not only the English language but also French. Ironically, precisely because Charleston afforded economic and social opportunities to enslaved and free people of color, their worlds were also fraught with danger. White laboring people resented competition from skilled pastry chefs, seamstresses, cooks, and washerwomen, and they railed against "a great number of loose, idle and disorderly" market women of color who bought and sold "on their own accounts what they please[d], in order to pay their wages, and [got] as much . . . for themselves as they [could]." One editorialist pointedly accused municipal authorities of failing to enforce slave-hiring regulations that affected "poor white people in a greater degree than is generally imagined." This anger occasionally turned violent, as when city watchmen began beating and "abusing" slaves who carried legitimate passes and were performing tasks assigned by their owners.[35]

Fear as well as economic competition and resentment precipitated periodic outbursts of violence against people of color (slave and free), so slave women learned to negotiate highly charged physical and emotional environments. In 1775 rumors of slave insurrection catalyzed an enlarged city guard, and periodic fires validated slave owners' simmering fear of arson. A destructive conflagration near mid-century confirmed one merchant's belief that white Charlestonians ran "the great Risque [of] an Insurrection of [their] Negroes." As war with the British approached, white residents listened in horror as some slaves appropriated militant declarations of liberty. Such incidents ratcheted up anxiety and fear, particularly among Charleston's wealthiest women and men, and innocent people of color frequently got caught in the crossfire.[36]

Before as after the American Revolution, white women of the laboring classes (including the destitute poor) frequently mingled with slaves and free people of color, and as they did they defined their roles and further distinguished themselves from ladies. These women's lives intertwined because of their positions at the bottom of the economic heap. White women tavern keepers, representing fully one-half of the dram shop operators, sold liquor illegally to slaves, and the white women who frequented such establishments reveled with slave men and women and occasionally conspired with them to commit crimes. One Catherine Malone, a white woman, received "25 lashes on the bare back" after the court convicted her of larceny. The "disorderly poor" also included "notorious bawdes [sic] and strumpets," like Mary McDowell and Mary Grant, who kept a brothel and "harbor[ed] loose and idle women" of all colors.[37]

Not all of the city's poor women engaged in nefarious endeavors, but women and men of the master class, nevertheless, rued the increasing numbers of "vagrants . . . and idle persons" who "infest[ed]" Charleston in the years preceding the American Revolution. These wretched economic and social inferiors simultaneously reinforced hierarchy (by obligating the ruling minority to assist worthy poor people, a duty integral to wealthy white women's identities) and quickened fears of economic and social disorder. In winter 1756, over 1,000 exiled French Catholic Acadians arrived in the southern port from Nova Scotia and were only grudgingly permitted to debark. In addition, the Seven Years or French and Indian War widowed and rendered destitute thousands of women who made their way to the city with children and little else to call their own. Orphans and prostitutes also swelled the population by the early 1760s. In excess of 300 indigents from Ireland exacerbated the "low circumstances" of Charleston's poor in 1767 by stretching church welfare funds beyond their limits. During this decade, Irish and German people also arrived from New York and Philadelphia, as immigrants turned southward when the cost of living doubled in those northern cities. Carolina's House of Commons began investigating Charleston's rising expenses for the poor. City relief rolls bear testimony to women's plight in particular. In three previous decades, old and infirm people had predominated among those seeking assistance from city churchmen, but after 1756, young women with small children requested food, shelter, fuel, clothing, and medical care in the largest numbers. Poor women of all colors faced grim prospects in the pre-Revolutionary years. Bare subsistence required ongoing struggle in the crowded, grimy, smelly, disease-ridden underworld of a city that nine of the ten wealthiest British mainland colonials called home, and where 10 percent of the population owned in excess of 50 percent of the wealth.[38]

Just as low-country planter and merchant families fashioned themselves into a ruling elite by the 1740s, the eighteenth century marked the slower evolution of a free brown elite. Small numbers characterized this group prior to the American Revolution. They represented less than 1 percent of the total city population during the 1770s and 1780s, and by 1790 that figure rose to 4 percent (or 7 percent of all people of color, slave and free). Their Carolina roots were planted firmly in slavery, but tenacity and hard work blossomed into freedom.

Low-country slaves ran to the city, "passed [themselves] for free," and started anew, establishing what would become Charleston's premier families of free brown elites. Mixed relationships between slave women and white men led to the founding of still other free brown families when some of those owners manumitted their slave lovers or their mixed-race children in the early eighteenth century. Still other slave women bought freedom through their hard work, often in concert with the earnings of their husbands, and bore their children into freedom. Carolina's wealthiest free people of color, Margaret Noisette and Ann Deas among them, descended from slave women and the white men who fathered their children.[39]

Women numerically dominated this small but economically and socially strategic group. "Amy, a free woman of color," purchased a building lot in one of the newly subdivided tracts of the city that was growing west and north across the peninsula from the original village limits. This urban development occurred in the late 1760s and early 1770s, so Amy had amassed resources sufficient to invest in real estate by that time. Her example reveals how the pre-Revolution decades constituted a formative era for Charleston's free brown elite and how, unlike women of the burgeoning master class, virtually none of these women lived lives of repose on the eve of the war for American independence. Their disparate realities simultaneously differentiated, defined, and connected these two groups of women. Like most of the city's free people of color, Revolutionary-era brown elite women labored as artisans and tradespeople. And like most laboring women of all colors, they lived modestly, often in the upper stories of wood or brick structures, the ground floors of which they turned into shops. Other women of color the wives of tanners, butchers, tallow chandlers, dairymen, or wood factors—lived on the fringes of the rapidly expanding city because their husbands' occupations posed a fire hazard, produced noxious odors, or simply required more space than compact city quarters provided. In contrast, a circle of leisured white ladies also called this city home, and the wealthiest among them already had few peers in mainland North America on the eve of the American Revolution. By the 1760s, marriage had cemented this low-country aristocracy. Its members maintained lavish residences in Charleston. About equally divided between women and men, the elite represented 5 percent of the city's white population of 5,000 and a mere 2.5 percent of the total urban population of 10,000.[40]

The French and Indian War affected people of the master class differently than it did newly widowed and destitute women of the laboring classes. Worldwide trade disruptions in the late 1750s increased demand for low-country rice, which netted hefty profits for Charleston's planter families. As their confidence in the economy soared, so did slave imports; more slaves meant more rice and thus more money for the master class. Consequently, Charleston ladies lived in elegant homes built at the tip of the peninsula, where they could best catch the cooling sea breezes on sultry days, and where they also could be seen by all who debarked in the port. They furnished their mansions with imported mahogany, brass, mirrors, Turkish carpets, and exquisite Chinese accessories. "Fine

Flanders Lace, the Finest Dutch Linens and French Cambricks . . . Silks, Gold and Silver Laces" also adorned these opulent homes, whose owners commissioned self-portraits to memorialize their achievements and high status. Their appetite for slaves was matched only by their passion for costly imported and domestic goods, and all these purchases lined the pockets of local merchants, importers, artisans, and shopkeepers. Women of the middling sorts—skilled dressmakers, proprietresses of dry goods stores, wives and daughters of silversmiths or cabinetmakers—in this way profited from the conspicuous consumption of the wealthiest residents who indulged in a spending frenzy during the 1750s and 1760s. The interdependence of women's lives sometimes proved lucrative and mutually beneficial as well as serving the purpose of defining who they were and were not.[41]

Ladies presided over Charleston's high social season, which was well established by the later 1760s. Dancing prevailed over politics from January to March, much to the disgust of one of the city's wealthiest men, slave trader Henry Laurens, who noted that assembly sessions were shortened "in favor of the ball." Even the Sabbath was "a day of visiting and mirth with the rich." In keeping with this aura, young girls were trained "in no professions at all, except Music and Dancing," one city visitor observed, so they made "very agreeable companions, but . . . expensive wives." Young mothers and their daughters avidly patronized the "more than twenty-three music, singing, and dancing masters," including one Ann Windsor who specialized in the harpsichord.[42]

In 1773, approaching war heightened political and social tensions, but ladies and gentlemen frolicked nevertheless, enjoying "the most brilliant season in the history of the colonial American theater" in a new "elegantly furnished" Church Street Theatre, reputedly the largest on the continent. The following year, a visitor reckoned Charleston "a gay place," replete with "dancing assemblies and plays . . . with horse racing about a mile off." The city's "genteeler sort" kept "handsome four wheel'd carriages," he noted, "and several carr[ied] their luxury so far as to have carriages, horses, coachmen and all imported from England."[43] Tenacious in their rollicking ways, it took a proclamation by the first Continental Congress to interrupt Charleston ladies and their escorts. In October 1774, the Congress resolved that "until relations between the British government and the American colonies returned to normal, all Americans should abstain from public amusements." Accordingly, master-class women and men suspended their diversions. Patriot ladies also began to distance themselves from their British-leaning counterparts by adopting the colonial cause as their own. Their political action manifested in sartorial changes; they donned "black ribbons instead of colour'd ones." By summer 1774, Charleston's social arbiters had taken further steps toward their own politicization. A group of "Respectable Ladies" organized a "Meeting of that amiable Part of our Species . . . to converse and agree upon some general Plan of Conduct with Respect to the Article of Tea." Ultimately they "renounce[d] the baneful herb" and went on to devise and promote a boycott plan directed at other city women. They were already accustomed to social dominion, and now they expanded their social roles into the public and political spheres.[44]

Black, brown, and white Revolution-era women lived during a time of urban growth and development, real estate speculation, population increase, and general economic expansion. In 1764 after a twenty-year absence, one city visitor swore the city was twice as big and had countless new public buildings and private dwellings. To this "humble Rhode Island[er], it seem[ed] . . . a new world." By the end of that decade, Charleston's wealthiest citizens, the Laurens and Manigault families among them, typically boasted a net worth that ran into the hundreds of thousands. All women of the master class celebrated and flaunted their wealth in a city populated overwhelmingly by slave women and other women of various shades who could boast of precious few material possessions. The wealth, social activities, and real and personal property of master-class ladies defined those women, just as the dearth (or absence) of all those things delineated slaves and poor women of all colors. Charleston women inhabited an economically dichotomized world and, because the slave trade boomed and European immigrants migrated to the port, women also lived in a racially and ethnically diverse world. However, white, rich, and leisured was the standard, and few women matched this ideal.[45]

In their daily endeavors and interactions, all of Charleston's women played integral roles in demarcating and reproducing urban slave society on the eve of the American Revolution. Women were the bearers of culture, not only because they bore children but also because they taught their children how to rule or how to survive under the rule of others. But the women of Charleston did not constitute a united confederation derived from shared female experiences. Because most were not of the master class, their relationships with men, their work and leisure, the ways they encountered the law, as well as their experiences of illness and death, all contrasted sharply to that of the city's wealthy white women. The very existence of most Charleston women served as a foil to (and reinforcement of) the lofty position of ladies. Together the city's women comprised disparate groups that were inextricably knitted together, yet separated by competing interests.

By late November 1775, a "heavy cloud" loomed over Charleston and "almost all the women and many hundred men [had] left town." A brief military engagement had turned the rhetoric of impending war into reality. The American Revolution, like virtually every encounter, enterprise, and experience of their lives, carried different meanings for the women of Charleston. Because master-class women had the most—in terms of material possessions and social status— they stood to lose the most. Slave women, on the other hand, had the least to lose and much to gain by exploiting war's chaos to their own advantage.[46]

2   Disorder and Chaos of War

The American Revolution precipitated near-total anarchy in South Carolina by unleashing fundamental conflicts—of race, color, condition, and economic position—forged in colonial slave society. The war disrupted two principal southern institutions: the household and slavery. As a consequence, war also temporarily eroded the social tenets that buttressed those institutions: patriarchal authority and deference. Established standards and customary practices lost their moorings as a result of war. It is an axiom that people behave atypically during the upheaval of war, and the striking social disorder precipitated by the Revolution drew Charleston women into the vortex. Scholars have analyzed, in particular, how war both here and abroad has historically affected women's lives and their roles. In the case of the American Revolution, the effects of chaos empowered some women who, by necessity or choice, acted in nontraditional ways and performed noncustomary tasks. These wartime experiences fostered new images, which endured long after the Revolution and altered women's self-perceptions. Some women began to reconsider their place in Charleston society beyond the family and household. During and after the war, women and men struggled to understand and redefine their relationships in this slave society within a new Republic that celebrated freedom. The creation of new, conflicting images and notions of women—whether self-styled or imposed by others—constituted a crucial part of this gendered task of postwar social reconstruction. Defining "woman" was integral to the individual and social work of bringing order to a city destabilized by economic, demographic, and democratic revolution. But there were limits to the changes wrought by war. Patriarchy and slavery survived the fighting. The American Revolution did not permanently alter the "culture of power" in urban slave society.[1]

The war accentuated women's entwined identities and their mutually dependent social positions. The Revolution magnified these entanglements of status and identity, which, in turn, were fundamental to the shifting, contested power relations at the heart of slave society. The war touched all women's lives in similar ways, but there were also differences, because women experienced the war distinctly depending upon their social group. Family loyalties (to crown or colony) and wartime activities of male kin also determined how the Revolution transformed women's lives. Few, however, remained untouched by war's attendants: dislocation, violence, destruction, and death. The Revolution widowed huge numbers of people and enraged and embittered many women. In these ways the war bequeathed a devastating emotional legacy.

In South Carolina, the war unfolded in four phases. After an early patriot victory in summer 1776 at Sullivan's Island (preceded by rumors about British incitement of slave and Indian rebellions), three additional stages of the war ensued: a period of intense suppression of loyalists; this was followed by British invasion of the low country in late 1778, capped by the conquest and occupation of Charleston in spring 1780; and finally, the British defeat and evacuation from the city in December 1782.

As early as 1775, Carolinians were divided, not only along the elemental fault lines of race, color, condition, wealth, and sex but also by splitting into "whigs and tories," who "pursue[d] one another with the most relentless fury killing and destroying each other whenever they [met]." Particularly in the back country, but also in the environs of Charleston, they cut "each other's throats" and rendered "the bands of society . . . totally disunited" by becoming "perfectly savage." While some city residents escaped the worst of this lawless guerilla fighting, many wealthy Charleston women knew the terror of flight and pursuit, particularly as they relocated between plantations and the city. Slave women were all too familiar with these horrors, because escape and pursuit constituted a regular part of life in slave society. Knowledge of this brutal civil war heightened rancor and precipitated brawls between Charleston patriots and those residents who remained loyal to the Crown. Approximately one-fifth of the state's free population became loyalists during the American Revolution, actively opposing the movement for independence by cooperating in some way with British authorities. As many as 9,000 or 10,000 loyalists—a group comprising people of color as well as white people—left the state. Mayhem reigned in city streets, where patriots of the laboring classes tarred and feathered British officials and suspected loyalists. The state Confiscation Act of 1776 and a 1779 city ordinance exacerbated this tension by legislating the expropriation of loyalists' property and the execution of people who joined or aided the British. Despite lax enforcement of both measures, the winds of enmity blew strong in Carolina, including its seat of government, Charleston, and these internecine feuds touched all women and men from the mid-1760s through 1783.[2]

Additional changes altered all women's lives regardless of social boundaries: social dislocation, trade disruptions, loss of property, and massive shifts in population. Although slavery and patriarchy persisted, authority alternated between patriot and British troops. Wealthy loyalist and patriot women, accustomed to submission because of their sex, also took turns being subjected to adversaries. In addition, household command shifted from patriarchs to wives and mothers, as husbands and sons departed for service to the colony or the Crown. Moreover, in excess of 6,000 militiamen and 200 Continental troops crowded Charleston early in 1776. This group was displaced by British and Hessian occupation troops in May 1780, which, in turn, were ousted thirty-one months later by patriot forces. While under British control, thousands of runaway slaves flooded the city seeking asylum, as did merchants from England hoping to reap profits under the occupation government. Before British occupation, loyalists fled what had become an intolerably hostile city, and thousands more embarked when the British evacuated Charleston in mid-December 1782. Although estimates vary widely on the numbers of fleeing slaves and free people of color, and no clear enumeration of enslaved versus free "evacuees" exists, it is likely that 7,000 or more Carolina slaves were carried off as well. These power and population shifts impinged on all city residents.[3]

War created opportunities as well as liabilities. What was one woman's problem was another woman's good fortune. The absent patriarchs, for example, created a power vacuum that slaves exploited to their advantage. They acted more "impertinent[ly]," refused to deliver wages to their mistresses, and ran away with greater frequency and impunity. Abandoned mistresses found themselves "in a ticklish situation," where slaves "entertained ideas that the present contest was for obliging [their owners] to give them liberty." In May 1775 one apprehensive city resident overheard a slave informing other people of color that "God would send Deliverance to the Negroes, from the power of their Masters, as He freed the Children of Israel from Egyptian Bondage." On the other hand, while the absence of male kin generated problems for master-class ladies, these women also discovered life-altering reserves of strength and ingenuity. Laboring women of all colors also stepped into the breach created by absent male kin. Necessity transformed them into businesswomen in their own right.[4]

In similar fashion, the presence of British and Hessian troops generated opportunities and liabilities for women depending upon their color and social station. Wealthy loyalist women reveled in the asylum from patriot persecutions, while their patriot counterparts, suffering insults and deprivations, seethed with resentment. Laboring loyalist women, including those from merchant families of modest means, reaped economic rewards from British occupation at the expense of laboring patriot women, who were denied the "liberty" of working. Slave women and some free women of color flocked to the British troops, anticipating special favors and freedom. A slave woman's chance for liberty was her mistress's problem and inconvenience. However, wealthy loyalist women occasionally benefited from this massive demographic upheaval, as when British officers rewarded loyalty with gifts of slaves. Slave women had the most to gain from war, but they also experienced the underside of opportunity.[5]

The war gave women of color the greatest opportunities for improvement, chief among which was escape. They took advantage of wartime bedlam by running from their Charleston owners in greater numbers than was customary. Some escaped temporarily—through truancy or maroonage—but others made that freedom permanent. Either course of action bore economic consequences for owners. No clear approximation exists of how many Charleston slaves (who numbered over 6,000) fled, but postwar advertisements of runaway slaves, slave owners' correspondence, and British records of "negro exiles" attest to their large presence in what became a massive migration. An estimated 25,000 slaves disappeared from South Carolina during the war, amounting to fully one-quarter of all low-country slaves.[6]

Many slaves defined freedom as the opportunity to reunite with husbands and other family members in Charleston and elude recapture by blending in with the port city's black and brown majority. Hundreds, perhaps thousands, of slave women from Charleston and the surrounding countryside remained in the city after fleeing their owners. When women known only as Rose and Amoretta ran from nearby Edisto Island into the city, their owner, much inconvenienced by their absence, attempted to entice them back with a promise to forgive them. On the other hand, one "likely young mulatto wench," approximately twenty-one years old, had run so many times that her owner declared his intention to sell both her and her three-year-old child. Likewise, Jenny fled with her young daughter, Phebe, and found refuge with other slaves or free people of color in Charleston, where she was said to be "well known." A skilled seamstress named Isabella was "frequently seen" in town, and her owner surmised that she was "harboured and employed by several persons." Because she was adept at needlework, Isabella likely supported herself by passing as a free woman of color or as a slave whose owner had granted permission to self-hire. The "visibly pregnant" Dido left her Charleston owner in the company of her husband, Stephen, an act of resistance perhaps made more urgent by the determination to bear her child in freedom. All these women proclaimed their sovereignty with their feet. They represented but a fraction of those slave women who scrambled for liberty through the window of opportunity provided by war.[7]

People of color also transformed islands off the coast of Charleston into "den[s] for runaway slaves." Hundreds of slave women and men formed maroon camps on Folly and Sullivan's islands in the shadow of both the city and its uneasy slave owners. By December 1775, one white resident estimated that 500 slaves had encamped on Sullivan's Island alone. These fugitives raided the mainland, robbed, and committed other "depredations" nightly. The presence of British men-of-war off the coast of Charleston and Crown troops on the islands emboldened people of color who exploited this opportunity to taste freedom, exact retribution on former captors, fill their bellies, and profit from the raids. What was to slave women and men an expedient policy was considered by patriot mistresses and masters as desertion to the enemy.[8]

Opportunities of war were not without risks, as the maroons on Sullivan's Island discovered in the early-morning darkness of December 18, 1775. State infantrymen disguised as Indians descended upon that island, set fire to houses, and killed or kidnapped some eight "banditti," as they called the slave women and men who were living there. After destroying food and water supplies, these raiders returned to the mainland. This dawn raid marked the first bloodshed of the American Revolution in low-country Carolina. Charleston slave owners applauded it as an utterly essential message to other renegade slaves and a means "to humble [their] Negroes in general." Female kin of the dead slaves likely viewed this incident through a different lens. The opportunity for slave owners "to humble the Negroes" translated into a life-altering trauma for these widows. Similarly, female friends and family members of slave refugees who had joined the "Negroe Dragoons"—a last-ditch scheme by the British to wreak havoc on low-country patriots before their 1782 departure—wrestled with mixed emotions of pride and terror each time their men departed on patrol and raiding parties. They may also have resented the king's use of their men as fodder for war and dreaded the prospect of losing their male kin.[9]

Thousands of other slaves attempted to leave Charleston with varying degrees of success. Evidence reveals that at least 110 slave women (about 2 percent of the city's total slave population) reached New York, an achievement that exceeded their modest numbers. In an exodus that began before the outbreak of war in 1775, gained momentum during the British siege and bombardment of Charleston in spring 1780, and continued into 1782, these slaves escaped their low-country owners and eventually boarded British vessels bound for St. John's, Port Roseway, Quebec, Annapolis Royal, and other Nova Scotian and Canadian ports, as well as England and several German kingdoms. Some women ran alone, others fled with their husbands, and still others carried children with them. Clarissa Channill was barely beyond childhood, at age thirteen, when she absented herself from her owner and ultimately made her way to Nova Scotia and freedom. The same was true of fifteen-year-old Charlotte Hammond and nineteen-year-old Sally Middleton. Catherine Drayton left her mistress "before the [1780] Seige," escaping with her husband, Samuel. Sarah Gordon also appropriated the revolutionary rhetoric of freedom, escaped from Charleston, made her way to New York, and, eventually, embarked for Port Roseway, Nova Scotia. She was just over twenty at the time, and took Jasper, her seven-year-old son, with her. More than a few women gave birth once behind British lines. These mothers, and British officials, considered the children freeborn. Their Charleston owners would have viewed these circumstances in a slightly different way. Lucia, described as a "stout wench," left Charleston in the year 1781. She informed the British that she was "born free." Lucia may well have been a freeborn or manumitted woman. If so, her experience provides evidence to support the contention that free people of color as well as slaves vacated the city immediately before and during the British occupation from May 1780 to December 1782. In the alternative, Lucia's declaration of independence may have been a reflection of her own self-perception and her determination.[10]

Actuated alternately by military necessity, genuine humanitarian concerns, and unadulterated greed, British officers early on initiated a systematic procedure for removing slaves from South Carolina. It is no surprise, then, that almost immediately upon taking possession of the city, they ordered 500 loaded aboard ships bound for service in the royal forces in New York. From late summer until mid-December 1782, British ships departed from the harbor regularly. At the end of October, a convoy of some forty vessels sailed with a large contingent of the British army, its supplies, and its plunder. Slaves constituted part of that booty. The British commander of the Royal Engineers in Charleston allegedly gained a fortune when he shipped 800 slaves to be sold in the West Indies.

Before Christmas in 1782, the last of the enemy troops embarked from Gadsden's Wharf, the city's largest pier, in over 300 ships. This massive exodus included some 5,000 to 7,000 slaves and free people of African descent. Over one-half were headed for Jamaica; others were bound for East Florida, St. Lucia, England, Halifax, and New York. The occupation commandant, General Alexander Leslie, had received orders from his superiors that any slaves who had been promised freedom, or who feared punishment if they returned to their owners, were to be given the option of accompanying the British. In a stunning example of a world upended, hundreds of slaves queued up outside the statehouse intending to vacate the city. Instead of being on the sales block in Charleston streets, these slaves were negotiating their own freedom. Instead of owners making provisions for the sale or purchase of slaves with vendue masters, white mistresses and masters personally petitioned their slaves in line, cajoling and attempting to convince them to remain "home." One master seemed surprised that his slave women and men informed him "with an air of insolence [that] they were not going back" and, indeed, meant to depart with the British. After this—the largest single, voluntary migration of slaves from Charleston— and after American troops regained control of the city, slave women and men continued to leave their owners in droves.[11]

Even when given this option to embark with the fleeing British occupation force in late 1782, slaves continued to define freedom on their own terms; not all of them quit the city. It is true that thousands departed. For many, however, the promise of freedom without their low-country friends and family was, to them, tainted liberty. Moreover, abandoning Carolina with loyalist owners simply meant enslavement in a new and strange location. More than one slave woman ran away and relied on a network of friends and kin to avoid embarking the next day. Their owners grudgingly set sail with other loyalists when it became clear that a quick recapture of their human property would be impossible.[12]

Flight was but one symptom of the changes the American Revolution wrought in the lives of women of color. Rebellion had many faces. Escape was one visage, but slave women also remained in their owners' households and seized upon other opportunities to engage in subversive activities both within and beyond the master's doors. At the least, their actions inconvenienced owners, destabilized Charleston households, and unsettled the larger social order. In its worst forms, rebellion by slave women brought violence and death to the doors of their mistresses. They not only rebelled more at home but also informed on and identified their patriot owners, as well as providing intelligence on American troop movements. As early as spring 1775, slave-owning women and slave women were left to fend for themselves when both European and African American men volunteered for or were dragooned into military service, and when American forces confiscated additional male slaves to dig trenches and construct abati outside the city. Charleston-area households were without their patriarchs and slave masters. This was the case in December 1778 when Savannah, Georgia, fell and the British rapidly fixed their sights just north. Carolina loyalists escalated their raids in the back country as British forces pushed relentlessly into the state. These maneuvers triggered fierce guerilla warfare in the countryside, including the immediate environs of Charleston. In the midst of this chaos, slave women collaborated with the British. As marauding bands of British and Hessian soldiers roved the area surrounding Charleston in 1779, slave women jumped at the chance to inform on their owners. An unnamed "negro wench" led one Colonel M'Girth and his sixty redcoats to a country home of the wealthy, slave-owning Wilkinson family. This "informer" looked on with satisfaction as the soldiers terrorized widowed patriot Eliza Wilkinson and her sisters. Perhaps this slave woman joined the pillaging and general anarchy and pocketed a trinket or two from the Wilkinson home, back pay for long years of uncompensated labor.[13]

War continued to present similar opportunities for those with the least amount of power and authority to appropriate a measure of both for a limited period of time and, simultaneously, to destabilize the society that had enslaved them. Each such occasion bore negative consequences for mistresses, who suffered economic losses as a result of slave women's "treachery." After her owner refused to identify the location of nearby patriot forces, one slave volunteered the information as her mistress stood by "seeth[ing] silently." The slave woman, possibly taunting her owner, subsequently asked permission to fetch food requested by the British officers. "I don't care what you do," snapped her mistress, "nor what becomes of you." From the drastically different perspectives of slave and mistress, this incident was a personal act of self-preservation, self-emancipation, revenge, or rebellion, but it was also a political act in the context of war. As one British officer stated, Carolina slaves did "ten thousand times more Mischief than the whole Army put together."[14]

Collaboration with the British took various forms, at times manifesting itself as spontaneous cooperation. Just two days after Colonel M'Girth pillaged Eliza Wilkinson's home, another British contingent ransacked Eliza's parents' home. In addition to looting this household, the soldiers drank all the wine and rum they found and invited "the negroes they had with them, who were very insolent, to do the same." This "insolent" group included slave women who collaborated in the impulsive drunken revelry. As these British and Hessian contingents roamed from house to house, enslaved women as well as men ran off to become willing camp followers. They sought freedom and, no doubt, revenge on former owners and other white Carolinians.[15]

Throughout the war, slave hiring remained integral to Charleston's social and economic order, and slave women maintained their central place in the city's economy. In this arena, too, slaves seized upon opportunities to exercise their own sovereignty. During summer 1775, five of eight Pinckney family slaves who hired out in the city labored as washerwomen. Bettina was pregnant, but was expected to continue delivering wages to the master after she delivered her child. Together with three male slaves, her work yielded a 6 percent return to their owner. However, this group quickly realized that absent masters, frequent household relocations, recurrent raids, and a British siege made it easier for slaves to do more of what they normally did in multiple ways on a daily basis: resist individual owners and bondage in general. The slaves of white patriots particularly capitalized on the British presence during the city's occupation. Slaves knew their owners were vulnerable because they were British prisoners either under house arrest, confined on prison ships, or allowed at large in the city only at the pleasure of occupation troops. The Pinckney family slaves "[did] now as they please[d] everywhere," and in general they "behaved so infamously [that] even those that remain'd at home [were] so Insolent and quite their own masters that there [were] very few purchasers" who would have them. Eliza Pinckney claimed her slaves "robbed" part of the pay before turning it over to her. In August one of the Laurens family slaves, named Chloe, took advantage of her relative autonomy as a self-hired slave. She held back from her owner fully three days' worth of her wages, stating she was sick during that time and could not work. The custom of slave hiring itself acted as a solvent to slavery's bonds, but the chaos of war exacerbated that corrosion. Two years later, several of the Laurens family's slaves still lived on their own in Charleston, and appeared to have established a relatively independent family life, thanks to the hiring system and their owners' preoccupation with war. A slave named Betty became "very troublesome" after her husband, Ishmael, disappeared while fishing. He was now said to be with a British privateer. It is unclear whether Ishmael joined the crew willingly or was shanghaied. Nevertheless, Betty's owner, the prominent Henry Laurens, complained that now he had lost both Ishmael's and Betty's wages. Betty, he said, had grown accustomed to working at home—keeping house for her husband while he earned enough wages to cover both of them—and now refused to hire herself out again.[16]

Betty and Ishmael were not unique in their exercise of de facto freedom during the war. Slave women hired themselves out as washerwomen, cooks, and needleworkers in addition to being hired out by their owners to specific households and to military men. Slaves also worked, lived, and intermarried with laboring free people of color, which likewise facilitated their formation of households separate from their owners. Historically this arrangement had proven profitable to slave owners. Yet in the context of war, white city residents experienced heightened anxiety and suspected an all-out slave uprising at any moment. In January 1778, a fire obliterated some 250 of Charleston's private and public buildings, leaving hundreds of people homeless. The fact that runaway slaves had already begun to expand the city's black and brown majority by this second year of war amplified the usual fears and suspicions of slave arson. The fire apparently originated in a kitchen that had been hired out to "some Negroes." More than a few white residents of the laboring classes as well as those of the master class pointed accusatory fingers at the city's people of color. This kitchen may have been one of the city's many catering businesses or the outbuildings of a residence. Either way, the people of color who had rented it were working or living without supervision by white people. Incidents like the 1778 fire confirm that Charleston's well-established hiring-out practice persisted during the war and that it increased opportunities for slave women to achieve a measure of autonomy.[17]

Women's centrality to Charleston's economy was nowhere more conspicuous than in the city markets and streets where market women continued to buy and sell a variety of goods throughout the Revolution. In February 1778, one observer "counted in the market and different corners of this town, sixty-four Negro wenches selling cakes, nuts, and so forth." White widows, in particular, customarily sent their slave women to market to sell home-manufactured goods and, indeed, these slave owners relied upon the resulting income. Enslaved women, in turn, counted on their percentage of the profits as well as the autonomy and freedom they exercised in the market. Slave women presided over these Charleston markets as they had for nearly forty years. War delivered to market women additional buyers—soldiers and civilians—for their wares. And much to the dismay of nervous white people, the markets were more raucous than usual because thousands of slaves from the surrounding countryside flooded the occupied city.[18]

While slaves pressed their claims for economic independence and other social freedoms by making alliances of convenience (with British troops, loyalists, and former owners), they also became easy prey. Ultimately white was white and black was black regardless of political allegiances, so the British occupation brought liabilities as well as opportunities to slaves. The king's soldiers deceived and exploited those whom they pressed into service or, worse still, shipped them to the West Indies for sale. When the British ravaged a plantation of the prominent Pinckney family on the Ashepoo River in 1779, they carried off nearly twenty slaves. A woman known only as Betty was among those who departed with the British. Her fate is unknown. If she was healthy and lucky, Betty may have managed to take advantage of this British incursion and to escape successfully into the pandemonium of wartime Carolina. However, a more likely scenario would have found her euphoria over freedom tempered by the sting of hunger; the British frequently abandoned slaves whom they could not put to good use.[19]

Of like mind with American slave owners on at least one matter, King George III and his minions proved themselves no true liberators. After May 1780, British occupation officers announced that "all the negroes whose masters have been declared prisoners [would be] listed and . . . counted in with the booty." They co-opted the labor of slaves, particularly those whose owners were patriots, and they considered slave women as objects to be exploited in a variety of ways. Female slaves worked as common laborers, nurses, and washerwomen for entire companies of loyalist troops. Some were coerced into (or willingly entered) sexual relationships after they "went off with the [British] officers." Observers noted that Charlestonians of both loyalist and patriot persuasion engaged in the common income-generating ploy of hiring out the "Negro girls" to British officers. Thus, both slaves and owners capitalized on the near-constant presence of military men by attempting to establish parasitic relationships—often sexual in nature—for personal gain. Slave women, however, were exploited more often than they were able to exploit this dubious opportunity afforded by war. They were lured by promises of wages never paid. They were raped and shipped off for use by troops headquartered in New York, kidnapped and sold for personal profit, and given away as gifts or compensation to loyalists.[20]

Overwhelmed by the numbers of enslaved people who flooded the city, unsympathetic British officials ultimately arrested many slaves and confined them to the "Sugar House," a contemporary euphemism for the city's workhouse and prison, where slaves were whipped and otherwise punished or held pending sale. Occupation troops alternately returned slaves to loyalist owners and complained of "the very great Inconveniences . . . found from Negroes leaving the service of their masters and coming to the British Army." Before returning to his New York headquarters, British General Henry Clinton commanded his replacement "to make such arrangements as will discourage" slaves from "joining" Crown troops. Hundreds of enslaved women and men died in prison or in nearby British encampments, where they drank water contaminated with raw sewage and huddled together without tents or blankets, exposed to the elements. One contemporary reported that "thousands of Negroes [died] miserably with" the small pox in 1780 when it spread rapidly through overcrowded army camps.[21]

Two realities exacerbated the vulnerable position of enslaved people during the war: the glut of slaves in Charleston, and the British perception of them as an "inconvenience." This double liability hampered slaves as they negotiated the terms of their service to military men. Slave women nevertheless rose to the challenge. One of the Pinckney family's slave women "join[ed] the British camp" and discovered her escape strategy actually improved her bargaining position in the ongoing give-and-take between owners and slaves. This woman's owner, Eliza Lucas Pinckney, counseled her injured son (a captain in the American army) to "employ" this unnamed slave—that is, to lure her out of the British camp with an offer of wages—because she could "be of great service to" him as he recovered from his wounds. Eliza urged her son to "prevail with her" to return to him. Here was another instance of British occupation overturning Charleston's social order and, in particular, destabilizing the power relations between owner and slave. Eliza Pinckney candidly if ruefully acknowledged this slave's ability to refuse service to her owner, to demand wages for her labor, and to choose whom she would serve.[22]

Free women of color as well as slave women relished the opportunity to play new roles in the capsized world of occupation Charleston. They seized every chance to displace the city's social avatars, the elite white ladies who were at center stage of the city's customary balls, dinners, and concerts. In February 1782, three free women of color—Hagar Roussell, Izabella Pinckney, and Mary Fraser—presided over a cotillion during which British officers danced with extravagantly dressed slave women. Sexual mixing of the races had long been customary practice in the city, but women of color supplanting masterclass women at major social functions represented an unprecedented reversal of Charleston's social order. In league with occupation soldiers, brown and black women intended to affront wealthy patriot women and their men. They staged the soiree at "a very capital private House," where enslaved and free women of color partook of an expensive supper. According to one contemporary account, "shameless tyrants [British officers] dressed [the slave women] up in taste, with the richest silks . . . waited on [them] . . . in carriages," and escorted these "powder'd up" women out to the extravaganza "before their mistresses['] faces." At this and other events, the American Revolution offered a fleeting opportunity for those who usually did the serving to be served. However ephemeral the role reversal, women of color briefly became much of what they were not—and some of what white ladies were—in southern slave society. Those who normally positioned themselves at Charleston's social zenith seethed and remained cloistered in the upper floors of their occupied mansions, that is, upstairs in the customary terrain of servants. The exchange of status and identity in this famous incident reveals how soldiers in wartime exploited women of all colors and social groups to humble the enemy and gain a psychological advantage. This incident also reveals the ever-shifting relations in slave society where those with the least power exploited their exploiters at every opportunity.[23]

Charleston's free laboring women comprised a middle ground between slaves and women of the master class. This diverse group included women of color and white women, non-slaveholders and slaveholders, women who hired slaves and those who did not, and women struggling to eke out a subsistence, as well as people who achieved moderate success and a comfortable living. Poorer laboring women of all colors mixed freely with slaves, but the wives of highly skilled artisans, mechanics, and merchants aspired to higher status and identified with their social betters—those of Charleston's master class. Laboring women, like slaves and people of the ruling elite, also differed in their political beliefs. Some were patriots and others loyalists.

While these differences affected the way they experienced the instability and turbulence of revolutionary Charleston, all laboring women shared certain realities that created parallel as well as disparate war experiences. All women of the laboring classes were acutely vulnerable to the economic dislocation war induced. They also shared a closeness to urban street life: physically walking the streets, immersed in the culture of laboring people, and privy to intelligence that spread at street level. This position set laboring women of all colors apart from wealthy women of the master class, and provided common ground (literally) with slave women. Freedom, however, served as the great divide separating the women, particularly free women of color from enslaved women. Unlike slaves, most laboring women (white, brown, and black) had some property to lose. But unlike master-class women, laboring women had neither enormous amounts of real and personal property nor the status of a ruling elite. Consequently, the war resonated differently among laboring women than among either slaves or master-class women.

The experiences of one white couple illuminate how the American Revolution transformed the lives of Charleston's laboring women. In 1771 Elizabeth Phillips married a Charleston bricklayer, William Samways. The timing was good, as the city was in the midst of a decade-long building boom from which artisan William and his new bride benefited financially. The young newlyweds established a comfortable household and cultivated a circle of friends among Charleston's mechanic community. That network included Elizabeth's sister, Massey, who married another bricklayer named James Graves. Since Charleston citizens had voted to end local boycotts prompted by the Stamp Act and the Townshend Duties, the port city's carrying trade with England was flourishing again, and as many as 350 ships lay at anchor in the harbor. While Elizabeth and William Samways numbered among Charleston's property-owning people, their modest holdings paled in comparison to those of the master class.[24]

The war catalyzed dramatic changes in the city that affected Elizabeth, William, and other laboring people. By 1775 the city's working men were joined by male slaves and militia recruits (free white men) who flooded in from the countryside and were put to work by patriot forces constructing earthworks and mounting guns on city wharves. William Samways, like many laboring men, had volunteered to serve in the Artillery of Charleston and, at the end of June 1776, shots rang out as a British fleet attacked the uncompleted fort on Sullivan's Island guarding Charleston Harbor. Now and for the duration of the fighting, war forced William and other line soldiers to leave their families several times. Elizabeth and William now faced separation and the very real prospect of his morbidity or mortality. Additional transformations were under way that disrupted their lives. By 1778 and 1779, embargoes imposed by the Continental Congress resulted in a dearth of imported goods and construction materials. The consequent inflated costs of available materials disrupted the building trades and forced many Charleston women and men out of business. These failures precipitated a chain reaction that adversely affected other city business concerns, including women shopkeepers.[25]

In addition, when the British seized Charleston in May 1780, occupation troops took hundreds of men as prisoners. If they had survived the siege and bombardment, most common soldiers were subsequently paroled and, like William, permitted to rejoin their wives at home. However, occupation law severely restricted them. Most working people who openly supported the American cause barely eked out a living during the occupation. British officials denied to "paroled" American prisoners the "liberty" of working. Whether engaged in artisanal trades, such as bricklayers, pastry cooks, and skilled seamstresses, or employed as merchants, Charleston patriots of the laboring classes were stymied by occupation regulations and opportunistic British merchants and tradespeople who flocked to the city.[26]

By late 1782, the Samways had endured separation, combat, British occupation, and economic hardship, but the Revolution precipitated further violence that altogether destroyed their lives. Despite his inability to work while British troops controlled Charleston, William Samways had been able to retain possession of a piece of property on nearby Folly Island. On the eve of British departure, William decided to check on his real estate. Elizabeth last saw him on the morning of December 7. Upon his arrival on Folly, "a number of armed negroes [runaway slaves], waiting to embark with the English troops . . . attacked, overpowered, and murdered her husband." Several days after the massive enemy embarkation from Gadsden's Wharf, friends collected the mutilated remains of William Samways for burial. While carrying out this grim task on Folly Island, the men encountered an African American who allegedly sported some of William's clothes. They executed him on the spot. Elizabeth now numbered among Charleston's widows who struggled emotionally and financially.[27]

Laboring women as well as men found their political voices during the American Revolution. Bitterly divided Charleston loyalists and patriots wrangled throughout the war and, during the edgy middle years after Carolina's invasion but before the city's occupation, a small group of loyalist women resolved to play an active role in the struggle. Persecution of other loyalists by city patriots only stiffened their resolve. Businesswoman and widow Eleanor Lester owned a grog shop frequented by sailors. She hid British seamen in her shop and "spoke 'freely' against the rebel cause." Similarly, shopkeeper Elizabeth Thompson allegedly carried letters through enemy (patriot) lines and even drove a British spy through an American camp. Particularly in the early years of the war, when patriot fervor ran high in the city, such actions risked harsh reprisals.[28]

In 1780, fifty-one women of the laboring classes penned a remarkable statement of the war's effect on their lives. Their petition constituted a highly personal and political action. Making neither excuses nor apologies for their husbands' actions and including none of the customary testimonials to the men's character or their own duty or devotion to these patriarchs, the women succinctly declared that they had been "deserted by their husbands [who had] gone over to the Enemy." The women requested that members of the South Carolina assembly release them from retributive taxes on "Tories," stating that a total of over two hundred children depended on them for the "necessaries of life," which they could not provide if taxed for their husbands' behavior. This petition may have manifested mere opportunism, an attempt to salvage some material benefit from their crumbling lives. In the alternative, the entreaty may have voiced genuine political loyalties and, therefore, split allegiances within families. Finally, the women's petition may have emerged from dual and conflicting motives. Notwithstanding this uncertainty about their reasons, these women acted politically to achieve the goal of household solvency.[29]

Not all wives whose husbands went "over to the enemy" had been deserted. Some loyalist women chose to stay in Carolina when their husbands departed of their own volition or after being exiled. That choice constituted both a personal resolution and a family strategy. The decision also entailed taking on new family and business responsibilities. Like slave women who remained in Charleston, these loyalist women had kin ties and networks of friends they were loath to abandon. They also stayed behind to try and protect businesses or property from confiscation. This choice eventuated in new political roles when loyalist wives began petitioning the state legislature. Mary Deas Inglis, the daughter of a Scottish merchant, and her four young children watched as her banished husband fled to East Florida. Mary subsequently apologized to the state general assembly for her husband's "Conduct," which incurred "the Resentment of the Country for which he [had] ever had the greatest Affection and Partiality." Her strategy of public contrition achieved partial success, because Alexander Inglis returned to South Carolina after the war and recovered his estate, minus a 12 percent amercement. Eleanor Mackey's husband, a Charleston cooper, was also banished from Carolina, causing his family to "[sink] under the pressure of accumulated misfortunes." Employing a slightly different technique in her plea to state legislators, Eleanor claimed that for eighteen years James Mackey "deported himself as a quiet industrious inoffensive Man [who] was never ambitious of . . . acquiring any higher Character than that of an honest industrious mechanic." But, because of "his simplicity and timidity," he was made "a miserable Dupe to the Suggestions & persuasions of more artfull [sic] designing and malignant Men." Eleanor succinctly informed legislators that she was a "native of this Country," that her "own conduct [had] been irreproachable and that she [was] deserving of [their] compassion." Although her husband had petitioned unsuccessfully on his own behalf, it was Eleanor's plea that enabled James's return to Charleston and recovery of most of his assets.[30]

Economic woes suffered by the likes of Mary Inglis and Eleanor Mackey were not unique to women whose husbands sided with the British, as was evident earlier in the misfortunes of patriots Elizabeth and William Samways. Their financial struggle reveals the way that frequent absences of husbands, aggravated by low and erratic militia and Continental army wages, created weighty financial burdens for patriot as well as loyalist women. Elizabeth Samways and her sister Massey Graves were unable to make ends meet. Mary Baker, the wife of a house carpenter, and Elizabeth Gabeau, whose spouse worked as a tailor, found themselves in similar dire straits. The British occupation transformed a bad economic situation into the worst of times for Charleston's artisanal families of the patriot persuasion. Under the "articles of capitulation," pledging allegiance to Great Britain, and promising to bear arms for Britain if need be, was the only way that civilians as well as soldiers could escape their prisoner status with its accompanying economic sanctions, restrictions on mobility, and general harassment by occupation soldiers. These pressures presented two grave choices to laboring men: they could maintain their patriot allegiance and flee, abandoning their dependents for whom they could no longer provide, or they could pledge allegiance to the Crown in hopes of gaining permission to work again. Elizabeth Beard's husband, a tinsmith, chose the latter option as did hundreds of Charleston residents. For some men determined to profit from the war, this decision to "tak[e] Protection under the British Government" came easily. Other men agonized over the prospect of publicly renouncing their patriot loyalties but found the enemy's economic sanctions too devastating for their families. When American troops regained Charleston, the new state government made few distinctions; they punished all "traitors." The state seized their property and banished husbands and fathers from Carolina. These families were twice punished, first by the Crown and subsequently by the state under patriot control.[31]

Wealthier artisan and merchant families were not immune to this same double economic jeopardy. Mary Cape's husband volunteered and fought with the Americans, for which British troops "destroyed [a] considerable part of his Property." But after being captured by British Colonel Banastre Tarleton, Brian Cape "took protection" from the enemy because his "large Family [was] in want and greatly distressed." Although he "truly and sincerely lament[ed]" his actions, Mary and Brian agreed that "he had no other Alternative." Carolina legislators later included Brian on the list of men whose property and assets were confiscated and who were exiled from the state.[32]

Laboring patriot women felt the sting of British control, household dissolution, and economic hardship in ways other than the banishment of husbands and seizure of family property. Mary Pratt refused to divulge to British authorities the identities of patriot men who confiscated arms and gunpowder from the statehouse where she worked as custodian or "keeper." Mary's refusal to speak, in fact, loudly voiced her political convictions. She also secreted supplies to American troops. For these patriotic actions, Mary lost her job and her living quarters for the full thirty-one months of British control.[33]

For many women, like ardent patriot Ann Timothy, their suffering at the hands of the enemy cut deeper than temporary family separation and economic loss. After the British captured her husband, they forced Ann and her children to flee Charleston. The Crown brooked little sympathy for the family's outspoken anti-British or "Whig" leanings, which the Timothys proclaimed in their newspaper and pamphlets. Although Ann eventually returned home and resumed the family printing business, by that time she had lost her husband and two daughters, all of whom had died before reaching Charleston. These experiences of loss are representative of the continuum of economic and emotional deprivation repeated in homes throughout the city over the course of the war.[34]

Charleston's poorest working women—destitute widows, wives of immigrant day laborers, and the displaced poor rendered homeless by the war—experienced multiple privations that intensified as the war progressed. Some tried to feed themselves and their children by sewing. Others peddled homemade goods on the streets, a practice customarily associated with enslaved and free women of color. When churches ran short of funds to ameliorate the lot of the city's white poor, some women were reduced to "begging their daily bread from door to door." With few avenues for employment open to them, desperate and poor women of all colors resorted to working in men's boardinghouses, where they supplemented meager wages by selling sex to soldiers, sailors, and civilians.[35]

While war bequeathed penury to some laboring women, it also lined the pockets of others. Women and children, indeed, comprised the vast majority of Charleston's indigent population during the American Revolution, and war swelled their numbers. However, women who worked in service industries made money from the war. Mary Sansum and her husband, John, owned one of the city's many taverns. During the Revolution, John served as a forage master in the state militia and, as a consequence, he was absent much of the time. It was Mary who kept their tavern open. Approximately one in every thirteen dwellings in revolutionary Charleston was a licensed tippling house, and many more dram shops operated without proper municipal permits. Women owned and operated many of those establishments, legal and otherwise, and reaped profits from soldiers and sailors stationed in or near the city. Before, during, and after the British occupation, troops of various allegiances and nationalities partook of the general debauchery available in Charleston's taverns and grog shops. Loyalist women in business, either independently or within family enterprises, reaped economic benefit from Great Britain's occupation. British officers rewarded and patronized only those businesses loyal to the Crown, and occupation officials penalized American competitors of these loyalist concerns. They either seized the concerns outright or taxed patriot owners out of business. Loyalists Barbara Mergath and her husband, who ran a bakery, and the widowed nurse Margaret Reynolds, were among those who profited during the occupation years, as did grog shop proprietor Eleanor Lester and shopkeeper Elizabeth Thompson.[36]

The Crown's terms of surrender churned the already vicious divisions between loyalists and patriots, which, in turn, strained normal social intercourse and heightened resentments. When loyalist women avidly took the British pledge and hailed occupation as a turning point in the war, patriot women seethed. When scores of patriot families turned "protectionist" ("took protection" from the British to safeguard their property and the integrity of their households), some acquaintances and family members shunned them. Charleston physician and contemporary historian of South Carolina, David Ramsay, maintained that 210 city inhabitants, the "greater part of whom had been in arms against the British during the siege" and whose ranks included "leaders of the popular [state] government," signed a congratulatory letter addressed to Sir Henry Clinton and Vice-Admiral Alexander Arbuthnot immediately upon Charleston's capitulation to the Crown. These early "protectionists" set a grave precedent for other patriots who longed for escape from British sanctions. But they also incurred the enmity of avowed patriots, and former friends were transformed into enduring adversaries. Similarly, when laboring loyalist women reaped economic benefits from the business losses of patriot artisans and merchants, they too made enemies of former friends.[37]

War ordeals inflicted deep emotional wounds that exacerbated the enmity between city patriots and loyalists. In addition to encountering economic harassment during British occupation, patriot women of all economic groups lived in constant fear that their husbands might die. In summer 1780, the enemy violated its own "articles of capitulation" when British officials arrested nearly seventy-five men on parole and warehoused them on noxious prison ships in Charleston harbor. Some died of typhus; others survived but never fully recovered their health. While none had violated their parole, they had refused the British oath. The occupation commandant, Colonel Nisbet Balfour, decided to make an example of them. By early September he exiled these soldiers to St. Augustine, Florida. Powerless to halt this exercise of arbitrary British control, city residents watched their husbands sail from Charleston Harbor. Ten months later Nisbet also ordered the wives and families of the exiles out of the city, declaring it "impolitick [and] inconsistent [that they] should longer be suffered to Rest on the Government established here." This blow to the city's patriot women was softened by the knowledge that they would soon reunite with their husbands in Philadelphia, where their men were to be released in a prisoner exchange. Still, Nisbet required laboring women (and some women of the master class) to leave family and friends and to abandon whatever property they still held. Forced to rely on the charity of friends in the North, many struggled to find and rent homes. The Charleston exiles were permitted to return in late 1782 and reached the city in early 1783.[38]

By the summer before the decisive British defeat at Yorktown in October 1781, Charleston's patriot women knew that their seventeen months of discontent were nearly over. The tables had turned, and now loyalist women feared harsh reprisals from embittered patriots. Their fears were realized by early January 1782 when Governor John Rutledge convened a meeting of the new state assembly in Jacksonborough, a town just outside Charleston. American troops now controlled nearly all of South Carolina, and by the end of that year, men of the master class had initiated the process of rebuilding civil government by electing state legislators. This Jacksonborough assembly forever altered the lives of loyalist women and others whose male kin were of the loyalist bent. Assemblymen denounced "conspicuous Tories," debated their punishment, and published their names. Legislators also banished many, and they confiscated and amerced or taxed the estates of hundreds of accused loyalists. One historian has estimated that fully 90 percent of some 425 loyalist families enumerated by South Carolina patriots on the 1782 lists were residents of Charleston. Although the legislature subsequently amended both acts, restoring much property to the owners, their wives, or their heirs, these measures speak to the retaliatory mood of patriot men and women as the war drew to a close.[39]

Patriot women of the working classes could not have been happier with the Jacksonborough proceedings. Emotions ran high because so many had endured enormous devastation and despair at the hands of loyalists before and during the British occupation. Unbearable grief consumed some women, whose realities turned on the bitterness of their war experiences and on the revenge they sought as a palliative. In this tumultuous era, patriot leaders spoke of honor and virtue. Military heroes celebrated women's spiritual inspiration and their quiet, gentle strength. But blood lust among laboring women surprised even the most patriotic Charleston men. One legislator wondered at women's role in fueling a "spirit of vindictiveness" at the Jacksonborough assembly, and another marveled that the "females talk as familiarly of shedding blood and destroying the [loyalists] as the men do."[40]

By the end of September 1782, British activity in Charleston indicated an imminent and long-awaited withdrawal. Loyalist families now feared for their lives. In late summer and early fall of that year, over 2,500 loyalist women—some of them women of the laboring classes—numbered among those who departed South Carolina on British ships. Over 900 more women, 1,000 children, and 1,800 men joined the final massive exodus of British troops, Crown officials, slaves, and free people of African descent in December 1782. Approximately two-thirds of this group of loyalists embarked for Jamaica and East Florida, while others headed for Halifax, England, St. Lucia, and New York. Many women took their slaves with them. Characteristic of earlier migrations, some loyalist women chose not to accompany their departing husbands. Once again some decided to maintain a claim on family property by staying in Carolina, or they simply refused to uproot their lives and abandon loved ones and property. They took their chances with vengeful Charleston patriots.[41]

Part of the Revolution's economic and psychological legacy lay in the numbers of women from the laboring classes who plummeted to the bottom ranks of the middle strata between slaves and master-class women. Embargoes, absent husbands, low or nonexistent military wages, lost property, and widowhood wreaked financial catastrophe. Economic deprivation rendered it impossible for some laboring women to hold their families together.

The war turned Charleston into a city of widows and orphans, and widowhood constituted another devastating consequence of the American Revolution from which some never recovered emotionally. The violence and death that spawned widowhood spanned the city's gaping social divides and fundamentally transformed nearly all of Charleston's women. A burning desire for revenge became the driving force for some. Fueling this vengefulness were the political divisions that fractured all social and economic groups. Whigs despised loyalists and loyalists reciprocated the feeling. Hatred and vengeance poisoned virtually all social relations in revolutionary Charleston.[42]

The American Revolution temporarily overturned Charleston society by toppling wealthy white women from their pedestals and creating terrible mayhem. Deferential order was the glue of slave society, so its opposite was abhorrent to Charleston's ruling elite, a minority in terms of sheer numbers. Mob action and impudent slaves frightened or infuriated ladies whose social inferiors of all colors defied them more freely. Moreover, women feared for their personal safety and that of their families. Beginning in the 1760s, "plebeians" (laboring people) took to the streets raucously advocating defiance of British economic measures that particularly impaired artisans. At the same time, "the noblesse [remained] perfectly pacific" and continued to prosper economically from lucrative ties to the mother country. Wealthy loyalists, in particular, longed for a quick resolution to continuing social upheaval. Elite loyalist women helplessly witnessed their husbands, brothers, and sons being physically abused. Aggressive persecution by city patriots, whom loyalist women perceived as riotous hooligans, confirmed fears of social anarchy, and rumors of slave insurrection roiled women's dread of a world gone awry. Scores of affluent loyalist families succumbed to this chaos and fled before the outbreak of war. By late 1775 and 1776, even patriot ladies abandoned their Charleston mansions fearing British invasion, which did not materialize for three years.[43]

While slave women were emboldened by the prospect of a distant king subjugating their owners, and "plebeian" (laboring-class) women enjoyed their newfound political voice, wealthy patriot and loyalist women of the master class felt inconvenienced and physically threatened by the war. In 1775 and early 1776, raw patriot militia recruits streamed into Charleston, and they took up residence in and ill-used some of the city's "best houses." To the horror of wealthy owners, back-country Carolina soldiers (both patriot and loyalist) "destroyed and even burnt as firewood such furniture as remained" after the occupants had fled to country estates. Many mansions suffered severe damage.[44]

By late 1778 and 1779, patriot women who had fled to their country estates in anticipation of a British invasion by sea experienced the full fury of marauding bands of British and Hessian soldiers who had invaded by land. The intruders stormed into homes brandishing firearms and bellowing curses. They plundered freely and loudly, destroyed personal items, snatched articles of clothing, and stripped earrings and wedding rings from the bodies of terrified women at pistol point. They pillaged and razed ancestral homes, decimating crops and carrying off all they had not destroyed. They kidnapped slaves and encouraged others to join them in destructive acts. "The whole world appeared . . . as a theatre," reflected Eliza Wilkinson, "where nothing was acted but cruelty, bloodshed, and oppression; where neither age nor sex escaped the horrors of injustice and violence; where the lives and property of the innocent and inoffensive were in continual danger, and lawless power ranged at large." Wealthy patriot women experienced further loss at the hands of their own troops, as in early 1780 when Mary and William Taggart were ordered to burn their house and all outbuildings in Hampstead, just northeast of the city, to prevent its use by the British as a staging area. The war reached inside wealthy women's homes, destroyed their households, transformed them into refugees, and utterly disrupted the well-ordered world over which they had formerly presided.[45]

The American Revolution also robbed patriot ladies of their customary authority. They no longer ministered to the needs of the worthy poor, for their property had been sequestered by the enemy or lay in ruins, their valuables had been stolen, and they had difficulty merely sustaining themselves. Ladies no longer controlled their own households because slaves ran off or "did as they pleased." It "seemed strange," one matriarch observed, "that a single woman, accused of no crime, who had a fortune to live Genteelly in any part of the world . . . should in so short a time be so entirely deprived of it." Her home lay "shattered and ruined, which left [her] little power to assist" her children. "Nor," she lamented, "had I in Country or Town a place to lay my head . . . all was taken out of my possession . . . nor was I able to hire a lodging." This elite woman was voicing more than self-pity over her financial losses. The war not only delivered devastating economic blows, but also interrupted social and cultural practices that distinguished ladies as a ruling elite. And each time slave women and free women of African descent basked in the attention of British soldiers and supplanted women of the master class at a public function, they inflicted more than minor insults. Thirty-one months of British occupation exacerbated this fundamental loss of social place and personal identity for ladies of Charleston's master class.[46]

On the other hand, wealthy *loyalist* ladies, like artisan women who sympathized with England, reaped monetary rewards and heightened status from the occupation. British authorities occasionally rewarded loyalty with gifts of slaves who had sought asylum with the king's troops. In addition, those who fought for the Crown sometimes received slaves in lieu of pay. After occupation, the British army also returned runaway slaves to their loyalist owners and periodically hired slaves from loyalists. If a slave died while in British service, occupation officials compensated the owner. In these circumstances, one woman (a loyalist) profited from the tragedy of another woman (a slave) whose husband had perished while working for the king's troops. Opportunity for one constituted liability for another.[47]

Although British occupation brought to elite loyalists (as well as slaves and free women of color) opportunities to exact revenge for previous persecutions, their revelry was tempered by lingering financial woes. Recall that in 1778 Carolina's revolutionary government had imposed severe economic sanctions by doubling taxes on all absentee loyalist property owners. Failure to pay resulted in confiscation. Margaret Colleton, widowed ten years before the Revolution and having relocated to England long before fighting broke out, nevertheless paid double taxes on her inherited Carolina property in order to maintain a legacy for her children. Even those loyalist wives who remained in Charleston were subject to this double assessment unless they could prove exclusive legal ownership of family real estate.[48]

Among the wealthy as among the poor, war inflicted emotional havoc in addition to political and economic chaos. Although Charleston women were well acquainted with disease and death, the war brought more frequent calls from these unwelcome visitors who were no respectors of wealth or position. By May 1781, upward of 800 American Continentals and militiamen had died after thirteen months' captivity on fetid prison ships in the city's harbor. They represented nearly one-third of the total number warehoused on prison ships and, under the British terms of surrender, most should not have been imprisoned at all. The ranks of Charleston's widows increased daily. The British continued to confine increasing numbers of men under conditions so abysmal that the latter "could not expect anything more but to perish miserably."[49]

Tribulations such as these also precipitated atypical actions, which, in turn, allowed master-class ladies to discover their true strength and to forge new self-perceptions. In summer 1781 several ladies boarded the putrid vessels, where hundreds lay sick and dying of smallpox and dysentery. Initially motivated by humanitarian interests, these ladies transformed a traditional female role—comforter and nonprofessional healer—into overtly political action. Avowed patriot Eliza Wilkinson, among others, swore she took "pleasure in giving a drink to even the most ragged, dirty fellow serving his country." She openly bragged of the prisoners' lofty spirits lifted still higher as the men enjoyed the attention and esteem of Charleston's finest ladies. One American soldier waxed poetic in extolling the selfless support of these women who "sweeten[ed] every sorrow [and] arm[ed] him with consolation to encounter every danger." The fact that these prisoners enjoyed "high favor with the ladies," Eliza boasted, gave "the proud conquerors the heart-burn."[50]

British occupation afforded master-class ladies occasions to step out of character and into comportment more typical of the lower sorts of women. They moved beyond benevolent tasks and began taking pride in publicly spurning and ridiculing British troops and defiantly celebrating patriot bravery. Although slave women and free laboring women of all colors were long accustomed to asserting themselves in public (after assessing how much they could get away with), this conduct was new to wealthy white ladies. Not alone in such actions, outspoken Eliza Wilkinson refused the arm of an enemy officer billeted in her city residence. He protested that she might fall on the uneven pavements, but Eliza coolly spurned his attentions and informed him that she could support herself. Moments later Eliza espied striped ribbon in a shop. Since the officer persisted in shadowing her, she inquired if he thought the stripes numbered thirteen. Emboldened by Eliza's taunting, the storekeeper entered the fray and suggested she buy black and white ribbons and "tack them in stripes." "I would not have them slightly tacked but firmly united," Eliza asserted. The merchant laughed, the officer gaped, and Eliza relished this opportunity to publicly voice her political sentiments and denigrate her foes.[51]

Women's outspoken patriotism occasionally reaped retribution from the occupation's commandant, Colonel Nisbet Balfour, whose infamy grew in relation to his exhibitions of "frivolous self-importance, and all the disgusting insolence which are natural to little minds when puffed up by sudden elevation." He wielded his power with gusto, and began confining women as well as men with little provocation and without any trial. Two sisters of the prominent Sarazen family served time in prison for what was described as a trifling offense. British soldiers escorted the Sarazen sisters to the forbidding, damp, "unwholesome" cellar of the Exchange building at water's edge, where the two "huddled up together in one common room" with male and female political prisoners and common criminals.[52]

Among Charleston women, American patriotism was much in vogue and genuine in fervor. Slaveholding women as well as men particularly prized liberty, because as slave mistresses they daily observed its antithesis within their own households. During the Revolution, patriot ladies espoused freedom's virtues on numerous occasions in correspondence with each other. "America, my dear native land," wrote one woman to her cousin and close friend, "may long . . . be distinguished as the favorite of heaven . . . [and] may humanity, piety, and tender sympathy be the distinguished character of every son and daughter of America."[53] Speaking for herself and on behalf of "her countrymen," city resident Miss Trapier exclaimed, "by our continued unanimity, in spite of all [British] base arts to disunite us . . . America determines to be free [for] it is beyond their force of arms to enslave so vast a Continent!"[54]

These women clearly viewed themselves as public-spirited patriots and full citizens in the new republic. Their letters and diaries reverberated with revolutionary rhetoric. "I would sooner bite my tongue off [than] designedly or inadvertently betray my friends and countrymen," one declared to rampaging British soldiers who sought information on troop movements. Eliza and her sisters discussed the latter topic and boasted, "Never were greater politicians than the several knots of ladies, who met together. All trifling discourse of fashions, and such low little chat was thrown by, and we commenc[e]d perfect statesmen . . . so well could we discuss several important matters in hand." On expounding the virtues of liberty, slaveholder Eliza exclaimed to her cousin how important, how sweet, and how worthy of battle was freedom. She confessed her "sympathetic ardor" and continued, "I won't have it thought, that because we are the weaker sex as to bodily strength . . . we are capable of nothing more than minding the dairy, visiting the poultry-house, and all such domestic concerns; our thoughts can soar aloft . . . [with] just [as much] a sense of honor, glory, and great actions, as these 'lords of the Creation.'"[55]

War afforded opportunities for women and men of the ruling elite to reify mutually dependent identities: the merciful, angelic, faithful lady on the one hand, and the conspiratorial, nefarious, treacherous slave woman on the other. These diametric images composed two sides of the same coin, with each image deriving full force and meaning in contrast to the other. By embellishing words and deeds, southern ladies became epic figures. They arose from the Revolution as "slender Columns . . . beauteous models of elegance and taste, erect and unimpaired notwithstanding the violence [and] desolation which surround[ed] them." Men of the master class lauded their ladies' "sensibility so exquisitely delicate," their "constancy so heroically firm" so as to inspire "admiration and delight" in "their enraptured Countrymen." Such notions became instrumental in raising elite ladies onto their pedestals after temporary displacement by women of African descent. This reinstatement—and the entwined antithetical portraits of women—became a keystone in Charleston's postwar social reconstruction.[56]

The American Revolution was both formative and transformative. The notion of virtuous and womanly women, perpetuated and embellished by the Charleston elite during and after the Revolution, glorified a constellation of female characteristics normally associated with middle-class women of the industrialized North. A rich body of literature has highlighted the changed notions of gender that developed when industrialization separated home from the workplace and relegated middle-class women to the former and men to the latter. Women in this group were characterized by their male peers and in prescriptive literature as selfless, compassionate, gentle, faithful, and virtuous. But these same Victorian images emerged decades earlier in the rhetoric of revolutionary South Carolina. Men of the master class described their women in identical terms. Charleston's "true women," however, came into their own during the

American Revolution and amid a non-industrial slave society. The portrait proved functional to ladies and gentlemen who were struggling to reconstitute urban slave society and to delineate their places in it.[57]

However disparately the war affected slave women, free women of color, white laboring women, and master-class women, all shared certain experiences, like the death of loved ones and temporary or permanent disruption of their homes. Because the city was besieged and occupied, all residents also experienced economic privations and physical discomfort, albeit to drastically different degrees. What was one woman's opportunity was another woman's liability, and one woman's bounteous blessing was another woman's tragedy. The commonalities knit women together, but the singular encounters differentiated and defined them as distinctive social groups.

Some changes proved only temporary, as when laboring women assumed control of family businesses when their husbands fled Charleston or fought in the war, or when slaves and free women of color supplanted ladies and danced at center stage during Charleston's high social season at the time of the British occupation. Other transformations (notably from wife to widow or slave to free woman) were permanent and life altering.

3 Rebuilding and Resisting

After the war, women of all colors, conditions, and economic status had to re-build their lives and ascertain their places in the new state. While engaged in this process, their interests often clashed. Yet at other times their needs and goals converged and complemented one another. One reality was constant. As they reconstructed their worlds, they did so in a city that was still chaotic and often dangerous, at the heart of a slave society that simultaneously entwined yet separated women. Even before the Paris peace treaty had been signed, men of the master class set about renovating slavery and patriarchy. These efforts im-pinged daily on the lives of all women, who worked to recreate their worlds and also resist measures that encroached on their reconstruction efforts. Women of color, in particular, resisted and adapted to an increasingly tight web of con-straints as men and women of the ruling class closed ranks and reasserted their dominance.

Although peace would not be declared until September 3, 1783, the British evacuation nine months earlier marked Charleston's liberation and the begin-ning of its physical and social reconstruction. Women of the master class held a great stake in this urban slave society and were eager to reassert their pre-scribed authority. Members of the master class reconstructed their city in two primary ways: by reasserting supremacy through pageantry and cultural forms and by restoring sanctions fundamental to slavery. Women were essential to both of these reconstruction strategies. As the British contingent departed by sea in December 1782, and 5,000 Continental soldiers triumphantly entered Charleston by land, it was significant that the wives of Governor John Mathews and Generals Nathanael Greene and William Moultrie rode down Broad Street in the stately victory parade. Wealthy white women, "many of whom had been cooped up in one room of their own elegant houses for upwards of two years," emerged ready to take back Charleston from their inferiors (particularly women of color) who had had the temerity to mimic and supplant them.[1]

Women of the master class derived from the American Revolution a stronger sense of themselves as full participants in the body politic and an awareness that they were excluded from realizing their new roles. Men "won't even allow us the liberty of thought," complained widowed slave owner Eliza Wilkinson. "I would not wish that we should meddle in what is unbecoming [to] female delicacy," she pronounced, "but surely we may have sense enough to give our opinions . . . without being reminded of our spinning and household affairs . . . I won't allow it, positively won't."[2]

Women of the master class were barred from full citizenship, but they infused into their traditional role as arbiters of Charleston's social scene a quickened patriotism, fashioning a new political role for themselves as civic hosts. These wealthy, white women repositioned themselves in Charleston society by expanding their traditional female mandate as quintessential hostess into the world of politics. Accustomed to being on display, whether at the annual round of winter balls, at St. Cecilia concerts, or riding through city streets in elaborate equipages on Sunday afternoons, patriot ladies had shunned the public eye during the British occupation. Indeed, their refusal to attend loyalist dinners and other social events was a form of political protest. Conversely, in the closing years of the eighteenth century (and continuing for a half-century after the Revolution), ladies figured prominently in civic pageants. Particularly during this time of reconstruction, public pageantry was crucial, not only defining what it was to be an American but also redrawing social and political boundaries.

En route to Charleston at the end of April 1791, President George Washington stopped first in neighboring Georgetown, where several of Charleston's wealthiest families owned plantations. The press reported that amid the great joy of the occasion and the multiple functions, including a public dinner, "nothing was more conspicuous than the patriotism of the ladies . . . [who] vied with each other in shewing [sic] him marks of the highest respect." Master-class women hosted their own state function—a tea party for the president—donning sashes imprinted with the seal of the United States. These civic hosts also "wore head dresses ornamented with bandeau, upon which were written, in letters of gold, either 'Long life to the president,' or 'Welcome the hero.'" Observers reported that Washington was "introduced to all the ladies present [and he] . . . entertained several of them in succession."[3]

During his weeklong stay in Charleston (2–9 May 1791), President Washington attended at least eight grand festivities in his honor. Women figured prominently in more than half of these social/political celebrations. But the city's civic hosts did not simply attend as appendages of their male escorts; they evidenced self-perceptions as political as well as social beings. They wore "ribbons and girdles with different expressions of their respect and esteem for the president, such as . . . 'Virtue and valor united.'" A ball at the governor's home served as yet another forum for the city's civic hosts to don ribbons with political and patriotic messages. At yet another elaborate dinner, hosted by city merchants and attended by all the "best" Charleston ladies and gentlemen, one of the toasts offered was to "the fair daughters of America." Two years later, when municipal officials organized a lavish ceremony to commemorate the fall of the Bastille, Charleston ladies again played a focal role. Public, political displays such as these were integral to the city's postwar reconstruction. Ardently patriotic ladies and gentlemen of the ruling elite were redrawing parameters of race, gender, and class upon which slave society was built.[4]

Charleston ladies appropriated a second political role during the early republic and, like the role of civic host, it emerged from their intensified patriotism during the war. Like women in the North, they adopted the role of "Republican Mothers." Embracing revolutionary rhetoric and envisioning themselves as "custodians of civic morality," women of the master class "domesticated . . . political virtue" by commandeering the task of educating virtuous future citizens, a crucial responsibility in the fragile republic. Eliza Lucas Pinckney typified this role. She was a successful agriculturalist, wife of a chief justice of South Carolina, and mother of three children, two of them heroes of the Revolution. When her daughter-in-law died soon after the war, Eliza became a surrogate mother to her three granddaughters. Inculcating the patriotic values she so treasured, yet reflecting her vivid memories of the horrors of war, Eliza addressed one of her grandsons in the immediate postwar period. "Though I hope your Country will never want your aid in a Military capacity," she wrote, "may you be guided by the same principles of true honour and real virtue that have always actuated [your parents]. . . . May your conduct in publick and private life Emulate the Example they have set you, and give your mother a comfort which nothing clsc can." Young unmarricd ladics imbibcd such admonitions and spoke in similar terms before they became mothers. One such woman, Miss Trapier, addressed herself to "her countrymen" and exclaimed, "Heaven interests itself in favor of those who have Virtue to assert the birthright of mankind, Divine Liberty!" Eliza Pinckney and Miss Trapier took seriously the task of instilling integrity and virtue in their "countrymen," their children, and their grandchildren. Their words resonated with the values associated with republican motherhood.[5]

The American Revolution divided Charleston's ruling class according to political allegiances, so some ladies were excluded from full participation in the new state not only because they were female but also because they were accused loyalists. A 1789 legal ruling reveals the intensity of persistent anti-loyalist enmity. In that year, the courts ruled against a basic tenet of common law: a woman's right to one-third of her husband's property. The presiding jurist vowed that:

> the widow of a person attainted of treason forfeits her right of dower . . . for the common law goes upon the idea, that husbands are oftentimes influenced and governed by the sentiments and conduct of their wives. If, therefore, they [women] do not exert this influence, by example and dissuasion, they are considered in the law, as having incurred such a degree of guilt, as to forfeit every right or claim under their husbands.[6]

Given this enduring antipathy, loyalist ladies found that the path of postwar rebuilding led to the male forum of the state legislature. Like their artisan counterparts, loyalist women of the master class·confronted state authorities over the issue of property confiscation. Unlike laboring women, however, ladies couched their petitions in terms of their roles as wives and mothers rather than as people with political identities. They framed their appeals in notions of female dependence, emphasized their ignorance of things political, and pled innocence. They beseeched state legislators to pardon their husbands and permit their return to Charleston. Ann Legge, for example, chose this tack of domestic entreaty. However, knowing full well that the legislature might refuse to absolve her husband, Ann also importuned the House to "prevent her & her three poor innocent children from experiencing those Calamities which a total Loss of her little remaining property must eventually produce, by *Vesting that property in her or her children*."[7]

Ironically, women like Ann who pleaded "dependency" had already stepped beyond the bounds of their dependent domestic roles in the very act of publicly protesting confiscation and amercement, and in requesting relief from the state assembly. They had already acted as *femes sole*—women who possessed legal identities apart from their husbands—rather than as the covered women (*femes covert*) that they were under South Carolina's rendering of English common law. Moreover, in soliciting transfer of property to her name, Ann Legge had applied de facto for *feme sole* status. Although Margaret Brisbane, wife of a banished loyalist, described the position of women as "weak and Defenceless [*sic*] . . . [and] whose Opinions seldom avail," she also added that her own "Sentiments with regard to the present Contest never coincided with, but were always contrary to her Husbands."[8]

Part of the postwar reconstruction process involved a closing of the ranks as the affluent master class turned more exclusive. It is true that the proportion of white residents who owned slaves increased during several decades following the Revolution. However, the wealthiest among them, who ruled Charleston and, indeed, all of South Carolina, restricted access to their elite faction. In the colonial era, successful working people had acquired land and slaves, intermarried with the great planter families, and were embraced by the nascent ruling class, who welcomed them into the top economic, political, and social echelons of Charleston. Before the American Revolution, slave traders, ships' captains, and merchants became planters, and some planters engaged in trade. The great families of Charleston also respected British and Scottish tradesmen, as well as Jewish merchants from London and Amsterdam (whose expertise in the indigo market proved valuable in that trade), and absorbed them into the city's self-made aristocracy. However, during the Revolution, Charleston patriots came to associate all merchants with the enemy. Exacerbating this rift, from approximately 1795 to nearly 1820, only one of the city's twenty-one leading commercial companies was owned or managed by a native Carolinian. After the Revolution, mercantile activity was spurned as an occupation unworthy of a patriot and southern-born gentlemen. Thus, after the war, Charleston's wealthiest women and men looked down their noses at parvenu merchants, including tradesmen in general and the city's Jewish businessmen in particular. In so doing, they evinced the class-based elitism of the Carolina aristocracy, lingering anti-British sentiment—for British businessmen had monopolized Charleston commerce—and anti-semitism. Well before the 1820s, regional antipathy came into play as well. In the first decade of the nineteenth century, northern merchants at first supplemented and then supplanted British merchants. "The only thing worse than a Jew," decried one city resident in 1818, was "a Yankee."[9]

Ladies participated in this entrenchment, which was fundamental to the rebuilding process of the master class, because ladies had a vested interest in re-asserting and securing their position near the apex of Charleston society. But their active participation—verbal and otherwise—in this process of reasserting the supremacy of the master class incurred open enmity. In 1785, rowdy members of the "Marine Anti-Britannic Society"—which included artisans, laborers, sailors, and disgruntled or displaced transients—publicly castigated wealthy women as spoiled, useless, and a drain on society. One caustic critic decried them as mere "Pretty little Misses at Home." Women as well as men of the master class responded in kind in this increasingly rancorous class war. Margaret Izard Manigault, wife of one of the state's wealthiest men and a privileged slave owner in her own right, openly expressed contempt for "those reptiles of the Patriotic Society," who presumed to meddle in politics. Margaret and other wealthy women loathed the destabilizing influence of these "lower sorts" who, they believed, had set out to destroy the city. In their demeanor, elaborate dress, exclusive social functions, ritualistic carriage rides, and other contrived cultural forms, women of the master class routinely conveyed utter scorn for their social inferiors. They publicly paraded their own wealth and high social status. These actions confirmed and provoked resentment and anger. While Margaret Manigault's words, and other women's denigration of lower-class men, primarily manifested their insularism, these actions also revealed a political awakening. The ladies perceived themselves as part of a political citizenry as well as a ruling elite group, and they appropriated from the Revolution license to express this identity.[10]

As the master class became more exclusive, it alienated other city residents, deepening chasms between ladies and laboring women. After all, the "reptiles" and political upstarts that Margaret disparaged had mothers, sisters, and wives. Charleston was home to hundreds of laboring women as well as men. This elitism of the master class engendered a world of intimate strangers. Milliners, pastry cooks, mantua makers, bakers, and other women in trade needed and catered to the city's wealthy women, who, likewise, relied on the services of laboring women. These relationships were mutually dependent, but the parties were not equal. In addition, the intractable commitment of the master class to slave-based agriculture resulted in dire consequences for the city's women, regardless of their social standing, because Charleston's relative economic position in the new nation declined as other cities eclipsed the southern port. Nineteenth-century visitors increasingly characterized Charleston as a grand, aristocratic, but "infirm, decrepit, bedridden" old woman. This grande dame of a city rested on a foundation of slavery, so it afforded few economic options to free women of the laboring classes.[11]

Another crucial piece of the post-Revolution reconstruction project undertaken by elite women and men of the low country involved retooling the institution of slavery. In this enterprise, perhaps more than in any other, the entwined, mutually dependent status of African Americans and European Americans becomes clear. Although men (primarily but not exclusively of the master class) legislated slavery's reinforcement, slave-owning ladies helped implement these measures. Old political affinities continued to divide members of Charleston's master class, but they were united as slave owners. Patriot and loyalist ladies did not go out of their way to mend fences, but safeguarding slavery took precedence over political grudges. After the Revolution, the city was plagued by enmity between patriot and loyalist, rich and poor, low country and back country, planter and entrepreneur, native Carolinian and immigrant, but a patina of solidarity smoothed over these ruptures. In the years of the early republic, however, racial tension was the issue that riveted the interest of Charleston's ladies and gentlemen.

In 1783, the state's general assembly took two giant steps toward rejuvenating slavery. First, it renewed in perpetuity the Negro Act of 1740. In taking that step, legislators reaffirmed all colonial slave laws and actually set the state on a path toward intensifying its black code. In March of the same year, the assembly also enacted a collective slave hunt or dragnet act. This law aimed at staunching a flood of runaway slaves precipitated by the recent war and restoring slaves to their rightful owners by penalizing those who either harbored fugitive slaves or appropriated runaways as their own. Legislators vowed to "punish such as shall embezzle, conceal, or neglect to render an account" of all "Negroes . . . not their own property." The law gave individuals four months from enactment to report "borrowed or stolen" human property in newspapers, and it required people to run each notice for four weeks.[12]

Women of African and European descent actively negotiated the strictures imposed by this 1783 slave hunt. After the Revolution, slave women's unwavering determination to establish their own parameters on mobility, on where they lived, and with whom was matched by the dogged exertions of owners to thwart such liberty. These antithetical goals clashed and intruded on women's lives. In early 1784 Mary Russel "Forewarn[ed] Captains of vessels from carrying off" her slave woman, Frances. Mary offered a reward of "ten dollars, if a white person, and Five [if] a Negro," to "whoever [would] take up, and deliver the said negro" to her. One year later, three generations of women ran off to Charleston together hoping to establish their own household. Matriarch Jenny "had a permit . . . to seek a master in the city," but her daughter, Dido, and granddaughter, Tissey, accompanied Jenny when she departed. Their owner concluded that the two women (with the infant) would be "lurking about town" and offered a reward for their capture. Likewise resolute about living on her own terms and reuniting with family or friends, a woman named Nancy had been gone two years, during which time she had been in Charleston where she "washe[d] and iron[ed] for a livelihood" while "pass[ing] for a free wench." And another woman, Tinah, lived with her sister "at Mr. Tunno's" house in Charleston. Like Nancy, Tinah was "well known" in the city and likely "pass[ed] as a free woman." The problem was that Mr. Tunno was neither her owner nor had he hired her. Runaway advertisements were not, of course, unique to the war and postwar years, but the huge number of slaves who fled was unprecedented, and the new 1783 dragnet law buttressed the determined efforts of slave-owning women and men to retrieve their property.[13]

Legislation like these 1783 measures reveals that, as a group, the master class enacted a comprehensive system of repression that could not be wholly implemented or enforced. In this city of 20,000 people, 51 to 53 percent were of African descent (both slave and free), so it was feasible for runaways to pass as free. They could also pose as slaves whose owners had granted permission for them to "work out"—to find employment on their own and remit wages to their owners on a regular schedule. In theory, all wartime runaways should have been returned to their owners because the 1783 dragnet put muscle behind this goal. In practice, however, the goal itself was unattainable.[14]

When the slave-owning elite sold slave women, men, and children to regain economic solvency, they quite literally rebuilt their world on the backs of their human property. Postwar Charleston was both a city of widows and a city in which many members of the master class—some of them formerly the richest in the American colonies—found themselves temporarily without shelter, food, and clothing, as well as without their customary luxuries. After the war, they reestablished order in their personal lives by trying to capture runaways and sell slaves to generate quick cash. During the six months between 22 March and 2 September 1783, area residents placed 300 announcements in just one of the city's papers, the *Gazette*, in their efforts to apprehend runaway slaves and notify the public of impending sales of their human property. They further indicated this resolve to restore the slave system by complying with the state's newest law concerning fugitives. They published names and descriptions of hundreds of other people's slaves whom they had apprehended. During this same six-month period, city residents placed a total of over 2,400 advertisements of various sorts in the *Gazette*, and of this total, fully 21 percent advertised slave sales, requested help in finding their own slaves, or notified the public of "stray slaves" in their possession. Women figured among these frenzied advertisers, but their numbers are not easily identifiable. Many declined to place their names on newspaper advertisements of slave sales, instead specifying that readers should "Enquire of the printer." Countless women also employed Charleston firms like Cudworth, Waller, & Co.; Sam Prioleau, Jun. & Co.; Webb & Bounetheau; or Colcock & Gibbons to conduct slave sales at private and public venues. In addition, male executors oversaw estate sales for widows, thereby keeping the women's names out of all public notices. By comparison, of a total 767 ads appearing in the *South Carolina and American General Gazette* during six months before the British occupation, only fourteen (or 1.8 percent) were placed by women who were selling slaves or attempting to recapture runaways.[15]

South Carolina's reopening of the Atlantic slave trade in 1803 and the importation of thousands of Africans into Charleston harbor constituted another centerpiece of slavery's regeneration. Before this deluge of slaves, the master class had undertaken much of its post-Revolution rebuilding—restoration of the black code, implementation of additional regulations, and demonstration of dominion through pageantry and other cultural forms. But the African trade revitalized slavery and fueled the city's longest boom. During the entirety of the slave trade, from its colonial origins until its legal termination in 1808, roughly one-fourth of all Africans transported to mainland North America entered through Charleston harbor. Between 1782 and 1810, traders and smugglers imported nearly 90,000 slaves into the city. Over 4,000 arrived in 1784 alone. Less than one-third remained in the low country. Most were transported to the Carolina backcountry, New Orleans, frontier regions of the new southwest, or the Carolina sea islands. This African infusion did not permanently alter the city's demography and culture as it did on the plantations where these new African slaves resided. But the enormity of the trade (the equivalent of over 3,000 Africans entered Charleston annually for a period of twenty-nine years), and its trappings, supplied striking reminders of slavery's extreme power relations and likely precipitated greater resentment, enmity, and dissembling among the port city's slave women. What better way for ladies and gentlemen to affirm their commitment to slavery than to ensure that slave ships routinely rode low in the harbor, that holding pens remained packed with slaves, and that vendue masters conducted brisk public trade in the city's streets.[16]

Ironically, the reopening of the African trade simultaneously revived slavery (as was intended) *and* exacerbated white Charlestonians' apprehensions about their status as a racial minority. So advocates of slavery accomplished their goal, but then they worried about the legacy of the achievement. This angst affected all women but in different ways depending on their race, color, condition, or wealth. In 1792, when some 500 Saint Domingue refugees arrived in Charleston, they encountered suspicion from slave-owning residents who feared the adverse influence (on the city's slave population) of the emigrants' "infected slaves." White residents assumed that these transplanted Caribbean slaves must be tainted by the seditious influence of slave rebellion. A visitor to Charleston in 1795 reflected the convictions of many slave-owning women when he observed that "a vast number of French Mulattoes and Negroes [were] ready for any mischief[,] and since arriving in the city," he continued, "there [had] been three or four different attempts to set the Town on Fire." On one of those occasions, "they so far succeeded that three houses were on fire." Petitions to the new state legislature also voiced white Charleston's anxiety about people of color, both female and male, but particularly expressed their suspicion of émigrés from the Caribbean. Supplicants urged enforcement of "successive laws prohibiting the importation of Negroes," because they were convinced that "[m]any Negroes of the worst description and most desperate and dangerous dispositions and characters [were] continually smuggled from the French and other West India Islands and disposed of in this State." The reopening of the trade, and consequent increased numbers of black and brown people in a city where they already outnumbered white residents, exacerbated uneasy race relations. That tension, in turn, spread to all people of color and likely heightened tensions between mistresses and slaves, between free white laboring women and slaves, and possibly between white laboring women and their darker counterparts.[17]

This contagion of distrust manifested in further restrictions on all people of color, whether slave or free, African, West Indian, or Carolina-born. The ruling elite enacted a systematic, incremental curtailment of the rights and freedoms of all people of color that continued from the end of the Revolution until (and after) the Civil War. This affected relations among the city's women. It also disrupted the lives of all Charleston's people of African descent. In 1793 city officials created a larger city patrol, whose job it was to enforce curfews and other laws regulating the mobility of every city resident of color. They funded this measure by further penalizing free people of color: Charleston established an annual per capita tax on all free people of color. It was a two-dollar head tax on all free persons of color ages sixteen to fifty. This "capitation tax" fell especially hard on non-slaveholding free women of color who derived no income from hired-out slave labor; they worked hard for every cent, and for them two dollars represented a huge sum. This regulatory crusade bespoke chronic fear of slave insurrection that had intensified during and after the Revolution. The increased restrictions also reflected white residents' anxiety about the city's increasing population of free black and brown people. Between 1790 and 1800, the number of free people of African descent in Charleston increased by 75 percent (from 586 to 1,024), which far exceeded the growth rate of slaves and white people. From 1800 to 1810 their ranks grew by 44 percent.[18]

In the first decade following the war, Charleston's wealthiest women and men rebuilt their own existence by narrowing the lives of the city's people of color, regardless of their status. Restrictions on the latter soothed the insecurities of the former. Slaveholders were not omnipotent—slaves made it so—but they tamed the chaos wrought by war, in large measure, by reshaping and reanimating the malleable system of domination that undergirded slave society.

While slaveholding women and men reinvigorated slavery and repositioned themselves at the pinnacle of Charleston society, slave women resisted the strictures imposed on them by the master class. Their post-Revolution rebuilding paralleled that of other groups of women in some respects. They, too, had been displaced by war and had lost husbands and other family members. Like white women, slave women imbibed the revolutionary rhetoric of liberty, so they resisted constraints imposed on them and determined to establish their own places in Charleston. Often these attempts clashed with the goals of the city's free people, particularly slave owners. The actions of female slaves during and after the war had heightened slave owners' suspicions about slave treachery that, in turn, hardened their resolve to constrain people of color. So slave women had unwittingly catalyzed slave owners, who tenaciously tightened restrictions. On the other hand, sometimes slave women's aspirations and the needs of other groups of women turned out to be mutually beneficial. Postwar rebuilding occasionally made for motley bedfellows.

Slaves manipulated people and the 1783 slave law—the slave dragnet—in order to reconstitute kin ties and escape intolerable physical conditions or owners. When an unnamed slave woman and her partner fell captive to Charleston resident Daniel Cannan, they professed to have the same owner, a man whom Daniel did not know. This slave couple likely did not attain freedom, but by naming a fictitious owner or one who had been exiled or whom they knew to be dead, they might have bought additional time together in hopes of remaining united under a new owner. Slaves used the 1783 Carolina slave law to find loved ones, avoid recapture, establish new homes, and find better owners. The same legislative act that mandated publication of the names of captured slaves, in effect, provided free advertising to slaves who wanted a former owner to find them so they could be reunited with family. Slave women and their kin asserted their own volition even as slave owners intensified efforts to rob them of it.[19]

With a tenacious but fragile grasp on freedom, and pursued by slave owners determined to break that grip, Charleston slave women turned to their free black and brown relatives and friends for help. In 1783 a free woman of color named Hannah Norman sold thirteen female and male slaves, but she transacted this deal with a buyer sympathetic to her desire to allow these thirteen slaves to live virtually free. Hannah retained exclusive use of the slaves (who may have been family members) under the terms of the sale, which stipulated that they could not be seized as payment for any financial debts her husband incurred. Hannah's fear of this outcome, as well as her desire to provide tacit freedom to the thirteen women and men, probably motivated the 1783 sale.[20]

However, benefaction did not drive all slave sales negotiated by Charleston's free women of African descent. As with white slave owners, some were propelled by profit. Hannah Norman's additional sales transactions reveal these mixed motives. During a postwar recession, Hannah sold her slave Lucy for £35 sterling. This sale was wholly unrelated to her 1783 sale of thirteen slaves. Hannah and other slave-owning widows of color, like their white counterparts, sold slaves when they needed cash. A transaction that reaped security for one woman sowed havoc in the lives of others. Particularly because Charleston was a nexus for local slave trading and a center for slave importation, sale loomed as a real possibility in every slave woman's life, and each sale bore potential disaster. As the 1808 federal curtailment of the slave trade approached, Charleston surged forward as a leading slave-importer, and approximately 10,000 slaves annually passed into the city's harbor. Notwithstanding the loss of some 25,000 slaves from South Carolina between 1775 and 1783, the number of Charleston slaves doubled between the Revolution and 1800. Private and public slave sales were everyday occurrences in the city, and increased demand for labor in the back country and in the deeper South rendered slave women vulnerable to grasping traders who might transport them far from loved ones. One historian has convincingly documented the speculative character of much local trading within the city of Charleston. Resident urban dealers, auctioneers, and commission agents often acted as intermediaries for slave owners who wished to sell or buy human property. It is estimated that, combining local and interregional sales statistics, South Carolina slaves faced a 14 percent chance of being sold.[21]

The postwar reality of slave women also entailed a continuation of their customary vital role in the city economy. The Revolution appears to have had little effect on women's near-monopoly of Charleston markets. By the wharves, as well as in the centrally located Four Corners area at the intersection of Broad and Meeting streets, and in their own "Slave Fair," hundreds of women sold baked goods as well as other domestic items as they had "for several years past." White residents and magistrates complained about the number, practices, and attitudes of Charleston market women as they had done in colonial times. In 1799 the city's Grand Jury recommended that "the [existing] laws against fore-stalling . . . be put in execution, as this grievance [had] grown to a very great magnitude." Magistrates also ruled that "the clerk of the market . . . be empow-ered to remove the number of negro hucksters from about the markets." The market women were not "removed," at least not permanently, because similar complaints and court rulings recurred into the 1830s.[22]

Because market women and other slaves so effectively resisted attempts to limit their independent productive activities and constrain their movements, work, and domestic arrangements, slave owners charted a path of subjugation tempered by negotiation. They resolved to reinvigorate slavery through conces-sions as well as strictures. But the relative autonomy of wartime had steeled slave women. They had gained confidence in their ability to negotiate the pro-scriptions of slave society. They also recalled their owners' weaknesses during the war and, indeed, the vulnerabilities of slave society as a whole. This double consciousness altered the balance of power in postwar Charleston. Slaves knew they possessed greater latitude to bargain; owners knew they had to make more deals. When Judy ran away with two other slaves in spring 1783, her owner ad-vertised that if they returned within three days, "and if they [chose] any[one else] to buy them," that he would sell them to a new owner. This prospect of allowing slaves to choose another owner represented an adaptation, born of necessity, of the common colonial practice of promising to forgive slaves if they returned of their own volition. In a sample of runaway advertisements in ten newspapers during the period 1783 to 1806, one historian has found 144 examples of promised forgiveness and the option to choose new owners, com-pared to only 40 such advertisements—chiefly promising forgiveness—in the entire colonial period. These statistics reveal that even as gentlemen and ladies of the master class reasserted their power, slaves pressed for accommodations to their own demands for greater autonomy.[23]

This postwar convention of allowing slaves to choose their owners persisted and became woven into the fabric of customary practice in postwar Charleston. As one historian has suggested, this protocol may have signaled the transition from the "distance, autonomy, and violence" of colonial slavery, to the "closer and more controlling, if less overtly brutal . . . paternalism" of post-Revolution slave society. It continued well into the nineteenth century, and expanded be-yond its original use as an enticement to runaway slaves. In 1822 the Yates family's slaves, Mary, Diana, and Billy, were "much dissatisfied and beg[ged]" their mistress to sell them. It is likely they had a prospective owner in mind. In addition, slave owners began stipulating in their wills that certain slaves were to be sold for profit, but with the privilege of selecting their masters. A member of Charleston's free brown elite community, Barbara Maria Bampfield, made precisely that provision for her slave Fatima in a final testament. Ironically, concessions like Barbara's to Fatima manifested a relative victory for slaves yet also revealed the vigor and adaptability of slavery. The master class had protected and expanded the institution into a flexible social system that accommodated a slave's assertions of autonomy and an owner's insistence on racial oppression and dominion. Free women of color, who straddled both worlds—slave and free, black and white—contended for a berth in this postwar order.[24]

Post-Revolution Charleston tendered opportunities and frustrations in nearly equal measure to free women of color. As they established their niche in a city committed to slavery, with one hand members of the master class promised a place in Charleston society to free people of African descent, but with the other hand they crushed their aspirations. Maintaining the lowest rate of slave manumission in mainland North America, Carolina nevertheless experienced a short-lived spate of emancipations after the war. Low-country slave owners freed more slaves in the 1780s than in the three previous decades. Only 14 manumissions by Charleston slave owners were recorded in the 1750s and 29 in the 1760s. By contrast, just over 53 percent of the 222 manumissions by Charleston owners from 1750 to 1790 were listed in the ten years after 1780, and fully 81 percent of them took place from 1770 to 1790. However unlikely the prospect of manumission for low-country slaves, urban women had a greater chance at it. Charleston slaveholders signed more than half of all recorded manumissions in the state, and two of every three persons manumitted were women. These facts are not coincidental. Revolutionary oratory inspired at least a small group of mistresses and masters. In March 1783 one Hagar and her child were "ever-hereafter deemed . . . free persons . . . and for ever delivered and discharged from the Yoke of Slavery." Her emancipation was a gift from the Carolina state legislature to her husband, Antigua, a slave whom they had employed as a patriot spy. Antigua had "obtained very considerable and important information from within the enemy's lines, frequently at the ris[k] of his life," and legislators judged it "reasonable that . . . Antigua should receive some reward for the services which he has performed." Manumissions, combined with the thousands of slaves who freed themselves by running away during the war years, laid the foundation for Charleston's free brown and black populations. Although free people of color constituted the smallest population group among Charleston's residents (as they would until the Civil War), their numbers increased dramatically from a mere 24 in 1770 to nearly 590 in 1790, when census enumerators counted a total city population of 16,400. The years between 1775 and 1800 marked a passage from slavery to freedom for many.[25]

Most manumission in postwar Charleston, as throughout South Carolina, was not so much a harvest of the Revolution's libertarian principles as it was a consequence of familiar relationships between slave women and their masters. Women predominated among those manumitted. That manumissions were recorded in the city partially explains the skewed statistics, but also important are the facts that most Charleston slaves were women, that racial mixing was common practice in the city, and that sexual relationships between white owners and their slave women constituted a principal stimulus for manumission. Slave owners freed favorite slaves who had furnished many years of loyal service and with whom they had been intimate. Some of these connections were reciprocal and grounded in affection. Others were not. Nevertheless, personalism and sex spawned Charleston's free black and brown communities.[26]

When juxtaposed with state law, the significance of this personalism shines brighter. In 1783 men of the master class made "perpetual" the 1740 slave code. Legislators chose not to change the law's title, so it remained an "Act for the Better Ordering and Governing of *Negroes and Other Slaves*"; symbolically and on paper "Negro" equaled slave. And despite the legislature's recognition that some "negroes, mulattoes, and mustizoes . . . [were] now free," the code's provisions frequently conflated slaves and "free blacks." Lawmakers made clear that South Carolinians would not blithely pave the way to freedom, so slave women's intimate ties with their owners became all the more precious as a means to attain liberty.[27]

As further evidence that women of African descent trod uphill as they reconstructed their lives after the Revolution, the pages of statute law offer glaring evidence. In 1800 Carolina's general assembly enacted the first restriction on manumission. Its members rationalized this legislation through assertions that, for years, owners had been ridding themselves of burdensome disciplinary problems by freeing slaves of "depraved character." Bent on halting this unsavory seepage, legislators initiated the first in a series of legal protocols to thwart the movement from slavery to freedom. It was a portent of the future for Charleston's slave women and, indeed, for free women of color. Some white residents believed the notion of "free Negroes" was antithetical in a slave society. Although free black and brown people constituted only 4 percent of the city's immediate postwar population—and never exceeded a high of 8 percent, reached in 1850—their rapidly growing numbers and anomalous status as free people of color in a race-based slave society bore an importance beyond their numbers.[28]

The experience of Sally Seymour reveals a typical pattern during this formative era. In 1795 Sally's white male owner, and likely the father of her children, manumitted her. She was a skilled pastry cook and applied her talents to support her mixed-race children. Seven years after being freed, Sally bought her first slave, a woman named Chloe, for $400 and set her to work in the pastry shop. In 1814 business was booming and Sally needed additional help, so she purchased her second slave, Felix, an investment of $800. All told, this successful businesswoman purchased four slaves, two of whom she later sold to her daughter Elizabeth (or Eliza), a Charleston mantua maker, for the nominal sum of $5. When Sally died ten years later, she left an estate worth in excess of $1,600.

In addition to her transformation from slave to slave-owning entrepreneur, Sally Seymour's legacy was typical of the formative brown elite in another respect. Although Sally's skin was black, her children, Elizabeth, Charlotte, and William, were of a lighter hue, and all three married light-skinned spouses. A skilled artisan in her own right, Elizabeth married a tailor, and Charlotte wed a barber from the city's brown elite community. William married the light-skinned Mary Warren. Sally Seymour recast her culinary talents, honed under slavery, into a prosperous concern enabling her to support her children financially. Then she attended to her children's social prospects by insisting that they marry well, and in Charleston "well" meant light-skinned.[29]

In the first two decades after the Revolution—precisely when the city's palest and wealthiest free people of color were constituting themselves into an elite group—the hard work and savvy planning of women like Sally Seymour rendered them indispensable to the building of Charleston's free brown and black communities. It was not just men, like bricklayer Thomas Cole, who labored diligently and saved money religiously in hopes of purchasing themselves and family members out of slavery. In 1782 one unnamed woman paid her owner a specified amount in return for her owner's "pledge" that she would be freed at his death. Two years later, another woman borrowed money to purchase the freedom of her three children, trusting that she could earn enough money to prevent their repossession. A slave named Grace postponed her own freedom in that same year and applied her savings to the purchase of a young girl named Hagar. Women bought this freedom for themselves and their children at enormous personal and monetary cost.[30]

Self-purchase was not foolproof. Slaves could not legally hold property, so their owners lawfully claimed all their earnings. Both they and their money legally belonged to the mistress or master. Consequently, women drew upon every possible resource to achieve and preserve freedom. Some sought white people's help. In 1782 "a mulatto girl named Jane" enlisted the help of a white man, Robert Ballingall. Jane paid Robert to purchase her, and he subsequently fulfilled his part of the bargain and legally manumitted her. In essence, she used Robert as an agent in purchasing herself. During the period 1737 to 1785, 105 of 379 recorded manumissions involved a financial arrangement between slaves and owners, and of those 105 (fully 59 percent of which occurred in the ten years after 1775), the majority were transacted by slave women. These women quite literally built Charleston's free colored community.[31]

Legislative petitions from free women of color attested to the American Revolution's inspiration on Carolina's marginalized people. After the war, free women and their men voiced grievances, fully expecting that the new republican state government would listen. In one rare instance, legislators did. In late December 1789, eight former slaves (four African couples, possibly from Morocco, who had recently purchased their freedom "by the greatest industry") petitioned the general assembly for official recognition and a guarantee of their rights as free people, particularly the right to a trial by jury should the need arise. Although these women and men were now free because of their own hard labor, they, like all people of color, remained subject to Carolina's black code with its separate "Negro" courts, which were presided over by white property holders rather than by judges and juries. Fatima, Flora, Sarah, Clarinda, and their husbands repudiated this subjection to "the negro law." Legislators granted their request, vowing that laws governing the treatment of slaves would not apply to them. The ruling was extraordinary and exclusive to these eight petitioners. The new Carolina government likely had no desire to precipitate an international incident or otherwise to wrangle with an African "Prince [ruler of the petitioners' unnamed country of origin] now in Alliance with the United States." Notwithstanding the singular nature of this petition and its outcome, the incident is important because these women and their husbands had drawn courage from the recent democratic revolution.[32]

As they established their places in Charleston society and forged their own communities, free women of African descent (as well as slave women) were caught in regulatory nets thrown wide by master-class men, but they drew upon their war experiences to defend themselves. After Charleston municipal officials established the annual "poll tax on all free Negroes and Mulatoes" in 1793, free people of color protested. In an unsuccessful 1794 appeal to the state general assembly, three women and thirty-one men declared that the recent head tax imposed by the city "pose[ed] a special hardship on those free people of colour with large families, and women scarcely able to support themselves." In addition, all petitioners claimed citizenship as free people. They proclaimed loyalty to the new republic and to the state of South Carolina and, on these grounds, they requested repeal of the tax as an unjust measure. Like the male signatories, the three women, known only as Mildred, Genelazier, and Catharine, believed themselves undeserving of this treatment as denizens. Distinguishing themselves from the loyalist ladies who couched petitions in the language of dependence (wives and children dependent upon a patriarch for support), Charleston's free women of color framed their entreaty with the perception of themselves as hard working laborers in the new republic.[33]

Free women of color numbered among the war's myriad economic victims, and their community building emerged from exigency as well as diligent labor and quickened political convictions. In order to relieve "the distresses of [their] widows and orphans" and other worthy poor in their hours of sickness and death, five members of St. Philip's Episcopal Church—all men of mixed race and part of Charleston's "brown elite"—founded the Brown Fellowship Society (BFS) in late autumn of 1790. A principal catalyst for this organization was the exclusion of free people of color from burial in the church graveyard. But these "bona fide free brown men of good character" also determined to function as a charitable organization to aid their members' needy widows and children.[34]

Brown Fellowship men and their wives entwined the lives of Charleston's brown elite women and white ladies through emulating the patriarchal relations undergirding master-class households and slave society in general. In this case, patriarchy manifested in women's exclusion from the BFS. Brown elite women patterned themselves after master-class ladies in deferring to their men in the work of benevolence, and their compliance enabled brown elite men to imitate white gentlemen who oversaw church as well as public charities like the city's Poor House, Orphan House, and paupers' clinics. Although white ladies eventually supplemented the work of their men, no evidence exists of similar formal groups within the brown elite population. There was no BFS women's auxiliary.

Neither did women of the brown elite form separate female charitable organizations as did white ladies. Consequently, men of the brown elite exercised nearly exclusive control over benevolence. In 1803 seven BFS men formed the Minor's Moralist Society to educate indigent orphans of color. They, too, excluded women from membership. These institutions provided rare arenas in which men of color did not submit to white men and, indeed, where others acceded to them because they made the rules.[35]

Society members also mimicked ladies and gentlemen of the master class in their fastidious color awareness and caste consciousness. During this formative era, when brown elites struggled for a place in a black-and-white world, they distinguished themselves from the "black masses" by chiseling places in the interstices between black and white. By emulating Charleston's master class, the city's wealthiest free people of color distanced themselves from both slaves and free people with darker skin. Although brown elite women outnumbered their men (as did slave women and less-affluent free women of color), the wealthiest among them acquiesced to exclusion from benevolent societies and to their compliant, domestic roles, because doing so disconnected them from slave women and poorer free women of color. It rendered them more like white ladies, the model to which they aspired.[36]

Free brown men also attempted to control women sexually, as did their white counterparts. Sexual mixing between white, brown, and black people remained as much a part of post-Revolution Charleston as of the colonial city, but BFS men condemned women who consorted with white men. They sought an end to the practice responsible for their very existence because this custom smacked of enslavement. Control of women's sexuality defined the brown elite by differentiating women of that group from other women of color. Women complied because, in Charleston, sex defined who was black and white, slave and free, wench and lady. The wealthiest brown women adopted genteel white protocols of sex because affluent brown women repudiated the slave-wench identity and aspired to the status of lady.[37]

As with all city residents, women of the laboring classes undertook the process of rebuilding personal lives and reconstituting Charleston society. This process was enacted on shifting terrain, because, for more than one decade after the American Revolution, chaos and violence reigned in the city. Patriotism was one sentiment precipitating daily verbal and physical confrontations. Other divisive issues included heightened class antagonism and white people's chronic, quickened fear and suspicion of the black majority. While this violence affected all women, those of the laboring classes found themselves at particular risk, because city streets were not safe. And unlike women of the master class who could remain indoors or send their slaves out to market, women of the laboring classes were forced daily to navigate rowdy, volatile public places. They encountered frequent brawls among large numbers of poor and frustrated militiamen. The city drew thousands of impoverished men and women who loitered in public places hoping to pick a few pockets.

At war's end, women of the laboring classes still inhabited a kind of diverse middle ground between slave wenches and master-class ladies, but they had been politicized by the war. Many laboring women now perceived themselves as political beings. For white women of this class, their postwar rebuilding task involved restoring their property as well as their lives. Although they had not possessed and lost enormous holdings like elite white ladies, Charleston's laboring women did own businesses, land, slaves, and other personal property. At war's end, they struggled to regain that wealth, a process that often pitted them against slave women and free laboring women of color. It also led them into the male domain of state politics and required the use of their recently tuned political voices. Their political participation was sporadic, personal, and reactive, but they were, nevertheless, claiming "membership in a community beyond [the] household."[38]

After British evacuation, loyalist women of the laboring classes challenged state confiscation and tax penalties levied against their husbands, as did master-class women. They petitioned the state assembly for restoration of (or compensation for) expropriated property and for the return of their exiled husbands. A substantial 19 percent of the surviving 202 petitions from South Carolina women were submitted by loyalist women of Charleston. Their petitions reveal two class-specific strategies. Some emphasized the traditional, dependent status of woman in which they existed only as extensions of their husbands. Most of these were submitted by women of the master class. Their pleas evinced an exclusive concern for home and family. Other women, however, framed their petitions in more overtly political terms and portrayed themselves as people with identities separate and apart from their husbands. The women in this latter group were definitely not "apolitical" as some scholars have concluded. Florence Cooke claimed that she had helped purchase the confiscated property by her "Domestic toil, frugality and attention," and that because of her "sincere affection for the independence and freedom of her Country" she was guilty of no crime. Florence further maintained that her husband, "a laborious hardworking man in a Mechanic employment," had pledged allegiance to the crown only when conditions in Charleston became "too powerful for his Situation and Circumstances to withstand." Moreover, Florence underscored her achievements as a republican mother who inculcated in her daughter "a real attachment to the liberty of her Native Country." Had she borne sons, Florence asserted, she would have applied "all the influence & Care of a Mother, to render them fit for the defense and Support of their Country." Likewise distancing herself from the "political errors of her late husband" (a deceased Charleston tinsmith), Elizabeth Beard informed legislators that it would be unjust for them to punish her because of the actions of her husband. Both Florence and Elizabeth likely agreed with fellow Charlestonian Catherine Read's assertion that she did not "always think it necessary to think as [her] Husband" did.[39]

Accused loyalist women were not the only ones who entreated state legislators for assistance. Patriotic Whigs Ann Timothy and her husband, Peter, ran a printing concern and were exiled by the British for their vocal promotion of the

American cause. When Ann returned to Charleston after the deaths of Peter and their two daughters, she found it difficult to collect fees due her for services provided as a state printer. Obliged to work without "compensation for her own services," she vowed "cheerfully" to provide "any service which [was] in her power to render the State, by Printing for the Public in Charleston." Her "patriotism," Ann proclaimed, "would induce her to serve the public for no other reward than the satisfaction she would enjoy in the reflection of having served her country." Although the assembly did not act immediately on her January 1790 petition, it did partially settle its accounts in subsequent legislative sessions.[40]

Excluded from citizenship, women petitioned because it was the only formal political procedure or forum available to them, and Charleston's free laboring women, in the aggregate as well as individually, expressed a strong sense of themselves as economic and political participants in the state. But their appeals also revealed women's entwined and symbiotic relationships, and occasionally exposed their clashes with men of the master class, whose goals diverged from Charleston's laboring women. The collective response of one group of white women to a state sanctioned municipal measure in spring 1783 reveals these intermingled and clashing interests. The law prohibited "Negroes and other slaves" from selling goods in the market. Its goal was to constrict slave women's independent economic activities. Along with many white residents, city officials beheld social and economic chaos in the comparative freedom of mobility that Charleston's African American market women enjoyed and their monopoly of the city's markets. More than this, the market provided a daily venue for interaction among free people of color, slaves and white people of the lower classes; this sort of mixing conjured the specter of rebellion. However, from the vantage point of many white women, particularly widows, the 1783 law disrupted customary practice and adversely affected their livelihoods and the well being of their families. Women protested. In early August 1783, nine "Sundry Widows of Charles Town" remonstrated to state legislators that "the [Charleston] Commissioners of the Markets" had lately prohibited slave women from peddling their "wares and merchandize" in the city streets, "under penalty . . . of having their goods seized and sold." The slave-owning petitioners protested on two grounds. "From a long and Accustomed time" these white women had "been us'd [used]" to sending "their servants" out "to expose [various goods] for sale"; it was an established practice. In addition, the women depended upon this custom to "Obtain an Honest livelyhood [sic] in defense of their fatherless Children"; they needed the income.[41]

Ultimately, state legislators neither repealed this municipal sanction nor ensured its enforcement, so market women and hucksters persisted as essential players in the city economy. Well into the nineteenth century, Charlestonians spoke of the women of color who sold an assortment of foodstuffs, basketry, and other goods. One resident recalled that "July Fourth was a very grand fete for the negroes. . . . On Meeting Street . . . and along the South Battery the sidewalks were crowded with booths kept by old negro maumas, and many more were under the trees on the Battery. The viands they sold were mostly sweet, and the drinks cooling."[42]

However, throughout the years of the Early Republic and periodically until the Civil War, the independence of market women and other enslaved and free people of color remained a source of contention among white people. In 1796 the general assembly passed another measure to quash independent economic activity, this one fining "Shopkeepers, Traders and Others" who purchased "any . . . article whatever" from slaves who did not have "Tickets from their Owners." On paper, market commissioners and state legislators had won, but in reality slave women continued to buy and sell for their mistresses and "on their own accounts" on street corners and in city markets as they had since the 1690s. White slave-owning women were complicit in safeguarding slave women's monopolistic control of Charleston's market trade. Mistresses expected to continue deriving income from their slave women's "labour and industry," and slaves considered their market activities an established right. In this particular battle, white mistresses and their slave women united because both parties derived mutual benefits.[43]

Other laboring women also acted in ways that demonstrated their willingness to make the personal political. In 1784 Charleston baker Mary Simpson added her voice to a group protest of state and municipal economic policies and, in so doing, manifested her membership in the political community. Mary and fourteen other (male) bakers petitioned to raise the price of bread. In winter 1788, sixty-seven "Sundry Seamstresses of the City of Charleston," half of them able to sign only with their marks, vented personal concerns. They stated that "by the loss of their husbands" or other relations "during the War; they [were] reduced to indigent circumstances and obliged to earn subsistence . . . by their needles." Unable to earn enough, they were forced "to apply to the Public for assistance." The women attributed their "want of sufficient employ" to the "great importation of ready made Clothes." They caustically critiqued Carolina trade policy by adding that, if given the opportunity, they could make the clothing "which [was] exported to [Charleston] by a Nation [England] whose policy it [was] to employ their own industrious poor." The general assembly rejected the women's proposal that South Carolina levy "a much larger duty" that would "give employment to [the] Petitioners." State legislators' interests would not have been served through increased import duties, since they were the ones purchasing imported "Shirts, Socks . . . Waistcoats & Breeches . . . & millinery of every kind." Two years earlier an exchange between "Julia" and "Cornelia" proposed that it was "high time for the women to try their skill in politics," since they might "do better than the men [and could not] do worse." It is likely that the sundry seamstresses of 1788 agreed with this political observation.[44]

Unlike ladies who channeled much of their rebuilding effort into reinvigorating the city's lively social and cultural institutions, Charleston's destitute white women engaged in a daily struggle for survival. In this respect, they tasted a bit of what fugitive slave women endured. Laboring women in the postwar era inhabited a world characterized by crime and street violence as well as by economic volatility and political, class, and ethnic factionalism. From 1793 to 1796, Charleston became a primary base of operations for French privateering. The population swelled with soldiers of fortune, "swaggering filibusterers and privateersmen . . . [who] elbowed citizens off Charleston's narrow sidewalks." Drunken revels degenerated into riots and hooliganism. Destitute female residents and other free laboring women, as well as slave women, daily navigated city streets that were more dangerous than usual for Charleston. Postwar rebuilding for them, unlike for wealthy white and brown elite women, meant trying to stay alive.[45]

Throughout the 1780s and 1790s, the Charleston Alms House quartered nearly twice as many women as men, and women consistently composed a majority of the petitioners for "out door [sic] rations" as well. Dwelling at the Alms House was the choice of last resort because of its wretched living conditions and the social stigma attached to its "inmates," so women tried to avoid admission by cobbling aid from church and secular charities. A pregnant Margaret Ramley knocked at the door of the dreaded Alms House because she had no other recourse. Board members allowed her to remain, but forced her to confess paternity as a condition of her admittance. A blind woman, Rebecca Streeper, staved off admission and received "one out door [sic] ration per day"; the Alms House board granted Mrs. Esther Quigly the same, plus "one quarter of a pound of tea and two of sugar." Mary Magdalane Combey, "confined to her house and bed for a number of years," also required food from the Alms House to live. Likewise a Mrs. McNeil petitioned for assistance for herself and her five children, and Mrs. Grossman, another "outdoor pensioner," requested and received firewood. The plethora of private charitable institutions and the high incidence of women's names on lists of beneficiaries of those organizations attest to the poverty of white women in the post-Revolution era.[46]

Indigent white women also turned to male associations for assistance. Like the BFS, these white, all-male institutions reinforced the patriarchal foundation of slave society by validating women's dependence on men. Women of German extraction petitioned the German Friendly Society for money, food, and clothing. They also asked for help in paying tuition for the education of their children (primarily boys). Men of that organization filtered weekly appeals and decided who was a proper object of charity and, therefore, worthy of assistance. Mary Sigwalds, Susannah Sheets, Mrs. Peterman, Hannah Rossberg, Mary Shutterling, and hundreds of other women turned to the Society because they found themselves and their children "in a very distressed situation and in want of all the Necessarys of Life."[47]

In a perverse way, Charleston's destitute widows and abandoned women served a fundamental role in the reconstruction of Charleston society, albeit not one of their own choosing. Although they drained both public and private coffers, they also provided an opportunity for nearly all free Charleston men to reconstitute themselves as patriarchs. Notwithstanding the temporary nature of war's disorder and loss of control, the fact remains that the American Revolution disrupted men's dominion—particularly men of the master class—and by reasserting jurisdiction over benevolence, they partly reasserted their dominant positions in slave society.

But even patriarchs on the make (or remake) had their limits, and wealthy residents grew increasingly annoyed at the sheer quantity of Charleston's poor. Destitute women encountered the rancor of those who tired of helping them. "The number of beggars which have lately appeared in the streets of Charleston has become highly disagreeable to the Inhabitants," opined city intendant John Huger in 1793. In that same year city council members requested state authority to establish "a Bettering house." Here, they declared, the poor might be "kept at labor" and out of sight. The institution would also serve to relieve respectable city residents of a financial burden as well as the distress of stepping over poor people in city streets. Two years later, municipal leaders remained irritated and persistent in their complaints to state legislators about the burgeoning numbers of beggars, who wandered the streets of Charleston, drained city and state coffers, and were generally bothersome to the inhabitants. What municipal officials sought was legislative approval of forced labor; they wanted destitute people off the city streets and working for their own subsistence. Women constituted a majority of those poverty-stricken street beggars about whom city leaders vociferously griped, and the Charleston streets they "wandered" were dangerous places to be.[48]

Regardless of their social stations, women reconstructed their lives largely in the shadow of master-class men, who began anew by reconstituting the old. Gentlemen reasserted their position at the pinnacle of slave society, and all women struggled to define themselves and demarcate their status in the new Republic. The process by which white women reestablished a place in reconstruction Charleston corroborated white men's authority. When formerly wealthy loyalist women petitioned for clemency and assistance, they, like destitute laboring women, provided ample opportunity to reenact the deference and paternalism central to slave society. Both ideology (paternalism) and reality (petitioning women) emphasized woman's dependence on man. Ladies had the most to regain by supporting their men in rehabilitating patriarchy and slavery, while slave women had much to gain by resisting. Free women of African descent, caught in Charleston's social interstices, alternately resisted and emulated the ruling elite. For free women of color, the master-class lady both exemplified their ideal and loomed as their nemesis.[49]

After the American Revolution, as during wartime, all facets of women's lives were entwined, mutually dependent, yet segregated. As city residents recovered from war's chaos and reconstructed urban slave society, women's braided relationships were evident in and demarcated every aspect of women's lives: their relationships with men, their work and leisure, their legal status and experiences with the law, and their encounters with illness and death.

Part Two.   *Defining Women,*
Defining Their
Braided Relations

4 Marriage and Cohabitation within the Aristocratic Paradigm: Wealthy White Women and the Free Brown Elite

In relationships with men, as in all defining aspects of their lives, the different aspirations, possibilities, realities, and practices of Charleston women derived from their interdependence. Women's marital identities were formed in daily interaction with each other and in ongoing social dialogue that differentiated the ideal married woman—the good wife of the master class—from all other Charleston women, who could rarely equal the ruling paradigm. Often the dialogue was oblique and implied, but it can be teased out of personal correspondence, newspapers, court reports, and other contemporary writings. Women did not make a habit of pronouncing, "My marriage is what it is because I see and hear what it (and I) should *not* be." Nevertheless, their relationships with men and with other women manifested that interactive dynamic: distinctive experiences with men defined each group of women, and women's entwined relationships, in turn, influenced the character of those experiences. This constant contrast of women and notions of woman (suffused with particular notions of race and class) influenced when and if women married, who they married, the nature of their marital or other sexual relations, and the level of protection they received when caught in abusive relationships. Appreciating the potency of these contrasting ideas yields a fuller understanding of marriage in slave societies and of the impact of different marital ideals and practices on women's lives.

To grasp thoroughly the significance of southern women's relationships with men also demands recognition of both the historic role of marriage and its special role in the slave South. "All marriages are entered into on one of two considerations . . . love or interest," one chancery court judge intoned in 1809, "and the court is induced to believe the latter is the foundation of most of them." From Charleston's earliest days, marriage cemented the new society. Throughout the eighteenth and nineteenth centuries, matrimony united people whose families knew or were already related to one another. In addition, Carolina's ruling class germinated, matured, and perpetuated itself through intermarriage. Women and men of Charleston's master class, and those who emulated them, paid special heed to marriage because this institution helped build, maintain, and rationalize patriarchy and slavery as well as wealth.[1]

In the slave South, marriage served a second essential function: its power relations were modeled on those of the larger society. Dominant yet benevolent husbands governed and protected their wives just as paternalistic masters controlled and guarded their slaves and other property. Any curtailment of the husband's power and authority over his household imperiled the larger social bonds. Within this paradigm, however, not all wives were equal. Distinct notions of gender, race, and class determined specific norms and conduct expected of each social group. These behavioral expectations gave rise to commanding ideologies that conveyed contrasting messages to women of the master class, free women of color, white women of the laboring classes, and slave women. Scrutiny of what married women were supposed to do and be, and of what women actually encountered in their marriages and non-marital relationships, exposes not only the conflicting expectations and realities of Charleston's women but also the ways that people rationalized their power through resort to entwined images of women.

Statistics do not tell the stories of people's lives, but brief snapshots of the Charleston population aid in understanding relationships. When the first United States census was taken in 1790, nearly 16,400 people lived in Charleston, over 3,700 (23 percent) of them white women. While over three-quarters of all city residents lived in households headed by white men (who slightly outnumbered white women), white women headed 285 (14 percent) of the city's nearly 1,900 households. Nearly 8 percent of Charleston's white women were not married (widowed, never married, abandoned) at the time of the first census. Although women presided over nearly 60 percent of households headed by free people of color, the same conclusion about marital status cannot be drawn regarding these women. Some of them were, indeed, married, but they were married to slaves. Throughout the antebellum years, both slave women and free women of color substantially outnumbered their male counterparts, thereby reducing the pool of potential partners and requiring them to look beyond the traditional family forms for husbands or lovers. Other obstacles combined with this sexual imbalance to create a higher percentage of unmarried women of color than white women.[2]

A special 1848 census ordered by the city council included brief commentary on Charleston's "domestic condition," and reviewed patterns of white marital status near mid-century. While marriage was expected for white women, particularly ladies of the master class, it was not the dominant relationship for the city's white women because well over 50 percent of them were not married in 1848. Although 45 percent of the nearly 4,800 white women over age fifteen (defined as adults) were married, over one-third (37 percent) remained unmarried, and nearly one-fifth (almost 19 percent) were widowed. Moreover, among white women twenty years of age and older, fully 50 percent were either unmarried or widowed. In 1848 nearly 1,200 women over twenty were unmarried and 877 women in the same age category were widows. Together they constituted 50 percent of all white women twenty years of age and older. Even allowing for statistical errors—a factor in virtually all census data—one conclusion remains valid: for the city's white women, expectations and aspirations conflicted with demographic reality.[3]

Among those white women who attained the ideal by taking marital vows, most wed men older than themselves. In Charleston, social stability hinged on preserving the power of the patriarch, and each additional year that separated the ages of husbands and wives likely strengthened the image of the man as a sovereign caretaker and the girl or woman as a childlike dependent. As other historians have noted, these roles bore powerful connotations for marital politics. Nearly 10 percent of Charleston women between the ages of fifteen and twenty were married, but not one single man in that age category could make the same claim. Moreover, 45 percent of women between the ages of twenty and twenty-five were married (and 2 percent of them were widowed), while only 12 percent of men of the same ages had wed. And 66 percent of women aged twenty-five to thirty were married (and 6 percent widowed), but just over one-half of that percentage (35 percent) of men in the same age grouping had married. It was not that white women outnumbered white men in all these age categories. The opposite was true. In all categories but two (ages forty to forty-five and fifty to fifty-five) up to age sixty, white Charleston men outnumbered white women. White women simply married earlier than white men (and earlier than northern women), and white wives were younger than their husbands. What is clear is that the expectation of marriage defined all white women, and the master-class ideal paired brides with older grooms. Furthermore, this ideal—central to the maintenance of that ruling elite—loomed as a marital mandate for all respectable women, brown as well as white. It served as one means of distinguishing wealthier ladies from lower sorts of women.[4]

Charleston's master class set the marital standard by which all others were judged, and this ideal changed little during the eight decades between the American Revolution and the Civil War. It included tenets familiar to wealthy northern women but also principles unique to southern society. According to this paradigm, negotiating a good marriage was more than an expectation, and even more than a social prescription for women. Marrying well and ensuring success of the marriage constituted a woman's life. From the time of their births, little girls of the master class were groomed to fulfill this singular goal.

As was true in other states, North and South, Charleston's dominant marital ideal was grounded in the English common-law tradition of coverture. The marriage contract was founded "on the weakness of the [female] sex," a debility that justified granting "great advantages . . . to the husband." Once a woman married, her legal and economic identity formally became subsumed under or covered by her husband as the two became one person. A wife could not execute contracts, convey property, prosecute lawsuits, or act as an estate executor absent the consent and cooperation of her husband. Free women shared with slaves these legal disabilities. After marriage a woman also lost control of all her property and the power to act as guardian of her own children. Her "very being or legal existence" disappeared, subsumed under her husband's "wing, protection, and cover." However, responsibilities adhered to his enormous rights. The husband incurred a reciprocal obligation to uphold his side of the marital contract by financially maintaining his wife.[5]

While not unique to slave society, this legal tradition furthered the mastery of wealthy white men. The pact fashioned them (and all would-be masters) as benevolent despots who justly governed their wives and other inferiors. Within the confines of the marital agreement, wealthy Charleston wives did, in fact, expect something in return for their covered status. Precisely because they received "maintenance," or theoretical exemption from work, elite women gained elevated status above slaves and other laboring women. In essence, master-class ladies traded away their property and their legal and economic identities and rights in return for presumed lifetime security.[6]

The American Revolution confirmed the legal principle of coverture, and Carolina legislators did little to ameliorate women's disadvantaged legal status. Unlike northern and even southern states, South Carolina legislators bestowed on no court the power to grant divorces, *a mensa et thoro* (from bed and board), which included the right to remarry. Throughout the late eighteenth and nineteenth centuries, South Carolina statute and case law reaffirmed this proscription against any and all forms of divorce. Legislators, primarily men of the master class, believed their policy "wise" because it "shut that door to domestic discord." Even if a man married his niece, the court affirmed that this marriage could not be voided. Carolina patriarchs tenaciously held to this stance because they believed any loosening of marital bonds would diminish their own power and authority, which, in turn, would presage a slackening of the social order and probable social chaos. It would also endanger the sexual freedom white men enjoyed; the absence of divorce in South Carolina enabled, or at least did not jeopardize, men's adultery. This prohibition of divorce, coupled with coverture's uneven marital pact and a sexual double standard, meant that patriarchs committed adultery with little risk of losing the marital right to their wives' property.[7]

South Carolina statute and case law ruled that a man could legally compensate a woman with whom he lived in adultery as long as such conveyances did not exceed one-fourth of his estate. This 1795 law limiting—not criminalizing—gifts and property conveyances from married men to their mistresses or illegitimate children provides one of the clearest expressions of the way in which the state legislature and court system privileged white men over all others in society, occasionally penalized lawful wives, and provided legal largesse to unexpected beneficiaries. In 1818 when a Mrs. Cusack and her husband asserted their legal title to a slave named Amy, the court upheld their claim. Amy had been a gift many years earlier, from a married man (Daniel White) to his lover, then the widow Pilkerton, now the remarried Mrs. Cusack. In this court dispute, White's lawful heir was attempting to recover that property, claiming Amy as the rightful possession of his mother (White's lawful wife at the time) and her children and other blood heirs. The court dismissed his appeal and affirmed this gift (to an extramarital lover) as legal and valid. One judge averred "that every man

[was] a free agent" and could dispose of his property as he wished. This extreme commitment to the power of the patriarch, evidenced in the 1795 act, occasionally led judges to support gifts to the African American lovers of white men and their mixed-race children. However, in all cases in which enforcing this legislation necessitated ruling against lawful white wives and heirs, judges rationalized their decisions through resort to images of paternalistic patriarchs. They asserted that the law did not encourage the practice of adultery, but instead supported the mandate of gentlemen to provide some protection or "bounty" to the objects of their "criminal intercourse." Judges also ruefully acknowledged that sometimes property would be taken from a "virtuous wife, and an amiable family of children, to support a dissolute and profligate mistress."[8]

This 1795 law also reveals the way that gender and race served as crucial vehicles for demarcating and sustaining power in South Carolina's legal system, because in practice, and in law, the act authorized adultery for white men only. Case law made quite clear that an adulterous woman would be "barred of dower." Judges intoned that a "common woman" could not "sustain injury" to her reputation and was, therefore, "entitled to no reparation" from her husband, the courts, or any other party. In order for wives to qualify for any court remedy in the form of separate maintenance, they had to prove conspicuously outrageous behavior by their husbands. Discreet male adulterers had little to lose, but the marital ideal demanded fidelity of their wives. While Charleston's prevailing marital paradigm specified a husband's marital obligations as well as his rights, it endowed him with incomparable domination by mandating women's singular role as the pure and faithful good wife and by decreeing that "the marriage contract [was] . . . indissoluble by any human means." South Carolina legislators and judges set themselves apart by their rigorous judgments on matters of domestic law.[9]

Southern domesticity shared with its northern counterpart a commitment to the notion of separate female and male characteristics. With the subtlety of a Carolina hurricane, the popular press trumpeted gendered traits as fixed and ordained by some higher power. Women were "timid, confiding, and submissive," but men were "bold, arrogant, and self-willed." Women "limit[ed] their wishes to the precincts of home, to the innocent prattle of [their] 'little ones,'" but men "court[ed] the bustle of the world and its loud praises" and aspired to "thrones and large dominion." Woman was "queen of the household; her diadem the social affections; her scepter, love; her robe, chastity, pure as the driven snow . . . her measures [were] those of peace; her ministers, the virtues; and her smiling subjects, the children of [her husband] to whom she owe[d] fealty, as the paramount lord of her heart and her treasure."[10]

But the master class also infused marital expectations with their southern brand of the doctrine of domesticity, a credo that defined and prescribed distinctions of race and class as well as gender. Southern domestic ideology was distinguished by its need to balance precariously between rationalizing (white) men's preeminent power and protecting (white) women's position. Proponents of northern ideology juxtaposed men's physical and mental superiority with women's moral superiority. Slave society could not resort to men's physical superiority as sanction for women's relegation to a finite sphere. This explanation, when taken to its logical conclusions, might imply that the physical strength of slaves rendered them superior to white women. Consequently, proponents of southern domesticity—including South Carolina jurists—faced the challenge of justifying "both white women's inferiority (in terms of gender) and their superiority (in terms of race)."[11]

In constructing and reaffirming southern domesticity, both men and women of the master class adjured their daughters and sisters to "have the grace to be a good wife," employing this phrase so ubiquitously that the colonial "Goodwife" came alive in antebellum Charleston. But they had robbed "Goody" of her vital economic role. Unlike her seventeenth-century forebears—married women of ordinary status—the dutiful, master-class daughter-turned-Goodwife no longer distinguished herself through her own hard work and economic partnership within the household. Instead she devoted herself "heart and soul to promote the good of her husband," arising early to set "her maidens to work."[12]

The Charleston Goodwife's social success turned, in part, on her ability to perform effortlessly her role as hostess, and that skill required effective management of household slaves. The implications loom significantly: a Charleston lady could not fully realize her life's goal without exploiting enslaved women. Prominent Charlestonian John Berkely Grimball recorded his and his wife, Meta's, pleasure when mother-in-law Amarantha made all guests feel welcome in her new home, which presented an aesthetically pleasing impression. Amarantha had superintended her slaves' preparation of all the correct foods, and their prompt and appropriate service. She "[accomplished these] honors with great propriety," John glowed. Amarantha had proved herself functionally decorative, proficient in slave supervision, and, therefore, a fit wife. Her success derived partly from her slaves' hard work; a slave woman's actions and demeanor determined the reputation of the Goodwife.[13]

An unrelentingly compelling chorus of women's and men's voices specified a sure path to marital success when they advised potential wives to be amiable. Just as John Grimball lauded his new mother-in-law's amiability, other of the city's social leaders clearly expected wives to manifest a particular constellation of traits embodied in this potent descriptor, "amiable." Good wives were to be agreeable, likeable, pleasant, congenial, friendly, deferential to their betters, kindly to their inferiors, decoratively useful. Their proper conduct explicitly excluded engaging in "intercourse unhallowed by the bands of matrimony" even if their husbands were regularly so occupied. Above all, a wife should never "confront [her] Husband by opposition, by displeasure, or any other mark of anger." Woman's "pride should be, to convert home into paradise . . . for this [was] her proper place, wherein she shine[d] most and [was] every where [*sic*] else a stranger." So, while men garnered "many ways to show themselves clever fellows"—notably through political or military service—women could prove themselves estimable only within the family and only if they acted a certain way. While the "consent of mankind conceded" to men "a moderate neglect of home and family" if they excelled in another area, "mankind" countenanced no negligence by women. The contentment of her husband, the orderliness of her household, and the burden of ensuring marital success rested on the narrow shoulders of the amiable Charleston Goodwife.[14]

The notion of "good wife" not only designated an ideal—the marital paradigm of the master class—but also constituted a means by which wealthy Charleston women distinguished themselves from myriad women of all colors who could not live up to that ideal. Men and women who constructed and perpetuated this southern ideology of separate spheres, with the Goodwife at its center, relegated women of color as outsiders with their repeated paeans to "golden-curled," rosy-cheeked, "white armed," loving wives. According to the master class, true womanhood was race specific. South Carolina law supported this pale southern domesticity by granting protection more readily to ladies than to other Charleston women. Legislators and judges worked in tandem with public and private speech.[15]

Finally, the marital ideal of Charleston's ladies and gentlemen perpetuated a trenchant image of woman as acquisition and possession in addition to a precise constellation of female personality traits plus the notion of woman's duty. Marriage bonded the master class and served as a means of capital formation. Infused with patriarchy, this latter function tended toward the commodification of girls and women in daily casual conversation and correspondence. In 1809, while setting her daughter's wedding date, Alice Izard boasted that the future groom, Mr. Smith, "expresse[d] the utmost anxiety to be in possession of his little treasure." He informed his future mother-in-law of his desire to "devote himself entirely to the care of so interesting an object." Alice reiterated this theme two months later in a letter to one of her sons. She gloried in daughter Georgina's match and expressed delight in Mr. Smith's satisfaction "with his acquisition." In both her mother's and husband's eyes, young Georgina was a cherished possession as well as a beloved girl. Alice Izard, like most of her counterparts, habitually identified all her daughters as appendages of their husbands. Rather than informing her husband that she had visited with Margaret and her family, Alice reported seeing "Mr. Manigault and our daughter." On a similar occasion Alice wrote, "Mr. Manigault and his family just left me to proceed on their journey." Such references were commonplace among Alice Izard's peers, and each mention reinforced the notion of ladies as the property of their husbands.[16]

The image of women that Alice Izard and her son-in-law expressed so openly was also acted out in the posting of wedding banns in which men gave women to other men. Late eighteenth- and nineteenth-century newspaper announcements uniformly named the groom first and specified where the man was from: "Married Dr. Matthew Irwin, of the State of Virginia to Miss Mary Bulline, Daughter of the deceased John Bulline, Esq." The banns appended the bride's name to two men, her husband and father. Mary Bulline's mother received no mention in this wedding announcement. Thus, in print, in law, and in fact a woman passed from one man's possession to another man's dominion. Public notices of marriages, births, and deaths also reflected and buttressed women's status as legal nonentities, and their wording further reduced wealthy slaveholding women to the symbolic status of property.[17]

Little had changed at mid-century when prominent, white Charlestonian, Robert F. W. Allston, contemplated how best to prepare his niece for marriage. Robert reiterated prevailing standards for female comportment as he waxed eloquent on the traits that would most attract a potential suitor, and he drew on his considerable experience in horse breeding and racing as he described the ideal wife. The good wife was "a thoroughbred lady," he declared. A gentleman would seek "one who will not only grace [his] table . . . but will also be able and find it agreeable to do the honors of important soirées, in courtly style, and with design'd effect." Like a well-bred champion racehorse, a Charleston wife was valued for the cachet she brought to her husband when she performed well and looked good doing so. Marriage comprised a complex mixture of desires, emotions, expectations, and goals, but the master-class ideal, particularly in the context of this urban slave society grounded in patriarchal power, fostered the notion of women as "acquisition[s]."[18]

Elite men and women imparted this marital ideal to their daughters from an early age. Some women lived the prototype; ideology and reality fused as they manifested the ideal in their daily conversation and actions. In fact, wealthy slave-owning women assimilated gender prescriptions and perpetuated the marital mandate each time they inculcated its values and traits in their daughters. Alice Izard's letters to her eldest daughter, Margaret Izard Manigault, resounded with gendered wisdom. "The name of the family always depends on the sons; but its respectability, comfort, and domestic happiness, often on the daughters." Alice maintained that "the rank of a good woman in society leaves her little to complain of" for "she guides where she does not govern, and acts like a guardian angel by preventing the effects of evil desires, and strong passions and leading [men] to worthy pursuits." Alice further asserted that women should accept their separate and less prominent place in society, and "enjoy the internal sense of their own abilities" rather than aspiring to a different role. She concluded her lesson on woman's role by reminding her daughter that "no one is happy without a good Wife."[19]

Eleven years later, Alice Izard's lessons reverberated back to her in a letter from daughter Margaret, who had skillfully mastered her role. The two women encouraged each other in times of stress, sadness, or disappointment by hearkening back to this theme of woman's obligations. "Happiness consists in the exact performance of our duty," penned Margaret to her mother, for "it makes us happy at the time and enables us to look back with pleasure to our past lives." When it came time for her sister to marry, Margaret confidently informed her friend and cousin that "Georgina [Izard] is accustomed to consider what is her duty and to follow that, and not her inclination." With "such a wife," Margaret continued, "a man . . . cannot run the risk of being unhappy."[20]

But not all girls longed for the frenetic round of parties designed to show (and marry) them off to potential suitors. Young Sally Elmore felt herself "quite disinclined . . . for a girl's society enjoyments." Much to her mother's chagrin, Sally "resist[ed] the St. Cecilia Balls, and all gaiety except Opera." And, on more than one occasion, Charleston novelist Susan (Sue) Petigru King vented her own frustrations through the voices of her characters and narrators. Girls "are taught French, music, drawing, geography," but "what is the use of study? . . . Somehow every one marries too early," and "as soon as they marry, they shut the piano, never open a French book, give all their paints away." She concluded this social critique with one of her most memorable lines: "We sell a slave with more hesitation to a new owner than we give our girls in marriage." Sue Petigru King's perception of women's reality veered wildly from the neat master-class paradigm in which amiable young women willingly obeyed their parents' (and husbands') wishes.[21]

This marital ideal packed force in the form of family members determined that their girls adopt it, so despite misgivings about their roles and destinies, few young women of the master class tread alternative paths. They were well versed in their duty. Georgina Izard, the younger sister about whom Margaret waxed so eloquently, "entreat[ed] that she may not for a long time hear of marriage," but within one year of that plea to her mother, Georgina succumbed to familial pressure. From nearly the moment of her birth, all roads pointed toward one defining goal. Her busy and relatively carefree childhood would culminate in a triumphant debut, followed by an economically and socially advantageous marriage. Fifteen-year-old Georgina had already vicariously experienced this social compulsion while watching her older sisters waltz through the rite of passage, and now it was her turn. In December 1807, her widowed mother, Alice Izard, accompanied Georgina to a ball and, if all plans flourished, this and other ballrooms would serve as a staging area where Georgina whirled from girlhood to good wife. Alice promised that her youngest daughter's nuptials would "not take place before she was seventeen." Instead of keeping her word, Alice orchestrated what she deemed an advantageous match and, with her son, negotiated her daughter's marriage to a man twenty years Georgina's senior. The distraught girl implored her mother to postpone the marriage to Mr. Joseph Allen Smith, who pressed Alice for the wedding date. But Georgina Izard fulfilled her destiny on the first of May, 1809. The marriage took place in her bedroom, where Georgina was still recovering from a horseback-riding fall and the doctor's treatment of "copious bleeding." Apparently oblivious to her daughter's sensibilities, Alice gushed that "it was with real satisfaction that I found Mr. A. Smith entitled to the appellation of my Son." Alice expressed pride in "my little Georgina's behavior," which "on the solemn occasion was calculated to raise her in the esteem of all who saw her." So, despite her fears and against her wishes, Georgina Izard Smith acquiesced to social coercion on that spring day. She donned the ideal (in her demeanor and actions) by bidding farewell to her carefree days as a girl and exchanging wedding vows with Joseph. The potency of this marital paradigm, coupled with the specter of becoming a "withered, ghastly, old maid," transformed most girls of the master class into some variation of the good wife.[22]

While Alice Izard and her daughter Margaret Manigault embraced and embodied the master-class marital paradigm, and Georgina apparently grew slowly into it, many women of the master class well understood the ideal, but knew their own lives deviated wildly from that prototype. Indeed, their reality belied the ideal of patriarchal protection. Nowhere was this divergence more evident than in the domestic court cases arising from women's allegations that their husbands abused them or otherwise violated the marital contract. Each good wife who sought legal redress exposed cracks in the veneer of paternalism, and judges constantly counterbalanced their desire to protect "ill-used" women with their dogged defense of the patriarch's power. The secret for wives lay in simultaneously proving severe ill usage and documenting their own praiseworthiness. In their attempts to negotiate this tricky path, women of the master class revealed how far afield their lives wandered from the ideal. Judges appraised the wife's demeanor, economic circumstances, ethnicity, and the number and character of witnesses on her behalf as much as or more than they weighed the husband's behavior.

South Carolina might best be described as hyper-patriarchal. Even within the slave South, this state stood alone in its extremist positions, including its stance on domestic abuse and divorce. Throughout the antebellum period, state legislators and judges steadfastly refused to legitimate the dissolution of marriage for any reason, gross neglect and violent abuse included. "Nothing short of the actual or presumed death of one of the parties," thundered one judge, "can have the effect of discharging [the] obligation and legal effect" of the marriage contract. This stance on wedlock placed the state "in a class by itself in the Anglo-American world." The rigidity of the law actually trapped elite white jurists between two conflicting imperatives: their determination to safeguard the authoritarian position of white men at the apex of southern slave society, and their desire to protect most women. In adjudicating civil and criminal cases in their courts of chancery (equity) and law, South Carolina judges trod a thin line between preserving the sovereignty of husbands, yet punishing men who egregiously violated southern ideals of white manhood.[23]

A close examination of case reports concerning domestic abuse (or alleged abuse) in its variety of forms reveals how judges navigated this precarious, potentially explosive philosophical tightrope; it reveals their desires, anxieties, biases. These cases are instructive, also, of how and why courts intervened in household affairs and of the criteria—the combinations, types, and severity of abuse—that triggered legal enforcement of paternalistic care. A case-by-case analysis also yields the advantage of uncovering a part of women's actual experience that, because of its private and painful nature, usually remains hidden from view. Most domestic abuse (then as now) never came to light because most women did not seek legal help. Those who did file suit provide a small window on their values, aspirations, and frustrations, as well as their treatment by spouses and the legal system. And each of their case reports (the transcript summations and court decisions) bears enormous importance beyond one woman's situation and her appeal, because every case served as a vehicle by which attorneys and chancellors patrolled the parameters of power in slave society, boundaries expressed in terms of gender and class as well as race.

Neither legislators nor judges charted a course of malicious persecution of women. Most men of the white ruling caste took seriously their status as southern gentlemen, a role freighted with responsibilities of paternalistic protection. Throughout the antebellum period, they recommitted themselves with a vengeance to the old-world (and Puritan New England) notion of divinely ordained organic hierarchy—that God had made some higher and some lower—which knit society together into a mutually dependent and symbiotic whole. As stewards situated at the apex of this social order, these gentlemen remained cognizant of their duty to safeguard those whom God had created for subordination, notably women, children, and "Negroes." "Hard indeed would be the lot of the fair sex," one chancellor decreed in 1801, "if . . . from the fear of infringing on the marital rights of the husband, the wife must be obliged to submit to all his brutal treatment without any redress whatsoever." However, jurists intervened in domestic affairs only when other men made a mockery of paternalistic patriarchy by egregiously violating the gendered protocols of slave society.[24]

Domestic violence in its most extreme form—murder—posed few dilemmas in the courtroom. But most of the relatively few cases of domestic abuse brought into the public record through legal action fell short of murder. And among those white women who sought legal action for some form of abuse (women of color could not bring suit in the state's law or chancery courts), most sought "alimony" because divorce was not an option in South Carolina. Alternately referred to as a "separate maintenance," alimony was an economic remedy available only through state courts of chancery (not law courts) in which husbands were ordered to pay toward the support of their wives who would, thereafter, live apart from them. But courts awarded alimony only under specified conditions: cases of legal cruelty (defined as "ill usage" beyond an acceptable level), desertion, or "obscene and revolting indecencies practiced in the family circle." In addition, judges also required that the wife's behavior be "unimpeachable." Throughout nearly sixty years beginning in 1801, cases of domestic abuse heard in state courts of equity/chancery (and appeals in equity) reveal combinations of behavior on the part of husbands that triggered court-ordered alimony. One clear judicial pattern emerges. Jurists penalized open, adulterous intercourse with other women, *but only* when combined with additional "intemperate" behavior of husbands toward their wives, like extreme physical abuse or desertion. This is significant because, before the Civil War, many state legislatures (including many southern states) granted divorce to wives who could prove their husbands' adultery. In South Carolina, judges made clear that adultery alone neither constituted an indictable offense nor qualified as "ill usage," so mere adultery was not grounds for alimony. In 1811 Judith Williams successfully proved that her husband, Josiah, abused her physically and kept a mistress in his house before the eyes of his own legitimate children. A judge deemed this intolerable cruelty, flagrant misconduct, and grounds for awarding guardianship of his children to his wife. Following the mandate of state law, the two remained married, but the court ordered Josiah to make payments toward a separate household for Judith and the children. In subsequent cases, judges upheld this standard of punishing adulterous men only if they had doubly mistreated their wives.[25]

While this legal precedent reveals one prototype of court intervention in the household, jurists examined and assessed each woman's domestic situation on a case-by-case basis, which led them to make exceptions to their rules or to establish new legal precedent. One particular exception sheds light on the ways judges used the courts to uphold customary practice as well as law in slave society. In 1801 a court of chancery unanimously concluded that Elizabeth Jelineau had suffered "extreme ill usage" by her husband, Francis, despite the conspicuous lack of physical abuse or abandonment. Jurists indicated that Elizabeth's maltreatment exceeded mere beatings. Francis Jelineau had treated his wife "with great indignity and impropriety, and had degraded her in his language and deportment, *below his slave, the mother of his Mulatto child.*" He not only openly cohabited with an (unnamed) slave woman, but he also publicly lavished great affection on his "mulatto" child while constantly insulting Elizabeth and encouraging his slave partner to do the same. In court testimony, Francis also reproached Elizabeth through allegations of licentiousness, dishonesty, and general failure to uphold her marital obligation of submissive comportment. The court dismissed these disparaging accusations against his wife with unprecedented swiftness, and sent a clear message to Francis Jelineau reiterating expected social standards: Francis's dishonor was precipitated neither by his adulterous affair, nor his liaison with a slave, but rather by the fact that he had crossed the color line in an unacceptable way—openly—and then compounded this flagrant violation of southern sex etiquette by refusing to support his lawful wife and newborn son. Accordingly, the court ordered Francis to make provisions for the separate maintenance of Elizabeth and their son.[26]

Notwithstanding exceptional cases such as that of the Jelineaus—often involving extenuating issues of race and class—judges remained committed to the notion that authority, command, and coercion constituted the rightful perquisites of every patriarch. This commitment influenced court action in disputes alleging domestic abuse. It also gave rise to another pattern of legal intervention or, in this case, nonintervention, coupled with reiterations of the patriarch's sovereignty. Many women who sought court enforcement of the protection and maintenance promised them in the marital bargain/contract quickly found themselves on trial.[27]

In 1810 an unidentified woman filed a complaint of "ill usage [and] gross neglect" against her second husband, and she requested court relief in the form of a separate maintenance. The court declared that its ruling hinged on "whether the plaintiff [was] entitled to alimony on account of her good conduct as a wife." Testimony by two female witnesses revealed that this widow lived in "the greatest comfort" before her marriage to the defendant, and did not want for the "necessaries and luxuries of life." Now, they claimed, she suffered greatly, "was scarcely provided for, and sometimes nearly destitute of the necessaries of life." She and her husband often quarreled, and "their conduct towards each other" reflected these frequent fights. The complainant's husband left her for three or four months at a time, when she "was obliged to sell trifling articles" in order to maintain herself. During the periods they did live together, the husband's "jeering and ridicule . . . was of the most provoking and offensive kind, and calculated to wound her feelings." He gloated to his wife that he had purchased a new plantation that "would afford him a good pretext for leaving" her. He further declared "that she was a virago and he could not live with her," but that he "would visit her at stated periods [and] see that she was provided for." To contradict this testimony, witnesses for the husband asserted that he was "a humane . . . good tempered, benevolent man," who was "esteemed and respected" by those who knew him. He "lived well" and never deprived his wife of "comforts and necessaries of life" even during his absences from home.[28]

Testimony in this case directly contradicted the marital ideal. It is possible that "Anonymous" was, as the court decided, a mean-spirited spendthrift, a nag, and an altogether unpleasant woman, and that her husband was a dutiful, loving man driven from his own home by this "virago." The truth probably lay somewhere between the two extreme portraits sketched in court. The presiding chancellor admitted that the she-said, he-said nature of case testimony rendered a decision "one of difficulty." He lamented that the wife's two witnesses "had not descended to [more] particulars" of her husband's "inattention, indifference and the want of affection." Nevertheless, his decision bears attention for the way that it substantiates the law's conflicting drives. He affirmed patriarchal prerogative in asserting that the "complainant herself drove [this] defendant from home to seek refuge from her bickerings," and that evidence of her ill treatment at his hands fell short of a necessary standard of "severity or cruelty." The court declared its proclivity to "refuse to grant [Anonymous] any thing [sic]." However, the husband admitted "it [was] not his intention to take his wife back," and he retracted an earlier offer to pay his wife one-half the net income from the estate she brought to the marriage (now under his control). The court lamented the man's refusal to reconcile with his wife and, for this action alone, "bound him by his [earlier] offer," and ordered him to pay his wife one-half the profits from (her) property. These annual payments constituted her separate maintenance. Clearly both wife and husband fell short of the marital ideal. "Anonymous" missed the mark by not being amiable, and her husband violated the marital pact by publicly refusing to take "Anonymous" back.[29]

But even "blameless" wives who patterned the aristocratic ideal could not count on consistently favorable treatment from Carolina judges, who jealously guarded patriarchal power. The struggles and disappointing outcomes of several women who came to court further illustrate the ways that jurists balanced justice (for wives) and power and status (for husbands). Ann Taylor (1811), Catharine Threewits (1815), and Marion Converse (1856) all proved, to the courts' satisfaction, that they had endured unkind and cruel treatment in the form of insulting, abusive, overbearing, and violent behavior. Witnesses corroborated their allegations of being punched in the face, kicked, dragged by the hair, bruised and bloodied by their husbands, threatened with death, even of fleeing and hiding like "trembling fugitives" from their homes on more than one occasion. Ann's husband threw furniture at her, whipped her, and beat her so badly that he knocked her teeth loose and left six-inch-wide contusions on her limbs. Catherine's husband had lunged at her with a knife, but because he was drunk and unsteady at the time she was able to fend off the blow and escaped with a cut on her hand. Marion's husband had, on one occasion, constrained her on the floor of their (outdoor) piazza in a painful position throughout most of a damp and chilly night. When their daughter attempted to free her mother or at least cover her with a blanket, A. L. Converse threatened her with violence as well.[30]

In all three of these cases, courts acknowledged the level of misconduct as gross, outrageous, and worthy of court intervention on the women's behalf. Yet the judges also limited their protective intervention in ways that reaffirmed the supremacy of a husband's position within the household. Ann Taylor, whose married daughter predicted that her father would eventually kill her mother if she returned to his house, received court-ordered maintenance or alimony. Ann would receive one-third of her husband's income paid twice yearly, but only until the court decided that she could "return in safety to her husband." While Taylor may never have reformed to meet this court standard, it is significant that a judge included the caveat at all, particularly given the repeated pattern of extreme physical abuse. In fact this doctrine had already been embedded in legal precedent: severe ill-treatment justified a wife leaving her husband and petitioning for alimony, but if the husband offered to take her back—and gave "sufficient assurance" that his behavior would change—she was bound to return to him. As one attorney succinctly summarized this principle of law: "if the husband [shows] that [his wife] is obstinate and will not return, though he is willing to receive her, the alimony will be revoked."[31]

Beyond this court ruling in Ann Taylor's case, a similar pattern of judicial decision-making emerges in all three of these examples from the first half of the nineteenth century. Catherine Threewits, like Ann Taylor, received a separate maintenance, but the judge allowed—"preferred"—the terms of the settlement to be proposed by her husband, Lewellin Threewits, rather than (as was customary) by a court-appointed official. This judge further decreed, against Catherine's wishes, that the older Threewits children would remain in their father's custody and awarded Catherine custody of only their youngest child. While this judge followed customary practice and legal precedent in privileging paternal custody, doing so affirmed patriarchal authority. Marion Converse also received legal assistance tempered by court reiterations of her husband's sovereignty in the marital relationship. This judge acknowledged that the physical abuse she had endured justified separation from her husband, but he denied her petition that the court return to her sole use properties inherited from her father and her former husband (a Mr. DeVeaux). She appealed this ruling, arguing essentially that her husband had violated the marital agreement and, therefore, had lost his contractual right to her land. Three of nine chancellors agreed with Marion's assertion that A. L. Converse should be denied any claim on "the bounty of his wife," but she lost again. The majority opinion overruled these dissenting voices and confirmed the lower court's finding that if a husband inflicts personal violence upon his wife—even when she is forced to flee and seek protection—that does not divest him of his marital right to her estate. "It is one of the highest triumphs of justice," intoned one of the appellate judges, "when the worst of men . . . can have his just and legal rights awarded to him by judicial tribunals, irrespective of his character, conduct, or position."[32]

Women of the master class sounded a mixed and ironic message when they initiated court action against their husbands. The women's behavior and their accusations (publicly airing spousal abuse) repudiated the ideologies of domesticity and paternalism, and manifested a mini-rebellion: they entered the all-male arena of the judicial system and focused public attention on the failure of Charleston's marital ideal, itself a model for and miniature of slave society. However, the remedy they sought from the courts (maintenance) constituted a fulfillment of the very marital pact that legally, economically, and sexually subjugated them. These women simultaneously denied and confirmed the fundamental concepts about marriage that they, their mothers, and their daughters helped reproduce.

The city's most affluent free people of color—the free brown elite—replicated the master-class way of marriage, notwithstanding its color-specific southern ideology of domesticity and blanched definition of the good wife. Throughout the antebellum years, this exclusive group guarded their privileged position by intermarrying. Brown elite families like the Bonneaus, Dereefs, Holloways, Sasportases, and Westons patterned manners and rituals of courtship and marriage after prominent white families like the DeSaussures, Grimballs, Izards, Manigaults, and Petigrus.

Like wealthy white belles, girls of the brown elite debuted at balls—albeit separate galas from those of the master class—where they could be seen and presented to eligible men. Also like affluent white parents, these mothers and fathers groomed their daughters to fulfill the defining role of wife and mother, and they planned parties, lavish receptions, dinners, dances, and springtime picnics as venues for showcasing their girls. The brown elite excluded all but light-skinned men from the pool of potential suitors and required proper courting rituals. In 1832, Jacob and Mary Kougley conveyed to a young man their "approbation for . . . visiting the house" to court their daughter. They were "perfectly acquainted with . . . [his] standing in life," and "hope[d] it [was] with the approbation" of his family that he "addressed [their] daughter with respect."[33]

When all proceeded according to plans, these young women, like Charleston's true [white] belles, married in the prominent St. Philip's Episcopal Church and other city churches whose members included the best brown and white families. In November 1859, just before the height of (white) Charleston's social season, Eliza Ann Johnson and her husband, James, attended an extravagant wedding.

Marriage and Cohabitation within the Aristocratic Paradigm 91

Like Eliza and James, many of the guests that autumn day hailed from the city's free brown elite, a group of light-skinned people knit together through extensive kin ties. As among the master class, elaborate social rituals such as this cemented them as a group and reiterated the distinction between their group and slaves or free black people. Twenty attendants preceded the bride and groom down the aisle of St. Luke's Protestant Episcopal Church, where the (white) Reverend Christopher P. Gadsden performed the ceremony. A free man named Nat Fuller prepared a sumptuous dinner, complete with oysters and champagne. Nat catered many social events of the city's white aristocracy. Indeed, in numerous ways this grand event mirrored nuptials soon to take place during Charleston's renowned winter season.[34]

Precisely because their festivities, customs, and notions of woman's role replicated the dominant marital ideal, and because colored elite parents inculcated these customary practices and beliefs in their children, they periodically incurred the enmity of outspoken white residents, who reminded the brown elite of their marginal status in Charleston society. In taking aim at another recent wedding celebration, one white slave owner in 1859 vented frustration at what he perceived as an ominous slackening of the social order. In a venomous tone, he decried the "nuptials of blacks [that] are celebrated in a spacious temple of the most High." Continuing his harangue, the editorialist complained that "a bridal party of a score and ten . . . [were] transported . . . in gay equipages" to the gala. Worse yet according to him, "hundreds of others, robed in extravagant costumes, witness[ed]" the elaborate proceedings "possibly with eyeglass in hand." Fully aware of the brown elite's caste and color sensitivity, this editorialist purposely used the term "blacks" to demean and rank them with Charleston's dark-skinned residents.[35]

Charleston's brown aristocracy further emulated their white counterparts, and distanced themselves from slaves and poor free people of all colors, by expecting their children to make economically advantageous marriages. The prominent Bonneau, Holloway, and Weston families united in marriage, forging business ties as well as wedding bands that laced them together. Fulfilling her mandate, a young Joanna Dereef, daughter of one of Charleston's richest free men of color, married another light-skinned resident, Michael J. Eggart. Like Joanna's father, Michael actively participated in the Brown Fellowship Society. He held office in both the Friendly Moralist and Brown Fellowship societies, where he distinguished himself as an outspoken advocate of "our people," a term freighted with commitment to maintaining a separate "mulatto identity." Joanna's social life and her aspirations appeared to duplicate the master-class paradigm. She and other wealthy brown elite wives internalized the notion that marriage was their destiny, and that they must remain unerringly faithful, devote themselves wholly to their proper domestic sphere, and inculcate these same values in their children.[36]

Charleston postmaster Alfred Huger characterized the brown elite as "darker copies of their white counterparts," for they augmented their own wealth, comfort, and social position through slave labor and, in widowhood, presided over estates improved by their parents' and husbands' bequests. In 1814 Barbara Tunno, daughter of free woman of color Margaret Bettingall and white Scottish merchant Adam Tunno, married an artisan and member of the Brown Fellowship Society, John Pierre Barquet. Like her mother, Barbara (with John and their seven children) attended St. Philip's. Under the terms of her father's June 1831 will, Barbara inherited $2,500, and she acquired slaves and more money under the terms of her mother's will drafted some eight years later. In 1830 Barbara Barquet headed a household of twenty-two persons, nine of whom were slaves. City records in 1840 and 1841 recorded Barbara, now a widow, as head of two different Charleston households. In similar fashion, Jennet (or Jeanette) Bonneau also inherited property, including slaves. She and her husband, Thomas, actively participated in St. Philip's Episcopal Church, where their children were baptized. Bespeaking their esteemed position in the brown community, the Bonneaus sponsored the baptisms of many free brown children. For nearly thirty years prior to his death, Thomas headed a school for children of the brown aristocracy. He also founded the Minors' Moralist Society to educate free brown orphans. In 1831 when he died, Bonneau specified that his plantation holdings be liquidated (if a "fair price" could be attained), but that his "slaves in town . . . Fanny and Mary" as well as Scipio be retained "to be subservient to the wishes of my beloved wife Jennet Bonneau and children." Modest roots notwithstanding, former slave Maria Weston rose to the position of Charleston's wealthiest person of color and progenitor of one of the brown elite's anchor families. In 1860 Maria paid taxes on over $40,000 in real estate holdings and fourteen slaves. Her wealth far surpassed that of the city's other people of color and many white residents.[37]

In their own eyes, the Westons, Bonneaus, and other prominent families attained the aristocratic marital ideal. Among the wealthiest brown elite, their prosperity, values, and social lives mirrored those of the master class. But these affluent brown residents understood that white people disagreed, and the brown elite knew that they occupied "a middle ground," terrain bordered by "the prejudice of the white man . . . [and] the deeper hate of [their] more sable brethren." They also recognized that prejudice, manifested in southern domesticity's snowy version of the true woman, forever barred brown elite women—in the eyes of white Charleston—from genuine good wife status. As one New York newspaper correspondent reported in late 1860, regardless of the affluence, education, respect, and admiration (particularly within the brown elite) attained by Richard E. Dereef and his children, "if one of those daughters [wore] a [veil] over her face [a privilege] accorded to the white girl, with no negro blood in her veins," a policeman would rip it off. Even when they knew who and what they were, another reality daily intruded to remind brown elite women and men who and what they were not. That wake-up call manifested in the form of a white policeman, or the free negro capitation tax, or a court's refusal to hear their testimony.[38]

Charleston's marital ideal affected all women's lives even though most women did not live that ideal. White women married and were transformed into good wives, or so the aristocratic paradigm dictated. This prototype loomed as the paramount goal for all elite women (and all who aspired to that status), even when as many as 50 percent of adult white women were not married. The ideal had staying power because of its centrality to Charleston society and because the combined force of statute and case law upheld it. Wealthy women of the brown elite could never fully realize the master-class paradigm as envisioned by its framers. They were the wrong color, but they emulated the paradigm because it was a road to respectability and differentiated them from other women who were poorer and darker than themselves.

5 Marriage and Cohabitation outside the Aristocratic Paradigm: Slaves and Free Laboring Women

While Charleston ladies were commodified in the sense that marriage was integral to capital formation, the city's true commodities—legally considered *chattel personal*—were slave women. A slave woman was the reverse image of her white mistress; one was forbidden by law to marry because of what she was, and the other was compelled to marry in order to fully realize who she was. As they accommodated to their condition and sought relationships with men, slave women fashioned a counter ideal of the relationship between women and men, infused with pragmatism and tempered by the reality that they were first and foremost chattel laborers.

Excluded from the ruling marital paradigm, most slave women nevertheless wanted to form stable connections with men and to rear families. Some of them adopted and adapted the aristocratic ideal of marriage. Bondspeople as well as some slave owners and judges used the terms "marriage," "wife," and "husband" when speaking of slaves' relationships, even though those words had no force in South Carolina law. Other slave women, however, openly rejected this ideal by flaunting their sexuality and sexual behavior; they lived up to their status as the antithesis of white ladies and reveled in doing so. Whether allied to or repudiating the prevailing ideal, slave women forged their marital and sexual identities in juxtaposition to this ideal. One identity depended upon the other, each deriving greater clarity from the very fact of being entwined.

Charleston slave women faced myriad obstacles to family formation. Not only did state law refuse to recognize slave marriages but also customary practices mitigated against lasting slave partnerships. Because slave owners valued slave women primarily for their labor and reproductive capacity, owners routinely separated slave couples, temporarily or permanently, as the need or whim arose. In one of the more tangible examples of how women's lives entwined in mutual definition, the nuptials of a mistress or master often severed slaves' kinship ties, including those of wife and husband. The marriage of one could effectively end that of the other, as when Miss Margaret Bell married. Her parents gave to the bride as a wedding gift five-year-old Josephine Steward and her mother, but not Josephine's father. As former slave George Woods explained, "it was the custom in slavery times that a slave be given to the son or daughter by the white people when they got married." George's mother and his grandfather were both given away as wedding gifts, in each instance separating them from the rest of the family.[1]

Sale menaced slave families as well. After Charleston's colonial heyday as the largest entrepot for slaves on the British-American mainland, the city remained a center of the interregional slave trade. City businesses included over thirty slave-trading firms at mid-nineteenth century. Slave women married at the pleasure or whim of slave owners, and their marriages endured or ended on these same terms. As one woman succinctly put it, "no minister nebber say in readin' de matrimony 'let no man put asounder' cause a couple would be married tonight an' tomorrow one would be taken away en be sold." As a young girl, one slave personally witnessed such a separation. She watched a young bride's mother run into the Charleston streets the morning after her daughter's wedding and listened as the mother "cursed de white woman [the slave's owner] fur all she could find," shouting, " 'dat damn white, pale-face bastard sell my daughter who jus' married las' night.' " When confronted by her daughter's owner who threatened to call the police, the enraged mother-of-the-bride screamed, "I redder die dan to stan' dis any longer." She was still yelling as city police dragged her to the workhouse, and "what became of 'er, [she] never hear."[2]

Slave society proffered daily images of female slave laborers but few of slaves as wives, so another impediment to marriage came in the form of social expectations opposite from those of master-class women. Unlike her mistress, the slave was not bombarded with advice adjuring her to pledge "fealty" to her husband, "the paramount lord of her heart and her treasure." The only real "lords" in Charleston were white patriarchs. Instead, a slave girl battled against ubiquitous negative stereotypes. While her white counterpart was encouraged to nurture her "good heart and a good understanding," a slave girl heard incredulity in white voices advertising a "remarkably honest Negro woman," who, against all natural inclinations, had "never been found guilty of the smallest theft."[3]

Enslaved girls were taught household skills from the time they were toddlers, and youthful slaves learned early that their lot in life comprised hard work and an endless quest for self-preservation rather than balls and parties followed by marriage. At age eight a "very handy, tractable . . . likely Negro Girl" found herself on the sale block, where she heard auctioneers and buyers placing dollar values on her talents and on her potential as a laborer. Likewise a sixteen-year-old "Mulatto Girl" would not recall her life-altering debut in a crowded ballroom, but rather a cacophony of voices debating her strength, work skills, and, perhaps, her potential for childbearing when her owner sold her at public auction. As a little girl, Josephine Steward did not attend parties and go horseback riding like Georgina Izard. Instead, Josephine "mind[ed] de flies off de table wid a brush made out of peacock tail-feathers," and she helped her mother in the kitchen. These daily images and realities conveyed a potent message and constituted a pragmatic tutorial on a slave woman's identity and role.[4]

Slave girls discovered another obstacle to marriage when they observed sexual assaults on family members or friends as well as consensual sex between slaves and masters. These realities served as crash courses regarding their own sexual vulnerabilities, but also revealed the power of sex for survival or advancement, revealing how different they were from their white mistresses. Slave women's intentional exclusion from the pedestal, where their mistresses were extolled as dutiful wives, demeaned slaves as a different order of woman, defined them as workers and sexual objects rather than as future wives and mothers, and rationalized sexual assault. These social images of slave girls and women constituted a fundamental part of the larger social project of defending and promoting slavery as well as diminishing the importance of a slave woman's family ties.[5]

The corrosive effects of slave women's segregation as a separate species from white women are also evident in cases where slave men were the abusers. In 1834 a slave woman named Kettura was murdered by her husband Isaac. Isaac's owner petitioned the state legislature for lenience, claiming that "the Case is not distinguishable from many others of conflict between people of this description." This slave owner further avowed that fights "between a negro and his wife [were] of frequent occurrence" and worthy of only "moderate correction." The state concurred with this owner's contention that "the death of Kettura may be regarded in some measure as accidental." Legislators reduced Isaac's sentence from death by hanging to twenty five lashes and three months in prison.[6]

A final obstacle to successful slave marriages was Charleston's population composition. An imbalanced sex ratio produced many real-life consequences for slave women. One of these was the comparatively small group of men from which they could choose marital partners. Exacerbating this disproportion, free women of color outnumbered their men by a greater margin, so they sometimes married slave men. Faced with this demographic barrier, some Charleston slave women married plantation slaves whom they saw only when their owners' seasonal migrations took them back to the country. Although slave women occasionally married free men of color, the comparatively smaller numbers of both male slaves and free men of color meant that slave women faced a greater chance of never marrying than did white women.[7]

Despite these formidable deterrents, slave women made choices about marriage, their sexual activity, how best to sustain or escape from relationships with men, and whether or not to remain faithful if they did marry. Some slaves struggled against their owners, social mores, and the law to form stable partnerships in a society that idealized married women as white. Although customary practice in Charleston ravaged slave marriages, convention occasionally worked in favor of those unions. Some slave owners disliked the idea of separating slave families on the auction block, and made concerted efforts to sell wives, husbands, and children together. At noon on a hot July day in 1783, "a good House Servant [who was] very attentive and careful about Children" and her "Husband . . . [who excelled in] breaking and managing horses" stood outside a Charleston store with their eighteen-month-old baby girl. Their owners hoped the new mistress or master would buy them as a family. This and many other slave sales and runaway advertisements reveal the breach between South Carolina law, which strictly forbade slave marriage, and customary practice, in which owners not only advertised openly the sale of "husbands" and "wives" but also allowed or encouraged those unions. These good intentions notwithstanding, it was common in the city's many auction venues to see only a mother and her children for sale.[8]

Particular problems arose when slave couples confronted two different owners as they strove to preserve the integrity of their marital bond. Slave owners often viewed such marriages as a hindrance, as well as a potential labor and economic problem. Sammy, one of the Petigru family's slaves, married a slave woman owned by another prominent Charleston family. Sammy and his wife longed to live together, and they convinced his wife's owner to attempt a business transaction with his owner, James Petigru. She would offer either to buy Sammy or to sell her slave (Sammy's wife) to the Petigru family. James inclined toward respecting his slave's wishes in this matter, even though Sammy's wife "would be of no use to [him]." Doing so made good economic sense: Sammy might remain at work rather than running off frequently to visit his wife. Ultimately, however, James Petigru declined to help, claiming he had "no right to sell Sammy" who belonged to his wife, Jane. Petigru expressed doubts about Jane's willingness "to make a sacrifice for the marriage union as I [would]." Sammy and his wife remained separated.[9]

When they could manage it, slave women and their partners circumvented owners like Jane and James Petigru by simply living with their spouses, permission granted or not. But owners begrudged slave women for devoting time and energy to their families, rather than celebrating these efforts as they did for master-class wives who acted similarly. Consequently, numerous Charleston couples like Sammy and his wife were forced to live apart and steal moments together whenever they could. Estimating their numbers is nearly impossible precisely because the law did not sanction their marriages, most of which were, as a result, not recorded. This customary practice—the separated unions of slave couples—put slaves at odds with owners who coveted their time.[10]

Slave-sale advertisements provide evidence of the power struggle between slave women, who were determined to appropriate family time, and owners bent on efficient household management. These ads also reveal the inverse connection between slave and owner marriages. In 1783 an unnamed "exceeding good Washer and Ironer [and] good Cook" was up for sale. Her husband and the father of her child also resided in Charleston, but not with her. To spend time together, this slave had to rendezvous with her husband somewhere in the city, which meant time away from her owner's household and her myriad duties. Her owner chose to sell her knowing that the woman would continue shirking her duties to spend time with her husband. The sale advertisement obliquely acknowledged as much and suggested a remedy: this "very valuable Negro woman," would make a "most excellent servant to any family residing in the country" (where she could not easily sneak away to meet her husband), because "absence from town may remedy the fault for which she is sold." Ironically, this slave's tenacious commitment to her family ultimately disrupted her marriage. Owners relied on the hard labor of slave women (and men) to turn a good profit, which subsequently yielded material comforts to those slave-owning families. When a slave persisted in running off to spend time with her husband despite warnings and punishment, her owner suffered an economic loss. Selling that woman and reinvesting the capital in a more compliant slave represented a rational fiscal decision. In a fundamental way, then, the disruption of one woman's marriage (the slave's) improved her owner's economic position (by improving productivity with a new slave), which, in turn, could enhance that slave owner's conjugal happiness.[11]

Sometimes these contests between slaves struggling to safeguard their families, and owners bent on extracting a full day's work from each slave, terminated in permanent separation. Phillis Gladney and George Stitt had endured a separated union—a marriage with no shared household—for several years. Like the Charleston woman sold to the country, Phillis had stolen time to meet her husband and he had done likewise. Together they "slipped in and out 'nough of times to have four chillun." Their marriage ended when George's owner sold him south to Arkansas. Phillis never saw her husband again and his former owner profited from that separation. "Plenty more good fish in de sea," Phillis recalled her owner informing her, just "set your cap, and maybe you'll 'tract one dat'll give your heart comfort, bye and bye." This heartless attempt to console Phillis, even if well intentioned, illustrates how many slave owners perceived slave partners as interchangeable, and slave marriages as inherently different from their own, just as they theorized slaves to be fundamentally distinct beings.[12]

When slaves wed free people of color, fragility characterized their relationships, as with marriages between two slaves. In this respect, their unions contrasted just as sharply with the master-class ideal. However, these partnerships between a slave and a free person wielded a significant advantage: despite considerable obstacles, the couples were better able to amass the funds necessary to purchase the enslaved spouse. Even before 1820, the year that state legislators forbade manumission except by special petition to that body, it was no easy matter to secure a spouse's freedom. If an owner expressed willingness to sell, earning sufficient cash took many years of work. If the free partner was the wife, she earned less than a man and took longer to earn her husband's market price. After 1820 the state legislature effectively closed all avenues to legal freedom, so the best possible outcome would be de facto freedom realized in purchasing the enslaved partner. The case of a slave known only as Doll and her free husband, Robert Bass, reveals how years of hard work sometimes yielded only Pyrrhic victories. Robert and Doll had married sometime in the 1830s, and before they saved enough money to purchase her (virtual not legal) freedom, Doll's white owner, one James D. Lyles, relocated to North Carolina taking Doll with him. Risking his own freedom, Robert left Charleston sometime in 1838 or 1839 to buy his wife from James. Upon his arrival in North Carolina, Robert insisted that James sell Doll, declaring that, "she was his wife." James capitalized on the situation and accepted Robert's payment of five hundred dollars, a sum at least five times higher than Doll's market value. By this time Doll was seriously ill and she died soon after her husband reunited them. Robert's desperate actions, his vehement assertion of their union, and the tragic end to their marriage constitute poignant testimony to the strength and delicacy of unions between Charleston's slave women and free men.[13]

This same fragility characterized relationships between free women of color and slave men, unions that also bore no legal sanction but that rendered free any children born of the partnership. These women worked long and hard to buy their spouses, who, after 1820, remained their slaves (in the eyes of the law) as well as their husbands. The adversity Elizabeth and John Cline encountered exposes just how vulnerable virtual (or de facto rather than legal) freedom really was. In 1833 free woman of color Elizabeth Cline initiated court action against a white man, Daniel Caldwell, who had seized her husband, John. Elizabeth and John had worked many years to purchase his freedom. They had succeeded, at last, when Cato Gallman, a free person of color, bought John from Joseph Caldwell in 1828. Cato subsequently resold John to Elizabeth as they had arranged. However, when Joseph Caldwell died soon after selling John, Joseph's brother, Samuel, inherited the estate, and when Samuel died, his widow declared that Samuel had never recognized his brother's conveyance of the slave. Accordingly, she contested the legitimacy of that sale (and Cato's sale of John to Elizabeth), claiming she was John's rightful owner, by virtue of inheritance. Elizabeth and John ultimately won their fight to remain together as wife and husband (owner and slave), but the court's grudging decision in Elizabeth's favor turned more on its determination to guard the sanctity of contracts rather than to protect Elizabeth and John's relationship. The presiding chancellor ruefully acknowledged that "there may have been an inchoate intention to set John free," and that "indeed he may be virtually a free man, when the slave of his wife." But the court also noted, "the claim is not for John's freedom; he is claimed as the slave of the plaintiff [Elizabeth Cline], by regular conveyances of the legal title." Finally, the court ruled that John had not been "allowed to be at large without an owner, [so] he could not be legally captured."[14]

Elizabeth and John's experience points to an irony: state laws simultaneously prohibited and protected Elizabeth and John's marriage, as courts wrestled with opposing drives—to subjugate slaves and free people of color (the legislative prohibition on their marriages) and yet safeguard the integrity of contracts. In the cracks between these conflicting impulses, couples of African descent negotiated marriage and sometimes virtual freedom, but not without encountering dreadful roadblocks, often in the form of greedy former slave owners and their heirs. Ensuing legal disputes, like Elizabeth Cline's, illustrate the unstable, shifting ground upon which slaves and free people of color built their marriages, as well as the extraordinary measures they took to protect their families. The court battles also show that Charleston's people of color cultivated and relied on white friends and benefactors, like the attorney who helped Elizabeth and John file and win their case at law.[15]

Slave women neither uniformly wanted to emulate the master-class ideal of marriage nor internalize the notion of marital fidelity. Some women adopted a more pragmatic approach to relationships, in part born of the instability of their lives and the reality of commonplace separations. Slavery did not easily lend itself to life commitments. The city's slave women engaged in a variety of relationships with men. Late in the eighteenth century, a slave runaway named Nanny was seen nightly in town. Nanny's nocturnal activities manifested her own sexual self-expression as well as resistance against both her owner and the slave regime. Others shared Nanny's attitude toward relationships with men. Around dawn on a city wharf approximately ten years later in 1804, a group of nearly forty slave women and men disembarked after spending the night on nearby Sullivan's Island. When a bemused white resident inquired of another bystander what was going on, he found that the slaves "had been dancing and carousing from Saturday night, until near sun-rise" with a group of people about one hundred strong. Another "gentleman" whose slave had run off one week earlier had staked out the quay, and "caught his wench" as she stepped onto the wharf. Despite unrelenting messages from slave owners that slaves did not attend parties like their young white mistresses, slave women partied nonetheless. Dances like the one on Sullivan's Island likely served as venues for courting as well as "carousing."[16]

Among Charleston slave women who spurned the master-class marital ideal, with its dictates of premarital chastity and marital fidelity for women, were those who pursued sexual relationships for pleasure and gain. When they did so, Charleston's black and brown slave and free communities tried to enforce behavior closer to the very model these women had rejected. In 1822 six percent of all slave women enrolled in Sunday classes at Trinity Methodist Episcopal Church were expelled for adultery.[17]

Slave women also jettisoned the edict of marital permanence and, when they could, slaves abandoned both unsatisfactory marriages and particularly abusive husbands. Unlike white women, slaves could not seek protection and a separate maintenance from South Carolina courts of equity and law. Their solution was to remove themselves physically from danger, and often they achieved this goal by exploiting customary practice rather than running away. Some requested a permanent assignment in Charleston rather than, as was common among the wealthier low-country planters, seasonally migrating with their owners in and out of the city, from rural plantation to the urban residence. In this way a bondswoman might escape from a spouse who lived permanently in the country. Others exited an unwanted relationship by volunteering to accompany a newly married mistress who was about to relocate. On the occasion of her mistress's marriage, Susan Hamlin's mother was given the option of relocating from Edisto Island to Charleston with the newlyweds. She and her children left Susan's father behind on Edisto. Susan's mother became intimately involved with her (white) master—with no overt indication of coercion—and subsequently bore at least one child with him.[18]

The evidence from Charleston is mixed. Slaves and slave owners alike attested to slave women's desire for stable partnerships with men of African descent, slave and free. Couples risked harsh reprisals to protect these relationships. Moreover, their peers—fellow church members—attempted to enforce marital fidelity, and slave owners averred (at least publicly) that they tried to avoid separating slave wives and husbands. Whether they did or not, some owners recognized that slaves considered their own marriages to be long-term commitments even if slavery negated such resolutions. But evidence from Charleston also indicates that slave women waged uphill battles in forming and maintaining their marriages with men of color. Some gave up or patently rejected the master-class paradigm. And among these slave women, some formed alternative stable partnerships with men of European descent, while others used sex to gain favors and gratify their own physical and emotional yearnings. The testimony is suggestive rather than conclusive, but the dominant relationship within Charleston's slave community seems to have been a pragmatic and loose adaptation of the master-class ideal to their own shifting, precarious, and (sexually) vulnerable status as *chattel personal.*

Charleston's free black, brown, and white women of the laboring classes were caught between the master-class marital ideal and slaves' adaptive relationships with men. They were neither one nor the other, and so constituted a third strand of women's entwined realities. The unifying and distinguishing characteristic of free working-class women and working-class marriages—whether black, brown, or white—was that the women's labor was necessary to sustain viable households. The women were deemed "as able to work as [their] husband[s]," and their families depended on their "exertions" for support. Precisely because of these realities, free women of the laboring classes muddled, even threatened, slave society. They did not fit the dominant marital ideal of dependent wives and yet they were not slaves.[19]

Although the great divide of race distinguished white women of the working classes from laboring women of African descent, poverty created parallel experiences of marriage and other sexual liaisons. Unlike slaves, the unions of free women of color were legal (unless they wed slave men), and they did not risk separation due to the sale of their partner. And a primary motive for the nuptials of working-class women, whether black or white, was not capital merger, as for ladies of the master class, so laboring women were not commodified as were the city's wealthy white women. But women of the laboring classes, regardless of their color, were simultaneously excluded from yet compared to a marital standard they would never attain. They were appraised (by the master class) as a lower order of woman, and some lived down to this expectation. Charleston's laboring women rejected the rigid proscriptions on comportment and sexual practices imposed on ladies and leaned more toward the pragmatic, even rough-and-tumble marriages and liaisons of slave women. Like slaves, their marital standards arose from the hard reality of their lives. These women did not perch on the pedestals of domesticity (theoretically or otherwise) because they were working hard in and out of their homes to feed themselves and their families. Moreover, some found a certain measure of sexual freedom in their exclusion from membership in that elite group of good wives and pure women.

Judges publicly decried intimate relationships between people of African

American and European descent, but antebellum South Carolina law decreed the nuptials among free people of color and "their marriages . . . even with white people [were] legal." This law lingered as a vestige of the colonial era, when free people of color mingled daily and intimately with white workers, as they continued to do throughout the antebellum years among the laboring classes. Not until 1865 did South Carolina outlaw marriage across the color line. Despite this legal sanction, case law and custom held white laboring women and women of color in lower esteem than good wives of the master class, regardless of whom they married.[20]

The different legal treatment accorded laboring women of all colors emerged within a caldron of negative stereotypes tainted by ethnic and racist elements as well as class-based elitism. Elite men (and women) stirred this potent blend by starkly contrasting ladies and workingwomen, as they did slave wenches and patrician ladies. The preemptive, exclusionary strikes—by contributors to literary magazines, private correspondents, and newspaper writers—that portrayed loving wives as "golden-curled," "exquisite[ly] fair," "lustrously blue eye[d]" ladies with "brows more delicately white and soft than the blanched almond," also excluded all women of color, whether slave or free. And these public portraits of perfect wives resolutely excluded many white women of the laboring classes, who, regardless of their skin tone, did not meet this delicate standard. Writers who detailed wives as "delicate" discriminated on the basis of class as well as race as they constructed and perpetuated a narrow ideal.[21]

Public commentary, often in the form of crime accounts or court reports, buttressed these glaring comparisons among different groups of Charleston women by elaborating negative traits of free women of African descent as well as slaves. Common themes echoed through city streets: women of color could not be trusted; they connived, defrauded, stole from honest white people; and they were inclined toward troublemaking. Thus, free women of color were tarred with the same brush as slaves and decried as "tricky" and prone to "negro violence."[22]

Popular literature and other public and private commentary also demeaned courting and marital practices of laboring white girls and, in so doing, circumscribed their lives, mocked them, and entwined all Charleston women's lives by contrasting and comparing different groups of women. One magazine serial, "The Vigil of the Bridegroom," featured a disobedient, willful white girl, Thiennette, whose Dutch father was trying to marry her off to a fellow immigrant and butcher. Through trickery and deceit, Thiennette circumvented her father's wishes and eloped. The implication seemed clear: this working-class girl acted like a woman of color because she was "tricky" and "artful" instead of "amiable" and "dutiful" like a proper lady. Stories such as these sustained city intelligence that "a bad white woman [was] a sight worser and more low downer than a bad nigger woman can ever git to be in dis world" because she betrayed her race and the white ideal. Real-life city residents as well as fictionalized characters exemplified and fueled these notions of "low down" white laboring women. Grace Peixotto was the "notorious" and "demoralized" daughter of a former Beth Elohim *hazan,* or synagogue official. She was not only disobedient or willful but also kept a Charleston brothel "where harlots of all shades and importations" plied their trade.[23]

Negative images became reality for laboring women of European and African descent, partly because the circumstances of their lives denied them a leisured life and the cultivation of courtly manners. Since privation crossed the lines of color and status, children of free laboring families, like slave children, began working and earning their keep before age ten. One city slave owner matter-of-factly stated that the free "negro [girls] in town . . . [were] well trained" and "put to sewing school or trained as pastry cook[s]." Slave owners and non–slave owners alike expected little girls of African descent to work. They had no choice but to support themselves and their families. George Bedon, a free man of color, specified in his 1794 will that his daughter "be bound to a [discreet] and careful Mantua-maker" when she turned fourteen. Likewise, poor white girls were expected to earn their keep. In the Orphan House they were "put out" to learn a trade at age thirteen or sooner if their "capacities enable[d] it." Like slaves, these girls would never debut as Charleston belles, nor would most of them marry men who could support them while they planned dinner parties and "[did] the honors of important soirées in courtly style."[24]

Before they came of age, poor white girls and free girls of color also realized that their sexual encounters and marital lives would depart radically from those of their wealthy counterparts. In late 1826 or early 1827, a young white girl named Mary Evans was "put to live" with Susan, the wife of William Wheeler. William "debauched" Mary when she was not yet fifteen years of age. She soon married another man, but returned to live adulterously with William, a relationship that culminated in separation from his wife, Susan. Even if they had not been raped or otherwise sexually assaulted, the hard circumstances of laboring women of all shades negated any chance for them to achieve the aristocratic paradigm of marriage.[25]

Because free women of African descent outnumbered their men by a greater margin than slave women (they constituted an average of over 60 percent of all free people of color), four of every ten of them would not find a free husband in Charleston; if they married, they wed slaves. Exacerbating the demographic imbalance, color mattered in Charleston, as members of the brown elite made clear, so most light-skinned free men avoided free women with darker skin when choosing their mates. They did not want to risk darkening their children's skin. In addition, free black women tended to be poorer than lighter-skinned women. Thus, color mattered economically as well as socially, so men possessed double motive to marry light.[26]

An additional fact sealed the immutable exclusion of Charleston's laboring women from Goodwife status: many of them, like many slave women, consciously rejected comportment demanded of true wives. One historian has shown how working-class girls and women in New York City acted differently from their middle-class counterparts and, in fact, constructed their own culture in opposition to the new bourgeois values of the nineteenth century. Working within a "dialectic of female vice and female virtue," they "turned certain conditions of their very subordination into new kinds of initiatives." A similar dynamic was at work in the antebellum South as laboring white women and women of color rejected a model imposed by the ruling class. In 1788 a Charleston resident, Elizabeth Chapman Lyon, wife of a Polish immigrant tailor, engaged in such "scandalous [behavior]" that her husband claimed he "could not with any propriety cohabitate with her any longer." The specifics of Elizabeth's conduct remain a mystery, but apparently she acted so badly that Mordecai Lyon successfully petitioned the synagogue's ecclesiastical court (the *bet din*) for a letter of divorce and separation (a *get*) in accordance with Jewish law. Elizabeth "cordially consented" to the divorce and renounced "all the rights and titles of a wife." Under Jewish—not South Carolina—law, wife and husband were free to remarry, which Mordecai did just two years later. Elizabeth's marital status after her ecclesiastical divorce is unknown. The Lyonses' ecclesiastical divorce, neither recognized nor disputed by secular law, represents one of only two recorded in Charleston's history. The other occurred in 1840, when Beth Elohim Synagogue granted Sarah and George Prince their divorce.[27]

A quarter century after Elizabeth Lyon's outrageous actions, a Mrs. Torre "eloped" from her husband, took a lover, and moved in with that man. In July 1815, Mr. Peter Torre had watched, stunned, as another man bodily picked up his wife and kissed her. Peter also eavesdropped on their conversation and heard this Mr. Summers promise Mrs. Torre that, "when rich enough he and [she] would live together." This came to pass sooner than expected, likely because Peter confronted his wife. By the next month Mr. Summers and Mrs. Torre were, in fact, cohabitating. Peter initiated court proceedings against Summers charging "criminal conversation" with his wife. A jury awarded him $5,000 in damages, a substantial sum upheld on appeal. At trial, Peter was quick to point out that prior to the time his wife moved in with Summers "in evident adultery, she had criminal conversation with other men." Under South Carolina law, adultery by a wife resulted in the loss of her dower rights, so Peter eagerly emphasized his wife's repeated transgressions to ensure release from this patriarchal responsibility.[28]

Elizabeth Chapman Lyon and Mrs. Torre (whose given name remained unstated in the court records) were not alone in failing to reign as chaste, loving wives who paid fealty to their husbands. Charleston newspapers and court records reveal others who rejected requisite wifely subservience, eschewed the "peculiar ornaments of woman . . . modesty, retirement, meekness, moderation, [and] purity," and who committed adultery and conspired to assault, rob, and even murder other Charleston residents. Their relationships with men represent the extreme on a continuum—ranging from Goodwife to murderess—that encompassed all women of the laboring classes (not merely a few anomalies) and the destitute poor. These women deviated from and were contrasted to the idealized good wife created by the master class, whose members subsequently decried them as "women of . . . worthless and abandoned character, and such bad repute" as to render them unworthy of paternalistic protection.[29]

Like slaves, laboring women abandoned their husbands rather than enduring loveless marriages or abuse, an action taken by few ladies of the master class because it would jeopardize their economic and social positions and constitute rebellion against not only the marital ideal that governed their lives but also a social structure that positioned them near the top. But women of the working classes had little to lose, or much less than ladies of the ruling elite, so they abandoned their husbands and lived with other men. In 1783, when Lucy Schooner did just that, her husband responded by placing an advertisement in the city paper—similar to slave runaway ads—admonishing city residents "not to credit her." He forewarned that Lucy "may perhaps call herself Mrs. Dutchfield, which is false." Following Lucy's departure, her husband publicly demeaned her as an undutiful wife and a woman of loose morals who had wronged him. Instead of petitioning city residents to aid in her recapture, as in a runaway ad, he attempted economic sabotage by adjuring shopkeepers and all city residents to shun her. Ironically, Lucy's husband rebuked her for not attaining the marital ideal she had long since repudiated in the act of leaving him to live with another man. It is difficult to determine even a rough estimate of the numbers of women who cohabited with men rather than marrying them. Such cases surfaced in historical records only when, as in Lucy Schooner's case, an outraged husband publicly advertised his marital problems, or when a property or inheritance dispute arose. In 1829 a court denied dower to a Mrs. William Bell (the court report did not state her given name) because "she had eloped, and lived in adultery during the life of the husband." Jurists acknowledged she "was compelled by the ill treatment of her husband to fly from his house," but because he offered to take her back (and she refused), the court nullified her dower right.[30]

Although laboring women deemed their rebellion a logical response to unacceptable marital relations and, indeed, common practice among their peers, state judges contested this assessment. South Carolina case law balanced along a familiar line regarding the practice of cohabitation: judges preserved the sovereignty of patriarchs, yet punished men who blatantly and egregiously violated the paternalistic ideal. And courts wielded free rein in determining if and under what conditions cohabiting partners deserved the legal privileges of married persons; state statute law intentionally made no provisions for common-law marriage. Absent any guidelines on what constituted common-law marriage and what responsibilities and benefits accrued from such relationships, courts alternatively supported and denied the validity of unions based on case testimony and court assessments of the characters of the two people involved.[31]

In 1838 a laboring woman named Elizabeth Bath discovered that judges neither shared her notions of marriage nor granted Revolutionary War widows special consideration or paternal support if doing so jeopardized the court's preeminent goal of safeguarding white men's autonomy, including laboring men. Elizabeth's first husband had disappeared in 1776 after the battle of Fort Moultrie, and Elizabeth alleged she had received word of his death when Charleston fell four years later. In the interim, Elizabeth had met one William Wightman who promised repeatedly to marry her. She and other reasonable people presumed her first husband dead, so she entered into a relationship with William that endured approximately five years. Elizabeth bore the first of their three children in 1779, and baptized little "Sally Wightman" in the German Lutheran Church. Elizabeth considered herself married to William and, upon his death, she turned to the law for help in securing part of her husband's estate to which she believed she and their children were entitled. The court dismissed Elizabeth's claim. Prior judicial decisions had established and facilitated a husband's freedom to have sex with women of color. However, Elizabeth's case was the first in which a court explicitly extended that liberty to include sex with "artful" white women (to whom they were not married) with few if any legal obligations to those women.[32]

In deliberating Elizabeth Wightman's case, the court rationalized its decision not to afford a white woman paternalistic care by positioning Elizabeth outside the protective ideology of paternalism. Judges impugned Elizabeth's character and motives. The chancellor of record declared that she was not "induced to enter into this intercourse [with Wightman] by any promise of marriage." The court also demeaned Elizabeth by implying she was a manipulative and sexual creature, characterizations customarily applied to slaves. "It might be of dangerous consequence," the judge intoned, "that every careless promise drawn from an infatuated man, in the course of a criminal [connection] by . . . a licentious and artful woman, should have the effect of fastening her upon him as a wife." Concluding his decree, the judge proclaimed that, "when a promise of future marriage is made between parties living in a state of concubinage, the continuance of that intercourse will not transform the [connection] into marriage."[33]

Because courts easily dismissed them as "persons of ill-fame and reputation, and of wicked, corrupt, and depraved dispositions," laboring women who petitioned state courts for protection and support had to demonstrate greater public mistreatment by their husbands than did ladies of the master class. Domestic disputes in which both spouses were of dubious character, and where the wife proved indisputable mistreatment by her husband, were particularly vexatious for South Carolina judges. And workingwomen who alleged abuse occasionally provided officers of the court opportunities to reinforce status distinctions. These cases exhibit a pattern of nonintervention, rationalized through resort to images of class as well as gender. Judges often expressed reluctance to award alimony to women of the laboring classes, and transformed their courtrooms into public venues for faulting the unladylike behavior of the complainants. Adjudicators actually elaborated a class-specific notion of womanhood, then employed that ideal to justify withholding paternalistic care. But in the process, judges also reaffirmed an ideal of patriarchal authority that *bridged* class distinctions among men by granting to all of them a similar measure of domestic dominion. When Nancy Boyd applied to a court of equity for alimony, her daughter served as the principal witness to corroborate allegations of physical violence and adultery. The chancellor dismissed this second charge, ruling that only a "few suspicious circumstances" of adulterous activity had been shown.

The primary charge (ill usage) also failed because it depended principally on the daughter's testimony and she "did not see the blow given, but only heard the quarrel, and saw [her father with] a piece of board in his hand, and saw a cut or bruise" on her mother's head. John Boyd asserted that he never struck his wife, he only pushed her and she fell. Moreover, he said, his wife had struck him the day before and called him a liar. The judge accused Nancy of being much at fault. Her husband, he said, was a "poor waggoner . . . of rude manners and given to intoxication" but that he had not exercised "so much continued cruelty" so as to warrant a separate maintenance. In addition, the justice asserted, any alimony award would have to come out of the husband's daily labor, "and *the wife appears to be as able to work as the husband.*" Nancy Boyd appealed her case and lost again. "Her own conduct was impeachable," decreed four appellate judges, and "the violence offered by the husband had been provoked by her." This constituted sufficient reason, they declared, for refusing assistance.[34]

The legal system did not withhold help to every workingwoman, but judges did make clear that class mattered. In 1845 Sarah Prince convinced judges in two courts that her husband had abandoned her and their child and now lived "in open and unconcealed profligacy with a concubine, leaving his family dependent for support on [Sarah's] exertions." George Prince advanced a creative but ultimately unsuccessful defense. He denied that he had ever married Sarah, stating that "he did not give her the ring with a view of remaining [with her]" but that "he had been frightened into it." George claimed further that he had cohabitated with Sarah, and "in consequence of this he had married her," but that he had "substituted words of cursing" in place of the marriage vows. Confounding the proceedings, the alleged marriage certificate was written half in Hebrew and half in German, and various alleged expert witnesses gave conflicting testimony on "the Hebrew law of marriages."[35]

The court's ultimate postponement of a decision in Sarah Prince's case exposed the uphill battle many women faced even when they presented clear proof of a husband's combined infractions (in this case, desertion plus open adultery). Deliberations also manifested the tug-of-war between patriarchal prerogative and paternalistic protection. Initially the court questioned Sarah's character and ordered a separate inquiry to determine whether "[her] child [was] the child of the plaintiff [George]." Several judges pondered whether they could assist her, given the relatively humble economic circumstances of Sarah and her husband. If "the condition in life of the parties is such that neither had property, and they were both to labor for subsistence," they said, "it is very questionable whether a case for alimony is presented." Another judge pointedly decreed, "if the parties are laboring people, the wife needs less." Despite questioning Sarah's worthiness, the Equity Appeals Court ultimately affirmed that George had, by his own admission, abandoned Sarah and their child. Worse still, George expressed no remorse and no intention to be more discreet in his "illicit intercourse . . . with another woman." This admission constituted the determining factor. The court considered George's stance unacceptable, given "that [the] law, which almost enslave[d] the wife, [made] the husband liable for her support." Even in the face of this matter-of-fact recapitulation of Sarah's disabilities and vulnerabilities (having found her "blameless"), and her husband's obligation of support, the court still wavered, for this was no lady and idealized good wife. The presiding judge awarded Sarah no fixed maintenance payment. Instead he ordered a reappraisal of George's income (previously assessed at four or five thousand dollars per annum), to be submitted to the court at a later date.[36]

Court debate in this case smacked of class anxiety, replete with fears of the lower order running amuck, wriggling out of their duties, and leaving the master class to pass the hat and foot the bill to support abandoned, working-class wives. "If the wealthy man denies to his wife the duties of the marriage relation," one justice observed, "there is no difficulty in compelling him to sustain her out of his property. But [should] the poor . . . desert their duties with impunity?" Further discussion suggests that the presiding chancellors were driven as much by their determination to ensure social order and economic stability as by their desire to protect Sarah Prince. It is not clear from the record whether the court ever ruled in Sarah's favor or not.[37]

An exceptionally potent patriarchal ethos pervaded South Carolina society and influenced how and when court officials interceded in the "delicate kind" of differences between husbands and wives. The adamant state prohibition of divorce, even in cases of extreme abuse, bespeaks this inimitability. Particularly in slave societies, where any subversion of the expected obedience and subordination of inferiors loomed as one step down a slippery slope to social chaos, courts and legislatures buttressed the power of husbands/masters. Many women found no help or achieved only partial victories in their legal quests for separation and alimony precisely because judges anxiously guarded the primacy of white men, or, as one chancellor expressed it, he preferred to "refrain from lifting the veil which concealed from public view" the private and often abusive matters of the household. On the other hand, courts did intrude in private domestic affairs when other men, by extreme and reprehensible behavior, belied the alleged superiority of their organic, highly hierarchical world. Judges struggled to reconcile the twin imperatives of gentlemen patriarchs— unquestioned sovereignty and caring protection—on which they had built slave society. Legal precedent concerning alimony and the rules and patterns of awards to abused women reveal that this balancing act yielded unexpected court decisions. They sometimes denied or limited help to "blameless" wives and affirmed the legality of gifts to "common strumpets," whether white or African American. Women confronted idiosyncratic justice in the hands of judges, attorneys, and witnesses who frequently appraised and dissected their character and social position as closely as they examined the facts of each case.[38]

From the late eighteenth century until the Civil War, women like Elizabeth Chapman Lyon (the immigrant tailor's wife), Elizabeth Wightman (the Revolutionary widow), Sarah Prince (the apothecary's wife), and others violated and/or rejected the marital model established by Charleston's master class. If they wound up in court, the outcomes turned on court assessments of their personal conduct and character as judges drew on a fixed notion of the amiable good wife.

Analyzing marital prescriptions (the aristocratic paradigm), juxtaposed with Charleston women's marital experiences (real lives), reveals how women gained their identities by playing off the different expectations and roles they had been assigned. Different sexual and marital experiences defined each group—slave women, free laboring women of all colors, brown elite women, and ladies of the master class—and their diverse goals and verities, in turn, were influenced by what type of woman they were.

6 Mixing and Admixtures

White men in eighteenth-century Charleston boasted publicly in doggerel verse of their "taste . . . for dark Beauties" and of the blessings of variety in "kiss[ing] black or white." Variations on this theme persisted into the next century, when intrepid British traveler Harriet Martineau commented on "the very general connection of white gentlemen with their female slaves," and city patriarchs continued to "laugh over their nocturnal adventures in Mulatto Alley." Observations like these speak to a fact of life in the slave South: daily sexual mingling or mixing occurred between women of color and white men.[1]

Slave society—distinguished by its reliance on chattel laborers who vastly outnumbered free, waged workers—celebrated marriage and family in the abstract. Southern patriarchs bragged about the care and attention they provided to their people, including wives, children, and slaves. They touted their paternalistic southern way of life as far superior to the impersonal, exploitative waged labor of the North. However, one form of racial mixing—the sexual abuse of slave women—belied these claims of paternalism and mocked the institution of slavery that they praised. Sexual mixing between women of color and white men facilitated goals integral to Charleston society because sex constituted a visceral show of patriarchal power, and sexual protocols helped define who was black and white, slave and free, female and male. In addition to the pattern of sexual abuse, some slave women and free women of color engaged in consensual sex with white men within relationships stimulated by genuine affection, physical attraction, or a powerful drive to gain some advantage in a world that daily disempowered them. The socially prescribed sexual license of slave women, like the sexual restrictions on wealthy women of the white master class, fundamentally shaped their identity. Many women of color extracted tangible benefits from sexual connections with white men. They transformed sexual vulnerability and sexual license into effective tools of accommodation and resistance.

The antithetical yet interdependent sexual ideals and practices of slave women and white ladies defined and governed sexual practices of all other Charleston women. Because the code of behavior regarding sex defined color and condition, it took on great significance to free people of the brown elite, a group that jealously guarded its hard-earned social respectability. Indeed, female chastity loomed as important for the brown elite as for the white ruling class, precisely because people of the brown elite navigated on shifting and sometimes treacherous terrain between the worlds of slave and free, black and white. The brown elite had more to prove. The centrality of sex in demarcating race, class, and condition also impinged on non-slaveholding women's lives. Poor Charleston women of all colors who owned little or no stake in slave society (black, brown, and white residents of the laboring, destitute, or disreputable poor) became sexual rebels and seized the sexual liberty ascribed to slave women. They had nothing to lose. Other laboring women, however, clung to and emulated the sexual ideals and practices of the master class. They not only celebrated and esteemed chastity, but also repudiated the notion of sexual mixing, a practice that distinguished them from black women. Whatever their choices, sex defined and distinguished Charleston women.

The common practice of sexual mingling in the slave South complicates facile definitions of concubinage and prostitution, consensual sex and coerced sex, sexual victimization and empowerment. Sex between white men and black women was coerced; it was consensual; it was a combination of both. Drawing on autobiographies of former slaves, transcriptions of interviews with former slaves, letters and diaries of slave owners, travelers' accounts, and other contemporary sources, scholars have documented the sexual exploitation of enslaved women and have enriched the literature on slavery in the (North) American South, the Caribbean, and South America.[2] But researchers are just beginning to explore the ways in which slave society—where certain human beings were legally defined as chattel—confounds the ideas and acts of concubinage, prostitution, and rape. Traditional definitions do not capture the reality of sexual customs in the slave South. Concubinage is commonly understood to mean the cohabitation of a woman and a man without formal or legal marriage. But at what point did a house slave, whose owner legally enjoyed access to her body as well as her labor and who routinely exploited and raped her, become a concubine? If the key is *voluntary* cohabitation, what are the measures of acquiescence and coercion? Few women of color in the slave South were so unencumbered by sexual and racial prescriptions so as to render truly free their choice to become a concubine. Put another way, when and how did the concubine become (or cease to be) her own sexual agent? Similarly, prostitution is defined as the practice of engaging in sexual intercourse for money. But was a slave a prostitute because she provided sex with the expectation of material rewards for herself or her children? Had not the institution of slavery already prostituted her with its customary sexual protocols? How could a chattel slave (herself property) sell part of that property, and which forms of sexual mixing constituted prostitution?

Turning these issues on their heads, the reality of widespread sexual mixing in the slave South, including concubinage, prostitution, and rape, complicates our understanding of the institution of slavery by revealing sex at the center of the ongoing power negotiations within slave societies. Scholars have exposed the centrality of gender (meanings attached to sexual difference) to the processes by which white men of the master class forged and perpetuated their supremacy: they created and promulgated specific notions of "woman" and "man" to empower themselves.[3] But sex as well as gender also proved essential to the acquisition and maintenance of power by white men of the master class. Just as important, many enslaved women and free women of color used sex as a survival mechanism. Examining the nature of sexual relations between women of color and white men reveals the *mutual exploitation* at the heart of social relations—power relations—in slave society. The partners were unequal and the negotiations were carried out on shifting, dangerous terrain, but enslaved and free women of color participated in this constant jockeying for a measure of control.

Consensual sex (itself a contested notion) between women of color and white men dated to Charleston's earliest years as a rough, frontier town and continued throughout the Revolutionary era and antebellum period. Particularly in the closing decades of the eighteenth century and the beginning of the next, some of these sexual relationships resulted in freedom for the women and their children. Indeed, before 1820 slave manumissions and assisted self-purchase contributed to the growth of the city's free population of color. In thirty years between 1770 and 1800, the number of Charleston's free people of color rose from 25 to just over 1,000, and between 1790 and 1810 their numbers increased over 151 percent. Significantly, about two of every three slaves who achieved freedom through manumission from 1700 to 1800 were women, and sexual mixing with white owners was a principal reason. It is difficult to document precisely which manumissions resulted from sexual connections and trickier still to speculate about what percentages of these sexual relationships were voluntary or coerced. Nevertheless, the point remains that sex proved useful as a survival mechanism.[4]

In Charleston, the distinction between housekeeper and concubine blurred, so when slave women and free women of color assumed the position of housekeeper, most understood the role to include sex and expected to derive material rewards for the extra service. In mid-eighteenth century when Sylvia's mistress died, her master never remarried. For over twenty-five years, Sylvia continued to serve as housekeeper to this wealthy Charleston merchant. When he died in 1781, Sylvia received her freedom and a substantial yearly income. Likewise, in the closing years of the American Revolution, Rebecca Kelly persuaded her owner to emancipate her in exchange for "housekeeping." By dint of hard work and savvy negotiations with her owner and a subsequent sexual partner, Rebecca Kelly had won her freedom by 1794. She then applied skills learned in slavery—as a household manager and mattress-maker—and prospered as a free businesswoman. A slave named Jenny received money and freedom for herself and her son when her owner died in 1801, while ten years later one Rebecca Thorne and her son were emancipated and continued to live with their former owner, a white man named John S. Thorne. Thereafter, Rebecca bore five of John's children. When John died, Rebecca and her children inherited a house and four slaves who provided her with a steady income. A housekeeper named Celestine bore five children with her white owner, a French immigrant from Saint Domingue, Philip Stanislas Noisette. In 1835 Philip freed their children in defiance of South Carolina's 1820 prohibition of slave manumission except by special petition to the state legislature. This law rendered his declaration of freedom illegal and non-binding. However, twenty years later their daughter,

Margaret, owned sixteen acres of farm land on the edge of the city limits, plus other real estate in Charleston. Although legally enslaved, Margaret Noisette lived as a free person, paid Charleston's free Negro tax, and was listed in 1850 with six other family members at the "Noisette Farm" on King Street Road.[5]

Prominent Charleston politicians and businessmen also granted favors to slaves who became their lovers. By the 1790s, a slave named Hagar was involved in a sexual relationship with General Arnoldus Vanderhorst, who served with Francis Marion in the American Revolution, became Charleston's second intendent (mayor), a state senator, and, in late 1794, governor of South Carolina. Although Arnoldus had six children with his (white) wife, Elizabeth Raven, Hagar bore him two (perhaps three) more children, Eliza and Peter and possibly Sarah. Arnoldus emancipated Hagar and the three children and provided for their maintenance and education. Aware of the vulnerabilities of free people of color, Arnoldus made provisions for his second family. In October 1813, two years before he died, Arnoldus conveyed to two of his white sons land, a house in the city, slaves "together with the . . . issue and increase of the females," and other personal property, including clothing and household items, all "for the use and benefit and lookout of Hagar, a free woman of colour and her two children Eliza and Peter formerly the property [of Arnoldus Vanderhorst] but whom he hath lately manumitted." In addition, Arnoldus stipulated that his estate pay for "the maintenance, education and apprenticing [of Hagar's] three children, Sarah, Eliza and Peter" throughout Hagar's lifetime and that of the children and their "issue." Also cognizant of the chicanery of executors and guardians, Arnoldus made some bequests to his white children contingent upon their upholding Hagar's emancipation and that of her children. In 1819 and 1820, Hagar Richardson paid city taxes on real estate valued at $3,000 and also on seven slaves whose work provided her income. She died a free woman in late May 1820.[6]

Other women's negotiations with former owners yielded mixed results and their success manifested in shades of gray. Many women foundered as they negotiated the shoals of inequality, often entangled in the nets of their lovers' (and former owners') "meddling" white heirs. In 1831 Charleston immigrant John Fable bequeathed most of his property "to [his] children, whom [he] acknowledge[d]." Although the 1820 statute prevented John from emancipating his progeny, he directed that his real property be sold and the invested proceeds be applied to the "support of [his] son, John, and daughter, Elizabeth." None too pleased with this situation, John's white heirs contested the will. The confounded presiding judge ruefully admitted that "there [was] no attempt at emancipation in the will." Moreover, the court found nothing illegal in John's direction to sell the bulk of his estate to support two slaves with the resulting income. "Suppose the testator had directed the executor to expend one hundred dollars annually, in support of a favorite old horse, for past service," the judge mused, "could his distributees or residuary legatees legally object to it? I think not." As in numerous Carolina inheritance disputes, this case placed the issues of sexual mixing and the distribution of property to mixed-race heirs at center stage and subjected them to public scrutiny. Five judges wriggled uncomfortably, caught between three conflicting drives: their inclination to uphold binding legal trusts, their abhorrence of legal precedent that created loopholes in the state's 1820 emancipation prohibition, and their sensitivity to heightened northern criticism of slavery. The court upheld John Fable's will and trust.[7]

A legal dispute in 1848 reveals that Carolina courts did not uniformly uphold white men's efforts to provide for their families of color. A woman known only as Tenah, who already had one daughter from a prior relationship, bore five of her white owner's children. This master, John Dougherty, stipulated in his will that Tenah and all her children "be left free under the guardianship of [his] executors, and . . . have a reasonable support from [his] estate." He left other slaves to his niece, making no similar demands. In late 1844 when John died, his white son, Joseph, contested the will and, because John had explicitly stated his (illegal) intention that Tenah and her children be "left free," Joseph prevailed. The court voided John's bequest of freedom and ordered that "the negroes . . . must be delivered up to the complainant [Joseph]." Joseph Dougherty acquired the valuable property he sought, plus his five half-sisters and half-brothers as well as their mother, his father's former lover. Forging links with white men, even when infused with genuine affection, did not guarantee protection.[8]

These cases of Hagar Richardson, John Fable's longtime lover (who remained nameless in all court documents), and Tenah were not rare in eighteenth- and nineteenth-century Carolina. Many women of color derived for themselves and their children concrete advantages from intimate relationships with white men, rewards that grew oddly and ironically out of their innately vulnerable position as women of color in a slave society. They inhabited a world in which their skin color constituted a marker of sexual promiscuity. Their alleged heightened sexual drives, in turn, were indicators of bestiality, according to white, southern apologists of slavery, who concluded that black women were, in essence, born to be concubines or prostitutes as well as laborers. Consequently, white men granted to black women greater sexual latitude than they did to white women, whose sexual activity they tightly constrained and protected. Slavery apologists alleged that white women were so delicate and moral that they must be nearly asexual by their very nature. Antithetical notions of female sexuality—aggressive, tainted black women and passive, pure white women—rationalized the sexual exploitation of slave women. State law upheld the force of these racialized notions of gender in a variety of circumstances: white men were not prosecuted for raping slaves; only white women could be accused of bearing a bastard child because bastardy was assumed to be common among "Negro" women; white women could be denied the benefit of spousal support if they had engaged in promiscuous (adulterous) behavior that was deemed "Negro" comportment. However, many women of color turned these sexual and racial stereotypes to their advantage. They were said to be highly sexual creatures that engaged in sex with slave men, free men of African descent, and white men. Many enslaved and free African American women exploited this ideology when doing so yielded material benefits to themselves, their children, or other family members.[9]

Despite the fact that women of color resourcefully negotiated social and sexual relations that were extraordinarily exploitative, many also succumbed to rape or sexual intercourse under physical force and duress. A few white southerners acknowledged this reality. "Some among us," slavery apologist William Simms reluctantly conceded, "make their slaves the victims and the instruments, alike, of the most licentious passions." In 1829 a "broken hearted" Lydia Frierson confessed to her minister that her married white owner "compel[led] her to live in constant adultery with him" and "threaten[ed] her most dreadfully if she resist[ed] him." According to church discipline, the minister should have "read [Lydia] out" of her membership from the pulpit during a Sunday morning service. However, female relatives of Lydia's master also attended First Baptist Church of Charleston, and Reverend Basil Manly had no wish to humiliate them by making public John Frierson's actions. Instead, he recommended to Lydia that she "remonstrate kindly with her master; and firmly . . . tell him that she could not consent to sin." Basil encouraged Lydia to "be resolute and firm" in her resistance, which would "surely . . . prevent the evil." John continued to rape Lydia until he died four years later. Rape manifested a murky but persistent feature of patriarchal control and a screaming repudiation of paternalistic ideology.[10]

Several factors conspired to create conditions ripe for sexual exploitation of Charleston slave women. The urban household constituted an intimate, walled compound unto itself. It comprised a single residence, a yard, and separate outbuildings. If extraordinarily spacious, the entire property measured 117 feet wide by 200 feet deep. In short, slave owners and slaves lived in close and intimate proximity, and even if slaves slept over the kitchen or stable, they were just steps from their owners at all times. Exacerbating the close dimensions of urban living space, many slave owners ruefully admitted the fact that young men of wealthy families spent years after school or college, and before marriage, "in perfect idleness." This inactivity, combined with a youthful urge to sample the perquisites of their authority, resulted in "licentious intercourse with slaves," an outcome common enough to spawn "anxiety of [white elite] parents for their sons." This changed little from the American Revolution to the eve of Civil War. Early in 1847, one of Charleston's many visitors observed "men of a more than doubtful morality" pressing around "a pretty young mulatto girl" up for public auction across from the Customs House. Made an "object of criminal lust," this young girl "turn[ed] red with shame and modesty" as the "cynical" bidders surrounded her and posed "indecent questions." Ultimately she was purchased at "twice her worth by a professional gambler who planned to put her in a lottery." Like their fathers and grandfathers before them, patriarchs-in-training understood that sexual access to slave women came with their positions of power and authority.[11]

Although the sexual exploitation of slave women consistently hallmarked the institution of slavery and Charleston society from the colony's founding until after the Civil War, its interpretation altered after 1822. In the eighteenth century, city slave owners, city guests, and southern apologists matter-of-factly recounted white men's "fornication with their black slave women," and spoke of these sexual exploits as commonplace. This is not to say that all city residents condoned such exploitation, but aside from occasional voices decrying this "too common practice" of rape, public observation in the eighteenth century focused on white men's prerogative to enjoy women of color. By the 1830s, in post-Vesey Charleston, white residents and visitors had shifted attention away from the joys and focused on the hazards of sex with slaves. Denmark Vesey was the former slave who allegedly masterminded an abortive 1822 slave insurrection. Hysteria reigned after a slave disclosed the plot, in which both slaves and free people of color were implicated. Thereafter, public voices warned that "connections" between white men and their female slaves augmented an "ominous . . . bastard population" (some of them free), whose growing numbers could prove dangerous. Others cautioned that sexual mixing "blight[ed] domestic happiness" within white households. By the mid-nineteenth century, with slavery under increasing attack by northern abolitionists, white men no longer boasted openly of their sexual exploits. Many still bragged about their sexual escapades but they snickered among themselves in private. The disparate tenor of eighteenth- and mid-nineteenth-century observations notwithstanding, two constant characteristics spanned more than one hundred years of public commentary on this subject: slave owners displaced onto female slaves their own licentiousness (maintaining that slave women encouraged sexual advances of white men); and, whether recounting bawdy details or relating how sexual mixing demoralized white mistresses and debased young sons, public observations focused primarily on the effects upon white people. In effect, slave society defined rape as the norm for slave women (even if some ladies and gentlemen lamented or decried it), and because slave women were acceptable targets of rape, white women, by contrast, were officially off limits. In this way, rape entwined Charleston women and abetted the process of constructing abstract notions of "woman."[12]

Laboring free women of color were defined by sexual beliefs and practices akin to those of slave women because sexual possibilities and practices demarcated color as well as condition. Unrestrained by sexual proscriptions imposed on (white) ladies, Charleston's laboring free women of color capitalized on the sexual freedom defined by the master class as black behavior. In some instances less vulnerable than their enslaved counterparts, free black and brown women reaped similar material rewards from sexual relationships with white men. In 1778 a visiting road surveyor particularly commented on the elegant dress and polite behavior of Charleston's light-skinned women of color, who lacked for few material goods so long as they enjoyed the favor of the city's most prominent white men. While "in keeping," they provided sex in return for this special treatment.[13]

Throughout the eighteenth and nineteenth centuries, free women of African descent entered into relationships with white men, some of which endured for decades. When Samuel Simons died in 1824, he bequeathed $1,400 and two slaves to his housekeeper, a free woman of color named Maria Chapman. Seven years later another single white man, Benjamin Davids, left generous bequests to Elsey, a free woman who had provided long and "faithful service" to him. Charleston businessman Sherry Sasportas publicly recognized a free woman of color, Catharine Maria, as his lawful wife in 1817, and provided her a maintenance. Only six years later, a white newspaper editorial stigmatized unions like those of the Sasportases. "There is not a white person in the community," he ranted, "who would hazard a defense of it." While acknowledging its legality, the editorialist declared that "a white person so acting would be considered . . . degraded" for committing what "amount[ed] to an indictable offense against the public decorum and public morals." Sherry Sasportas was not part of the master class and, thus, had not risked expulsion from that ruling clique, but he had jeopardized his economic position. He likely suffered losses but continued to enjoy the support of most city residents, who transacted business with him while sneering behind his back.[14]

Not surprisingly, most mixed relationships in Charleston were never legalized even when they were of long duration, like that of Margaret Bettingall and Adam Tunno. Scottish immigrant and de jure bachelor, Adam Tunno, never violated white society's sexual protocols. Yet from at least the closing decade of the eighteenth century until his death in late 1832, he cohabitated with "a fine looking [brown] person" named Margaret Bettingall. According to some black and brown city residents, Margaret not only served as "the head and front of [Adam's] household but also was his "wife." Members of the white elite preferred to speak publicly of Margaret as Adam Tunno's housekeeper; in private they whispered that she was his concubine. Margaret bore Adam two children, one of whom died in infancy. The other, Barbara Tunno Barguet, found a niche within Charleston's brown elite community, a status she attained because her father educated her (and her first son) and left her $2,500 as well as slaves and other property, and because her mother also bequeathed money and slaves to Barbara. Margaret Bettingall derived substantial material benefits from this long-term relationship with Adam, for he left Margaret, her children, and her grandchildren a total of nearly $6,000 plus slaves and other personal property. Adam Tunno, the public bachelor, provided well for his family of color. However, during this more-than-forty-year relationship with Margaret, Adam remained a prominent member of the city's mercantile community and active in one of the city's foremost social and benevolent organizations, the St. Andrew's Society. Charleston's municipal leaders formed the constellation of Adam's (public) social sphere. He achieved this because he crossed the color line in a socially admissible way—that is, discreetly, behind the walls of his East Bay residence—thereby allowing members of the master class either to pretend he and Margaret were not a couple or, in private, to decry such women who lived "in disgraceful intimacy" with white men. These different interpretations of Margaret and Adam's relationship by the city's black and white communities reveal concubinage and prostitution (so labeled by wealthy white Charlestonians) as contested notions in slave society, because many people of color clearly viewed the Bettingall and Tunno liaison as marriage.[15]

The idealized dictate of ladies' sexual purity and the alleged sexual license of slaves initiated business opportunities in Charleston: a likely and logical coupling of the city's extensive slave-hiring system and the sex trade. Unlike New Orleans, Charleston did not formalize prostitution into a system of *plaçage*, replete with a class of "fancy women" whose mothers contracted formal arrangements of concubinage between their daughters and white men. Nor did most city residents overtly condone or tolerate sexual liaisons between people of color and white people, as one historian has found in upcountry areas of antebellum Virginia and North Carolina. However, evidence points to the use—by both slave owners and slaves—of Charleston's ubiquitous practice of slave hiring to facilitate the provision of sex for remuneration. At least two scholars investigating Caribbean and South American slavery have uncovered a "domestic subculture of prostitution . . . linked symbiotically to the legitimate" urban practice of hiring slaves. In nineteenth-century Rio de Janeiro and Bridgetown, women were hired out as prostitutes in addition to serving as their owners' concubines and performing domestic tasks within private households. The pecuniary benefits to be derived from this covert sex market "made slave owners keen to keep at least one woman so employed."[16]

Several elements point to a similar nexus of slave hiring and prostitution in Charleston. Slave labor drove this city's economy, enslaved women outnumbered their male counterparts, and the work of slave women constituted an essential element of Charleston's economic life. Moreover, within this urban work environment where women figured prominently, there existed few public or private settings closed to slave women. Their labor took them throughout the city and they often worked (or not) without white supervision. Slave women also comprised an essential component in the ubiquitous custom of slave hiring, a system elaborated on in greater detail in chapter 7. As one visitor observed, "many people ma[de] comfortable incomes in this way out of the labour of their slaves." The city came alive during its winter social season, and business owners as well as private householders advertised their need for temporary help. Charleston slave owners obligingly filled these demands and made a profit in the bargain.[17]

Most of this industrious activity by slave women comprised legitimate enterprises, but some slave women turned to full- or part-time prostitution as a pragmatic economic choice, and the city's hiring system facilitated their decision. Both customary practice (hiring slaves out and allowing slaves to hire themselves out) and the relative autonomy often achieved as a hired slave expedited prostitution. On a weekly or monthly basis, slaves performed varied tasks and delivered their earned wages to mistresses and masters who specified what dollar amounts they expected. Therefore, whenever a slave chose to provide sexual services for pay, the entirety of that income constituted clear profit for that woman. Despite Charleston's nightly patrol, resourceful slaves could stay out past curfew, rendezvous with paying customers, and sneak back into their owners' homes. One mistress complained that "if locked out at ten o'clock," her slave woman "jump[ed] the fence and force[d] a window open to get into the house." Another owner lamented that his "pretty lusty . . . young . . . yellowish wench," named Silvia was "so well known in and about Charleston that she need[ed] no further description." And a slave runaway named Nanny was seen, "every night in town." The infamous "Negro dance[s]" of Revolution-era Charleston continued at least throughout the final decades of the eighteenth century and yielded benefits to slave women and free women of color as well as to the men who participated.[18]

Additional evidence points to the ways in which slave women were simultaneously sexual victims and their own sexual agents, sometimes trading sexual favors for protection from abusive owners. Slave owners and slave society had already defined slave women as "lusty" and "cunning," so some slaves exploited their sexuality for gain. Near mid-nineteenth century one "young quadroon" who worked in a Charleston boarding house flirted with the secretary and valet of a visiting French pianist. Quite the ladies' man, this valet swore to the slave that "there [was] no sacrifice [he] would refuse . . . to merit [her] affection and esteem." The woman inquired, "you will buy me . . . and when I am free you will take me with you to Europe?" The valet, Monsieur François, vowed to do this "without any haggling" over her purchase price because he found his "pretty colored girl . . . ravishingly charming and spirited." In jubilant response, the young woman declared François "more than a lover [and] an angel descended from heaven." This woman's attempt to trade sex for freedom failed; the rogue departed with his employer for New Orleans and left his "dearest pretty girl" in Charleston with her owner. Her situation reveals slave women's vulnerability to exploitation and their determination to make choices about their sexual activity, inclusive of trading sex for promised freedom or other gain. When working to buy real or de facto freedom for themselves, for their spouses, or for their children, other women likely resorted to occasional prostitution. Most slave women in Charleston routinely ran errands for owners or otherwise performed tasks that daily took them into the city streets. They, too, had opportunities to engage in occasional prostitution. Urban slave women possessed both motive and opportunity to sell sex for profit even if they could not achieve immediate or complete emancipation.[19]

Much of the lively sex trade flourishing in Charleston was grounded in exploitation and premised on the ability to realize a "superordinate level of accumulation" from a slave woman's labor, prostitution, and reproduction. That is, a slave owner could reap triple returns from enslaved women who completed necessary household tasks, performed sexual acts for money, and bore children into bondage. As in most busy urban ports, numerous brothels lined certain Charleston streets and alleys, like Beresford (later Fulton), Archdale, Chalmers, Friend, and Clifford or "Mulatto Alley." Slave-owning proprietors of those establishments, like Mrs. Grace Peixotto, were known to offer women "of all shades and importations." Many profited handsomely from the fact that white men in South Carolina refused to outlaw prostitution. Throughout the eighteenth and nineteenth centuries, a woman could not "be indicted for being a bawd generally" because "the bare solicitation of chastity [was] not indictable." If nearby residents complained of constant noise and fights at a bawdy house, the proprietor could be charged merely with creating a "common·nuisance." In 1852 business had been brisk enough to allow the prosperous Mrs. Peixotto to enlarge "the Big Brick" at 11 Beresford (later Fulton) Street in Charleston's ward four. She also requested that the city council pave the area in front of her house with flagstones, since she had dedicated that space "to the citizens of Charleston." Grace still owned her Beresford property in 1860 (then valued at $15,000) plus seven slaves.[20]

Charleston residents did not confine their sex trade to the conspicuous bawdy houses. Less obvious businesses fronted for Charleston's sex industry as well, and evidence points to a pairing of covert enterprise with respectable city businesses. In the 1830s, a grocer named Dietrick Olandt gained notoriety for several years when citizens protested to the mayor that his store was "an improper and disorderly house." Investigation by municipal officials revealed that Dietrick worked "several females . . . [in] the upper portion of his house." A white man, Cornel June, operated one of Charleston's myriad boardinghouses, a legitimate option for travelers and other visitors particularly during the busy winter season. However, Cornel's establishment catered to the waterfront trade, and he prostituted slaves and free women of all colors out of his boardinghouse on Bedon's Alley. It would have been an easy matter, and profitable, for other male or female boardinghouse keepers and tavern owners to reserve one room in an otherwise respectable house for special services, and to keep one slave woman employed in this manner. The proprietor of the Planter Hotel, a Mrs. Street, "daily and hourly . . . beat her servants, male and female, either with her fist, or with a thong made of cow-hide." When one of her slave women "had disobliged her, [Street] beat her until her own strength was exhausted, and then insisted on her bar-keeper" continuing the punishment. It takes little imagination to envision Mrs. Street whispering with interested male guests to negotiate the terms of sexual services to be rendered by one of her maids or serving women. Slave owners and potential slave hirers often settled their contracts personally and made arrangements by word of mouth, so sex could be sold in the same way with city residents paying little heed. Charleston's ubiquitous slave-hiring system aided not only slave women who opted for extra money by providing sexual services but also slave owners who longed to increase profits by sexually exploiting their slaves.[21]

It is unlikely than men like Dietrick Olandt and Cornel June had cornered this particular aspect of the sex market. From the era of the early Republic to the mid-nineteenth century, Charleston's primarily white proprietresses owned and operated boardinghouses, hotels, punch houses, taverns, and coffee houses. While most of these tradeswomen ran wholly legitimate concerns, some probably possessed both motive (greed) and opportunity (a ready clientele) to enhance their incomes by hiring out women sex workers to sailors, travelers, and local men.[22]

It is also likely that a nexus of sex and the city's extensive practice of hiring slaves for various tasks constituted a regular part of the city economy. Charleston slave owners and hirers were bent on wringing every dollar from their enslaved laborers, and if occasional cruel treatment of slaves excited little interest or inquiry, similar indifference was plausible over the practice of discreetly hiring out slave women for sex. Within this context of routine exploitation, prostitution probably complemented Charleston's pervasive slave-hiring system. It also provided a discreet alternative to the city's more notorious bawdy houses and afforded yet another means for slave owners to maximize their investments in human property. On the other side of the ledger, slaves were equally resolute in exploiting hiring situations to their best advantage. During the eighteenth and nineteenth centuries, the city's heavy maritime activity and its status as a habitual stop on tours of the United States assured a constant sex market. Enslaved women and slave owners alike doubtless tapped into this steady customer base of pirates, soldiers, sailors, visitors, and city residents.[23]

Some white women—sexual rebels—rejected the white ideals of female chastity and fidelity and engaged in extreme rebellion against the dominance of white men by having sex with men of African descent. When white women breached Charleston's protocols of sex in this way, they sexually rejected white men and violated the fundamental doctrine that white men singularly enjoyed sexual access across the color line. Moreover, when white women sexually mixed, they turned Charleston society on its head by rhetorically painting themselves black and reducing themselves to the status of "slave." Precisely because this particular type of mixing was anathema (and, therefore, a taboo subject), the frequency of sexual relations between Charleston's women of European descent and slave men or free men of color may never be determined definitively. Nevertheless, white women engaged in sexual liaisons with black and brown men. Partial proof resides in whispered stories as well as in recorded court proceedings.[24]

Perhaps the most sensational of these relationships involved one of the city's skilled carpenters, an ill-fated slave called Zampo. In need of a slave to "wait on table," and impressed with Zampo's honesty and intelligence, a Charleston lawyer purchased Zampo at public auction in early 1847 for $800. After only a few months in this new household, Zampo fell in love with his owner's wife. Fearing a catastrophic outcome, he begged his new master to sell him. When the master refused, he ran away and was caught the next day. This slave owner sent Zampo to the "sugarhouse" for a hundred lashes, but he stayed the slave's sentence, claiming, "I pardon you because of the prayers of my wife." Just three months later the mistress awakened her household with "cries for help," and when questioned by her husband, "let fall from her hand a tuft of . . . the hair of a Negro."

Suspicions fell on another household slave who was about to be tortured to extract a confession when Zampo admitted his presence in the mistress's room. He was summarily accused and convicted of rape, a capital crime "in a country where the respect of the black for the white is required as a guarantee of order and general security." City officials assembled over 300 slaves to watch as they administered a punishment designed "to instill a salutary feeling of terror in the minds of the other slaves." They tied Zampo to a tree at the edge of a forest and ordered another African American man, the "appointed official executioner," to set him on fire. According to city lore, he crushed a vial of "fast-killing poison" with his teeth before the flames reached him, and allegedly cried out, "to you . . . merciful woman . . . I address my dying breath." Evidence points to a consensual affair. The "merciful" mistress cried rape because she and Zampo had been discovered or someone was about to expose them. Unable to save Zampo without dishonoring herself and her family, she sacrificed her lover, but quickened his death by providing the poison.[25]

Most relationships between white women and men of color took considerably less sensational forms, but each liaison denoted a rejection of white women's sexual ideals, expectations, and practices. White women of the lower classes routinely mingled with slaves and free people of color in Charleston's teeming waterfront areas, crowded alleys, and, particularly, the city's myriad taverns. These women "were made wenches by a combination of poverty and loss of self-control that blurred the distinctions . . . between black and white females." In addition to gambling, exchanging stolen goods, and getting drunk, white wenches also engaged in sex with men of African descent. Women like Louisa Uttes, Elizabeth Buckley, Ann Peterson, Maria Swords, and Catherine Lowry plodded a dreary path from sailors' boardinghouses—where they could earn drinking money by prostituting themselves—to makeshift living accommodations and the city's Poor House.[26]

Men of the master class reluctantly acknowledged this unthinkable form of sexual mixing when confronted with it on the bench. An 1829 court ruefully conceded that "the [color] taint in the blood" could derive from the *father* as well as the mother. In that same year, another judge incorporated into his ruling a public admission that the offspring of a *white* mother and a "negro" father was "a mulatto." This fact rendered the young woman in question subject to the 1740 slave code that established separate courts of magistrates and freeholders for enslaved and free people of African descent. Just four years later, another chancellor explained that the "free mulatto" plaintiff in his courtroom was "descended from a white mother." Likewise, an 1835 court specifically referenced the white wife of a mixed-race man. Rueful recognition, however, did not imply acceptance, and men of the master class never sanctioned this form of mixing as they did white men's sex with women of color. As they well understood, sexual independence conferred a measure of power, so white women who mingled sexually with men of African descent posed a danger. In a patriarchal slave society like Charleston, "femaleness" as well as manual labor and dark skin connoted inferior status. Therefore, white women who exercised sexual freedom threatened southern patriarchy and the southern social order because they were subordinates who undermined their subjection.[27]

Sexual relations between white women and men of African descent presented another thorny problem in race-based slave society. Unlike the progeny of white men and slave women, all children born of white women and men of color were free and, as one judge succinctly stated in 1854 during a period of increased racial tensions, free people of color violated the "rule on this subject" that "the distinction [between slave and free was] founded on color . . . [and] the people commonly called negroes . . . have been deemed absolute slaves." Accordingly, all "admixtures" should have been "absolute slaves," but those born of white mothers were not. This jurist voiced the extremist views of a small but increasingly vocal group of white Charlestonians in the decade of the 1850s. White men had never sanctioned or tolerated white women's sexual mixing (a constant reality from the eighteenth through the nineteenth centuries) but white people's anxiety about the results of mixing did change over time. While many city residents tolerated law-abiding free people of African descent, goodwill had its limits. The unsuccessful 1822 Denmark Vesey slave revolt had ratcheted up white people's fear of all residents of color, terrors that gradually dissipated only to be reawakened and fueled to fever pitch by northern abolitionists in the three decades before the Civil War. "A free African population is a curse to any country, slave-holding or non-slaveholding," intoned one chancellor in 1854, "and the evil is exactly proportionate to the number of such population." White women's "amalgamation" menaced the dominion of white men and potentially augmented Charleston's "curse[d]" free population of color.[28]

The prevalence of sexual mixing was so great that white legislators and judges took upon themselves the task of assigning race and condition to "admixtures," the progeny of mixed sexual connections. Just as this urban slave society simultaneously entwined women yet strictly separated them, so, too, did it relentlessly distinguish between white and black yet refuse to impose a strict standard for classifying the races and "admixtures" in particular. Neither statute nor case law specified what percentages of a black person's and a white person's blood produced a mulatto. Neither legislators nor judges decreed a legal definition of the term mulatto. One judge observed that "[t]here is considerable difficulty in laying down an exact rule on this subject [and] it may not perhaps be necessary to do so." Instead, courts deemed different individuals with like parentage (and grandparentage) as white or mulatto according to ancillary facts of each person's life. In South Carolina race was a social construction, and judges, legislators, and common people turned neighborhoods and courtrooms into their building sites. "Not every admixture of negro blood" produced a person of color, cautioned jurists. One court attempted to lay down the singular rule that where "a distinct and visible admixture of negro blood" existed, "the individual [was] to be denominated a mulatto, or person of color." Just four years later, in 1835, another court contradicted even that simple test by ruling that "the condition of the individual . . . [was] determined . . . by reputation, by his reception into society" and not merely by "the distinct and visible mixture of negro blood." Further muddying the waters, yet a third court touted the harsh line that, under South Carolina statute law, "every person of color [was] presumed to be a slave, and the onus of proving freedom [was] thrown" on them. This ruling reflected fears that without a rigorous delineation between white, black, and brown, slave society's race barriers might, in reality, be "nothing more than a rope of sand." In sum, South Carolina statute law clearly stated that the presumption of slavery shackled every "Negro" and "mulatto." However, in elaborating case law, judges exercised latitude in determining who was mulatto and who was white.[29]

The law presented both opportunities and obstacles to free, light-skinned Charleston women of mixed race who aspired to whiteness, but to avoid being "reduced . . . to the state and condition . . . [of] that degraded class of people" denominated "mulatto," women had to follow the sexual protocols of white ladies. Men of the master class purposefully left indistinct the designation mulatto and appropriated to themselves the case-by-case task of assigning mixed progeny to different "caste[s]," some black, some brown, some even white. This is because some "admixtures" had married into reputable white families, they were "respectable . . . [had] always been received into society, and [were] recognized as white." To denominate such persons as members of the degraded class after they had exercised the privileges of white people was unthinkable.[30]

The experience of Elizabeth Cleviand Hardcastle illustrates how women of color exploited Carolina's malleable notions of race and mutually dependent gender ideals. In the late 1740s a little girl journeyed to Charleston with her father, an English merchant and slave trader. Elizabeth's mother, the daughter of a West African king (himself half-English and half African) had been given in marriage to Elizabeth's white father. This woman did not accompany her daughter to South Carolina. Upon arrival in the busy port, Elizabeth's father placed her under the protection of some of the "principal families" of the city. Raised as an affluent white girl and educated in England, she married Dr. William Hardcastle, a slave-owning former surgeon in the British army, just prior to the American Revolution. Elizabeth Hardcastle socialized freely with her white affluent neighbors and participated in Charleston's famed social scene. Like others of the master class, she and her husband divided their time between the city and their rice plantations, which were located approximately fifty miles north of Charleston. One can only imagine the full panoply of gossip among certain city residents concerning Mrs. Hardcastle's lineage. Some acquaintances circulated vague stories about her brother, a man banished from white society who lived in the world of "free negroes." Others besmirched Mrs. Hardcastle's virtue in private and flattered her in public. Nevertheless, Dr. and Mrs. Hardcastle's material wealth—and Elizabeth's adherence to white sexual and social ideals—bought public toleration of her mixed parentage. Heir to considerable wealth, the widow Hardcastle continued to mingle with affluent white planter families. But after her husband died many members of the master class shunned and refused even to speak with her.[31]

Notwithstanding Carolina's idiosyncratic attribution of race in the eighteenth and nineteenth centuries, in which luck and wealth secured for some women of mixed race a comfortable, perhaps happy existence in the world of the master class, most free "admixtures" chose or were relegated to one of Charleston's other subcultures, the spheres of black or brown free people. Furthermore, freewheeling race construction had its limits even in South Carolina. An enslaved individual could be paler than members of Charleston's first families; but "admixtures," born of a slave mother and never legally emancipated, usually remained slaves regardless of their pale hue. With the large number of light-skinned people in Charleston—"proof of a [vitiated] taste," according to one early visitor—it was inevitable that occasionally slaves as white as the city's social arbiters were "exposed for sale" in public markets and streets. When this occurred, visitors and residents alike "turned away from the humiliating spectacle." [32]

In addition to producing strife between slave-owning wives and philandering husbands, sexual mixing forged sexual competition and jealousy that pitted ladies against wenches. Few Charleston residents openly acknowledged this emotional undercurrent that tinged relationships between women, but writer Susan Petigru King, who closely patterned her work after her life in the port city, wrote it into her fiction. She incorporated themes of men's deceit and their power over women, and of women's jealousy of each other. She also repeatedly contrasted fair women and dark women. Her motifs did not emerge in a vacuum. Susan had only to read the city newspapers to imbibe dichotomous images of white purity and black sexuality. She did not have to look far to see her own themes played out in Charleston households. In her novel, *Lily*, Susan conspicuously and repeatedly contrasted the blond, innocent, pure, eponymous heroine to a dark-eyed "siren" with black hair, Lily's voluptuous cousin Angelica. Susan infused their interactions with an undercurrent of competition and "color-coded . . . these ostensibly white competitors . . . in black and white." *Lily* concluded with a murder and suicide, quintessential archetypes of victimization. On the eve of her wedding to a philandering planter, perfect Lily was poisoned by a seamstress who had just completed the finishing touches on Lily's wedding dress. This "dark beauty" was a former lover of Lily's fiancé. Since a woman of color could not escape, unpunished, after murdering a white woman, the seamstress threw herself into the Ashley River. From Susan Petigru King's perspective, and from that of contemporary analysts of slave society, mixing victimized all women to varying degrees. Women of color existed "at the bottom of a malevolent system that disempowered all women, even those who were rich and white," and slave women inhabited the extreme "negative end of a continuum of power on which white women also occupied positions of relative powerlessness and exploitation."[33]

7   Work and Workers

All but an elite few Charleston women and girls worked, and that work—or free-dom from work—configured women's self-perceptions and public attitudes to-ward women. Recreation constituted the hallmark of the master class, so lei-sured ladies did not and could not labor for wages without jeopardizing status and reputation. Slave women's regular hard work formed a second strand of women's entwined economic realities. Their labor enabled the mistress's leisure. Where the lady could not work, the slave woman could never work hard enough or long enough. These diametric economic possibilities, practices, and aspira-tions of elite ladies and slave women determined the economic realities and identities of all other women. The wealthiest among the city's free brown elite aspired to the much-esteemed status of lady and risked shattering this image if they worked for pay. Few achieved the goal of becoming a lady. In contrast, most free women of color supported their families or supplemented the family economy. They took pride in their achievements and, in fact, were respected by many fellow city residents, but their work separated them from women of the brown elite and the master class. Likewise, the hard work of white laboring women defined and differentiated them from other Charleston women. In slave society, the work of the "degraded [negro] class" enabled the "civilized" leisure of their white owners. But this axiom broke down, weighted by another reality: myriad white women also labored outside their households, which confounded role expectations forged in dichotomies of black and white, slave and free. The labor of one woman threw into sharp relief the expected work or leisure of an-other, and all Charleston women were identified, in part, by the fact that they did not perform the same work as the others.[1]

Several features of Charleston work and workers effectively frame this analy-sis, foremost among which is the fact that women's work and women work-ers were essential to the city economy. At the time of the first federal census, women of European and African descent headed nearly 20 percent of all Charles-ton households, and most of those women worked for wages. Eighteenth- and nineteenth-century city directories indicate that substantial numbers of women of color and white women worked in and beyond their households even when they owned slaves. While flawed (like most early censuses), the special city census of 1848 constituted the city's first systematic attempt to collect infor-mation regarding occupations of its inhabitants. In that year, enumerators listed a total of nearly 4,700 white, "black" (slave), and "free colored" women workers, or over 38 percent of all city laborers (see table 6). They were boardinghouse keepers, midwives, shopkeepers, madams, pastry cooks, teachers, house ser-vants, mantua makers, market women, tailors, and more. While these figures

Table 6. Women's Occupations, 1848.[1]

	White	Slave	Free Colored
Clothing Trades:			
Dry goods dealers	39	0	0
Hair braiders	2	0	0
Laundresses	13	0	45
Mantua makers	38	4	128
Milliners	44	0	0
Seamstresses	87	20	68
Tailoresses	6	0	6
Worsted dealers	1	0	0
Washerwomen	0	33	0
TOTAL	230	57	247
Education:[2]			
Music teachers	5	0	0
School teachers	47	0	0
Dance teachers	2	0	0
TOTAL	54	0	0
Food Trades:			
Bakers	1	0	0
Boardinghouse keepers	40	0	0
Confectioners	4	0	2
Cooks	0	11	0
Fruiterers	9	1	1
Gardeners	1	0	0
Hotel keepers	1	0	1
Housekeepers	0	0	4
Hucksters	0	11	0
Market women	1	6	4
Milk vendors	8	0	0
Pastry cooks	1	1	16
Planters	25	0	0
TOTAL	91	30	28
Furniture Trades:			
Crockery dealers	1	0	0
TOTAL	1	0	0
Health:			
Botanic practitioners	1	0	0
Midwives	5	0	0
Monthly nurses	7	2	0
Nurses	0	0	10
TOTAL	13	2	10

Continued on the next page

Table 6. *Continued*

Unclassified:[3]			
Apprentices	5	8	7
Clerks	3	0	0
House servants	100	3,384	28
Housekeepers	13	0	0
Keepers, public institutions	2	0	0
Laborers	0	378	2
Storekeepers	4	0	0
TOTAL	127	3,770	37
Superannuated & Disabled:	0	54	0
TOTAL	0	54	0

Totals of Population Listed as Working in 1848 by Race, Condition, and Sex

	White		Slave		Colored		Total	% of
	No.	%	.No.	%	No.	%	No.	Wkrs.
Total Women	516	11.6	3,859	53.1	322	55.0	4,697	38.2
Total Men	3,923	88.4	3,406	46.9	263	45.0	7,592	61.8
CITY TOTALS	4,439	100	7,265	100	585	100	12,289	100

Notes:

1. Classifications listed are those assigned by enumerators and compilers of Charleston's special 1848 city census. The data are useful as an indication of the breadth of occupations; the numbers (as in most early census data) are unreliable and drastically undercount people in every category. Dawson and DeSaussure, *Census of the City of Charleston*, 29–35.

2. Census enumerators listed no free people of color as "contributing to education" because the state outlawed schools for "free colored" people in 1834.

3. Term assigned by compilers for all other occupations.

underestimate the numbers of Charleston workers, the tally reveals laboring women's centrality to the city.[2]

At least eight additional attributes characterize work in Charleston: (1) it was gendered; (2) it was wrapped in race-specific ideas of sexuality; (3) it was seasonal; (4) distinctive work venues offered opportunities for mobility; (5) there was much opportunity for sabotage; (6) slave hiring was central to the economy; (7) *feme sole* traders were also at the heart of the economy; and (8) benevolent work of the master class was important to the economy.

Work was gendered. That is, city residents determined task assignments partly by notions of proper activities for women and men. However, no evidence indicates that divisions between women's work and men's work bridged a massive gulf between mistresses and slave women, or between slaves and free women of

African descent. Charleston slaves and their owners did not engage in communal, female tasks like quilting or sewing clothes as occurred on some plantations. As the following pages will reveal, little opportunity existed to forge the kind of cross-racial gender solidarity that some historians have found on large plantations. In fact, a prevailing citywide fear of slave insurrection, coupled with a fundamental distrust of African Americans, separated black, brown, and white Charlestonians into their appointed, distinct social places.[3]

Work also came wrapped in race-specific ideas of sexuality, a second defining characteristic of labor in this city. With puberty came additional tasks for female slaves—cooking, cleaning, washing, ironing, wet nursing—as well as the appellation, "wench." The onset of menstruation bore ramifications for slave women's work as well as their sexuality. The term "wench" set apart slave women as subservient laborers (an underclass) and denigrated them as a lower form of female, utterly distinct from white ladies and, therefore, legitimate targets of sexual exploitation by their owners. In Charleston only slave women were wenches; that identity distinguished them from white women of the laboring classes. "Active, overtly, and available female sexuality was explicitly identified with black wenches, in whom it was tolerated, expected, even encouraged."[4]

Charleston work was seasonal, a third characteristic. From January to March the great master-class families participated in a frenetic round of balls, horse races, concerts, and theatergoing. These events were experienced differently by those who held the silver serving trays. For slave women, "the season" meant extra rooms to clean, more fires to tend, more women to wash and dress, more dresses to launder, more food to cook, more trips to the market through muddy, foul-smelling city streets, and more messes to clean up. The domestic work of urban house slaves encompassed multiple tasks, and the rhythms of urban society dictated that slave women and girls perform several different jobs as the need arose. All city workers in service industries (hotels, taverns, boardinghouses, or catering firms) worked harder and longer during the season than during Charleston's languid summers.

Charleston's stratified and hierarchical world pressed slave women to the bottom, but city life created distinctive work venues and afforded unique opportunities for wide social intercourse as well as comparative autonomy. This fourth characteristic of, particularly, slaves' work derives from urban geography and population density. The tasks of hotel cooks, servers and maids, city washers, ironers, and caterers brought them into contact with thousands of slave and free city residents, and with the outside world in the form of northern and foreign visitors. "Girls that waited on the tables, [and] the ladies' maids . . . pick[ed] up everything they heard and pass[ed] it on to the other slaves." Messengers and market women gleaned this news as well and they walked city streets freely and enjoyed hours of relative autonomy.[5]

Like work on the plantation, labor in the city provided daily opportunities for slaves to defy and endanger the lives of owners and to destroy property, a fifth attribute of Charleston work. Crowded city compounds and urban density afforded ideal conditions for inflicting personal injury. Slave women took full advantage of their close proximity to owners and their children, and wreaked constant havoc, a reality that will be explored in this chapter.

Three additional characteristics of urban work round out this general backdrop on women's labor. Slave hiring constituted a mainstay of Charleston's economy, and women actively participated as *rentiers* (owners who profited from renting out their slaves), hirers (non-slave owners and slave owners who rented slaves from others) and laborers. Also central to its economic life were the many *feme sole* traders, who lived and labored in this southern port. These unmarried and married women of all colors obtained legal sanction to execute contracts and own and operate businesses in their own names (married women did so with their husbands' permission). A final important trait is that the work of benevolence was crucial to the city's economic survival. This responsibility claimed the interest, monetary support, personal time, and labor of the city's preeminent ladies. In the act of performing this job, women of the master class conserved municipal resources and contributed materially to the city economy. They also reified their own identities and those of women on the receiving end of charitable endeavors.

In this city where most women worked, and where slave women comprised the principal labor force, master-class women constituted Charleston's paramount leisure force. Urban ladies—unlike plantation mistresses—defined themselves by not working and by being of service in benevolent ways. By reputation, custom, and practice, elite ladies relied on the service of their slave women who attended to every personal and household detail. The calculated contrast between leisured ladies and working wenches was a thread in every aspect of life; the axiom was fundamental to slave society. Black, brown, and white Charlestonians assimilated it as toddlers. In the city, more than on plantations, women of the master class lived up to this ideal, particularly during the high social season. All who aspired to the lofty status of lady coveted a life of relative leisure. Notwithstanding the leisured ideal, Charleston ladies also defined themselves by prudent attendance to their families' needs. Not working, it seems, entailed a considerable amount of work, and ladies worked hard at their role as "directresses" of Charleston society. They bore and raised children and they participated in and managed the many household tasks performed by slave women. In these endeavors and their ritualized social events and visiting, church activities and charitable work, elite ladies reinforced women's mutually dependent identities by bolstering race, caste, class, and gender boundaries.[6]

A primary task of Charleston's social arbiters lay in rearing their daughters and other female kin in the proper role of the lady, that singular identity distinguishing them from all other women. Daughters of the city's wealthiest white families commenced these lessons early. Nearly from infancy, affluent girls learned, and helped their mothers to perform, the earnest work of entertaining. The hard labor associated with parties, balls, and informal social gatherings fell to slave women and girls, to be sure. Nevertheless, ladies schooled their daughters in the arts of slave management, conversation, home decoration, and entertaining. Entertainment was Charleston's hallmark and a vital part of its society and economy. Visitors journeyed to the southern port each winter to experience the city's famed high season and to spend their money in the city's retail and hotel establishments. Few failed to comment on the city's belles, who, during this season, honed the skills necessary to perform as the quintessential hostesses under their mothers' tutelage.

Benevolence was the purview and responsibility of the wealthy, and benevolent ladies negotiated this social arena adeptly, maneuvering between the private and public spheres, creating a distinct social sphere that bisected both. Although men managed much of the public and private poor relief in Charleston, ladies carved out their own niche in social service, despite (or at the pleasure of) patriarchal control. They ameliorated human suffering and, in the process, reenacted the "the highly ritualized paternalistic relationship between master and slave" that characterized all social relations in Charleston. They consciously and unconsciously inculcated hierarchies and social boundaries in their children while easing the economic burden on municipal and state coffers through their charitable work. Benevolent women sought not to overturn or even to reform their world, but rather to buttress it by fulfilling their role as charitable directresses of society. Benevolent ladies aided and abetted their male counterparts in perpetuating the hegemony of the master class.[7]

In the work of benevolence, as in entertaining, rearing daughters into their proper roles fell to the capable hands of Charleston ladies, who performed this task earnestly. Under their mothers' watchful eyes, girls of the master class imbibed, echoed, and fulfilled this "peculiar duty of females" in alleviating human misery. They learned that "females alone under[stood] and [could] enter into the minute details necessary" for completion of the endeavor. Daughters, nieces, daughters-in-law, and granddaughters accompanied female kin to meetings of the Ladies Benevolent Society (LBS), the Ladies Fuel Society, and the Female Charitable Association. They assisted in monthly visits to indigent and sick women and helped their mothers raise money to support these charities. One LBS charter member, Mrs. C. Broughton, attended meetings with two daughters. Two Mrs. T. Corbetts, a senior and junior Mrs. J. Huger, and Mrs. Lydia Bryan and her daughter Eliza C. Bryan also participated in 1813 meetings of that organization. Six Dawson family women, three Blake sisters, and mother-daughter circles of Alstons, Grimkés, Mottes, Yateses, and many other families joined the LBS.[8]

Founded in 1813, the LBS anchored female benevolence in the city and, in both membership and activities, it served as an archetype for subsequent organizational work. Society members and their activities amplified precisely the characteristics that differentiated elite women from all others: they possessed the time and money to engage in charity work. The society's 125 charter members, all from prominent Charleston families, publicly pledged "to relieve the distresses of the poor, and administer comfort to the sick." Emulating men's benevolent organizations, each lady agreed to pay an annual fee of five dollars. They applied the interest on that capital toward helping worthy recipients. Members formed themselves into visiting committees to "assist those persons . . . considered as proper objects of the bounty of the Society; visit them, where they [could] with propriety, and send relief to them in the way they judge[d] necessary." On the occasion of their eleventh anniversary, the LBS board congratulated its membership on relieving "the wants and misery of 2,916 destitute sick poor—from the Infant in the Cradle, to the old Man of an [sic] hundred and five!" They boasted that society ladies had "visited the sick and forlorn in their wretched hovels without shrinking from the inclemency of the weather." The LBS board also resounded its genuine religious impulse. "Christ has set us an example of visiting the sick and needy," they declared, and LBS members "fulfil[led] this duty" for which the society had been "expressly instituted."[9]

Simultaneously the products and the conservers of their slave society, LBS members bespoke their entrenched commitment to a world starkly divided by race and class, one in which ladies worked to distinguish yet entwine the separate identities of lady and woman. Ladies of the LBS aided "a respectable old [white] Lady" named "Mrs. Bridic," as well as an old crippled "free black woman" (not lady) named "Clarissa" (no last name mentioned). In the very words they employed to catalog their acts of benevolence, they affirmed women's mutually dependent identities and taught their daughters how properly to maintain the distinctions.[10]

The numbers of destitute black, brown, and white women swelled as Charleston's population increased in the nineteenth century, and ladies organized additional social service agencies to meet basic needs. In 1824 members of the newly constituted Female Charitable Association (FCA) determined to limit its assistance to "the Relief of Sick Poor of Charleston Neck," an area north of the city's commercial and social center. During the opening decades of the nineteenth century, stately mansions and their slave quarters coexisted with a plethora of cheap, wooden housing and noxious butcher pens in "the Neck." But by the close of the first quarter of that century, the Neck had gained a reputation as Charleston's low-rent district, home to rising numbers of poor Irish and German immigrants and numerous self-hiring slaves who lived apart from their owners. Undeterred, ladies of the all-white FCA determined to visit and supply the unfortunate sick and poor of this area. Like LBS ladies, FCA members elected officers, appointed task-related committees, and formed themselves into visiting assemblies. They donated clothing in addition to their time and membership dues and, like their sister group, FCA women solicited funds from private citizens, social organizations, and churches.[11]

The association's ladies also expressed a learned commitment to divinely ordained inequality. One visiting committee member opined, "we are sensible that one of the most effective means of exhibiting gratitude *to Him who maketh to differ* consists in sharing our own comforts with those who are destitute." However, not all FCA ladies wanted to share equally among all the destitute. Only three months after its formation, members wrangled over the issue of bestowing charity on the Neck's free people of African descent. Those opposed to cross-racial philanthropy won a close first vote on the question, but members debated the issue every meeting for the next eighteen months. In January 1826, FCA president Caroline Gilman again proposed that "the free Blacks be included as objects of our Charity." Her persistence and lobbying skills overcame lingering opposition, and the FCA began assisting sick and indigent free people of color.[12]

This hotly contested issue of extending charity to free people of African descent eventually evolved into FCA common practice. In 1835, ten years after the FCA founding, Charleston Quaker John M. Hopkins bequeathed to the FCA's sister organization (the LBS) the equivalent (in property and bank shares) of several thousand dollars "in trust for the relief of the sick & infirm poor free persons of color residing in the City & Suburbs [the Neck] of Charleston." Because the FCA already ministered to many free people of color in the Charleston Neck, the LBS requested FCA assistance. Ladies of the FCA agreed to this cooperative endeavor, and they accepted responsibility for distributing the Hopkins funds. Not all FCA members concurred in this organizational decision, but the two women's organizations cooperatively dispersed this money in tandem over the next twenty years.[13]

In 1830 the founding of a third major benevolent organization, the Ladies Fuel Society (LFS), bespoke an increase in the city's poor. It also revealed the social mandate and appeal of charitable work: these endeavors ordained masterclass women as Charleston's economic and social superiors. Members of the LFS set out to buy and supply firewood to needy, cold city residents when the price of fuel overreached their means. Like the women in the LBS and FCA, LFS ladies enlisted the cooperation of city clergy of all denominations, who issued appeals from the pulpit. Mirroring its sister organizations in another way, LFS members debated the issue of extending their charity to people of African descent. Those in favor of assisting people of color triumphed over the opposition, but the subject caused persistent tension.[14]

Genuine humanitarian impulses and notions of religious accountability and female duty, as well as a learned assumption of their innate preeminence, drove benevolent ladies. In 1827 the FCA's secretary and treasurer, Miss Elizabeth Robertson, voiced this constellation of catalyzing values when she proclaimed that it was "a great thing for the wretched poor to be visited by refined females." The three principal female benevolent societies, and several smaller female organizations, all ministered to very real physical needs of the city's poorest people. The Ladies Auxiliary Christian Association (founded 1857), the Female Missionary and Education Society (1848), and the Ladies Ursuline Community (1835) represent just a few of these charitable concerns. Ladies also instituted the Sisters of Our Lady of Mercy (1835), the Charleston Bible Society (1810), the Charleston Protestant Episcopal Domestic Missionary Society (1824), and the Gregorie Society of St. Philip's Church, all of which focused part of their attention on Charleston residents. In addition, master-class women individually administered to the needs of those less fortunate than themselves, usually remaining within color and ethnic lines. Charleston residents Miss Jones and Mrs. Gilliland distributed money to the city's poor Irish. Jewish women contributed money to the all-male Hebrew Benevolent Society. The Misses Folker and Boyd collected funds and purchased and distributed clothing for inmates of the Charleston Alms House, and volunteer "Lady Commissioners" oversaw the care and apprenticeships of Orphan House girls.[15]

While Charleston's wealthiest free brown elite women emulated the master-class ideal of proper women's behavior in most respects, they did not establish women's associations. Instead, ladies like Jeanette Bonneau, Elizabeth Mishaw, and Gabriella Miller played active roles in St. Philip's, St. Michael's, Grace Episcopal, and several other city congregations. With their husbands, they sponsored baptisms of their peers' children and actively participated in church socials. However, these women left to their men the task of ministering to the material needs of those less fortunate; men ran the two most prominent social and charitable organizations among free people of African descent, and they explicitly excluded women from their memberships. Women of the brown elite instead defined themselves, in part, by their avoidance of less affluent free women of color, slave women, and laboring white women, and by their engagement in church-sponsored social activities. They could never attain the status of lady, but they approximated that lofty identity by avoiding behavior and venues that would have relegated them to lesser social strands.

An expectation of constant work defined slave women, who represented the diametrically opposite image of Charleston ladies. As young children, slaves understood that their identities as female laborers contoured their lives, and they quickly discerned that the type, locale, and unremitting nature of their work derived from the color of their skin, their status as property, and their sex. This economic reality—as the polar opposite of her wealthy mistress's opportunities, practices, and aspirations—largely delimited a slave woman's destiny.

Beginning their work lives at the age of five or six, slave girls and boys under the age of eight performed many of the same chores. Both fanned flies and gnats from the table and off the bodies of napping owners and their children. Both toted water, filled wood boxes, and swept fireplaces, and both helped serve the mistress or master at informal meals. At an early age, however, slave girls also took on gendered tasks. Unlike boys, young girls sewed clothing and draperies, helped wash and dress young mistresses, rocked babies, and combed and groomed the hair of white children with whom they grew to maturity. They helped their mothers, sisters, and other slaves in the kitchen, learning the multiple and time-consuming tasks of eighteenth- and nineteenth-century cooking and homemaking. Little girls observed their mothers washing and ironing, they waited at table, and they cleared and helped wash the dishes after meals. Slave girls also dusted the furniture, swept and scrubbed floors, polished the brass and silver, and made beds. They trailed after young masters and mistresses because it was their job to "look after" their white counterparts.[16]

Most slave girls worked under the tandem supervision of other female slaves and white women. Slave mothers oversaw many tasks and disciplined their daughters when they saw fit or when an owner ordered them to punish the children. One of young Adeline Johnson's tasks was to tend fires. Overwhelmed by the weight of a coal bucket, she accidentally blackened part of a mantelpiece. "They ma[d]e mammy do de lashin,'" Adeline remembered, an indication that her owners held Adeline's mother accountable for the child's work.[17]

Slave girls also answered to white children in the household, an arrangement that implanted, early in life, the reality that slaves worked and that slave owners—even toddlers and children—gave the orders. Little Victoria Adams had to "keep de house clean[ed] up and [to] nurse de chillun." But Victoria also took orders from her young, white counterpart, "Missy Sally." Rebecca Jane Grant's owners expected her to defer to their three-year-old boy as well as care for him. Rebecca learned this lesson at the stinging end of a cowhide strap. "You can't say 'Marse Henry,' Miss? You can't say, 'Marse Henry!'" she remembered her owner screaming at her as the mistress chased Rebecca up the stairs, whip in hand. Rebecca learned quickly to call the little white toddler, "Marse Henry," but she ruefully recounted that he was just a baby who "come 'bout halfway up to me." Physical proximity to their mothers only partially insulated girls from these harsh realities of slavery.[18]

The wealthiest among Charleston's master class maintained substantial numbers of town servants, so sizable retinues migrated seasonally into and out of the city with the great planter families. These peripatetic households included as many as fifty slaves. One wealthy mistress complained that her family "actually mov[ed] an army every time" they relocated from their Georgetown plantation into Charleston. "We cannot possibly separate husband and wife for six months," she claimed, "so Harry, the coachman, has to have his wife and children, and the same with the cook, and the butler, and the laundress." If a slave gave birth, her owners often incorporated this new property into the extended urban household and its labor hierarchy. The arrangement yielded mutual benefits. The slave mother reared her child, the child received some degree of protection, and the mistress gained help training the next generation of slaves. In effect, the slave mother performed three jobs: she labored as a full-time cook, laundress, seamstress, or maid for the mistress; she provided basic infant and child care to her own children; and she trained and supervised future household slaves. Slave mothers who labored as supervisory housekeepers, the urban variant of a plantation driver, shouldered additional responsibilities in overseeing all other servants in the household, a particularly taxing workload. This labor-intensive administrative position brought with it considerable accountabilities. When a plantation slave known only as Cynthia was promoted to "supervisor of indoor work," she reported to the mistress, who expected Cynthia to do her own household work plus oversee the labor of other domestics. The census label "house slave" failed to describe adequately these increased and varied tasks that fell on Cynthia's shoulders and those of slaves with similar responsibilities. During Charleston's high social season from January to March, these personal and supervisory tasks likely doubled or tripled.[19]

When they deemed it necessary, slave owners also separated mothers from their young daughters, a wrenching experience that reminded young slaves of their status. The identity of "worker" took precedence over that of "little girl." As a youngster Genia Woodberry felt isolated in her owner's house, where she worked as a children's nurse. Genia longed for her mother and felt robbed of her own childhood. She gently rocked "de chillun to sleep . . . eve'y evenin' [on] dat big ole joggling board dere on de front piazza." When Genia sang "one uv dem baby song[s] to de child" it soothed her tiny charges, but the lullaby made Genia "hu't lak in [her] bosom to be wid [her] ole mammy." She "wus jes uh child den," and she yearned for the happiness of being "raise[ed] up wid [her] mammy." Although Genia longed to be cradled in her mother's arms rather than "joggling" white babies, at least her owner had not sold Genia or her mother out of the state as some Charleston slave owners did. Genia learned as a youngster that while she was defined by her work, her charges, in contrast, were defined by their lack of it.[20]

Throughout their lives, slave women continually confronted the stark contrast between their unceasing toil and their mistresses' relative leisure. One common category of house servant, a lady's maid, remained on call nearly twenty-four hours each day. Mistresses expected their maids to rise early and attend to their every need and whim. A lady's maid tended her mistress's personal hygiene, clothed and unclothed her. Slave women were bidden to wash feet; rekindle fires; adorn, unfasten, and comb hair; run errands; carry messages; and, finally, to remain at the foot of the mistress's bed in constant attendance throughout the night.[21]

These defining, mutually dependent identities of laboring wench and leisured lady impinged daily and in multiple ways. The quality of a slave woman's work affirmed her mistress's status as a proper southern lady. Each time that a slave owner presided over one of her many social functions, both her image and the degree of her success depended almost entirely on the work of her slaves. Quite literally the mistress's reputation as a proper southern lady rested, in large measure, on the maintenance of a decorous and genteel home, and on the quality of her finely polished and heavily laden dining table. Precisely because her persona hinged on her slaves' work, the mistress carefully assigned tasks, set performance standards, and expected slave women to measure up. To assure quality control, mistresses periodically tested their slaves' competence. The severity of punishments for failing these tests turned on the mistress's personality and whims, but they ranged from a few harsh, demeaning words to beatings and increased surveillance of a slave's every move. Always the Charleston Work House or "Sugar House," a darkly ironic colloquialism, loomed as a possible sentence. Once behind its forbidding iron door, slave women were whipped, tied to the treadmill, or thrown into solitary confinement. It was all quite civilized, because slave owners who availed themselves of the Work House could always boast that they never beat "their people."[22]

A slave woman's success or failure in performing assigned tasks and placating her owner also bore implications for where she lived. Owners manipulated work assignments as a form of punishment. Sophia Watson demoted Lucinda by sending her "down to the plantation." Sophia suspected Lucinda, the children's nurse, of being "unkind" to the baby, although Sophia did not offer any proof of this accusation. Lucinda may or may not have carelessly treated her white charge, but the mistress acted swiftly, nonetheless. Sophia sent Lucinda out to the country and penned to her husband the afterthought, "besides, I am ashamed to have her about." Evidence suggests that Charleston slaves expressed pride of place and clearly perceived themselves as more privileged, and their status higher, than the plantation's field slaves. It is possible that Lucinda orchestrated her own punishment—even relegation to fieldwork—in order to be reunited with family on the plantation. However, it is also true that a slave might resent such a demotion because it compromised her identity as an urban nurse.[23]

The city's numerous boardinghouses, taverns, hotels, boarding schools, and bawdy houses required the labor of slave girls and women. The orphanage and almshouse utilized slaves in maintaining their inmates. Owners of these public facilities depended on enslaved cooks, washers and ironers, maids, waiting girls, and pastry cooks, whom they owned or hired from other Charleston residents. In spring 1837 at the Planter's Hotel, Harriet Martineau commented upon waking in the morning with "two or three black faces staring" at her "from the bedpost." In public places like these, slave women encountered and interacted with a cross section of city residents. In Charleston's public work sites, slaves were distinguished from other workers not necessarily by their work or even by the measure of that labor. Slave women and free women of color performed similar tasks. Instead, different economic aspirations and prospects set apart the skilled slave pastry cook from her free counterpart. Census enumerators in 1848 counted slaves, free women of color, and white women all laboring as washerwomen, laundresses, mantua makers, and seamstresses. The city's fruiterers and pastry cooks also comprised slaves as well as free women of African descent and white women, and all three groups of Charleston women were represented among the ranks of house servants. Free women pocketed the fruits of their labor and could aspire to life as an independent caterer or shop owner. By contrast, their enslaved coworkers kept only part of their wages, if any, and their hopes of purchasing freedom were crushed early in the first quarter of the nineteenth century by state prohibitions.[24]

In addition to these restraints on economic prospects, slave women also endured restrictions on mobility in the forms of city ordinances, patrols, and owner surveillance from which white workers were immune. Slaves nevertheless proved resourceful in escaping the prying eyes and incessant, needful voices of masters and mistresses. Potential lucre as well as relative autonomy drew "swarms" of women of African descent into the city streets and public markets, down to the wharves and out to the Battery, a popular promenade overlooking Charleston Harbor. From their booths and makeshift tables, they peddled crafts, sweets, and drinks. Huckstering women heaped impossibly large quantities of fruits and vegetables upon their turbaned heads, and hawked their wares to black, brown, and white city residents of all ages. Charleston's slave and free market women, fruiterers, and hucksters facilitated social intercourse and economic transactions that extended into the countryside and beyond the city's harbor. Whether selling or buying, market women and peddlers absorbed news from travelers and exchanged information with slaves and free locals of all colors and economic positions. They transacted business with the city's free people of African descent, Irish and German immigrants, slaves from nearby farms and plantations, and even runaways who sought the anonymity of a heterogeneous urban environment.[25]

Charleston's public markets dated to the 1730s, and soon thereafter enslaved and free market women and peddlers dominated them. White residents unwittingly testified to the economic centrality of market women when, in the last quarter of the eighteenth century, they complained about the "excessive number of Negro Wenches [who bought] and [sold] about the streets, corners and markets." One visitor to the city expressed amazement at the close "connection with and influence" of these market women "on the country negroes who c[a]me to" Charleston. This stranger accused slave women of "thoroughly monopolizing transactions," insolently "wrest[ing] things out of the hands of white people, pretending they had been bought . . . for their masters or mistresses" and subsequently reselling those items for their own profit. They engrossed items peddled by other city slaves. Slave women also presided over the "slaves' fair," their own Sunday market instituted by the end of the eighteenth century (moved to Saturday evenings by the next century), located at the tip of the peninsula where the Ashley and Cooper rivers converge. It, too, drew slaves from surrounding plantations and farms who arrived toting garden produce, animal products, woven baskets and mats, and manufactured goods to trade and sell. They mingled and bartered, applying "great quickness in . . . making change, [with] rarely an error in the result," reaping returns for themselves and their owners. Through prior negotiations with their mistresses, and the force of customary practice, market women and street peddlers pocketed any weekly profit over six dollars. This economic gain complemented the temporary, nominal freedom and ephemeral dominion slave women achieved at market. The weekly ritual provided both "amusement and profit" to city and country slaves alike who enjoyed the "fun and bustle of the market, and look[ed] with complacency on any white customers" who attended it. Meanwhile, many a mistress enjoyed the revenue and pointed to the market "merriment" as assurance of slaves' "satisfaction with their condition," and proof positive that people of color realized "their true happiness" as slaves. Specious as that conclusion was, it is true that the diversity and profusion of their tasks positioned slave women at the heart of the city economy where they exhibited striking autonomy.[26]

Charleston never developed its industrial sector, as did Richmond, but slave women probably labored for a time in several of the city's short-lived industrial concerns, where they would have been supervised by men. Near the turn of the eighteenth century, a Mrs. Ramage owned a cotton cloth manufactory on nearby James Island. In 1802 two ropewalks operated near the city limits. Six years later, entrepreneurial businessmen established the ill-fated South Carolina

Homespun Company, which failed in three years. In 1812 a clock-making enterprise thrived for a short time in Charleston. Although each of these forays into urban manufacturing crumbled within five years, they likely utilized slave women and men during their short periods of operation. In addition to these transitory industrial jobs, Charleston's status as a busy southern port yielded additional, atypical labor for the city's slave women. Nancy Williams, slave to a ship's captain, worked as a "stewardess" on one of her master's ships. The locus of Nancy's work was the coastal sea on packets plying the eastern seaboard.[27]

In both private and public venues, slave women engaged in daily, ongoing resistance, the effects of which ranged from minor annoyances to lethal outcomes. A "worthless servant" named Caroline burnt the lace off a new garment the first time she laundered it, and her owner griped that "no week passes that she does not destroy more clothing . . . than her neck is worth." In just three weeks, Caroline riddled her mistress's undergarments with "iron rust," "burnt a chemise" so extensively that it fell apart, and "mildewed 15 yards of cloth." Constant and close proximity to owners and their children provided opportunity for slave women to wreak bodily harm when they engaged in "crimes against the person." Charleston nurses pushed children down stairs and shoved or hit them. They adjusted gas lamps so that deadly fumes suffused a nursery, and abandoned toddlers while out walking with them.[28]

Arson and poison, known among white people as weapons that best suited slave women, also served as effective tools of resistance. Solomon Cohen's slave, "Bella," developed the disconcerting habit of "throwing pieces of fire about her room." Bella was not alone in this propensity. White Charleston residents repeatedly pointed fingers at slaves after "suspicious" fires ravaged homes and large chunks of the city. In 1779 city residents executed a slave for arson, and the decade after 1790 witnessed several conflagrations as well as rumors of slave rebellion. This pattern continued throughout the following century. Slave women were numerous, had ready access to fuel, and had plenty of motive to set fires, but arson was not the only weapon in their arsenals. An older woman named Peggy who cooked "for de Scotts . . . put poison in de coffee" because the mistress and master were "mean to her." Hotel and house slaves, market women and street hucksters, all prepared and served food daily to their owners and the general public. Although punishment was swift and severe if they got caught, slaves could derive a measure of satisfaction from inflicting physical discomfort if not death. Just as ladies taught their daughters how to be proper hostesses and benefactresses, slave women schooled their daughters in the ways of insurgency. By socializing their children in this manner, they reproduced and perpetuated urban slave resistance.[29]

The economic practices and prospects of all other Charleston women fell somewhere between the two entwined realities of working slaves and leisured ladies. White women who worked for wages were neither one strand nor the other. White but not ladies, workers but the wrong color for southern laborers, white women of the laboring classes complicated the social dictates of slave society. Southern dogma not only held that slaves worked to enable the higher pursuits of ladies, but also that white women and girls toiled either because of some inherent personal flaws or extenuating circumstances beyond their control. By implication, the interlocked opposition of slave wenches and master-class ladies denigrated white laboring women. The same principle held true for most free women of color who were inferior on two counts: their color and their labor. And they, too, confounded social mores of slave society: they were free but not white, and they were black or brown but neither slaves nor (usually) members of the brown elite. The possibilities and realities of their work enmeshed them with white laboring women, while skin color cast their lot with slaves.[30]

In Charleston, most girls and women worked. Necessity decreed that many little girls of European descent begin laboring before the age of ten and, like slave girls, they learned early that the role of worker was fundamental to their identities. Girls of European and African descent who were neither enslaved nor wealthy quickly became accustomed to long hours of toil if their families were laboring people. They performed kitchen and other housekeeping chores for family members who depended upon their contribution to the household economy. Before age eight, most girls in Charleston began assisting with the endless tasks associated with their mothers' work as boardinghouse owners, innkeepers, tavern keepers, confectioners, and shop owners. Early in life these girls learned needlework and cooking, not as ornamental accomplishments like Charleston belles or free brown elite girls, but as a means of survival. Abject poverty alone did not precipitate this labor. When the city economy fared well and their mothers and fathers prospered, girls of the laboring classes still learned a trade because it was expected and necessary. Most girls of European descent worked under the supervision of other white women and they continued to do so as they grew to maturity. In Charleston, no women of color supervised white girls.

Experiences of early hard work were painfully real to the city's orphans. The Charleston Orphan House—which excluded children of color—served as a temporary home to white children whose parents were "unable to support and maintain them." However, entrance into that institution was premised on the assumption of work. Each child was initially "bound to" the Orphan House commissioners, but "their indentures [were] transferred to such Mistresses or Masters as shall teach them [a] profession, trade, or occupation." Even before they were apprenticed to the city's female artisans, thousands of Orphan House "inmates" combined chores with their daily institutional routine. Girls assisted the institution's sewing mistress in making their own and fellow inmates' clothing. They helped in the kitchen and learned the rudiments of housekeeping. Those admitted as toddlers worked six or more years before they commenced their official work lives at age twelve or thirteen, when institution officers placed them on the "Binding Out List." A girl's apprenticeship continued until she reached age eighteen or until she married.[31]

When poor and orphaned white girls began to learn a craft at the direction of Charleston tradeswomen, they fell headlong into a life chock-full of hard, long labor. They were free, to be sure, but they also tasted a fraction of a female slave's vulnerability and constrained economic prospects. They were defined by this middle status. Girls experienced their apprenticeships differently depending on the character of their mistresses and masters. Life in the Orphan House was harsh—in the early 1790s, two white nurses employed to supervise the children drank heavily and battered their charges—but life beyond its walls was worse for some who fell victim to the avarice and cruelty of adults who sought cheap labor. Early in 1793, Mrs. Dupre, a needle worker and mantua maker, unceremoniously returned Elizabeth Margaret Somers to the Orphan House. Elizabeth was blind in one eye, and Dupre could not extract enough work from her to justify keeping the child. Similarly, Mrs. Joy applied to take a lame Elizabeth Moore into her home, but only on the condition that she could return her if she proved "unable to obtain subsistence by labor." Two years later, a Mrs. Speissegger so severely misused young Jane Fleming that the Orphan House board demanded her return.[32]

Anticipating trouble after these and similar experiences, the institution periodically declined requests for apprentices. When Mrs. Milligan applied for a girl, the board refused "on account of . . . the place of her [Milligan's] residence being conceived improper for a young girl to be brought up in." Commissioners' suspicions were well founded, because Orphan House girls became targets of sexual exploitation by unscrupulous men and women. The board bound out Theresa Harrigan to Peter Bounetheu (or Bonetheau), who claimed he had promised Theresa's father that he would care for her. A commissioner subsequently found Theresa "in the possession of a Mrs. Salts who appeared a very unfit person to bring her up." Peter had never intended to care for Theresa as "a guardian and friend," and the commissioner returned Theresa to the Orphan House. Although they never detailed why Mrs. Salts was "unfit," it is likely that she was a drunkard, a prostitute, or both.[33]

In these and too many other ways, white girls of the laboring classes, like slave girls, endured ill treatment at the hands of adults who should have been safeguarding them. Mothers and other real or alleged kin periodically snatched children from the Orphan House. Poor parents genuinely sought to protect youngsters from further abuse from institution staff or Charleston tradespeople. Alternatively, some mothers and fathers were not above exploiting their own children when they needed strong young arms to help put food on the table. They borrowed their daughters temporarily and then returned them to the Orphan House when the children became liabilities rather than assets. The residents of the Orphan House were neither belles nor wenches. They inhabited neither one world nor the other. But working-class white girls forged their self-concepts and understood their social expectations in juxtaposition to those two prevailing prototypes.[34]

The majority of Charleston's laboring women were skilled workers and tradespeople, not common laborers. Free women of African descent also figured prominently among these urban artisans. Whether black, brown, or white, these women labored alongside family members and supervised the work of free apprentices as well as hired slaves. Their social respectability notwithstanding, these skilled women shared with unskilled workers exclusion from the rank of lady because their work took them beyond the domains of domesticity and benevolence. Catering to the needs of, particularly, women and men of the master class and the free brown elite, these talented women plied their trades as bakers, confectioners, pastry chefs, basket makers, upholsterers, painters, jewelers, and silversmiths. Women of color and white women together dominated the clothing trades as milliners, mantua makers, needleworkers, seamstresses, and tailoresses. In 1848 free women of color comprised 46 percent, white women 43 percent, and slave women 11 percent of the 534 female artisans laboring in the sewing trades. Mantua makers and milliners crafted the latest European fashions for Charleston's wealthy women to display at balls, horseraces, plays, and concerts. Women of African and European descent labored in these trades, with the former controlling the mantua-making business and the latter dominating millinery. All had mastered skills that warrant their classification as artisans, not merely laborers.[35]

Among Charleston's white artisans, widows frequently labored in their husbands' skilled trades with the help of daughters, sons, and slaves. Seamstress Rebecca Weyman and tavern keeper Ann Hawes resumed their husbands' glass-grinding and painting businesses when Edward Weyman and Benjamin Hawes died during the American Revolution. Heloise Boudo's husband, Louis (a French native of St. Domingo), died in 1827. Shortly afterward Heloise announced her intention "to carry on the Jewelry Business, in all its various branches." Heloise enlisted the assistance of her daughter, Erma, and the concern prospered for ten years under her management. One year after Heloise's death, Erma reopened her mother's establishment. Elizabeth Dumoutet actively participated in the management and expansion of her husband's "jewelry business, millinery, and fancy store." Elizabeth and her daughter Jane did not retire from their livelihood until ten years after her husband's death. In 1822, two years after John S. Bird and his wife emigrated to Charleston from Middlesex County, England, they opened a shop in the city. The Birds imported jewelry and crafted functional and ornamental silver, enterprises that Mrs. Bird continued until her death during the Civil War.[36]

Unmarried female artisans, shopkeepers, and dry goods dealers of all colors joined these married women and widows as active players in Charleston's economy. Mary Bourgeois and Maria Isabella O'Brien opened jewelry stores in the first decade of the nineteenth century. Mary subsequently moved into the millinery business. A watchmaker and jeweler, William Ashton, relied on his two daughters to manage his King Street business. Slave owner Anna Miller plied her trade as a baker at mid-nineteenth century, and Isabel Peace, a mantua maker of African descent, oversaw the training and work of two slave apprentices, Lizzy and Martha, in 1855. With little variation from the late eighteenth through the nineteenth centuries, Charleston women earned livelihoods as artisanal shopkeepers.[37]

Another group integral to the city economy also comprised women of both African and European descent. These were Charleston's boardinghouse, hotel, and tavern keepers, as well as coffee house proprietresses who, like artisans and shopkeepers, supervised other women's waged and slave labor. From 1782 through 1802, city directories listed an annual average of twenty-five women in these accommodations trades, and in 1848 forty-two of the city's women owned and managed these facilities (see tables 6 and 7). Thousands of travelers visited the city, drawn to Charleston by their business interests, by its reputation as the South's cultural center, and by their curiosity about slavery. Like tourists today, those travelers required food, lodging, transportation, and other personal services. Charleston's businesswomen helped meet these needs. While ladies hosted parties and balls for prominent city visitors and wealthy guests, laboring women saw to the more basic needs of sojourners from various walks of life and made profits in the bargain. In 1783 a Mrs. Ramadge announced the opening of her coffee house at the corner of Broad and Church streets, vowing "to make it as completely agreeable as the most popular ones in London." Courting the city's merchants and other businessmen, Mrs. Ramadge declared the availability of private rooms for transacting business as well as the "public Coffee-Room." In spring of the same year, municipal officials granted to women fully 35 percent (thirty-three) of the ninety-three permits required by law to operate taverns, "punch houses," and other retailers of spirits. Ann Cross, one of those thirty-three women, managed her Charleston tavern at least four additional years with the labor of slave women and men. During that time, she also raised her son, Robert, accomplishing both tasks largely without help from her husband, Paul Cross, a slave trader who spent much of his time traveling the sea between the west coast of Africa and Charleston.[38]

Other businesswomen capitalized on the city's status as a busy port and the playground of the low-country master class. Catherine Coates successfully operated and expanded "Mrs. Coates's Tavern on the Bay" while her husband remained at sea. Toward the close of the eighteenth century, Catherine exploited the rising popularity of French coffee houses and established her own version, the Carolina Coffee House, on Tradd Street. It became a focal point of Charleston business and social activities. Another entrepreneur, Mrs. Calder, transformed a "large and roomy house" into the "superior . . . establishment of its kind in the Southern States." Under her management, Planters Hotel blossomed into one of the city's social centers. She "spared no pains or expense to fit it up . . . for the reception of the Gentlemen Planters and their Families from the Country, and also for the citizens of Charleston." In 1806 Calder refurbished Planters and secured the most "obliging, obedient and orderly" slaves to attend to her guests' every need. Three years later Calder relocated, secured the services of a renowned French pastry cook, and reopened with great success. Wealthy ladies and gentlemen migrated from their country plantations into the city, where they entertained extensively, so Mrs. Calder and other proprietresses effectively exploited the seasonal rhythm by establishing reputations for excellence, advertising, and cultivating this clientele. They derived their identities in

Table 7. Women's Occupations, 1782–1802.[1]

	1782	1790	1794	1796	1801	1802
Accommodations: boardinghouse keepers, hotel keepers, and tavern keepers	2	16	67	12	18	33
Artisans and Shopkeepers: jewelers, silversmiths, milliners, mantua makers, seamstresses, tailoresses, and upholsterers	2	34	58	20	39	119
Food Trades: bakers, confectioners, pastry chefs, caterers, produce/fruit hucksters, peddlers		2	2	4	9	13
Grocers: sellers of dry goods				2	11	6
Professionals: teachers, school managers		18	31	2	15	26
Professionals: midwives, nurses, physicians		1	4	3	2	8
Washers					4	17
Other:[2] cigar makers, state printers, madams, butchers, dry nurses, nurses, merchants, saddlers, planters, ravaudeuses, umbrella makers, wagon yard keepers, clear starchers		2		2	7	29

Notes:
   1. These directories enumerated a total of 5, 222, 192, 166, 309, and 450 women, respectively, in the years listed above, but included professions for only a small percentage of the total.
   2. In 1796, 2 women were listed as "madams." In 1802, 24 women were listed as "planters."
Source: Hagy, People and Professions.

large measure from these endeavors, profiting from the labor of wenches and the recreation of ladies, while themselves neither one nor the other.[39]

Another group of professional women—midwives—also labored independently of others' supervision and occasionally oversaw the work of assistants. Charleston ladies frequently used their services. Mrs. Thompson and Mrs. Murphy, *accouchers* (midwives) who attended affluent Meta Morris Grimball when she delivered six of her eleven children, earned thirty dollars each time they "officiated at Meta's confinements." Meta gave birth to most of her children without a doctor, relying on midwives and their slave or free assistants. The midwives' thirty-dollar fee represented four to five months' wages for Mary, the nurse of color who looked after the Grimball children. In 1848 city census enumerators counted five midwives, all of whom were white women. Doubtless many slaves and free women of color plied their trade in midwifery as well, but were excluded from the census. Other female professionals listed that year under the rubric of trades "contributing to health" included "monthly nurses" (two slaves and seven white women), ten free women of color who worked as "nurses," and one white botanic practitioner.[40]

Charleston's professional and artisanal women of African and European descent did not merely share a variety of occupations, but also competed against each other. This competition, exacerbated by the ready availability of slave labor, depressed wages that were already lower than what men earned, and slave-owning employers utilized this rivalry to gain an upper hand in wage negotiations. A white, English nurse, Harriet Davis, attended John Sidney Algernon Ashe Legare as a child, yet slave girls, like Genia Woodberry and Jessie Sparrow, commonly labored as children's nurses. Another slave, Susan (Calder) Hamlin, was hired out in this capacity at the beginning of the Civil War. Susan's "Mausa" (master/owner) received the seven dollars per month she earned. And free women of African descent performed the same work. A woman known only as Mary labored for several years as a children's nurse in the Grimball household. She earned six dollars a month. In late summer 1833, after working for the family at least one year, Mary asked Meta Morris Grimball for a two-dollar increase. Meta informed Mary that eight dollars was "entirely out of the question" but that she would consult with her husband about raising Mary's monthly salary to seven dollars. John Grimball bristled with irritation. "Today, our Nurse Mary gave Meta to understand that her wages were too low—that all Nurses in Charleston got 8 dollars per month and she would get the same sum." John groused that, "considering all things," the six dollars constituted "great wages for her," but he reluctantly increased that amount by one dollar because "a change just now would [have been] exceedingly inconvenient." However, he also determined to replace Mary with one of his slaves as soon as practicable. Meta convinced her husband to change his mind and Mary continued at her job for another four years until she married. Nonetheless, John Grimball retained the option of replacing her with a slave woman, a reality that eroded Mary's bargaining power and prevented her from earning a higher salary.[41]

The field of childcare was not the only occupation pitting Charleston's female laborers against one other. Near mid-nineteenth century, slave women, free women of color, and white women shared at least ten additional occupations. At least two, if not all three, categories of workers could be found toiling as laundresses, mantua makers, seamstresses, and common day laborers. They also shared work as hotel keepers, confectioners, fruiterers, market sellers, and pastry cooks. All three labored as house servants. Ann Deas, free woman of African descent, inherited a hotel from her father, Jehu Jones, when he died in 1833. She and her two partners (also people of color) successfully competed against the city's white hotel proprietors for fourteen years. A cadre of free black, brown, and white professional women—teachers and boarding school mistresses—competed against each other and male teachers. In the late eighteenth-century and throughout the next, white schoolmistresses taught most of the elite girls throughout the region, and the institutions they founded provided employment to other teachers, both female and male. Boarding school mistresses supervised their instructors as well as slave women and free women of African descent who labored in the kitchens and did other necessary household work. City directories included an average of twenty-two female teachers and school managers during the years 1790, 1794, 1801, and 1802. By mid-century, that number exceeded fifty-four female teachers. Numerous others likely went uncounted. Although men began to usurp women as "principal-proprietors" of southern girls' schools by the 1820s, Charleston women continued to operate schools and female seminaries and to employ other women as teachers. Education was the only employment considered respectable for ladies who encountered economic difficulties that "reduced" them to working for wages. By mid-century, the city's female educators instructed both boys and girls, earning as much as 300 dollars annually. Tuition costs at this time ranged from 35 dollars to over 140 dollars per quarter, depending upon the number and type of courses and lessons, so only children of the master class and brown elite could afford to attend school. Only they could become teachers in the future.[42]

Free women of African descent also taught Charleston girls and boys—and competed against their male peers—but in strictly segregated facilities. In 1822 four "colored" women—Emma Borduck, Sophia Ives, Maria Michael, and Maria Nell—taught children within their distinct social group. White ladies and gentlemen esteemed the city's schools and teachers, but this pride was race specific, particularly after 1822. In 1834 South Carolina legislators decreed that a white person must be present whenever free people of color were being taught, a measure designed to terminate most schools for children of color. The law also mandated a fifty-dollar fine and up to fifty lashes for free people of color who violated this dictate. In spite of these barriers, Charleston's free brown elite women (and men) continued clandestinely to teach children of color throughout the next two decades in direct violation of that law.[43]

Their labor distinguished every working woman—slave and free, black, brown, and white—from Charleston's ladies, but no class solidarity united all female workers. Free artisans, other tradeswomen, and professional women laid claim to a respectability that eluded skilled slave women and, indeed, they usually owned slaves in addition to paying hired laborers. These characteristics positioned them above Charleston's struggling, free, wage-earning female laborers as well as slave women. And among the free destitute poor of all colors, who attempted to piece together a subsistence but who languished in the futile effort, color further sifted them.

Charleston women of all groups profited from the city's pervasive, custom-ary, yet contested practice of slave hiring, a convention that entwined slave women, free women of color, white laboring women, and master-class ladies in complex relations of employer and employee, slave owner and slave, slave hirer and slave owner, lady and laboring woman, and belle and wench. In South Caro-lina slave hiring dated from at least the first decade of the eighteenth century, and complaints from white residents, as well as restraints on hiring, began al-most immediately. Legislative acts of 1712, 1722, 1822, and 1849 alternately prohibited and regulated self-hire (a variation on this labor practice), but failed to stop it; enforcement of the laws was costly and difficult, and many slave owners encouraged their slaves to hire themselves out in the city. Some white people feared the measure of autonomy slaves achieved in working (and some-times living) away from their owners' compounds. White people of the laboring classes objected to the competition or the mere presence of slaves "at large" in the city. Grievances and regulations continued through the 1850s, but repeated city ordinances passed to control—not abolish—the hiring system reveal that it persisted as a vital albeit troubled part of the city's economy. Slave-owning women of African and European descent rented out their slaves for gain. City residents hired slaves for a variety of tasks. Slave women and girls labored for the Charleston residents who hired them and, if they were lucky, saved a portion of their own earnings while their owners appropriated most of the money. Slave hiring yielded benefits to owners, hirers, and slaves, but the practice also carried risks to all parties.[44]

"The practice of letting [slaves] out to hire [was] very prevalent in Charles-ton," one visitor observed at mid-century. From September 1844 to August 1848, an average of two to three people per month paid for hiring advertise-ments. They were either attempting to lease their own slaves to other city resi-dents or to hire the services of slaves owned by fellow Charlestonians. Municipal ordinances required slave owners to purchase a tag or badge for each slave they hired out. The laws served two purposes. First and foremost, they regulated (or at least were intended to regulate) the amount of hiring and attempted to ensure close supervision of every slave. The badge requirement also enriched city cof-fers. In 1849 the city issued over four thousand badges to owners, a figure that underrepresents yet provides a rough idea of the extent of slave hiring. In that same year and the following one, city residents paid nearly $14,000 and $26,000, respectively, to the city treasurer for slave badges, and the hired slaves labored in virtually all Charleston venues. They worked in private homes, hotels, taverns, the Orphan House, and the Alms House. Hired slaves could also be found work-ing in the city market, retail shops, workshops, and boarding schools and on city streets as municipal laborers.[45]

Women constituted a visible presence on all sides of the hiring agreements. In addition to advertising in city newspapers, slave owners and potential slave hirers often negotiated their contracts personally, made arrangements by word of mouth, and validated their agreements with a simple, handwritten receipt. Tavern keeper Ann Cross hired out her slave, Moses, at the rate of ten dollars per month in 1789, thereby adding $120 to her yearly income. Frances S. Pinckney received forty dollars from the city paymaster general for the hired labor of "her carpenter fellow Anthony." Over a period of eight years beginning in January 1829, Mary Aldret paid an average of over four dollars per month to more than a dozen different Charleston women and men from whom she hired at least nine different slave women. The monthly wages ranged from a low of $2.50 up to $6.00. In the 1830s the going rate for a child's nurse in Charleston was $6.00 to $8.00, so Mary Aldret likely hired girls and women to serve as general housemaids, cooks' helpers, and nurses.[46]

A majority of the city's slaveowners, at some time in their lives, took advantage of Charleston's ready market for short- and long-term slave hiring. Although terms of hire varied, leases customarily ranged from one month to a full year rather than mere days or weeks. Slave hiring operated as both a lucrative strategy for slave owners to supplement their incomes and a practical way for slave hirers to meet seasonal variant labor needs. In 1783 one Charleston owner advertised five women and girls for hire by the month: "A young, healthy Wet Nurse . . . two good washers and Ironers . . . [and] two handy Girls." Less than two weeks later, a Mr. Colcock advertised his "sensible Negro Wench who [was] a good Cook and Washer woman" for hire "by the month." Many Charleston hotel, tavern, and boardinghouse keepers found slave hiring an expedient and cost-effective method of fulfilling their labor demands. In this way, they saved the larger expenses of purchasing more slaves and maintaining them year-round. Harriet Eddington's mother was just one of hundreds of slave women who "worked in town at hotels." Patterns of slave hiring also defined different women's lives. Not only was it an axiom that when ladies played their hardest, slave women worked the longest. It was also true that slave-owning women who rented out their human property increased their profits at the expense of the women whose lives were defined by that labor.[47]

In addition to this flurry of winter hiring, Charleston's seasonal rhythms generated a second variant of slave hiring that helped planter families maximize profits from their large investments in human capital. The approach of summer and its concomitants (yellow fever and other diseases) triggered annual anxiety and, hence, planter family migrations to the South Carolina sea islands, Virginia and West Virginia springs, or northern cities. Slave owners leased some of their slaves for the duration of these annual pilgrimages. In anticipation of summer travels in 1835, John Berkely Grimball casually noted, "we have hired out the Cook (Kit) to a Mr. Margrave at $12 per month." John and Meta Grimball also "placed a girl named Amy with Camilla Dunstan, to be taught pastry-cooking." John noted one additional new labor adjustment in his diary: "Patty & her child and Eve have . . . been sent into the country. Patty will work in the field doing however only so much as she can with ease—just enough to benefit her health and keep her out mischief."[48]

From John and Meta's perspective, making these arrangements was a minor irritation, "a difficulty" as he called it. From a different vantage point, they disrupted four women's lives with their travel plans. Kit, Amy, Patty, and Eve may have been separated from family; all of them were torn away from friends. John noted that he had sent Patty, a house servant, to the fields "for her health." This scenario played out in dozens of white households and wreaked yearly havoc in the lives of slave women throughout the city. Slave hiring bore the potential of altering slaves' work environments, their labor relations, and, in cases such as Patty's, even their identities as house and town servants.

Slave hiring proved a malleable labor innovation that entwined women's lives in labor negotiations and daily activity. Free woman of color Camilla Dunstan, the Charleston pastry cook to whom the Grimballs apprenticed Amy during the summer of 1835, participated in an alternate form of hiring that combined apprenticeship and leasing. Meta and John paid Camilla a nominal fee to train Amy, and Camilla agreed to provide room and board as well as instruction. In this transaction, Amy's newly acquired skill boosted her value, and the Grimball family simultaneously reaped the benefits of her culinary talents. Camilla profited from the arrangement because she acquired an extra pair of hands in her shop and received modest compensation at the same time.[49]

Many of Charleston's free female artisans of African descent owned slaves and entered into slave hiring at both ends of the transaction. They hired slave women, men, girls, and boys to assist them in their work, and they leased their own slaves to other city residents for the extra income. In addition to training Amy, the Grimball family slave, the confectioner and cook Camilla Dunstan also hired slaves until her catering business yielded returns enabling her to purchase Maria, Dinah, Phoebe, and Diana. Pastry cook Martha Vanderhorst hired out several of her seven slaves to augment what she earned in her King Street pastry shop.[50]

Among Charleston's thousands of residents who profited from this ubiquitous labor practice was a particular category of slave owner, the *rentier*. Predominantly women, *rentiers* derived their incomes almost exclusively from renting out their real (land and buildings) and personal (human) property. Free women of color and white women alike numbered among their ranks—ladies as well as laboring women—and an elite few "rose to positions of wealth and affluence through speculation in land and . . . slaves." Charleston's predominance of female *rentiers* derived from the city's uneven sex ratio, the large number of widows, and the reality that ladies (and would-be ladies) could not, themselves, labor for wages and maintain that status. In addition, master-class and laboring women and girls inherited slaves from their mothers, fathers, husbands, and other kin, so they possessed both the means (slaves) and the opportunity (urban labor demands) to become *rentiers*. Elizabeth Holloway, one of Charleston's brown elite, leased as many as seven slaves to other city residents, thereby supporting herself and her two daughters after her husband died. Similarly, Susanna Cole Raper's husband bequeathed to her nine slaves, several of whom she hired out for profit. Ruth Cole left her slave, Amey, to daughter Barbara Maria (Cole) Bamfield, fully expecting that Amey's leased labor would help support Barbara and her family. Caroline Laurens, one of the city's white *rentiers*, was widowed at age twenty-seven and hired out her cook, Clarinda.

Women purchased dray badges and hired their slaves to the city and private businesses to haul freight. Municipal regulations mandated that Charleston streets be kept free of rubbish and offal; women hired out their slave men to perform this unpleasant work as well. From September 1850 to July 1851, seven to nine city women received an average of thirty-eight dollars in monthly income by providing cartage service to the city. Charleston's black, brown, and white *rentiers* literally bequeathed to their female kin the ability to profit, as they had, from the hired labor of slaves. In this way, they provided support to their families even beyond the grave.[51]

As adaptable and profitable as slave hiring proved, this long-lived labor practice also afforded slave women opportunities to reappropriate their own time, their freedom of mobility, and the fruits of their labors. Census records and tax lists provide imperfect windows on the composition of city households (and often census enumerators did not distinguish between hired and owned slaves), so the actual numbers of slave women who "worked out" may never be known. However, letters and other private documents suggest that the practice was common and that women achieved relative freedom of movement and limited autonomy through this labor convention even if they still lived under their owners' roofs. In the eighteenth century, hiring also opened the possibility of achieving legal freedom. In the 1790s, a "negro wench slave" obtained permission from her master to "work out in town": to negotiate her own hiring arrangements and to work wherever she chose as long as she remitted monthly wages to her owner, a Mr. Beaty. By her industry, this slave woman "acquired a considerable sum of money, over and above what she had stipulated to pay [Beaty] for her monthly wages." She applied this profit toward the purchase of "a negro girl, Sally," for whom she had "an affection." The nature of their relationship remains unclear; Sally may have been the woman's daughter, but evidence points to some other close connection. Nonetheless, she bought Sally from Beaty, who owned them both. When this slave woman, and the guardian she had obtained for Sally, tried to remove Sally from Beaty's home in 1792, he refused to relinquish her. Sally's guardian successfully brought suit against Beaty for unlawfully holding the girl in bondage; the unnamed "negro wench" ultimately achieved her quest of Sally's freedom.[52]

The legal debate over Sally's status reveals conflicted attitudes toward hiring and, especially, the practice of allowing slaves to hire out their own time as quasi-independent agents. Beaty acknowledged that he had permitted his slave to "be at her own disposal, and work or hire herself out as she pleased." However, he argued "all [that] she gained was for his use," and "became a vested right in him as soon as she acquired it." He concluded fervently "of course, she had no right to manumit the girl [Sally], or do any other act to the prejudice of his interest." Counsel for the slave woman countered that after Beaty sold Sally, he had stopped paying property taxes on her and, in fact, had openly stated "he had no property in her." Debating eloquently and successfully, Sally's guardian maintained "the generosity of the act, and the strong affection the wench must have had for the girl, ought not . . . pass unnoticed." Moreover, he reminded the court of this woman's selfless act of "remain[ing] in slavery, in order to give liberty to" Sally. Lauding her "extraordinary . . . kindness and benevolence," he adjured the court "that to thwart or defeat the wench's intention, would be doing violence to some of the best qualities of the human heart." The jury concurred and set Sally free, but the selfless "wench" remained enslaved to Beaty. This 1792 state supreme court case, *Sally v. Beaty*, established an important legal precedent in granting to slaves property rights in earnings exceeding the amount required by their owners. However, in 1846, some fifty years after this landmark decision, a greedy (white) Charleston *rentier* laid claim to all her slave's earnings. Sympathetic judges concurred and as a result the court overturned long-standing customary practice and legal precedent established in that case, thereby eroding one of the most cherished rewards slaves reaped from hiring out. The timing of this retrenchment is significant. It came during a period of heightening racial tensions that, by the next decade, crescendoed into a wholesale constriction and elimination of the few remaining rights of both free and enslaved people of color.[53]

Even after statute and case law slammed shut the door to lawful freedom after 1820 and the prospect of legally saving excess earnings after 1846, Charleston slaves still exploited other opportunities inherent in hiring. They seized every chance to inconvenience owners and hirers. *Rentiers* griped about hired-out slaves who eluded them, disappeared for weeks at a time, and remitted "little or no wages." In 1822 slave owner Anna Yates wrote to her sister, absentee *rentier* Elizabeth Yates, "I really feel distressed what you are . . . to live on." Anna continued, "Mary is at our house and does little or nothing . . . she will not go to a steady place [of employment]," and "Billy has not been seen for months." Three months later Anna vented further frustrations. "Lavinia pays and she gets Fatimas to send [wages] . . . Sally will pay nothing, Mary has paid some [but] she is very ill. I think she may die." Utterly absorbed in their "servant problem," another sister suggested that Mary, Billy, and Sally's lack of productivity warranted "dispos[ing] of them next year." However, just weeks later, Anna proudly announced that Fatima and Lavinia handed over a total of twenty-eight dollars and that another slave, Emma, delivered eleven dollars to her mistress. Like most slave owners, Anna wielded both carrots and sticks in dealing with her human property. She rewarded Fatima with "a gown which [the slave said was] promised her" and gave four dollars to Lavinia. But she also threatened Sally with dire consequences if she failed to hand over her wages. Anna likely threatened to have her whipped or even sold. The tug-of-war continued between Yates family members and their slaves. Two years later David Yates reported to his mother, the absentee *rentier* Elizabeth Yates, that "Emma and Sally have not paid any wages for a long time." Not only could David not collect wages, but he was also "trying to find out where they stay[ed] that [he could] make them pay wages." It is clear that slave hiring slightly cracked the door to autonomy and economic opportunity, and slave women (like men) flung it wide by capitalizing on these openings.[54]

Hired slave women effectively wielded other common resistance strategies familiar to all Charleston slaves. They feigned illness when asked to remit earnings, informing owners they had been too sick to "make [their] wages." In reality, they either pocketed their hard-earned money or had chosen not to work and, in fact, possessed no wages to remit. Also common among the city's hired-out slaves was attitudinal resistance. Nearly all slave owners griped about slave "impudence," but Charleston slave women took this form to grand heights. In 1782 one master described his runaway slave, Lucy, as a "very good washer," but also as a woman who spoke freely and was impudent. Lucy's toddler, a child between one and two years old, was already "very forward" as well. The urban environment, in part, fostered a measure of independence evident in slaves' demeanors, and slave mothers reared their children to similar comportment. Near mid-nineteenth century, one observer commented that a "mulatto woman, Mary Ann . . . seemed to be mistress of her own time." A foreign visitor to Charleston reflected that "the negroes here have certainly not the manners of an oppressed race." In this respect, customary practices associated with slave hiring undermined slave society by loosening the one-on-one imposition of power—owner over property—at the heart of slavery. Ironically, this flexibility also strengthened the institution of slavery by offering slaves opportunities to acquire cash and purchase family members, which, in turn, gave them a reason to remain in the city. Hiring tightened the bonds by loosening them.[55]

Slave hiring magnified women's interdependence by further enmeshing their lives in economic and personal relations of antagonism or mutual toleration. The hiring system complicated the social relations of urban slavery, as when it enabled slave women to live out, hire their own time, and withhold wages from the owner. Slave hiring yielded to slave women (and men) the psychological and economic power that slavery daily eroded. In part, this is because the labor practice underscored the mistress's dependence on her slave, itself simultaneously a hallmark of slavery and one of its weaknesses: slavery disempowered slaves and empowered slave owners, but the owner's dependence on human property altered the balance of power; it transferred to slaves a measure of control. Nevertheless, the lucrative customary practice of slave hiring endured because it was at the heart of Charleston's economy and social fabric.

Among Charleston's female laborers was a particular type of businesswoman: the *feme sole* trader, also called sole traders or *femes sole*. The term *feme sole* (woman alone)—a legal, economic, and social classification—differentiated an unmarried woman from a *feme covert*, a covered or married woman. Unlike the latter, a *feme sole* in South Carolina could sue and be sued (a mixed blessing), she could own and operate a business and execute binding contracts, and the law held her liable for her own debts. Women attained this special status in one of two ways. Single, widowed, or abandoned women established themselves as sole traders upon opening a business and engaging in daily public transactions. Indeed, state courts supported sole trader status for women whose husbands had abandoned them, particularly if the men had been absent for a long time. Ruling case-by-case, the judicial system declared as *femes sole* loyalist wives whose husbands had been banished from South Carolina after the American Revolution. State courts consistently demonstrated their inclination to keep people off the public dole, and they perceived sole trader status as a strategy for achieving that goal. A married woman attained the status of sole trader (an apparent contradiction) "by deed under the hand and seal of the husband." By law, these wives were, simultaneously *feme covert* "yet . . . sole trader[s]" and transacted business under their own names. Whether married or not, state law required a sole trader to publicize her "intention to trade as a sole trader," in a kind of ongoing, monthly public announcement of her status. The statute never required all *femes sole* officially to register, so their actual numbers may never be known. Only those who advertised in city newspapers (an efficient way to comply with the 1823 statute) or those involved in court disputes emerged into the public record. Ann Pillans, for example, owned and operated a shop, but she never materialized in the city census or directory until her husband died in 1800. Similarly, sole trader Mary Repon kept a Charleston boardinghouse, yet city directories sometimes listed only her husband, Bernard. What is certain is that most (fully 83 percent) South Carolina sole traders lived in Charleston. They comprised artisans, artisans' wives, and women in the accommodations sector of the urban economy. The spouses of planters, merchants, slave traders, and professional men also numbered among their ranks. Although a small minority hailed from Charleston's wealthiest residents, women of the laboring classes (including the lower, middle, and upper echelons of those who worked outside their homes) dominated the ranks of *feme sole* traders. They were black, brown, and white, and represented a cross section of the city's occupations.[56]

Charleston women, and their husbands on their behalf, sought *feme sole* trader status for mixed motives, one of which was to escape relentless creditors. Husbands blatantly attempted to defraud creditors by transferring property to their newly constituted *feme sole* wives. In 1833 one judge proclaimed "there [were] but few [insolvent] married men who [had] not attempted to shelter themselves under this cover." Men were not the only ones who sought to defraud creditors; women adjoined in similar activities. As early as the second decade of the eighteenth century, state law authorized legal action against sole traders attempting to elude financial obligations by claiming *feme covert* status. In 1801 when milliner and shop keeper Martha Surtell attempted this ruse, the presiding judge ruled that Martha had transacted business "in her own name publicly . . . as a *feme sole* dealer" for upward of ten or twelve years. He made clear the state's commitment to protecting the integrity of all mercantile transactions. But not all women harbored nefarious designs in seeking *feme sole* status. Many viewed sole tradership as a legitimate means of materially improving their lives and, by protecting their inheritances, the lives of their female kin. In equal or greater numbers than the conniving Martha Surtells were women like Susannah Tennant, who obtained the signature of her future son-in-law on a document in which he agreed to make Catherine Tennant (Susannah's daughter) a sole trader when she reached age twenty-one. Samuel also agreed to a marriage bond stipulating that the estate Catherine would inherit from her mother would be "for her sole and separate use." In taking these two actions, sole trader Susannah Tennant established for Catherine the freedom to dispose of her inheritance and to earn and dispose of her own income as she saw fit. One decade earlier another woman, Catharine Megrath, also sought greater economic autonomy and maneuverability through sole trader status. Her husband, John, allegedly "acquiesced merely for peace sake, as she was of a violent temper."[57]

Regardless of their motives for attaining sole trader status, and notwithstanding their centrality to the city economy, Charleston's sole traders violated fundamental tenets of slave society. White *femes sole* transgressed southern domestic ideology mandating that (white) women remain sheltered within the household and under the protection and maintenance of their patriarchs. *Feme sole* traders of African descent, like Catharine Maria Sasportas and Dye Waring, also breached southern canon. In South Carolina, "it [was] . . . always presumed that every negro . . . [and] mulatto . . . [was] a slave." Whatever their color, sole traders were women out of place, concurrently integral to the city's economy and society and yet a threat to the slave order.[58]

Consequently, master-class men granted *feme sole* status when it suited their purposes, but they also increasingly constrained the privileges of sole traders. Because of the economic and social advantages inherent in sole tradership, Charleston gentlemen perceived sole traders as an erosion of their dominion. Particularly threatening were married sole traders. By the first quarter of the nineteenth century, state courts ruled as "contrary to the common law, and to the principles of our government," the custom of granting sole trader status to married women. Wary judges ruled the policy "at best doubtful." Sole trader status potentially "released [a woman] from the shackles which the Common Law imposes upon her by reason of her matrimonial contract." The prospect of releasing any shackles was anathema to slave society. The city's sole traders of African descent only compounded this perceived crisis of authority.[59]

Married *femes sole* activated fears of social anarchy because they represented "partial dissolution of the husband's authority over the wife." So, while *feme sole* traders had excited little judicial passion in the eighteenth century, beginning in the 1820s, courts repeatedly delineated and contracted their boundaries. The status "confers no power or privilege except that of suing and of being sued," judges thundered, and "it limits her authority to sue expressly to such debts . . . contracted with her as sole trader." Accordingly, courts required a husband to "conjoin" his sole trader wife whenever she sued, but "not where she is sued."[60]

As judges restricted the legal and economic privileges of sole traders, they even went so far as to re-label married sole traders as "*feme covert* sole trader[s]." This conflation of the safer *feme covert* with the now-threatening "sole trader" reverberated with the courts' apprehensions. In addition, judges pointedly limited sole trader status to those women "engaged in trade and commerce," adding, "it never was intended to authorize any other pursuit in which the wife might engage." Further testifying to their discomfort over a perceived erosion of white men's economic and social dominance, judges narrowed their definition of "trade" to exclude waged laborers. In so doing, they effectively eliminated many sole traders of African descent and others among the "lower sorts" of women. "A trader means a person engaged in merchandize [*sic*], or one who gets his living by buying and selling again for profit," one court ruled, and the status of sole trader "cannot be extended further."[61]

Both married and unmarried sole traders established themselves as central to their individual family economies and the larger city economy, a fact that Carolina judges did not dispute. But their very centrality discomfited men of the master class. Their insecurity manifested in the ways they increasingly de-limited sole trader status and privileges. Their discontent also became evident in the words by which they described women's roles. Sole trader status neither "constituted a new era in the history of family arrangements," nor "conferred any new power on married women," jurists declared. "It is utterly inconsistent with the duties of the wife to the husband and her children," an 1840 court pronounced, "that she should engage in business which would deprive them of her society and assistance." Resorting to race-based and class-specific shib-boleths of the southern lady, the court decried all roles that would necessitate ladies venturing out in "the busy world to mingle with all classes," where they would "lose that distinctive modesty of character which makes her at home and abroad the ornament and the directress of society." Wielding words and images like these, Carolina judges once again contrasted laboring women to idealized ladies—tightly entwining those two identities yet distinguishing between distinct groups of women—in order to shore up patriarchy.[62]

Women's work and women workers comprised an essential part of the urban economy and social organization, and whatever her tasks, each woman's work roles and realities crystallized the status of another Charleston woman. All work dramatized women's interdependent lives: the long hours of a young Orphan House apprentice underscored the leisure of a master-class belle, just as the la-bor of a slave woman and the merrymaking of her mistress formed two sides of the same coin.

8   Leisure and Recreation

Slavery afforded leisure to Charleston's wealthiest slave owners, leisure confirmed wealth, and the wealthy deliberately cultivated social and cultural activities to distinguish themselves as a ruling, aristocratic elite. While slaves worked hard and rarely played, wealthy white owners seldom worked and played earnestly to "keep ahead, to set the pace, and to adopt each new fashion in thought and theory as well as in dress." These intertwined realities of abundant and scarce recreation elevated women of the master class above, especially, slave women. The ways in which other Charleston women aspired to socialize and amuse themselves, and their actual opportunities for play, delimited one category of woman from another. Likewise, the diverse recreational activities they pursued, and the nature and frequency of those endeavors, constituted different but interwoven strands of women's defining experiences.[1]

By the mid eighteenth century, the master class dominated much recreation in Charleston and, indeed, had transformed the city into a social and cultural winter garden for all low-country planter families. Girls and women of the master class took center stage during most winter social activities, because mastering the art of entertainment distinguished a lady; leisure entwined with status and duty. Of equal importance, women of the master class (and the brown elite) capitalized on their customary social roles to carve out a public presence and exert a measure of influence in their patriarchal world.

Other city residents also played, notwithstanding the control of many forms of recreation by the master class. Slaves deftly recast work into leisure by visiting with friends and relatives in the city market, or by taking detours while delivering messages for their owners. Charleston slave women wielded their rare, sanctioned leisure time as an instrument of self-preservation or resistance, because they had learned how to negotiate slavery's uneven power relations to increase their survival odds. Slaves were not alone in manipulating the political uses of leisure. Excluded from citizenship as well as the cultural ventures of affluent white people, members of Charleston's free brown elite created their own, exclusive social spaces, often in the form of activities closely resembling those of the master class. The city's disreputable residents took advantage of recreational time by transforming play into profit; they picked pockets and bilked drunken revelers of their currency and valuables. Virtually all Charleston women enjoyed leisure and maximized the designing functions of amusement. As in all aspects of their lives, leisure simultaneously entwined women and separated them. What was one woman's play was another's hard work, and the social functions attended by one woman purposefully excluded another. The same fault lines of race, condition, class, and gender that divided all of

Charleston life also determined and segregated recreation. Leisure defined white and black, rich and poor, slave and free, male and female.

Charleston residents had progressed from brawling and eye-gouging in muddy streets to theatergoing. In the first half of the eighteenth century, the burgeoning master class forged itself into a European-styled aristocracy. Carolina's ladies and gentlemen delineated themselves through their culture—that constellation of habits and artifacts related to clothing, food, drink, architecture, landscaping, furniture, and mannerisms—and Charleston became their playground as well as their mercantile hub. With the 1762 founding of the St. Cecilia Society, a concert association named for the patron saint of music, elite Charlestonians established their city's reputation as a center of music and drama. More than a decade before the American Revolution, they boasted three theaters. Imitating the English aristocratic penchant for riding and hunting, Charleston gentlemen also formed hunt clubs, and the "Charlestown Races" gained renown as an aristocratic sporting and social event occasioned by dinners and balls. By the 1820s, the St. Cecilia Society had evolved from its eighteenth-century concert emphasis into an elite dancing club, in which membership became an inherited perquisite of prestige and power. A multitude of northerners and foreign visitors commented on the city's vibrant social scene and the young girls who whirled at its center.[2]

Girls and women played pivotal roles in this ongoing process of self-creation and self-perpetuation. Because intermarriage constituted an integral strategy for forging and maintaining economic and social dominion, much of the city's social life facilitated the fundamental goal of devising unions between Carolina's most affluent and powerful families. Travelers and residents alike acknowledged the "extreme youth" of Charleston high society, where "the belles [were] girls; the beaux . . . scarcely more than boys." The low-country elite (or elite aspirants) transformed this social scene into a kind of youth culture.[3]

From the era of the American Revolution until the Civil War, Carolina's wealthiest families of European descent played their hardest during the first three months of each year. They celebrated Christmas on their country estates, then journeyed to Charleston from plantations fifty or more miles distant. During this high social season, Charleston's population swelled and the town, according to one grandee, became "exceptionally gay owing to the combination of several seasonables, such as the Races." In addition to the host of social and cultural events, this annual rite of "transient gaiety," also furnished an opportunity for the master class to celebrate, display, and reinforce its economic and social dominion. Grandiose demonstrations of wealth and privilege accompanied each public and private ball, dinner party, concert, theater production, and horse race. The St. Cecilia Society sponsored three public balls on Thursday evenings in January and February. Dancing assemblies convened in private homes and public venues, and the Jockey Club hosted its annual ball marking the season's apogee. These social activities constituted more than mere frolic.[4]

In addition to providing recreation and demonstrations of power, the season quite literally facilitated reproduction of the master class, because social functions showcased young debutantes who married during a subsequent season. Only those families with young, marriageable daughters repositioned themselves in the city each winter, and only unmarried girls (and their mothers) attended "seasonables." Families with young sons (but no daughters of age) customarily remained on their country estates and sent their marriageable sons into Charleston to board with relatives or friends, while parents with girls of age reconstituted their households in the city to oversee their daughters' social debuts. Elite women commented on their own non-attendance at balls and dinners because their daughters were still too young, and travel accounts echo with the surprised scrutiny of European eyewitnesses who puzzled over the dearth of wives (without progeny) at Charleston social events. This custom bespeaks the centrality of the ritualized matchmaking season: it constituted a family project and an economic strategy in low-country Carolina. Each ball—the archetypal playground of the master class—attracted prominent, white, wealthy parents with matchmaking on their minds and young girls in tow.[5]

For more than two years beginning in May 1780, British occupation troops interrupted this important seasonal matchmaking ritual and usurped the master class as arbiters of the city's social scene. The British employed cultural activities to reinforce their control, just as the city's ladies and gentlemen of a patriot persuasion wielded leisure to demonstrate and cement their power. British occupation officers, in league with Carolina loyalists and other Tory sympathizers, hosted dinners and compelled the attendance of wealthy patriot ladies. They sponsored and encouraged other social events, like concerts, theater performances, and private and public balls. Loyalist women gladly participated, thereby evoking the abiding enmity of their patriot neighbors. Patriot women and paroled American prisoners of the artisan and master classes shunned occupation leisure whenever possible. From their perspective, the city's social life, like their personal lives, had been overturned. On at least one occasion, white patriots looked on with horror as women of African descent donned ball gowns and danced with occupation troops. Thus, in addition to bolstering their authority through cultural activities, British troops also brandished their control by intentionally pitting African-American women against white women, and loyalist and patriot women of European descent against each other.[6]

After the Revolution, leisure activities provided a principal means by which patriot ladies and gentlemen reconstructed their social and economic dominion, and women figured prominently in this reinvigoration of social and cultural forms and the reconstitution of authority. In late summer 1783 (before this social reconstruction), one traveler observed, "there is no theater or spectacle whatsoever," and "the only place women are seen in large numbers is in church on Sundays." While it was the off-season, this dearth of amusements indicated the city's need for a postwar rebuilding of leisure forms as well as a renovation with bricks and mortar. Victorious patriots addressed the task directly. Members of the master class infused their new political culture with traditional forms of leisure and exploited social activities to buttress the city's image as a premier urban center of the new republic.[7]

Elite ladies purposefully inserted themselves into this post-Revolution reconstruction process, partly because culture comprised customary female forums. But they also did so because they had been excluded from citizenship in the new American republic and had determined to fashion their own political roles. In preparation for President George Washington's May 1791 visit, wealthy, white ladies embroidered bandeaux with his portrait and a motto of welcome. Women hosted and appeared prominently at several breakfasts, dinners, balls, and concerts. The primary event during Washington's weeklong visit was not a speech or a political rally, it was a ball, and that grand event spotlighted women. Carolinians had just fought a bloody, guerilla war for independence against British aristocratic tyranny. But, ironically, Charleston's ladies and gentlemen were reconstituting themselves as a ruling aristocracy and envisioned their home as America's most genteel and sociable city.[8]

Over a quarter-century after President Washington's 1791 visit, the ruling elite persisted in its use of leisure as a means of perpetual self-construction, and women remained central to the process. Ladies planted themselves firmly in the center of these public shows. In 1825, just three years after the Denmark Vesey slave insurrection plot had convulsed the city, the Revolutionary hero, Marquis de Lafayette, visited Charleston. Social activities accompanying Lafayette's stay aided in Charleston's recovery process after the Vesey upheaval, because leisure provided venues for conspicuous displays of wealth and, most importantly, power. The Marquis's stop in the southern port occasioned several balls and dinners, a fireworks display, and a military parade. Visitors commented upon the elaborate appearance of ladies who decked themselves out in "brilliant as well as costly" dresses and "rich head-dresses with a profusion of diamonds and jewels." Richly adorned women served as conspicuous reminders to all city residents that the master class, though a numeric minority, dominated the city nonetheless. In this way, master-class women staked their claim to citizenship and performed a vital role in perpetuating the slave society in which they had so much invested.[9]

Affluent Charleston patriots wasted little time in repossessing the famed Charleston "season." As before the Revolution, the first three months of each year constituted Charleston's busiest social time, and young girls figured prominently in all venues. At first glance, the season appears a benign, albeit frenzied, round of social events, but contemporaries also characterized these activities as theaters of war and public markets, where fourteen-year-old girls were pitted against each other. According to one former belle, "seasonables" constituted "the first battle-field of our young Amazons" whose mission was "to conquer the male sex." Charleston writer Susan Petigru King ridiculed and unmasked these unsavory facets of seasonal fetes and the expected comportment of their coquettish stars. Although her biting social criticism materialized in the narrative voice of her novels, Susan spoke truths about how real (not fictional) belles were prepared for this rite of passage. Furthermore, Susan Petigru King was not alone in decrying the immense annual social pressure to "ensnare" husbands during the high season, nor was she the only one to critique expected, inculcated female behaviors. Popular and literary presses disparaged the belle persona and the potential psychological damage wreaked on young girls by the season. "Calculating all night, and dressing all day, their hearts get beaten up by the world like grist in a mortar," one social commentator wrote in mid-nineteenth century after observing seasonables. "When a man marries a [belle], he gets a body without a soul, and sometimes a dress without a body." Leisure in this port city elementally defined and influenced young girls.[10]

Contemporary accounts bear witness that winter amusements constituted serious family business as well as play. These accounts testify to the potency of social dictums mandating that a girl's future turned on her successful showing during the season. Elizabeth Grimball, eldest daughter of Meta Morris and John Berkely, was "introduced into company" in February 1850. Meta was ailing at the time and, in fact, had not been well for fully two months. John saw that his wife was physically weak, but neither he nor Meta ever considered curtailing the frenzied round of social events. Too much was at stake. Elizabeth had been "invited to all the parties—Public and Private," her father noted with pride. Meta went out every night, accompanying her daughter to several balls and private cotillions. Only when the season ended did Meta recuperate by returning to the country for the doctor-prescribed rest she needed.[11]

These "scene[s] of splendid confusion" induced trepidation that sometimes overshadowed the exhilarated anticipation of a debut. Not all girls enjoyed the prospect of their first ball. More accustomed to country life than the urban social scene, young Caroline Howard felt "shy and fluttered" as she and her young cousin followed her mother up the broad, intimidating staircase to the Jockey Club. Caroline "half shrank back as the light of the chandeliers burst upon" them. Gazing upon the "row of brilliant-looking ladies [who] lined the room," Caroline and her cousin "shrivelled up into almost nothingness" as they stared at the "easy, graceful, practised [sic] forms of the city belles." Caroline and Anna sat along the wall, "so long neglected that [their] nerves became excited." Struggling later to describe the intense pressure she felt, Caroline wrote, "I felt as if I was mocked; the sensation of anger" mounted. She longed to "scream, or weep, or grasp at something violently." The debut was a disaster. She hated the social ritual of this "painful event," and wondered how many other "aching hearts" filled the glittering room.[12]

It is no wonder that some girls feared this sink-or-swim proposition, and shuddered at parental and peer pressure to conquer Charleston society. Quite literally, a young woman's performance at a ball determined her future. "She is predestined to rule who finds herself engaged" to dance constantly "before she smooths out her skirts for her first quadrille." Conversely, a girl—like Caroline—who "passes her evening on one of those very hard chairs planted around the room" was doomed to disgrace. The stigma reached beyond the momentary discomfort of social rejection. Once shunned as unaccomplished or insufficiently amiable, a young girl disgraced her family and jeopardized prospects of making a suitable marriage. She became unmarketable goods.[13]

For all the emphasis on Charleston sociability, the ritualized "icy propriety" governing interactions between young women and men rendered balls insufferably stilted affairs. "Ladies and gentlemen appeared to be entire strangers to one another," marveled one visitor, and he watched as "the ladies . . . planted [themselves] firmly along the walls, in the coldest possible formality, while the gentlemen . . . stood in close column near the door." Perhaps this is why some mothers shrank from returning to the social stage, instead asking other female kin to escort their daughters to, particularly, the daunting Jockey Club and St. Cecilia balls. When Caroline Howard's mother attempted this strategy, Mr. Howard "insisted" that his wife personally introduce Caroline and her cousin Anna in public. "Mama" finally agreed.[14]

Young belles in attendance at balls and various other social functions of the season self-consciously displayed themselves and were cognizant that their parents were exhibiting them. The season served as a crash course in the centrality of women to proclaiming the wealth, status, and control of the master class. How these belles looked and what seasonables they attended starkly differentiated them from their female slaves and the women of the laboring classes, who merely watched as the elaborate carriages rolled by. Attired in "close, dark riding-dresses, with hat and feathers" chosen by her father, Caroline Howard and her cousin, Anna, were escorted by "Papa" to the race grounds just outside the city. The girls arrived in their father's "handsome equipage," as did all members of the exclusive Jockey Club. They donned red club ribbons and then Papa ushered the girls to a members-only box, a vantage point from which to view the races and the crowd. More importantly, in the grandstand, Caroline and Anna could "be viewed" clearly not only by other club members but also by attendees down below at the course-level. "Race Week" (an ironic appellation) had originated in the second quarter of the eighteenth century as a time during which planters transacted business with factors who bought and sold rice, cotton, and European goods on their behalf. However, by century's end, Charleston aristocrats had incorporated Race Week into their social season. The low-country love of horse racing endured, but the emphasis changed. In the nineteenth century, Race Week metamorphosed into yet another vehicle for exhibiting marriageable girls. The February races may have drawn thousands of racing aficionados from all walks of life, but hundreds of spectators came to be seen more than to view the horses and their slave jockeys. Moreover, when the Jockey Club instituted its annual ball, invitations to that gala became a coveted cultural commodity. Charleston women of the brown elite aspired to inclusion, other women dreamed of attending, but the doors of the ballroom swung open exclusively for master-class belles.[15]

Marriage was the paramount goal of a debut, so several elaborate weddings annually climaxed the Charleston season. The marriage ceremonies, as well as accompanying dinners and parties, also furnish added venues for displaying debutantes, affluence, and dominion. The grandeur of their weddings set apart these brides from all other women. Members of the master class spared no expense in producing these lavish nuptials; the opulence was calculated visibly to reinforce their positions at the pinnacle of low-country society. Some marriages, like that of Alicia Russell and Arthur Middleton in early March 1809, entailed a "succession of parties" in a solid month of celebration, during which Charleston's merchant and planter families hosted dinners, dances, and musicales in the couple's honor. A profusion of food, drink, and amusements added to the costs of entertaining. While not occasioned by a wedding, Meta and John Berkely Grimball's modest dinner party in 1849 provides a tiny taste of high-season entertainment in Charleston. The Grimballs served "jellies . . . custards, tarts, preserved fruits . . . a roast turkey and a boiled ham, three wild ducks, [and] four dishes of scalloped oysters." Later in the evening, "3 other hot ducks were brought in and the turkey gave place to a hot oyster pie." Attendees at their "small party" also downed four decanters of Madeira and two bottles of champagne. Courtship and marriage precipitated extended revelry each season, because these unions personified the reproduction of Charleston's ruling class and its culture.[16]

Wealthy women fancied themselves the epitome of hospitality, and their ritualized visiting, much of which was concurrent with the high social season, reinforced this image. Formal calls on acquaintances, friends, and relatives formed a common leisure pursuit among women and girls of the master class and an integral part of their social identities. In one of her trips to the city, Frances Kemble labeled Charleston women "miserable pedestrians" because they rode distances "of less than a quarter of a mile" to visit other ladies on the same street. Muddy and sandy streets aside—city thoroughfares remained notoriously bad through most of the nineteenth century—there was a logical explanation for this curious customary behavior. City matrons taught belles to avoid any appearance of the unladylike trait of self-exertion. Slave women worked hard and sweated, ladies did not. Moreover, just as "handsome equipages" bespoke a certain rank as they rolled onto the race grounds in February, carriage rides through city streets displayed the accoutrements of class and high status. Maintaining a carriage and horses required not merely the initial capital outlay, but also payment of an annual tax on the carriage and ongoing maintenance costs. The daily display of that vehicle, with its owners comfortably ensconced within, reinforced social distinctions so crucial to slave society.[17]

Selectively inclusive, city hostesses took seriously their mandated cordiality to visitors and included them in ritualized visiting and social functions. However, only those whose wealth, rank, or character endowed their Charleston patrons with *éclat* experienced the full force of southern congeniality. Letters of introduction from appropriately genteel, mutual acquaintances served as keys that opened doors to the best city homes. Accordingly, in 1838, Charleston ladies provided Louisa Minot a "most social and delightful time," thereby buttressing Charlestonians' reputation as "a most warmhearted, easy people." In particular, southern ladies perpetuated their profile as "pretty [and] easy, soft and kind in their manners." Louisa received calls from a half-dozen ladies in less than one week during the 1838 season. She promptly returned those visits, as custom dictated, and rode about town in carriages sent to her by prominent city residents, who also invited Louisa for tea or dinner. On yet another day during her winter visit, Louisa ventured out to "return [her] calls," and missed three other women who visited her that same morning. Louisa felt relieved when she later "found all except Miss Huger" at home and was able to reciprocate those attempted visits in short order. Nevertheless, she lamented that she still had "three more calls to make." Louisa's account conjures a comical image of women riding feverishly from house to house every morning with a checklist of requisite visits, and missing each other in the process.[18]

Mastering the art of performing as a proper hostess comprised just one part of the transformation from little girl to belle. The metamorphosis included many lessons and took several forms, most of which were related to leisure activities. Travel served as one method of tutoring young daughters, nieces, and granddaughters in the accomplishments of a lady, and also was a means of presenting them in public to test their "sociability." It is true that wealthy low-country residents traveled partly because they feared summer "miasmas." Prevailing wisdom dictated that one might return to the low country only after autumn's first "black frost," which signaled a safe environment. Nevertheless, expensive summer migrations earmarked Charleston ladies as members of the ruling class. With expenditures sometimes exceeding $1,400, these annual visits to the springs of South and North Carolina, Virginia, and New York served as costly reminders to observers of all ranks and colors, and to the travelers themselves, of who wielded social and economic power. In 1835 the Grimballs spent an average of slightly over ten dollars per day while on their four-month journey. Their daily expenditures exceeded (by three or four dollars) the monthly wages of a child's nurse. Meta and John evidenced no overt designs to impress observers with their money; however, the style in which they traveled, and the fact that they had the time and resources to take this trip, bore witness to their high place in Charleston society.[19]

In addition to maintaining and patrolling social boundaries, leisure pursuits also socialized the next generation of the master class. Dynamic daily lessons in social hierarchy were not lost on young girls (and the slaves accompanying these sojourners), who thus learned about their rank and roles in Carolina society. In 1839 little Harriott Horry Rutledge and her mother, Rebecca Motte [Lowndes] Rutledge, encountered the Trapiers, fellow Charlestonians, in the city of New York, and had been persuaded to accompany them to West Point. Bespeaking the educational value of this excursion, Rebecca relayed to her husband that Harriott had earned "great admiration and attention, and showed an astonishing aptitude at the science of Flirting." Rebecca boasted that "Harrie" was "decidedly the belle of West Point." Clearly, this northern jaunt was a proving ground for blossoming belles as well as an enjoyable diversion. Harrie and her young friend, Sally Trapier, competed for the attention of admirers as they soon would do for higher stakes in Charleston.[20]

If finances precluded northern trips, elite families relocated from plantations in May or June to their Charleston homes, or they rented city mansions from one of the traveling families. Summering in Charleston, like other jaunts, offered opportunities for little girls to master the arts, displays and role of city belles. Harriott Horry Rutledge learned her place in society by spending the summer of 1841 in Charleston with her maternal aunt and grandmother. She socialized with her peers, and accompanied her Aunt Holbrook to dinner in some of the city's most beautiful mansions. "Harrie" also took evening carriage rides on the Battery "with a servant." Down by the bay in Battery Park, Harrie watched other wealthy children play while their slave "attendants" waited for them nearby. At the Battery she also observed young ladies promenading with their beaus. Harrie listened and learned how to converse cleverly and "agreeably" with boys and how to command the slave girls and women who attended her.[21]

In these ways, leisure was didactic and crucial to the metamorphosis from mischievous, strong-willed child to amiable belle. Over the summer of 1841, Harrie vacillated wildly between the two poles, but her aunt and grandmother resolved that she would transform into the latter. Correspondence from Harrie and her aunt to Harrie's mother in Boston provides a fascinating glimpse of this transitional period of master class adolescence. One moment Harrie and her friend, "Miss Raven Vanderhorst," stalked a cat and "sprang out upon her" with "such a shout that Aunt H[olbrook] sprung [sic] to the door" frantic to discover what had transpired. Only hours later, Harrie the budding belle preened for a party at Sally Lowndes's house. Likewise, much to her aunt's frustration, Harrie defiantly refused to correct her penmanship, vowing that she would write a letter "in my own style" which "Mama would rather have . . . than an affected one." But the next moment, a compliant and amiable Harrie joined her aunt and grandmother in reading the Anglican service to "set an example" for slaves "Maum Kate and Maum Sue," who were "invited to come up" to the house. Her descriptions of such commonplace activities manifested Harrie's quick mastery of condescension as well as ladylike comportment. Young Harrie alternately exasperated and gratified her aunt, Harriott Pinckney Holbrook, but, despite minor setbacks, leisure served Aunt Holbrook, Grandmama, and Harrie as crucial venues of tutoring, in which Harrie-the-child metamorphosed into Harriott-the-belle.[22]

In addition to providing multiple arenas where little girls practiced the social graces, summering in Charleston and traveling with their mothers allowed girls to master the role of slave-owning mistress. Giving voice to her success in this area, ten-year-old Harriott Horry Rutledge proudly wrote to her mother. "I told Esau to clean [the grass] away," she bragged after ordering one of her family's slave men to trim weeds growing between the stones of their front piazza. "He said that he was going to do it." Watching her older kin and her peers, Harriott had learned to command, as she navigated the transition from child to slave owner.[23]

These annual peregrinations of the wealthy were so woven into the lives of area residents that they evoked little more than a line or two in diaries or journals, and the slaves who migrated with their owners likewise considered the migrations a normal part of their routine. "We spent the summers in Charleston," an unnamed slave woman recalled, and "winters on the plantation." Slave owners seemed oblivious to the menace their journeys created for slaves, and customarily thought little (if at all) about how such arrangements might affect their slaves' kinship ties or their sensitivities. In reality, these annual trips separated families for weeks or months at a time. Conversely, seasonal migrations into and out of Charleston occasionally reunited slave couples and other kin who had been segregated by their urban and rural assignments, or by their status as field (plantation) or house (urban compound) slaves. Nevertheless, annual migrations or extended travel by elite women differentiated ladies from the slave women who served them and, indeed, from most Charleston women who could not afford this form of leisure.[24]

When the wealthy played—and they played frequently—they usually created more work for others, particularly their slaves. But city residents of all colors and classes experienced some form of leisure, and these activities fulfilled divergent functions. Charleston slaves savored leisure as a precious commodity and relished the scant recreation time authorized by their owners and municipal law. They also generated their own forms of leisure, often combining recreation with work, and each hybrid of labor and entertainment offered the possibility of resistance: recreation occurred at the expense of work, which inconvenienced their owners.

During the frenetic high social season, slave women stood on the serving side of elaborate and heavily laden dinner tables. They worked long hours preparing their mistresses for endless social engagements. But some slaves derived small pleasures from this frenzied three months. The bedrooms of master-class belles became electrified with mixed emotions emanating from mistresses and slaves alike. Some slaves experienced vicarious pleasure at this hectic time as they adorned and coifed young mistresses whom they had raised or with whom they had played as youngsters. Caught up in the excitement of imminent balls, slave girls and women exerted great care in dressing their mistresses. For example, two slave women, Chloe and Flora, adamantly refused to allow a male escort to drape evening wraps over the pale shoulders of their young charges, insisting on doing it themselves. The two slave women wrapped their mistresses "with peculiar caution" before sending them off to the Jockey Club Ball. Although most slave women worked harder and longer than at other times, some combined fun (or pleasure and pride) with their work.[25]

Race Week, one of the season's biggest attractions, offered amusements for virtually all city residents, slaves included, but these mixed assemblies served multiple purposes. From the perspective of the master class, this superficial mingling of social groups emphasized and reinforced boundaries of race, condition, class, and gender in the very act of mixing. Such revelry may also have served as a release valve, acting as the bread and circuses of the slave South. "Negroes love the excitement of any public spectacle," wrote one longtime resident. This condescension aside, slaves did join those who thronged the racecourse, and took advantage of the socially sanctioned leisure time. Family and friends of the slave jockeys attended for the fun and as a show of support or solidarity. Slave women "often carr[ied] a white child" with them and, in this way, continued their work while enjoying the diversion. Race Week also induced "votaries of debauchery and drunkenness" as well as other "unholy pleasures." These base pastimes attracted certain slave women just as they did a cadre of other Charlestonians of both African and European descent.[26]

The December holidays and the period from January through March also generated unusual distractions for enslaved as well as free city residents. Animal shows and exhibitions of assorted oddities gained popularity in the late eighteenth century. In 1798 the "great WONDER OF NATURE," a 3,500-pound elephant, shared Christmas day with Charlestonians. The city charged no admission and allowed everyone to watch this pachyderm consume her personal holiday pudding, comprising nearly 115 pounds of rice, raisins, molasses, and cayenne pepper. Thirty years later, animal shows and exhibitions continued to amuse the masses. In 1828 "The Caravan"—an African lioness, a tiger and tigress, one puma, a llama, a lynx, monkeys, apes, and other creatures—stopped in Charleston. Whoever could afford the twenty-five-cent admission charge gained entrance. This fee represented one full day's wages for a children's nurse, but some slaves mingled with the free city residents of all economic stations and colors who paid to see the wondrous display. During another holiday season of the same decade, the city's Museum of South Carolina exhibited a whale, a huge snake, hundreds of birds, "panoramic views of public buildings in Europe," and a "New Zealander's head."[27]

Throughout the nineteenth century, panoramas of diverse lands and sights found favor with all city residents, regardless of color, condition, and class, but these public diversions also periodically reinforced racial boundaries. Some excluded slaves and free laboring people through their prohibitively high entrance fees. Others openly banned all brown and black residents. During January 1807, a 3,000-square-foot panorama of the "Battle of Alexandria in Egypt" toured England, Ireland, New York, and Philadelphia before making its southern debut in Charleston. The exhibition was "open to the public" for a fee of fifty cents, but "no people of colour |were| admitted."[28]

Although the master class controlled much Charleston leisure, slaves formulated and tenaciously preserved their own styles of sociability. By customary practice, slaves held a market every Saturday night, coupling fun with work. Slave women largely presided over this anchor of the city economy, peddling everything from sweet-grass baskets and baked goods to produce. They transacted serious business, to be sure, but from its inception early in the eighteenth century, the "slaves' fair" was a weekly social event. Women and men mingled by lamplight, visiting with friends and family, both slave and free. They shared news, commiserated, and supported each other. In this venue, work was leisure, and leisure functioned as a means of emotional self-preservation as well as just plain fun.[29]

While nuptials of belles advertised and celebrated the wealth and high social position of the ruling elite, slave women's weddings (and funerals) represented celebrations of life and provided brief, sanctioned respites from work. Slave women also transformed weddings into opportunities to draw boundaries of their own. A Charleston waiting maid named Flora secured the permission of her owner (who rued the loss of her "valuable [time and] services") to marry Kit, a city stevedore. The mistress suggested the ceremony take place in her parlor, but Flora "chose to have [it] performed in the wash-kitchen." Flora's choice of location is significant and her decision constituted a form of rebellion. She politely refused the mistress's recommendation, and planned and held her wedding as much as possible on her own terms and in her own social space. Flora chose the Methodist clergyman who would preside. She also oversaw the physical preparations. "The floor was nicely scrubbed, seats placed around, and the tin candlesticks on the wall ornamented with sprigs of green." The "bride's chamber" was decorated with white curtains and more evergreens. She and Kit appointed their six bridesmaids and groomsmen, the former adorned in white, like Flora, "with flowers, [ribbon and] tarnished silver and gold sprigs in their hair." Flora's owners and their children attended the ceremony and, as custom dictated, later received wine and cake sent by the bride and groom. However, the white people departed immediately, while slaves and free people of color "shouted forth a Methodist hymn" and continued celebrating until midnight. Those attendees without passes from their owners returned home at "the roll of the [curfew] drum" (at 10 P.M. in the summer, 9 P.M. in the winter). Despite these constraints, Flora maximized the celebration of her wedding by resisting her mistress's inclination to control the event.[30]

Slave funerals similarly occasioned rare release time from work, as well as socially sanctioned gatherings of slaves and free people of color, and women played a central role. Death brought temporary freedom of assembly for the living as well as permanent escape to the dead. City ordinances normally prohibited congregations of more than seven "grown negroes [slaves] or other people of color . . . *except when attending funerals.*" Many slave funerals were conducted "with great ceremony," particularly when the deceased had been a congregant at one of the city's many churches. Funeral garb united the mourners and bequeathed a kind of public license to act atypically and to participate in the public ceremony. Women donned scarves of black or white cambric or silk—the color and fabric depended upon the sex and condition (slave or free) of the departed one—which they basted and drew over their bonnets, or over one shoulder. These women, called "waiters," led the funeral procession through city streets. Like weddings, burials provided opportunities for people of color to control their social rituals, thereby appropriating a measure of sovereignty over their own lives.[31]

Slave women also routinely outsmarted and eluded their owners to enjoy stolen hours of revelry in taverns, alleys, or the slave yards of friends or family. A city noted for raucous gaming and drinking as well as its genteel balls, Charleston boasted one licensed tavern for every thirteen dwellings at the time of the American Revolution. That ratio altered over the course of the eighteenth and nineteenth centuries, but city residents maintained their reputation as being "addicted to spirituous liquors," and slave women and men numbered among those who frequented the city's "dram shops." One August Saturday in 1807, a group of slave women and men made their way to nearby Sullivan's Island (a customary summer playground of the master class), where they joined a group numbering "about one hundred" in "dancing and carousing . . . until near sunrise." Perhaps this frolic had become an annual event.[32]

Slaves also appropriated a few hours each Sunday for ritualized visiting. Many attended church, but during and after the services, city streets filled with slaves dressed in their "best attire." They strolled along, "apparently enjoying themselves," made "the most formal and particular inquiries after each other's families," and addressed one another as "Sir" and "Madam." One white visitor at mid-nineteenth century confirmed that slave women and men had established this Sunday stroll as a fixture of the Charleston social scene. Through jaundiced eyes, he observed that "Negroes and Negresses . . . promenaded wherever they pleased." Their attire "had something of the burlesque about it," he sneered. The men sometimes "dressed as dandies" with coats "folded back all the way up to the front" and they sported "watches without movements suspended from heavy copper chains covered with dozens of trinkets." They escorted women whose hair was "piled up in rebellious pyramids, like stubborn horsehair." Occasional fights as well as flirtations ensued during these extended jaunts, but were "invariably finish[ed] with a dance to the music of the banjo."[33]

Sundays brought yet another weekly amusement for slaves, but girls and boys presided over this favorite game. The diversion reveals that slaves learned at an early age what types of leisure they could pursue, where and when they could enjoy it, and what uses it served. After Sunday dinner, a group of slave children sang and shouted for the white children to come outside. "We were always in a big hurry to get through" the meal, one white Charleston resident related, and to "go out on the piazza . . . [with] a supply of biscuits and sugar to distribute to the little ones." This game afforded opportunities to procure food and ritualistically to overturn the social order, because the next step was to "choose" white children. Slave girls and boys examined each master-class child in the household and "claim[ed] [them] as their special property." Most white children considered this "a great compliment," and were "much pleased though a little embarrassed by the claiming of [their] dresses or shoes, or anything else down to [their] toes and fingers." The youngest slaves likely considered the game a fun means to a tasty end, but older girls (and boys) may have perceived the deeper meaning of the weekly ritualistic role reversal and upending of the slave order. While ladies and belles wielded leisure to reinforce social boundaries, slave women and children employed it to flout those borders. And while the excesses of master-class leisure demanded more time and work of slaves, slave recreation functioned to reappropriate what the mistress and master had taken.[34]

Like slaves, other Charleston women experienced frenetic winter festivities differently than did ladies around whom most seasonables swirled. The balls, dinners, weddings, February horse races, parties, and endless rounds of visiting among women of the master class reinforced unbridgeable chasms separating them from all other women, inclusive of the wealthy and refined women of the brown elite. Excluded from the city's elite social orbit, affluent women among Charleston's free people of color patterned their own debutante balls, parties, and other social engagements after the ruling class. They did so to distance themselves from slaves, from less-affluent free people of African descent, and from poor white people, all of whom they considered beneath them. Their style of recreating was central to their identities and fundamental to their savvy straddling of Charleston's black and white worlds.

While members of the brown elite emulated the social and cultural events of the master class, they did not compete with them. Brown elite parents planned elaborate winter weddings for their young debutantes, but they timed these ceremonies to avoid the frenetic partying of the Charleston season. In 1859 the prosperous Ellisons (one of the low country's distinguished families of African descent) celebrated a family wedding in mid-December. They displayed their wealth in the ceremony and reception, but timed the gala to avoid any appearance of presuming to vie with the January and February festivities. It "came off in style," and the "large and respectable crowd" feasted on oysters, champagne, and cake. Fully twenty bridesmaids and groomsmen participated in the ceremony, and the bride and groom departed for a "tour in the country" afterward.[35]

Apart from winter revelry, women of the brown elite played in a similar manner to their white counterparts. They retreated to Sullivan's Island and strolled its beaches to escape oppressive summer heat and, in the evenings, they entertained each other with dinners and parties. Some of them annually ranged further afield, traveling by steamers to Philadelphia, New York, and Boston. Usually they were not challenged upon returning to Charleston, despite 1820 (and subsequent) state prohibitions upon the entry (or reentry) of "any free negro or mulatto" into South Carolina. It was not until the late 1850s that these migrations of the city's brown elite excited much attention, and not until 1860 that they drew the ire of a minority of white Charlestonians. At that time, a former city police chief vowed to halt the travel. This out-of-state travel, he complained, "was too common with females especially," and these brown women "return[ed] . . . as coolly as whites."[36]

Like white ladies, wealthy brown elite women had honed visiting to a fine art as they traversed city streets in carriages, one of the traditional hallmarks of wealth. They groomed their daughters in the social rituals of "calling" and "taking the air." By the late 1850s, this leisure activity precipitated irate complaints from white residents who resented "black and mulatto" women who "assume[d] to themselves prerogatives and distinctions" that "separat[e] the classes." As war loomed imminently, white citizens took aim at the social protocols and behavior—not specifically at the money—that distinguished Charleston's brown elite. "Shall they, in silks and laces, promenade our principal thoroughfares, with the arrogance of equals" this critic thundered, making "the poor white woman to feel . . . below the slaves?"[37]

Color, economic status, and intermarriage with slaves drew most of Charleston's free laboring women of color to the same leisure activities as enslaved city residents. They attended weddings and funerals where slaves and free people of African descent celebrated together. Unlike slaves, they did not have to obtain passes from the mistress or master, but they did have to worry about being caught by members of the city guard if they stayed beyond the nightly curfew. Also like slaves, whenever free people of color gathered for "the purpose of dancing or other [merriment]," municipal regulations required that they obtain prior permission from the "Warden of the Ward in which it [was] to take place." Moreover, the same law—which prohibited assemblies of any kind involving "grown negroes" that numbered more than seven—applied equally to slaves and free people. City laws precluded large public celebrations like those of the master class. So, counter to regulatory intent, Charleston's middling and poor free people of color likely played in private and clandestinely. Unlike the brown elite, however, they had few ties to the master class, a position that left them more vulnerable to persecution from zealous white people. Consequently, it was expedient to maintain a low profile at work and at play.[38]

Clerical advocacy of slavery notwithstanding, religion provided African Americans moral and spiritual uplift as well as leisure time exempt from municipal limitations on assembly. Well over one quarter of the city's people of color (slave and free) attended services in fifteen Charleston churches. Wherever they worshipped, free women of color and slave women consistently outnumbered their men on membership rolls for church classes. However, men of African descent (despite being outnumbered by women attendees) led these racially segregated classes held on weeknights and Sunday mornings. Church furnished opportunities to meet with friends one night each week in addition to socializing before and after Sunday services. The city sanctioned these religious functions because most people of color attended white churches throughout the antebellum era. White lay leaders as well as clergymen wove into the church liturgy biblical justifications of slavery, and members of the free brown elite (in league with their white counterparts) monitored the behavior of other people of color. The notable exception to this rule, the African Methodist Episcopal Church founded in 1816 on Charleston's Neck, thrived and attracted thousands of congregants, but city officials demolished the building after defusing the 1822 Denmark Vesey slave insurrection. Not until some twenty-seven years later would people of color establish a second church independent of white control, but fearful white residents periodically subjected that congregation and its edifice to threats of destruction.[39]

Although church-sponsored classes, special events, and congregational social ties represented an important part of some women's lives, free people of color also were attracted to the same public amusements that slaves and white people enjoyed. Charleston's working-class women of African and European descent occasionally engaged in similar leisure pursuits partly because they shared a defining reality: none enjoyed enormous amounts of time for recreation, and all were excluded from the extravagant, exclusive endeavors of the wealthy. Quick and inexpensive (or free) diversions like the memorable visiting pachyderm of 1798, traveling panoramas, and sundry other displays drew mixed throngs of black, white, and brown residents who attended for the sheer fun of it. More rare were the virtually all-inclusive occasions like the annual May festival, where hundreds of rich and poor residents of all colors mingled and partook in "fun . . . of a novel [and] diverting kind." However, instead of uniting Charlestonians, each of these all-city pastimes bore the potential of emphasizing and reinforcing differences—particularly of color and wealth—that separated free working women of African descent and slave women from white laboring women and that also differentiated working women of all colors from the city's affluent white ladies and brown elite women.[40]

Less reputable mixed gatherings also appealed to women of the laboring classes. Often poor white people, slaves, and impoverished free people of color rubbed shoulders in Charleston's tippling houses, billiard halls, and bawdy houses, worlds apart from the glittering halls of the St. Cecelia and Jockey Club balls and staid parlors of the most affluent free brown elite families. In such humble venues, economic status took precedence over color, so the city's poorest women of all colors, free and slave, fraternized to enjoy themselves and to disconnect from bleak reality. Moreover, those laboring women who engaged in full-time or occasional prostitution profited from a form of leisure that many Charleston men pursued. What was one man's recreation was one woman's work.

Although economics dictated that working-class women of African and European descent frequently played together, the social schism of color sometimes positioned free women of color on the outside looking in. Ever vigilant in patrolling boundaries, municipal officials periodically barred all residents of African descent (slave and free) from various public amusements, like the popular traveling panoramas and exhibitions. The city's famed Vaux Hall also excluded free people of color as well as slaves. For a small fee, Vaux, which opened in 1799, proffered to white residents a potpourri of diversions, including instrumental and vocal music, fireworks, strolls through its gardens, refreshments at the cafe, and public baths. Each time a woman partook of Vaux Hall's eclectic pleasures during the nearly eleven years of its full operation, free women of color were reminded that their shared economic status with laboring white women had limits, and those boundaries were drawn in shades of black and white.[41]

Charleston women played in multiple venues, for mixed motives and in varied company, but always leisure activities defined and reinforced social distinctions. Different groups of women encountered unique realities, aspirations, possibilities and practices of leisure; their distinctive experiences defined and entwined them at play as at work. Each time they amused themselves—whether in mixed or segregated groups—those pastimes reminded women of their discrete identities and social ranks. The influence worked in two directions: social boundaries prescribed leisure by determining which category of woman could engage in particular forms of recreation, while at the same time, leisure buttressed those fundamental fault lines of race, condition, class, and gender. It was a reciprocal dynamic.

9   Women and the Law

Whether criminals or victims of crime, Charleston women encountered the law differently based on the color of their skin, their social standing, and their economic status. Who and what they were not, as much as who and what they were, determined how the courts treated them. Judges and legislators (primarily men of the low-country master class) justified idiosyncratic treatment by declaring who was and was not a lady worthy of deference. Court officials often appraised women of color as a lower order of female and, therefore, unworthy of the protection accorded ladies. White women of the laboring classes also usually fell short of behavioral expectations exemplified by master-class women; the shortfall produced unfavorable court decisions, in which judges rhetorically colored women black by treating them as something less than true southern ladies. This unequal treatment reveals multiple strands of the mutually dependent legal status of women.

In the process of meting out uneven justice to disparate groups of women, South Carolina courts were constructing gender as well as race, and this construction project was instrumental to slave society. Entwined, contrasting notions of "woman" proved essential to Charleston's social organization and to South Carolina law because gender served as a principal model for social hierarchy. Municipal regulations, state statute law, and case law strove to maintain order, but the law upheld the master's sovereignty over all his underlings. It codified the supremacy of male over female in addition to white over color. Jurists had a vested interest in perpetuating antithetical images of women because doing so justified idiosyncratic judgments, which, in turn, sustained the supremacy of the master class and fortified slave society.[1]

Ironically, when slave women and free women of color committed nonviolent crimes like theft, they confirmed perceptions about their castes that reinforced Charleston society. Although theft constituted a form of rebellion and certainly inconvenienced other residents, "thieving negroe women" conformed to precisely that stereotype (thieving negroes) that infused daily life, statute, and case law: white people were honorable, but black people were devious and criminal. Charleston slave women and free women of African descent were more likely to be indicted for theft (which was second after assault in numbers of South Carolina prosecutions) than were white women of all classes. During the twenty-two-year period beginning in 1786, no women of European descent were indicted for theft.[2]

When women of color came to court, they confronted a confusing institutional morass, with separate courts (unless the person of color was a third party in an action between white people) and distinct punishments for slaves and free people of color. South Carolina's black code—statutorily effective from 1740 until after the Civil War—restricted their testimony and other rights, outlined acceptable behavior for all people of African descent, and enumerated the disciplinary privileges of slave owners and non–slave owners alike. The 1740 slave code derived from Carolina's seventeenth-century slave laws (the 1691 and 1696 acts "for the Better Ordering of Slaves"), themselves gleaned from Barbados's statute laws and reflective of the Caribbean origins of a substantial number of South Carolina colonists. Under this code, "negro courts," or the Inferior Magistrates and Freeholders Courts, comprised one to two justices of the peace and two to five freeholders, depending upon the severity of the crime. These white men possessed the wherewithal to execute slaves and free people of color for more than a half-dozen offenses and to inflict corporal punishment at their pleasure. This is not to argue the impossibility of justice for "Negroes." Not all magistrates and judges were brutish and malevolent, and appellate courts did sustain appeals of judgments against slaves and free people of color. However, it remains true that special courts and harsher retribution underscored the subordination of Charleston's slave women and free women of color and widened the chasm separating them from white women. Localism and notions of gender also infused court interpretations of black law as they did the state's white law. Charleston's power politics—the ideological and institutional constructions of power—emerged from South Carolina's peculiar adaptation of English common law to slave society.[3]

The city's slave women and free women of African descent also encountered a formidable web of extralegal authority buttressed by customary practice as well as Carolina's separate penal code "for the better ordering and governing [of] negroes and other slaves." Extralegal and legal vigilantism (the urban variant of "plantation justice") was restrained, not prohibited, under state statute law, and it came to force when alternative sources of control failed. More often than not, the city's institutionalized repression, including curfews, restrictions on mobility, confinement in the Charleston Work House, bounties for slave catchers, police patrols, and fines for trading with slaves adequately suppressed the city's people of African descent. Both municipal and state laws tightly constrained the city's negro population.[4]

In addition to prosecuting slave women and free women of color, magistrates, trial attorneys, and plaintiffs also reinforced negative images of women of color in court proceedings and implicitly differentiated them from white women. Two days after Christmas in 1800, John and Harriett Mitchell, a free couple of African descent, "falsely, fraudently [sic], and deceitfully and by false arts" procured nearly $70 worth of Irish linen and other fine fabric from Edward Mortimer's dry goods store. Just two days later "a negro wench named Kate" flashed a forged note to obtain several items from John Robertson's store on Tradd Street. This shopkeeper claimed the appropriated merchandise totaled over $160. Court testimony alleged that the "free black," Harriett Mitchell, had colluded with a slave, Kate, in stealing fabric and clothing from city merchants.

The court indicted only Harriett in the "theft conspiracy" charge brought against both Harriett and her husband. The courts pointedly recorded Harriett's sex and race, precisely opposite customary practice in cases against white women, where judges conspicuously avoided addressing the troublesome issue of white female criminals. The undercurrent of this and similar court reports was that Harriett Mitchell and Kate were the right color for female criminals, they engaged in expected behavior, and were justly punished for their crimes. The tone of the court reports indicated that the women's conduct confirmed why black people were or should be slaves.[5]

Statute and case law also buttressed the front line of social control in Charleston: highly personalized daily relations between white people and people of color. The law created loopholes for "accidental" slave murder by mistresses and masters, thereby confirming slave owners' prerogative to "inflict . . . such punishment as may be necessary for the good government" of slaves. Under the 1740 black code, if a slave owner or hirer beat to death a slave woman or girl, that person would likely escape a "willful murder" charge and, instead, be fined for killing a slave "on a sudden heat or passion, or by undue correction." An 1841 amendment "to make the *unlawful* whipping or beating of a slave an indictable offence" maintained the crucial distinction between the mistress/master's "lawful" beating and the "unlawful" whipping of any slave "not under his or her charge." Clearly, slave women as well as men fell subject to a law that, while not willfully malicious, nevertheless jealously guarded the sovereignty of all white slave owners, particularly those of the master class. "Whatever may be the technical language of the law [of slavery]," intoned the Reverend J. H. Thornwell at an 1850 church dedication ceremony, "the ideas of personal rights and personal responsibility pervade the whole [slave] system." Thornwell's characterization of the highly personalized owner–slave relationship both reflected and accentuated Charleston's customary practices, a personalism that packed the double-edged potential to protect or injure slave women.[6]

Carolina's "Negro Law" reached beyond the governance of slaves and free people of color and even extended beyond the relationship between owners and slaves. The black code constituted a central tenet of women's places in Charleston society. It reinforced the alleged inferiority of all people of African descent, rationalized their subjugation, underscored the dominion of all slave owners, emphasized white people's superiority, and reiterated the contradictory status of slaves as both people and property. However, in so doing, the black code also celebrated the patriarch's dominion and his paternal duty to protect his inferiors, including slaves, women, and children. Negro Law shielded slave women from unjust punishment as a byproduct of the courts' determination to safeguard slave owners' property rights. In 1831 an unnamed slave woman was beaten cruelly by a white man who had hired her for a term of twelve months from her owner, Isaac Helton. After the beating, this woman fled and returned to Isaac. He, in turn, brought action against the woman's abuser, and a jury found in his favor. The assailant endeavored to avoid paying a court-imposed fine by claiming an owner could not maintain trespass on behalf of his slave.

The appeals court disagreed, ruling that a slave owner "reserves a right in his property," and if "it is injured by any immediate, and forcible act, destroying or materially injuring the thing itself, trespass may be sustained." Tempering his rhetoric of property, the judge also reiterated that slaves, although deprived of "all personal rights" by law, nonetheless "[were] moral agents, subject to the same feelings; and [had] a right to protection from abuse as other human beings." This slave woman had already suffered extreme abuse. Only after the fact did she gain protection as a side-effect of the court's affirmation of fundamental legal principles at issue in this case, which turned on property rights, the integrity of the hiring contract, and the right of a master to maintain legal action if his slave's injury resulted in a loss of labor.[7]

In Charleston the whip distinguished white women from black and brown women, and statute and case law effectively defined women of African descent (slave and free) as something less than "true" (white) women. Although slave law, when enforced, controlled individual dominion and tried to prevent wanton cruelty—cutting out tongues, putting out eyes, castrating, or "cruelly" scalding, burning, or depriving a person of limbs—municipal and state laws upheld corporal punishment throughout the antebellum era. Whipping served as a common punishment throughout the colonial and early national eras. Before the 1820s, statutory law delineated offenses punishable by whipping, regardless of the offender, so men and women of all colors were subject to public floggings. The lash remained gender- and colorblind during this period. However, during the third decade of the nineteenth century, whipping turned increasingly race-conscious. By 1825 case law had specifically exempted white women from corporal punishment (and imprisonment) for crimes short of murder. State law mandated that women of African descent were the only females subject to whipping and frequent incarcerations.[8]

Petitions and legislation during two decades preceding the Civil War concerning corporal punishment and, specifically, whipping, reified this distinction between true women and women of color. An 1858 act amending previous laws regulating trade with slaves specified that "any free negro, or free person of color" (white people were excluded) who gave or sold liquor to a slave "without permit from the owner" shall "be whipped not more than fifty lashes." Even when heightened fears of slave insurrection reigned and (returning to colonial custom) white men once again fell subject to the whip if they colluded with slaves, the law expressly exempted women of European descent from corporal punishment. In late 1857, Carolina legislators decreed that "any person . . . not being a white female shall," after the first offense, "be whipped not exceeding thirty-nine lashes."[9]

The whip was no mere symbol or idle threat. Charleston slave women, as well as men, endured brutal beatings. Some judges reluctantly yielded to and others embraced the periodic, strident demands of "sundry inhabitants" of the low country to protect the "practical necessity" of owners' total discretion in slave punishment. As late as 1854, a Charleston petition bespoke continued violence against enslaved women and men and the sensitivity of some low-country residents to escalating criticism by northern abolitionists. The appeal recommended passage of laws to curtail "the unlawful beating and stabbing and otherwise maiming of slaves," which practice was "increasing and becoming a very serious evil; to the injury of our property and . . . revolting to human nature." From at least the late eighteenth century until the mid-nineteenth century, slave women (and free women of color) remained caught between the conflicting drives of most slave owners to protect their property and of the ruling class to nurture its self-perception as benevolent caretakers while dominating southern slave society.[10]

In the last two decades before the Civil War, slave women's vulnerability increased as state courts further empowered increasingly defensive slave owners by turning customary practice into law. The codification of "insolence" as a legal offense in 1847 manifested this trend. It also revealed another means by which Carolina law distinguished slave women from all other Charleston women. A ubiquitous transgression in slave society, insolence routinely triggered mistresses, masters, and miscellaneous bystanders to whip slaves throughout the eighteenth and nineteenth centuries. But in 1847, a Mrs. Crook demanded the arrest of her slave for allegedly addressing her with "insolent language and behavior." At trial, defense counsel argued futilely that "there [was] no such offence in the whole of the slave code as 'insolent language and action'" and, therefore, the slave "was not bound by the law of the land to answer" these charges before the court. The appeals court annihilated this argument by decreeing "any conduct of a slave inconsistent with due subordination contravene[d] the purpose" of the slave code. Lest there be any confusion, the court further specified that Carolina's black code "contemplated . . . the subordination of the servile class to every free white person" in order to "enforce the stern policy which the relation of master and slave necessarily require[d]." After this precedent-setting decision, "insolence" became an offense for which slaves might legally—as well as customarily—be tried and punished. In this case, one mortified and indignant slave-owning woman served as the vehicle by which custom hardened into law, and the law further distinguished slave women from all other "insolent" Charleston women.[11]

South Carolina statute and case law trod a fine line between enforcing paternalistic care (characterized by an idealized close, fatherly concern for and control of all underlings) and safeguarding the brute white supremacy of patriarchal power. Fragile protective shields for slave women often failed, especially when protection conflicted with profits. In particular, slave women found themselves and their family members caught amid property disputes. Court rhetoric emerging from these feuds starkly enumerated differences between distinct categories of women, and case law upheld the distinction. In an 1809 ruling on a contested estate comprising slave children born after the intestate's death, a presiding judge opined that state law declared "the brood, or offspring, of tame and domestic animals . . . shall follow the condition of the mother." The identical principle applied to slave children, he said, "because as objects of property, they [stood] on the same footing as other animals, which [were] assets to be administered." The court's decision was unremarkable for the principles of law it reaffirmed, but its language reveals that Carolina courtrooms functioned as conduits for leaching a ceaseless litany of social control into public discourse and behavior. Often this discourse of power manifested in demeaning notions of women. Indeed, negative images of certain types of women were essential to the maintenance of social manipulation, and slave women were situated at the bottom of Charleston's pyramid of power relations.[12]

Every property dispute accentuated the contrast between slave women and free women, particularly when the law upheld sales and bequests of female slaves. A free woman, whether white, black, or brown, could bequeath property to a daughter; a slave woman or daughter frequently *was* that property. Daphna "and her increase" were bequeathed to several white children by their mother, Sophia, when she died in 1841, and one Mr. Hood became the white children's guardian. Hood hired out Daphna for four years, but decided it was too "difficult to hire at any profit." Consequently, he sold her and the two children to a speculator in slaves. At public auction in Charleston, the trader subsequently hawked Daphna and her infant together, but peddled Daphna's older daughter separately. Friends and kin of the deceased owner, Sophia, attended the slave auction, protested the breakup of this slave family, and subsequently contested Daphna's sale by a "guardian [who] had no legal authority to sell" the slaves. Resolute as he surveyed the disturbed crowd, guardian Hood defended his actions, and those of the slave trader, averring, "he must sell so as to git the most." Following this public confrontation, the bidding stalled. The crowd attempted to enforce what they considered customary practice: selling a mother with her children if they must be sold. In court, a judge reflected on the event, declaring he "[had] no doubt" that the public castigation of Hood and the slave speculator "contributed in some degree to chill the bidding and injure this sale." Ultimately, the court upheld both the legal principle that Hood and the slave trader could sell Daphna and her children and the actual sales. Nevertheless, Daphna and her baby sold for $350, less than Daphna's valuation alone, and the speculator pounded his gavel at $160 for the older daughter. Convention and law collided in this case, and a profit-motivated Mr. Hood won his Pyrrhic victory by selling Daphna and her children at a loss.[13]

Unlike slave women who sometimes received protection because they were valuable property, and unlike ladies of the master class who usually received protection from the law because of who they were, free women of color—including propertied women—often secured justice because of who they knew. Because of their skin color, free women of African descent were subject to the limitations, restrictions, and vulnerabilities of the black code, as well as the nefarious designs of disreputable residents. Free women were kidnapped. For nine years in the opening decade of the nineteenth century, a young Charleston woman known as Phebe was "detained . . . in the character of a slave" by one Bartholomew Clarke and his bride, the widow Mrs. Gibson. The Clarkes enslaved Phebe despite their knowledge that her mother was a free woman of color residing in Baltimore. Phebe's mother was free, therefore Phebe should have been free. Phebe finally escaped her unlawful enslavement by securing a white guardian who sued Bartholomew in January 1816. The court upheld Phebe's claim to freedom and ordered Bartholomew to pay her $400 in back wages and damages suffered under his "base attempt to consign to slavery, for life, this unfortunate being, whose very situation called loudly for the protection of every feeling and honest man."[14]

Free women of color were vulnerable in ways that slave women could empathize with and white women could not comprehend. The law alternately sheltered and sacrificed them. Although extremist proslavery orators—who advocated re-enslavement of South Carolina's free people of color—never attracted a wide audience until the 1850s, free women of African descent were subject to laws predisposed against them throughout the eighteenth and nineteenth centuries. First and foremost, state statute and case law assumed that all people of color were slaves, because the "presumption [of enslavement] . . . arises upon the color." Free women of color had to "assume the [burden] of proof" that they were not slaves, and they had to do so on a daily basis. In 1811 a former slave, named Susan, sued a white man, David Wells, for assault and battery. The court dismissed her action after another white man testified that he "heard she had been set free" but that he had only known Susan as a slave. The presiding judge ruled Susan "disqualified to sue" because the court lacked proof of her freedom. Her attacker escaped punishment and Susan was lucky to avoid re-enslavement. Precisely because of the peculiar vulnerability of free people of color, Susan's case was not unusual. For nearly thirty-five years beginning in 1809, "the old woman, Judah, and her family, had lived and passed as free." Nevertheless, at the end of September 1842, William Smith hired two men to seize Judah and her daughters, and for several nightmarish days it appeared that William's determination to enslave and carry them off to his Georgia holdings would triumph. Judah, Malinda, Tabitha, and Lizzy were lucky because a white neighbor heard of their plight, pursued the entourage, rescued the family, and filed suit on their behalf. One year later a South Carolina appeals court upheld a conviction for assault and battery against the women. Although Judah and her family ultimately regained their freedom, court records, contemporary accounts, and state statutes indicate that others—in numbers impossible to calculate—fell prey to unscrupulous, repeated attempts to tear the thin safety net of customary practice and municipal and state laws protecting the limited rights of enslaved and free women of color. Slave traders and greedy slave owners often found shelter under an act of 1800 that authorized "seizure and conversion of a slave illegally emancipated," so that any slave or newly arrived "free negro" might be "appropriated by another master."[15]

Case law reveals a pattern of capricious protection of the liberty and property of free women of color, in part because judges assessed the reputation and status of each woman's white advocates as much as the facts of her case. On this basis, the courts determined who was and was not worthy of protection. In 1831 Patience McKenzie Marshall, a woman of color, discovered the benefits to be derived from forging economic or social links with an influential white advocate. Patience's grandmother, free widow of color Martha Patience Morton, had subsisted on interest and dividend payments (derived from a bequest to her by one Joseph Morton) from 1823 until her death sometime before March 1831. The prominent white Charleston merchant, Adam Tunno, had served as Mr. Morton's trustee and, in this capacity, administered Martha's investment income. In the interim, Martha's granddaughter and heir, Patience McKenzie Marshall, had relocated to Philadelphia where she resided with her young children at the time of her grandmother's death. Patience could not return to Charleston to claim her inheritance, as a series of South Carolina laws prohibited free people of color from entering the state upon pain of enslavement. At Patience's request, Adam Tunno petitioned a Charleston court to transfer the trust fund to a Philadelphia trustee. After some quibbling over court jurisdiction —an overt attempt by at least one judge to stall the transaction—the court acknowledged Patience's right to the trust. Over one decade later, a subsequent court decision reiterated that "free negroes have all the rights *of property and protection,* which white persons possess[ed]." Judges enforced this legislative safety net at their pleasure and discretion. It is also significant that this same judicial ruling tempered its protection of people of color: "they cannot with force, repel force . . . by a white man and less provocation might excuse a white man in an assault and battery upon a free negro, than . . . in the case of [that upon] a white person."[16]

Poor women were not shielded by male champions as were ladies of the master class and some women of the free brown elite. Unlike slave women, free but destitute black, brown, and white women had no owners to protect them. Impoverished free women of all colors shared the reality that they constituted easy targets in this "verminous, stinking, overcrowded . . . brutal and crime-prone seaport." In 1788 a city newspaper responded to street violence by advising people to "be on your guard, and carry with you a heavy loaded whip, and a well charged faithful pistol." During eight decades between the American Revolution and the Civil War, periodic economic downturns, disparity between rich and poor, and the constant presence of privateers and sailors fueled unlawful activity in the city. Moreover, notwithstanding its reputation for gaiety and hospitality, this was a city "composed of two classes, which entertain[ed] a mortal dread of each other." Poor people were vulnerable because they resided in the same areas where burglars, robbers, pickpockets, drunken sailors, and assailants prowled. They were daily accessible to criminals. The social space they inhabited, their economic status, and their sex particularly imperiled destitute women. An unnamed white woman traversed Lynche's Lane one Saturday evening in early March 1788. Three sailors attacked, stripped, and raped her, then melted into Charleston's dark alleys and streets to escape retribution. Seven months later a pauper named Mary Buffin was beaten to death in the city almshouse. Her murderers also eluded the law. Municipal regulations and state laws did not effectively protect the city's impoverished women, regardless of their color. Many criminal acts, like this sexual assault and the murder, never found their way into the courts.[17]

Some poor women responded to their disadvantaged economic status and physical vulnerability by turning to crime. The city's indigent women comprised thieves, assailants, and murderesses of all colors; women perpetrated crimes as well as falling victim to criminal activities. In 1788, the same year that pauper Mary Buffin was killed, one resident complained that destitute "gangs of men and women lived like packs of wolves" in the city. Compounding this riotous atmosphere, during the early years of the Republic, frustrated and angry men who had lost most of their real and personal property during the American Revolution also engaged in mob violence. "We may talk what we please of liberty," lamented one anonymous citizen, "but tell me what kind of liberty is that [when people are] debarred of an evening retreat, merely from an apprehension of not returning safe home." The complaint was no exaggeration. Late-eighteenth-century visitors to Charleston observed bloody fights on the wharves as well as genteel teas in elegant parlors; they encountered not only exquisitely attired ladies and gentlemen but also grimy, noisome beggars and thugs. Many of the latter were women, and public discourse and court reports in the early republic reveal how women criminals, especially white women, incited judges to construct gender and race while rendering their legal verdicts.[18]

White women criminals particularly threatened society because their behavior diverged wildly from the ideal southern lady. Their actions repudiated the social order of urban slave society. In 1794 Cynthia Simmons, a white woman, conspired with her (white) lover and a male slave to murder her husband. The following year, another white woman, a Miss Arden, killed a Spanish seaman "by stabbing [him] in the throat and breast with a pair of scissors," while her alleged male accomplice assaulted the victim with a stick. When these two cases came to trial, court reports reveal the judges' discomfiture with the social dissonance these women created. They were neither proper ladies who thrived under the protective wings of their fathers and husbands, nor were they chaste, dutiful exemplars of conjugal propriety. In sum, the women behaved more like "conniving negroes." They challenged fundamental assumptions about gender and race that undergirded slave society. In both cases, state courts tried and convicted "the prisoner[s]" for murder, but the presiding judges circumvented the inconvenient fact of the women's sex and race by refusing to voice their names. This atypical procedure constituted their method of evading the vexing issue of deviant white women. Cynthia Simmons's counsel also tried, in vain, to divert attention away from Cynthia and her lover, Laurence Kitchen, by focusing on the role of the male slave in this murder. The attorney argued on a technicality inherent in South Carolina's separate "negro court" system. He claimed that the (white) court should have recited the full conviction (for the murder of Mr. Simmons) in a "negro court," and the prosecution's failure to follow this legal procedure rendered it impossible for his clients to controvert the guilt of this slave, and thus, to defend themselves as accessories to the murder. In the alternative, he continued, the court must throw out the indictments of Cynthia and Laurence because the principal (Cynthia's male slave) was a slave, and slaves are "personal chattels, and not persons having any civil or political rights attached to them, except as property belonging to others." A slave, like a cow or a horse, could not be held accountable for murder, he argued. It followed, he persisted doggedly, that the rule of the law dictated, "there could be no accessory to a murder perpetrated by a slave."[19]

Employing the opposite tactic, Miss Arden, the woman on trial in a 1795 murder case, highlighted her sex (precisely what the court wished to avoid) when she pleaded her belly, or claimed she was pregnant. State law forbade hanging a pregnant woman, so her strategy turned on both statute law and the outside chance that she might solicit paternalistic concern given her alleged delicate condition. Examination by twelve matrons belied Arden's claim, and the court sentenced the defendant to death for murder. Her accomplice was convicted of the lesser charge of manslaughter. The unwillingness of the judges in both cases to name the two women in court documents had nothing to do with a desire to protect their identities. Eighteenth- and nineteenth-century court reports routinely referred to women plaintiffs and defendants by name in property or domestic disputes. Flummoxed by these blatant violations of woman's role and womanly behavior, the courts set out to destroy the alleged murderesses, first by declining to identify them (except in the case report heading, which demanded at least a family name) and then by executing them.[20]

Nearly a quarter-century after these 1794 and 1795 murder cases, state courts remained constant in avoiding reference to the sex and race of white female criminals. In 1820, however, witnesses and a cadre of fashionable Charleston ladies foiled this judicial strategy in the sensational murder trial of John and Lavinia Fisher. As previously mentioned in the introduction, this white perpetrator wreaked havoc by her murderous designs, sparking public debate that turned on the entwined social constructions of gender and race. Ignoring the judge's aversion to remarks about the defendant's sex, alleged survivors of Lavinia's gang drew on the woman-as-temptress caricature when they testified in court about alleged homicides committed at the Six Mile House, a common stopover of wagoners lumbering in from the backcountry to trade in Charleston. The court condemned both Lavinia and her husband to death by hanging. This startling case reached its denouement during Race Week festivities of the high social season, so most of the state's wealthiest families were in Charleston at the time. Several of those elite ladies petitioned the governor unsuccessfully for Lavinia's pardon. They shared nothing in common with her except skin color, but the proposed punishment would obliterate one of the crucial social boundaries that distinguished all white women. The governor and presiding judge were intent on enforcing laws against highway robbery and murder to safeguard the city's trade routes and protect the region's mercantile economy. Nevertheless, the court also aimed to uphold the image of white women as congenial southern ladies. At trial and sentencing, the judge achieved these conflicting goals by avoiding all mention of Lavinia's race and sex.[21]

When confronted by white assailants, thieves, and unwed mothers, magistrates capitalized on courtroom opportunities to rationalize the existence of these out-of-place females. They consistently employed two principal strategies. The first was demonstrated by the judges presiding in the three murder trials discussed: they refused to discuss or record the sex and race of white female defendants. Although defense attorneys, witnesses, and some defendants frustrated this plan, judges, in essence, simply dismissed white women felons and scofflaws as anomalies. A second approach took the form of aggressive gender and race reconstruction: by deploying racist characterizations and negative class and sexual stereotypes—and selectively ignoring or justifying crimes perpetrated against women of the laboring classes—state courts metaphorically blackened white women and exploited their behavior to reaffirm the social order.

Unlike slave women, free mothers who bore children outside of marriage suffered double condemnation as degraded women and criminals who threatened to drain the city's economic resources. From 1703 to 1795, the law classed all unmarried free mothers as criminals, albeit not violent felons as were Charleston's murderesses and female assailants. South Carolina's 1703 bastardy law derived from English common law, the dual impetus of which was to control sexual behavior or morality and to avoid the financial burden of unwanted or unsupported children. This law criminalized all free women who gave birth to a child outside of marriage. Justices of the peace issued warrants to arrest unmarried mothers and coerced them into naming the fathers. The practice was common in the colonial years throughout mainland North America as in England, but unlike in the northern states, this convention persisted throughout the nineteenth century in South Carolina. By law, a pregnant unmarried woman was imprisoned if she could not pay a "surety," the goal of which was to compel her appearance at the next General Sessions Court. This provision intended publicly to identify the father, to fine him, and to order the reputed father to pay weekly sums to the commissioners of the poor—not to the mother—thus defraying public expenses for the child's maintenance. Nonetheless, in arresting, fining, and indicting unmarried free mothers, the bastardy law treated them as criminals and attempted to constrain women's sexual behavior. Moreover, if an unmarried mother cohabited with the father of her child, which relieved the community of financial burdens, local officials still fined her monthly until she married.[22]

In a fundamental way, unmarried white mothers and prostitutes of color were two sides of the same coin: the former were anathema to slave society and the latter were integral to it. In 1795 Carolina lawmakers codified these diametric women's realities. From 1703 to 1795, the state bastardy law had stigmatized all of Charleston's free women, whether of European or African descent. A crucial reality united this disparate group of women: their children were born free and, as a consequence, did not augment any slave owner's personal property holdings as did the offspring of slave women. In direct contrast, state legislators effectively decreed bastardy as the norm for slave women by not allowing slaves to contract marriage. But in 1795, South Carolina legislators made explicit their sexual dichotomy of white women and women of color by amending state bastardy law. In that year for the first time, the criminal code specified that "if any *white* woman be delivered of a bastard child," she was subject to prosecution under the bastardy law. With one phrase, lawmakers changed the status of free women of color. In effect, the amendment legislated antithetical white and black standards of sexual behavior for women. And, by openly defining bastardy as exclusively a white woman's crime, the law also facilitated white men's sexual exploitation of black and brown women by delineating colored women's extramarital sex (and pregnancies) as normal and legal, unlike white women's. In addition, the 1795 amendment released fathers of children born to women of African descent, slave and free, from all mandatory financial responsibility. Lawmakers also appended an additional clause that sanctioned gifts, legacies, and devises (disposal of personal and real property, respectively, in a will) to bastard children. Cloaked as a benign protection of lawful wives and children (by restricting gift amounts), this section of the bastardy law partially protected illegitimate offspring of European and African descent by legalizing the customary practice of bequeathing money and property to them. In practice, the provision codified white men's sexual dominion—including adultery—over all women in their households, white, brown, and black, free and slave.[23]

Assaults dominated South Carolina court dockets in the eighteenth and nineteenth centuries, and, unlike their black and brown counterparts, white women assailants muddled the social configurations of urban slave society. Charleston's working-class women of European descent (native Carolinians and immigrants) engaged in rowdy, violent behavior unbefitting ladies, and their actions stood in sharp relief against those of belles, benevolent ladies, and free women of the brown elite. In 1805 Catharine Parker "grossly assaulted" Madelaine Chatellon. Madelaine swore that Catharine tore her clothes, "violently beat, battered and bruised her." In June of the following year, Susannah Dupré "threatened the life of Jane Williams, and struck her with a brick bat." Later the same day, Jane enlisted the help of a Mrs. Hislop in retaliating. They entered Susannah's yard, "whipped her severely with a cowskin whip . . . beat her over the head with a brick bat," and then "threw a pitcher of scalding hot water on Susannah, burning her head and shoulders." This unruliness emerged from their urban street culture with its fluid boundaries between household and street. Violent neighborhood quarrels, replete with networks of cooperation and contention among women and men, persisted for days and weeks at a time. One September morning in 1806, Mary Appleton Grado assaulted Thomas P. Dillon, so later the same day, Elizabeth and John Dillon, assisted by Catherine and Michael Doyle, "struck several violent blows" on Mary. On the first day of April two years later, Christiana Mattuce (or Matoushe) assaulted three different women, Betsey Baxter, Charlotte Saunders, and Mary Wells. Just the day before, Jinah Mattuce had "grossly assaulted, abused and beat" one of Christiana's victims, Mary Wells. And, in 1813, another Charlestonian, Elizabeth Hart, allegedly struck Susan Salts repeatedly, and consummated the attack by biting

Susan's hand.[24] These incidences reveal a pattern of violent physical behavior among white women of the laboring classes that continued throughout the nineteenth century. When they landed in court, these rowdy females confronted chancellors with the realization that numerous white Charleston women (not just three anomalous murderesses) diverged from the congenial ideal of belle, wife, and mother.[25]

Several altercations indicate that ethnic and religious tensions motivated some of the city's warring women. In the nineteenth century, an increasing number of the city's Jewish people hailed from Eastern Europe and, unlike earlier immigrants, many of these Jews spoke German or Yiddish rather than English. This changing composition of the Jewish population triggered elevated enmity, just as Charleston's Irish immigrants (who also augmented the population beginning in the 1820s) spawned antagonism. In spring 1818, Rebecca Solomons allegedly attacked and grievously wounded Nancy McDowall by throwing "brickbats at her in her own yard." Rebecca justified her volley of hazardous debris, claiming that Nancy had thrown "a dead fowl over the fence and hit her in the face." When Rebecca tossed the carcass back, Nancy continued the fowl fling and insulted Rebecca by calling her "a damned Jew bitch." Carolina judges pointedly distinguished Rebecca and Nancy's encounter—as well as the behavior of other aggressive women—from the expected comportment of genteel ladies. However, they did so without naming the rowdy women in question.[26]

In these assault cases involving white, female perpetrators, judges endeavored to ignore the assailants' sex and color, just as they tried to ignore the femaleness and white skin of Charleston's murderesses. Although eighteenth- and nineteenth-century court reports consistently identified slave women and free women of color by name, the reports did not follow this customary legal practice with white women. The invariable distinction was no mere accident or clerical error. A palpable and perturbed silence bespoke the courts' annoyance at white women who acted black. The only exceptions to this general practice occurred when something intensified Charlestonians' deeply rooted fears of slave insurrection, as in 1822. In that year, the abortive Denmark Vesey slave uprising triggered tighter restrictions on all people of color, and anyone who breached these constraints (regardless of color or sex) was publicly condemned and identified by name. Judicial reluctance to name white women offenders evaporated into a haze of heightened fear. When "Mrs. E. Van Roven," a sole trader, answered charges of "selling spirituous liquors to negroes in the night," the court unhesitatingly named and accused her of violating a city ordinance vital to the peace and safety of its citizens. After the summer hysteria of 1822, state courts brooked no violation of the myriad proscriptions of the black code. If white women (or men) disobeyed municipal and state laws, the courts named those individuals.[27]

These 1822 exceptions notwithstanding, the trenchant division between white female criminals (who were problematic in slave society) and female criminals of color (whose behavior justified slavery) manifested themselves in jurists' continued preference to avoid naming white female defendants. It was as if in refusing to name them the courts willed their disappearance or willed them to be black instead of white. But, as in the previous century, nineteenth-century trial attorneys and defendants periodically thwarted this common practice. Indeed, some trial participants emphasized the accused's sex, hoping that racial solidarity and concern for the status of white women would triumph. In 1846 when Mary and John Parkerson were indicted for assault and battery upon another city resident, Mary Jane Adams, John appealed the court's guilty verdict by drawing upon fundamental notions of white women's place. He claimed his wife could not be "joined" with him in the prosecution of this crime because Mary was a married woman and he was her "master." When confronted with Mary's *feme covert* status, the judge admitted that in some cases coercion was "to be presumed from [the husband's] presence." Nonetheless, he ruled that a woman's coverture might be suspended and "rebutted by testimony." Unwavering in his determination to punish asocial behavior and resolute in his desire to enforce womanly demeanor, the judge dismissed John's plea to exculpate Mary. The court also refused to voice Mary Parkerson's name, instead treating her as an appendage of her husband.[28]

To justify not protecting white women of the laboring classes in the same ways that they shielded elite ladies, judges demeaned victims (as well as perpetrators of assault) as a lower category of female. The topic of domestic abuse has already been discussed in chapters 4 and 5, but it may be useful to reiterate here the constancy with which members of the ruling elite deployed contrasting images of women to rationalize their own opportunities and privileges and to restrict those of other groups. This comparative dynamic emerges clearly in those cases (elaborated earlier) where husbands assaulted their wives yet escaped retribution when courts ruled a wife's conduct "impeachable" and, indeed, responsible for the husband's violence.[29]

Laws and customary practice governing the treatment of prostitutes also reveal the centrality (to maintaining the social structure) of women's interdependent images and roles. The color of a prostitute's skin, not her work in the sex trade, determined whether she was tolerated or castigated. Black and brown prostitutes induced few if any condemnatory remarks, while white prostitutes were alternately pitied as victims of predatory scoundrels, or ignored because they constituted living refutations of the white lady/black wench dichotomy at the heart of slave society.

A confluence of events rendered eighteenth- and nineteenth-century Charleston uniquely suited to the business of prostitution. The British occupation from 1780–1782 boosted the business of sex, as did the city's position as a principal lair of French privateers in the 1790s. From the American Revolution to the Civil War, this urban port annually hosted thousands of sailors who provided another steady clientele for prostitutes. Moreover, prostitution (like adultery) was not a crime in South Carolina. Unlike in northern port cities, occasional grievances about women of evil fame never congealed into an organized moral crusade to eradicate prostitution. The state's attitude toward the regulation of moral behavior was one of laissez-faire. Whereas Massachusetts persistently attempted to legislate moral standards and conduct, South Carolina did not ban fornication or adultery because legislators and judges abhorred any public intervention in private behavior. Courts preserved white men's sexual license and couched that dominion in the language of individual responsibility. Consequently, in their trifold roles as masters, husbands, and fathers, gentlemen perceived themselves the ultimate arbiters of their own and their dependents' behavior. They decreed sexual freedom for themselves and their sons, fidelity for their wives, virginity for their unmarried daughters, and sexual subjugation for their slave women and girls. State law upheld their actions.[30]

Women of African and mixed descent plied their trade in rooms above stores, boardinghouses, city taverns, and large bawdy houses, but city residents only periodically complained about "lewd and disorderly persons" cavorting at all hours of the night and day. Municipal officials generally took little action precisely because they perceived prostitution as customary practice, not a crime. However, what did incite anger, fear, and intervention were "improper assemblages of negroes." In late autumn 1795, city guardsmen investigated reports of "a negroe dance." Night watchmen surrounded the house, requested admittance, and were refused. Forced entry revealed a motley and inebriated gathering of prominent white chancellors, "a number of mulatto and black wenches and some negroe fellows." The presence of white men sanctioned the gathering (the "negroes" were supervised); nevertheless, several white men and people of color, both female and male, dove out of windows to escape capture or identification. Guardsmen escorted other occupants of the house to gaol, not for their sexual activity, but for loud and disruptive behavior. The prostitutes were not prosecuted. All were women of color and, in the eyes of city magistrates, they were fulfilling one of their expected roles. In this case, a passion to regulate the mobility and activities of enslaved and free people of color, driven by longstanding fears of slave insurrection, precipitated the raid, not municipal or state regulation of morals.[31]

This confrontation between city guardsmen and the "mixed assembly" speaks to the bifurcated characterization of women. A stark and functional antithesis—white lady, black wench—buttressed the tacit acceptance of prostitution. It justified white men's infidelity and adultery and their sexual exploitation of slave women. Customary practice and the conspicuous silence of the law conspired to reify these diametric images of women and confirm near-total sexual freedom for white men. When, in 1824, state legislators specified that calling a white woman a "whore" constituted an actionable offense, the law turned on the racial rather than moral implications of the term. Labeling a white woman a "whore" painted her brown or black. But white prostitutes muddied this racial dichotomy. City residents normally resorted to the familiar strategy of dismissing those women as anomalous embarrassments to their race. Revealing a second strategy, an 1835 newspaper story sensationalized a particular group of white prostitutes as unsuspecting victims. This report alleged that one of Charleston's madams detained and employed several white women against their will, an explanation that conveniently explained why white women had stepped out of their appropriate place and into a black woman's role.[32]

Analysis of women criminals and victims of crime unlocks the issue of womanhood in eighteenth- and nineteenth-century Charleston, where slavery created distinctive moral and legal codes around gender, where different categories of women encountered the law differently, and where many elite white men wielded the law to distinguish their ladies from other women, a chasm critical to fortifying the pyramidal social structure of slave society.

10 Illness and Death

Illness, debility, and death cast continual shadows on Charleston women's lives and simultaneously knit women together yet segregated them. Women shared the uniquely female experiences of pregnancy and childbirth, and all received distinct treatment from medical men because they were women. However, women also endured disease, medical treatment, and loss differently, and the dissimilarities turned on race, legal status, and wealth. As they encountered sickness and demise, women were united by their sex but divided along the same social fault lines that ordered all of life in slave society. Consequently, women's experiences of illness and death were concurrently entwined and interdependent yet discrete.

From the American Revolution until the Civil War, Charleston residents fell victim to the city's frequent epidemics (see table 8) and endured heroic treatments grounded in undeveloped science that debilitated or killed patients. These shared horrors notwithstanding, women confronted disease and death distinctly from men. Numerous pregnancies and the multiple hazards of childbearing wore out their bodies and minds. Women's experiences with illness also affected them uniquely because medical views paralleled social views of women as distinct creatures ruled by the womb. "The uterus is the 'sine qua non' of the female organization," intoned one young physician. Another concluded that woman's "elevated excitability" derived from her "more abundant and less firm [than men's] cellular system," which created less energy "in the capillary circulation," explaining "the blush . . . that sacred emblem of virtue, innocence, and modesty." As medical men pondered "the Peculiarities of the Female," they disputed the enigmatic physiology of conception, and drafted dissertations on myriad female problems. These notions precipitated unique remedies for women, such as more aggressive bleeding for certain maladies.[1]

But Charleston doctors also theorized that people of African descent constituted a different order of being, and required distinctive treatments. The experiences of pregnant, ailing, or injured women of color were filtered through the twice-distorted lens of professional medical men. Regardless of their common experiences—"the shadow of maternity," frequent miscarriages and high child mortality, medical assumptions regarding woman—women encountered the unsavory details of illness and death differently depending on who they were and who they were not. Slave women operated under a triple bind, because their sex, race, and condition predisposed antebellum physicians toward particular diagnoses and treatments. Unlike their mistresses, pregnant and parturient slaves were perceived as coarse creatures that recovered quickly and required little special care. While white skin and wealth did not eradicate death's routine visits and attendant anguish, money and privilege safeguarded women of the master class from the putrid cells of the Poor House hospital and its maniac ward, where poor women languished. The treatment of one woman hinged on an implicit (and sometimes explicit) contrast to the handling of another woman. In addition, as medical men attempted to professionalize their craft, two results emerged: female healers (particularly slave practitioners) became further marginalized, and the appropriateness of various treatment options ("scientific" versus traditional techniques) further distinguished separate groups of women. Illness and death ordered women's tightly braided and mutually dependent lives.[2]

Sickness loomed large in women's lives partly because of where they lived. Mainland North America's southern colonies had quickly earned reputations as "sickly Provinces." Travelers deemed South Carolina notorious in this regard, and a physician once described the state as paradise in the spring, but "in the summer a hell, and in the Autumn a hospital." Charleston, in particular, never escaped its fame as one of America's deadliest port cities until late in the nineteenth century. Geography and climate were responsible for coastal Carolina's reputation for poor health. Insect vectors thrived in the low country's semitropical climate and its low-lying swamps and marshes. Antebellum scientists and medical professionals had not yet connected malaria, yellow fever, and typhoid fever to insect carriers (whose eggs never died as they did in northern climes), but all Carolinians associated fevers and "agues" with hot, humid weather, as well as stagnant bodies of water, and the exotic, hanging tree moss that thrived in semitropical terrain. These conditions created "miasmas," which, residents explained, rose from the ground carrying disease and death. Moreover, the port city functioned as an entry point for fevers and other contagions not homegrown.[3]

Charleston residents contended with poor sanitation as well as insect-borne diseases. Long, sweltering summers foiled attempts to preserve food, and high humidity and heat aggravated sanitary problems caused by inadequate removal of human waste and the byproducts of butcher pens. In 1798 citizens complained of the "noxious effluvia of Hides, Horns, and Ears" dumped in city docks and elsewhere, "where they become putrid and produce pestilential diseases." Such grievances about the ill effects produced by floating offal within city limits continued well into the 1830s. The city's low elevation and its network of creeks and marshes, with consequent standing pools, created additional problems. Attempts to remedy the problem of stagnant water by constructing tidal drains failed. The drains ran under Charleston's streets and relied on rainwater to flush them clean. Regular backups produced additional brackish ponds. Exacerbating this health problem, the subterranean vaults of city privies periodically overflowed into the streets, discharged into city drains, and contaminated ground water and the shallow (drinking water) wells of urban compounds. Not until the 1850s did city residents begin constructing cisterns to collect and store rainwater to replace their vulnerable wells. Contributing to this lethal brew of contaminants, numerous city cemeteries were constructed on low, marshy land, creating a situation in which, as one disgusted resident commented in 1838, Charleston residents drank a cocktail of "not only soluble filth, and excretion of men and animals, but the very mortal remains of [their] citizens."[4]

Even the hardiest of Charleston residents battled a dreadful disease environment. During seventy-nine years between 1781 and 1860, no fewer than fifty-one epidemics swept through Charleston. Nearly 3,500 inhabitants died of yellow fever in twenty-seven outbreaks of that dreaded plague; this "stranger's fever," as it was called, visited the city every three years on average (see table 8). In addition, smallpox periodically killed Charlestonians throughout the eighteenth and nineteenth centuries, as did typhus, influenza, and scarlet fever. Cholera killed over 400 city residents in 1836, which was the second visitation of that disease in five years. Thousands more children and adults succumbed to whooping cough, dengue or "breakbone" fever, malaria, and the most consistent killer, consumption. None of these diseases was unique to Charleston, but the regularity with which they struck perpetuated the city's "sickly" image. Indeed, few residents escaped untouched from this chronic inventory of lethal maladies. This fact eclipsed contemporary efforts to compare Charleston's mortality rate favorably to that of northern cities.[5]

Charlestonians who battled illness in the eighteenth and nineteenth centuries faced a formidable and frequently impossible task given their treatment options. Revolution-era residents of all colors and ranks relied on mothers, grandmothers, and other female family members to administer lotions, syrups, salves, and various additional home remedies during illness or after accidents. Town apothecaries also armed them with advice and tinctures imported from England. In addition, slave women shared with other women of color and white mistresses their knowledge of indigenous, plant-based remedies and other alternative healing practices. Imprecision tended to characterize all these treatments. In particular, practitioners did little to ease excruciating pain or lessen complications accompanying operations and childbirth.[6]

The era of the American Revolution marked the professionalization of medicine, a process that began during the eighteenth century and proceeded slowly. Charlestonian Alexander Garden and other scientists corresponded with European counterparts concerning their collections of medicinal plants and seeds. Early practitioners formed themselves into medical societies, and wealthy sons were sent to Leyden, Edinburgh, or Glasgow for academic training. Some returned home to practice and, eventually, to train other general practitioners of medicine. However, the Revolution curtailed imports of medicines, equipment, and advice books. In addition, Charleston was drained of physicians, as many loyalist doctors returned to England. The war also interrupted lines of communication and cooperation between medical men on both sides of the Atlantic.

As men professionalized the practice of medicine, they denigrated and displaced women practitioners and adopted invasive treatments such as bloodletting and purging, which, by the late eighteenth century and continuing into the

Table 8. Epidemics in Charleston, 1781–1860.

This list includes only the worst epidemics measured in terms of morbidity and mortality. Yellow fever actually struck Charleston at least twenty-five times between 1800 and 1860. During the thirty-seven years after 1821, it killed approximately 3,000 Charleston residents.

1781	typhus; smallpox
1785–1786	influenza
1787–1788	scarlet fever
1790	influenza
1792	yellow fever (four months/over 165 killed)
1794–1797	yellow fever
1799	yellow fever (summer/134–239 killed)[1]
1800	yellow fever
1800–1801	yellow fever (over 184 killed)
1802	yellow fever (96 killed); measles
1804	yellow fever (148 killed); hurricane flooded the city with several feet of water, mixing privy water and drinking water in shallow wells and cisterns.
1807	yellow fever (162 killed); influenza[2]
1809	yellow fever (64 killed); whooping cough (96 killed)
1810	conjunctivitis (in Orphan House)
1813	measles (in Orphan House)
1814	diphtheria
1815	influenza
1816–1817	yellow fever (272 killed, or 22 percent of total [1,249] deaths in 1817); influenza; smallpox
1819	yellow fever (176 killed)
1822	malaria
1824	yellow fever (three months/nearly 240 killed); whooping cough (Orphan House)
1828	typhoid fever; dengue ("breakbone") fever
1832	Asiatic cholera (introduced to New York from Europe; spread through Atlantic ports)
1834–1835	yellow fever; cholera
1836	Asiatic cholera (nearly 400 killed)[3]
1838	yellow fever (outbreak followed a fire that destroyed a large part of city)
1839	yellow fever
1840	yellow fever

Continued on the next page

Table 8. *Continued*

1843	yellow fever
1849	yellow fever (over 100 killed; thousands sick)
1852	yellow fever
1853	small pox
1854	yellow fever (over 600 killed; thousands sick; worst epidemic to date)
1856	yellow fever (nearly 250 killed)
1858	yellow fever (surpassed all previous records: 800 killed)

Notes:

1. Waring provides the conservative figure; a contemporary report estimated the higher death toll. Nearly 3 percent of all Charleston residents suffered from yellow fever during the 1799 epidemic, and over one quarter of them died (in excess of 46 percent if Shecut's higher figure of 239 deaths is used). Those deaths represented nearly 1 percent of the total city population. Waring, *A History of Medicine,* 130; J.L.E.W. Shecut, *An Essay on the Prevailing Situation or Yellow Fever of 1817* (Charleston, S.C.: Archibald E. Miller, 1817).

2. "September [1807] was, from sickness and death, the blackest month ever recorded in Charleston . . . at least one fourth of the inhabitants were affected with the influenza about the last of the month." Joseph Johnson, "An Oration Delivered Before the Medical Society of South Carolina, at their Anniversary Meeting, Dec. 24, 1807" (Charleston, S.C.: Marchant, Willington, and Co., 1808).

3. The overwhelming majority (85 percent) of those killed were people of color, among whom the death rate was 51 per 1,000.

Sources: Waring, *A History of Medicine;* Mills, *Statistics of South Carolina;* "Abstract of Mortality from Fevers in the City of Charleston, Each Year, a Period of Thirty-seven Years," *Report of . . . City Council . . . on Yellow Fever of 1858* (Charleston, S.C.: Walker, Evans, and Co., 1859), 47; Fraser, *Charleston.*

nineteenth century, were standard medical practice. Dr. Henry Rutledge Frost, a physician at the Shirras Dispensary for the poor, found that "the loss of as much as ten pounds of blood within twenty-four hours was not a bad treatment for certain disorders." These men also prescribed extraordinary amounts of laudanum (opium), medicinal alcohol, calomel (mercury), and rhubarb (a purgative). While myriad treatments were literally worse than the maladies, doctors also added to their arsenals new, propitious drugs like quinine as they became available. By 1830 new notions of hygiene and preventive medicine emerged from fresh knowledge of human physiology, much of the latter gleaned from an expanding interest in "morbid anatomy" and its concomitant, the practice of postmortem examinations.[7]

During this same period, Charleston physicians also pursued a specialized interest in the nature of "negro physiology." They studied alleged connections between skin color, ancestry, and the nature of species-specific diseases. This specialized subfield constituted a pseudoscientific justification of racial slavery. Women of color, slave and free, felt the effects of these theories when they fell ill and required medical care.[8]

Notwithstanding these new medical treatments—and often because of them—Charlestonians continued to suffer and die from diseases like tuberculosis, yellow fever, cancers, and cardiac problems, and women continued to suffer and die giving birth to their children. In this regard, Charleston fared no differently than other cities during the nineteenth century. In addition, mothers lost their infants and toddlers to gastrointestinal afflictions, tetanus, and fevers. In 1807 a city physician reported that "the proportion of deaths among children is [a] distressing one fifth, and in some years, one fourth of all that are born die under five years of age." Infant mortality remained high throughout the nineteenth century. As a result, if women survived childbirth, they became well acquainted with illness, debility, death, and grief.[9]

White skin, money, and lineage set master-class ladies apart from all other Charleston women, but illness and death were blind to lofty social positions. These unwelcome guests visited so frequently in the city's wealthiest homes that girls and women of the master class wove into their life's fabric a culture of illness and death. It was not a morbidly pessimistic perspective on life, but rather their adaptation to the relentless hammering of debility and death among loved ones. Women and girls constantly wrote about their own health problems and expressed undeviating concern for the well-being of their children, their husbands, other family members, friends, and acquaintances. Occasionally they also discussed illnesses and infirmities of their slave women as well as the city's poor free women. In this respect, elite ladies identified and entwined their lives with the city's darker and poorer women.

Pregnancy and childbearing ranked high among the topics addressed in these dialogues, because eighteenth-century Americans had gained a near-legendary reputation for high fertility. Despite variations by region, race, and class, women at the beginning of the nineteenth century bore an average of seven live children. High rates of miscarriages and stillbirths ratcheted up the number of pregnancies to as many as twelve or fifteen. "A possible death sentence came with every pregnancy," and this specter hung over most Charleston women.[10]

The omnipresence of illness and death becomes clear in the interaction between women of the extended Izard family. Through intermarriage, the Izard, Manigault, Middleton, and Heyward families solidified their fortunes and status as the most successful dynasty in South Carolina (rivaled only by the Allston family). Unique in this high position within Charleston society, the Izard women were, nevertheless, representative of the master class and its distinctive women's culture of illness and death, which comprised interminable talk of pregnancy, miscarriage, birth complications, deaths, and a plethora of minor and major ailments. Alice Izard, her daughters, and her daughters-in-law wrote weekly to family members or friends and nearly all letters mentioned health. Their behavior constituted a coping mechanism; it was their way of reconciling perpetual illness and loss.[11]

The genesis of this culture of illness and death among elite women becomes apparent in even a brief overview of troubles and losses within the extended

Izard family. Alice De Lancey Izard bore fourteen children and buried eight of them. She also grieved with her daughters and sons when they interred their children. Her husband suffered a stroke, became an invalid, and predeceased her by twenty-eight years in 1804. Alice never remarried. Two of Alice's daughters, Margaret Izard Manigault and Nancy Izard Deas, together bore at least fourteen live children. Four of Margaret's ten and three of Nancy's four had died by 1819, and a fifth child of Margaret died two years before she did in 1824. Margaret married at seventeen, became a grandmother at thirty-nine, and buried at least one grandchild in addition to the three daughters and one son she lost. Alice's three daughters-in-law also miscarried or lost infants soon after their births, and one of those women left behind five young daughters when she died. This general trend of loss was not unique to Alice Izard and her female kin. Indeed, their saga is representative of Charleston's master-class women.[12]

Although childbearing weakened all the Izard women, and issues related to pregnancy and birth figured centrally in their lives, Alice Izard and her daughters also endured a variety of chronic and acute illnesses. A painful, chronic skin disease, Saint Anthony's fire, periodically plagued two of Alice's daughters, Nancy and Georgina. In 1814 Nancy (Izard) Deas lamented that there was no more "distressing disorder . . . in the degree [she has] had it." She told her sister that "nothing but our dear Mother's kind attention has enabled me to go thro' it." Just one year earlier, Nancy's sister-in-law, Emma Izard, had died after a relatively short "life of pain and suffering." Emma left behind five small girls and a father who had no idea how to care for them. Consequently, his mother (Alice Izard) raised the children. Alice Izard's daughter, Margaret Manigault, lost her infant, Edward, and her beloved husband, Gabriel, in 1809. At Gabriel's death, Margaret wrote, "my existence is changed, and I look beyond this world now for happiness." Over a period of six years beginning in 1816, Alice Izard gained three grandchildren, lost two, and agonized with Margaret again—and Margaret's daughter—when the latter buried her second child, who was less than one month old. The saga of death continued. In 1824 Alice Izard buried her eldest daughter, Margaret Manigault. Alice died eight years later at the age of eighty-seven.[13]

Women of the master class did not merely discuss and correspond about their ongoing tragedies, they also cultivated a stoic, religious resignation to suffering, and instilled this philosophy in their children. In July 1807, when Henry and Emma Izard's only son died, the boy's grandmother, Alice, lamented this loss and acknowledged that "the stroke is severe," but she adjured them to "submit to it" and wait for another "existence" when "the book of destiny" would open their eyes and they would "bless the hand who has inflicted this misery." Alice also entreated her son and daughter-in-law to "acquiesce . . . under this great affliction," because it was "the unerring will of our Heavenly Father." Frequent "indispositions" (a catchall phrase for suffering) in Alice's extended family provided her ample opportunity to reverberate to her children and grandchildren this theme of pious submissiveness. The women learned it particularly well. They shared their sufferings, confessed the depths of their disquiet and grief, looked to each other for strength, "pray[ed] to be enabled to submit to [heaven's] decrees without murmuring," and lauded one another for properly resigning themselves to a loved one's death.[14]

But when elite white women discussed and corresponded about their families' and friends' myriad ills, and when they entreated each other to "submit" to these afflictions, they were not whining. It was a fundamental expression and reinforcement of who they were. Master-class women submitted to unwelcome but frequent visitations of illness and death because "submission [was] the duty of women." Their vocal, visible, gracious submission distinguished them as Charleston ladies, which set them apart from all other women even as they endured similar tragedies.[15]

Unlike women of the master class, Charleston's slave women, free women of color, and white women of the laboring classes did not chronicle and celebrate chronic struggles with illness and death. Nevertheless, minor annoyances and painful, mortal maladies also ordered their lives and the lives of their families and friends. Despite this commonality, slave women and free working-class women of all colors experienced sickness and death differently from wealthy white women. And while their poverty produced shared experiences among all laboring women—slaves, free black and brown women, and white women—differences in skin color and social condition (slave or free) produced distinct possibilities, practices, and realities as they encountered illness and death.

Charleston's slave women bore more children than did the city's white women, and the death rate was higher among slaves than among white city residents. Between 60 and 70 percent of slave women were of childbearing age. In 1856 one child was born for every thirty-six slaves, compared to one birth in ninety-nine for free people. One in every forty-three slaves died, compared to one death for every 121 free persons (white people and people of color). Consequently, many confrontations with illness and death among the city's slaves derived from complications surrounding pregnancy and childbirth. The "shadow of maternity" was longer for slave women, a reality that distinguished them from their mistresses and other free women.[16]

Infant mortality as well as overall mortality was substantially higher among slaves (and free people of color) than among white people throughout the antebellum period, ranging from a low of seventeen per thousand (1831–1840) up to twenty-two deaths per thousand (1841–1848). Even more than their mistresses, slave women regularly suffered the loss of their children in miscarriages or soon after birth. "Rachel has lain in and has lost her Child," Alice Izard informed her husband in 1792, when her slave's newborn died, and they "also lost a little [slave] boy called Harry." The grief that regularly revisited Alice with her own and her daughters' losses had struck Rachel and a second, unnamed slave woman in the Izard household. Over a quarter-century later, another Charleston slave owner provided a similar snapshot of ongoing loss. "Black Emma had a child a few days ago," one resident reported to his mother, "but it is dead, so Aunt Anne tells me."[17]

Exacerbating the rigors of childbirth endured by all mothers, slaves were torn between caring for their babies and fulfilling the work demands of owners, an experience that poor laboring women of all colors could relate to, but that few master-class ladies could understand. In April 1816, "old Mary's granddaughter" (Mary was a longtime Izard slave) went to the Izard family's home "three or four times a day to nurse" Elizabeth Izard's newborn daughter. Elizabeth "was so ill" following her delivery that her mother-in-law, Alice Izard, convinced her not to nurse the baby. Because one of their slave women had also just given birth, the slave was ordered to nurse Elizabeth's baby as well as her own. This young slave mother resided in another household—the extended Izard family occupied several in the city at various times of the year—so she had to care for her own newborn, attend to her household chores, and walk over to Elizabeth Izard's home to nurse their baby several times daily. However, another of the Izard family's slaves, Eleanor, was also pregnant, and Alice and Elizabeth Izard planned to put Eleanor to work feeding Elizabeth's baby as soon as this slave delivered her child. Eleanor was overdue (and Elizabeth Izard had been early), so she had temporarily thwarted Alice's original plan. "We have Eleanor in view for a continuance," Alice Izard wrote, "but she goes as much beyond her time as her Mistress was within hers." Eleanor gave birth to "a stout boy" just two weeks later, and Alice lost no time putting her daughter-in-law's baby to Eleanor's breast. Elizabeth feared that the slave would not have enough milk for both babies, but Alice maintained that Eleanor was "a stout healthy Wench" and that she would do fine.[18]

Like many Charleston bondswomen, these two Izard slaves were subject to their owners' determination to utilize all of their slaves' resources. While pregnancy and birth carried manifold physical and emotional meanings for all women, when a slave gave birth, she and her owner knew that she could be exploited in yet another way, a fact unique to slave women. While Alice and Elizabeth Izard's resort to a slave wet nurse was not universal practice, it was common in Charleston. Margaret Bryant's mother suckled Margaret and her twin brother as well as a white infant. "Me and Marse Allard suck[ed] together," Margaret explained pragmatically, "Me and Marse Allard and my brudder Michael." City residents advertised their desire to hire a wet nurse if one of their own slaves could not perform the task. Slave owners achieved supervenient capital benefits from pregnant slaves: they acquired new property when the child was born and also maximized profits by hiring out the new mother to breast-feed white babies.[19]

In this consistent resort to "stout healthy wenches" as wet nurses, Alice Izard manifested a common perception about slave women among members of the master class and medical men at the time. They believed that slaves gave birth more easily than did white women and suffered fewer physical complications afterward; the alleged ease of a slave's pregnancy and birth defined both her and her delicate mistress. In 1833 John Berkely Grimball contrasted his wife's difficult delivery to the easy birth of a Grimball slave. Meta Morris Grimball "suffered extremely" during more than seventeen hours of labor, but "it was not more than [three] hours from the first alarm to the birth of the child" when "[their] washerwoman Patty gave birth to a male infant." John may have recorded mere fact, but he likely inscribed his own preconceived notions of how diametrically white women and slave women confronted childbirth. Women and men of the master class effectively inculcated this stereotype in other Charleston residents and acted upon their assumptions in requiring new slave mothers to return quickly to their normal tasks. Millie Barber echoed this convention when she claimed that a "slave woman [had] a baby one day, up and gwine 'round de next day, singin' at her work lak nothin' unusual had happened." Not all new slave mothers were "singin'" about it, but "dey deliver de baby 'bout eight in de mornin' an' twelve had to be back to work." There is little evidence to support the contention that slave women (or free women of color) gave birth more easily than white women, but the notion justified a shorter postpartum recovery period for slave women than for their wealthy mistresses. This view also provided fuel for those who rationalized slavery by equating slave women's easy childbirth with that of animals; painlessness equaled savagery.[20]

Such notions about the opposite constitutions of white women and women of African descent also gave rise to correspondingly distinct medical treatments for conditions other than pregnancy, and sometimes this dogma of separate black and white physiologies worked to a slave woman's advantage given the invasive medical procedures employed in the eighteenth and nineteenth centuries, like bleeding, purging, blistering, and the liberal use of opium and sulfuric acid. A common treatment for menstrual cramps involved bleeding and purging, as well as oral administration of camphor, opium, and belladonna. Doctors treated puerperal fever by bleeding women with lancets or leeches, blistering the women, inducing vomiting with calomel, and drugging them with opium. However, many of Charleston's medical men agreed with prominent southern physicians, who maintained that slaves and free people of color should not be bled or purged as aggressively as white people because their physiological inferiority required less heroic measures. The "essential differences" between slave women and white women saved slaves from some of the lethal treatments that their white mistresses endured.[21]

More frequently than women of the master class and free women of the brown elite, Charleston slave women escaped—or tried to avoid—lethal ministrations of white male physicians by relying on women healers. Slaves (and working-class free women of color) learned from their mothers the art of boiling plant roots, leaves, bark, fruit, and gum resins into teas, and mixing those ingredients into poultices. These healers assisted women in labor and treated a variety of maladies, including colic, teething problems, and rashes, as well as ulcers, digestive problems, and snakebites. According to Nellie Lloyd, "when anybody got sick," the older women "made hot teas from herbs dat dey got out of de woods." In addition, slave women brewed an abortifacient tea from the root of the cotton plant. Some white residents suspected and feared that slave women also concocted poison under the guise of mixing herbal remedies. Slaveholders did not wholly dismiss all black practitioners. South Carolina surgeon

Francis Peyre Porcher denounced slave herbalists and healers as "charlatans" who merely memorized "the name of the plant and disease which it is said to suit," but he studied and published the botanicals "extensively employed" among slaves. Although he purported to place these remedies in scientific context, his publication, nonetheless, acknowledged the efficacy of this healing tradition.[22]

Although "niggers from way down in South Carolina" bore a "reputation as conjurers," and some low-country slave women, like "Maum Katie," were known as conjurers or fortunetellers as well as healers, most of Charleston's women healers were like Lina Anne Pendergrass. When Lina was a child, her mother taught her how to "make teas to cure folks' colds and ailments." Lina also assisted in birthing and sick rooms. "My ma made me . . . fetch her water and towels and other things while she wait on de sick folks. Dat's de way I was broke into nussing [sic]." Charleston's wealthiest women turned to male doctors, who excluded women from the medical profession, but the city's women of African descent preferred their own female healers and herbalists who nurtured daughters in the healing arts.[23]

Slave healers rarely administered herbal remedies to the wealthy white women or brown elite women who owned them, but slave women routinely provided basic care to their ailing mistresses. Moreover, slaves exploited those illnesses to achieve their own goals. In 1816 a slave named Beck, along with three of her daughters, accompanied Alice Izard on several trips from Charleston to the pinelands of Carolina, as well as up to Pennsylvania and New York. When seventy-one-year-old Alice took sick, it was Beck who nursed her back to health. "Beck has behaved so well to me particularly during my illness," Alice told her daughter, "that I cannot bear the thoughts of any other attendant." Beck's dependable nursing paid off (likely as she had planned) because a grateful Alice bought Beck's husband, Cuffy, and also one of Beck's daughters. Beck had capitalized on Alice's illness to unite her family. Regardless of their motives, slave women were expected to care for their owners during Charleston's frequent periods of illness, while also caring for their own families. This double duty marked them as slave women and delineated their owners as ladies.[24]

While master-class ladies accommodated to relentless ill health and death through resignation and submission, slave women manipulated or feigned illness, wielding it as an effective tool of resistance. In 1824 when a Charleston slave owner tried to collect money from his two hired-out slaves, Emma and Sally claimed they had been too sick to "make their wages." The two women may have been ill. In the alternative, they may have pocketed their earnings or simply not worked; either way, their frustrated owner was left empty-handed. Slaves also exploited or fabricated illness to escape tasks they disliked, and to procure assignments they considered preferable. Near mid-century, a slave woman named Jane on one of the Manigault family's Argyle Island plantations tenaciously "represent[ed] herself as being in a feeble state of health," and so ill that "she [did] not know what a well day [was]." Ultimately Jane wore down her owner, because she was transferred from the rice fields to the big house. Thereafter, she occasionally labored as a nurse and house servant in one of the Manigualts' Charleston homes.[25]

Unlike master-class women who realized their full character as genteel ladies, in part, by embracing infirmity as the visitation of a higher power, slave women repudiated their identities as *chattel personal* by exploiting illness to sabotage their own sales. They shammed physical problems or emphasized real infirmities. In 1827 a slave named Violet announced to all bidders that whoever bought her would lose their money because she "had a sore throat [and] rheumatism." Just over ten years later, another slave woman similarly stalled the bidding by declaring that she was deformed and unable to attend to her duties about the house. On the auction block in 1847, Judy complained of a sore foot that she exhibited to the crowd while explaining she "was sometimes laid up for months." One young doctor at mid-nineteenth century advocated "more careful investigation" of slave ailments "than those of whites" because of this "prevailing disposition to practice deception." He detailed various "tests" by which slave owners and physicians could trick slaves into revealing their true, healthy state. A low-country attorney warned that "negroes, when about to be sold, sometimes disfigure[d] themselves when they [had] a particular object in view."[26]

When slave women fell ill, that illness carried multiple meanings for owners as well as for slaves. A sick slave inconvenienced the mistress because of her inability to perform daily tasks. In 1824 Charleston slave owner Anne Yates complained that her slave, Lavinia, was "frequently sick," that this seemed to be "always the case," and that when Lavinia was well, then "her husband was sick and [Lavinia] could do nothing but nurse him." Worried or grieving slave wives, husbands, and other kin also might slight their chores to gather round the bedside of a seriously ill or dying family member. In the final few weeks of her term, a pregnant slave could not work to full capacity. In 1817 one Charleston owner sold his "healthy, young" slave "of good character" because "she [was] in a state of pregnancy; and too clumsy to do the work of a large family." Slave illness and pregnancy represented a nuisance to owners as well as economic loss of varying degrees. In March 1820, a man viciously beat Mary Lloyd's slave, Chloe, for being "impertinent" to him and allegedly stealing "a fowl" from his yard. Chloe miscarried as a result of the beating and was bedridden for one month. Her owner successfully sued to recover the cost of lost work time in addition to the amount of Chloe's medical expenses. To Chloe, her injuries meant pain and a laborious recovery; to her mistress, the wounds meant lost profits and inconvenience.[27]

Affection as well as annoyance also animated relations between mistresses and particular slaves, so illness triggered emotional as well as fiscal concern. A slave named Statira became sick while traveling with her owner during the summer of 1805. "Could I have foreseen this melancholy event," the mistress lamented, "how gladly would I have left Statira among her friends in Carolina!" Statira's owner vowed she was "willing to pay anything for any advice or assistance" that might help the ailing slave. Statira recovered from her illness and eleven years later she was nursing her owner's daughter-in-law and four grand-children.[28]

Concern for a slave's health and annoyance at lost service were not mutually exclusive reactions among mistresses. Ill slaves evoked mixed emotions. Upon her return to one of the family's country homes in February 1802, Alice Izard was greeted by an ailing slave. "Our good old Elsey got out of her bed to come and see us. She dressed our dinner the first day, but has been confined ever since." Elsey's owner was sympathetic, but that forbearance was limited by El-sey's inability to work. Fifteen years later, another Izard slave found herself caught between family tragedy and her owner's expectations. Betty, one of the daughters of a favorite Izard slave named Beck, had been commanded to join her mistress in New Jersey, where she was visiting family. However, Betty wanted to remain in Charleston because her sister, Rosetta, was dying, so she defied her owner and delayed departure from Carolina. When Betty finally arrived in New Jersey, her mistress, Alice Izard, was "too angry with her to see or speak to her." Only later did Alice express her condolences at Rosetta's death and confess that she felt sorry for the "poor little girl [Betty]" and the grieving mother, Beck. Similarly, a wealthy Charleston mistress empathized with her recently wid-owed slave, but subsequently rued losing valuable property when the widow "wasted away without any symptom of disease." These battles with disease and death concurrently triggered reluctant acknowledgment from mistresses of their slaves' humanity and underscored one woman's status as property and an-other's as privileged property owner.[29]

Relationships between slaves and mistresses comprised intricate and tangled feelings of affection and disdain, cooperation and competition, pleasure and pain, and sometimes the mistress inflicted physical torment and injury on her slave. By law all women of color were singularly subject to the agony of whip-ping, but in practice few free black or brown women endured this particular torment. After 1825, white women enjoyed legal exemption from the lash, and so, unlike most free women of color (rich and poor) and all white women, the city's slave women suffered the distinctive pain of flogging and its debilitat-ing aftereffects. This distinction partly defined them as a social group. A "high-tempered . . . mulatta" washer, named Clory, who "didn't take foolishness from anybody . . . bodily [threw]" her owner out the door after this mistress found "fault with de clothes." Although the mistress did not actually wield the lash in this case, she ordered Clory's "brutal whippin.'" All other slaves in the house-hold were "made to watch," and one reported that it was "de worst I ebber [saw] a human bein' [get] . . . beatin." Although "dere wusn't a white spot on her body," and many thought "she wus goin' to die," Clory slowly recovered. While Clory's whipping was extreme (to match her offense), Charleston slave women routinely received beatings, if not from their owners, then at the Sugar House, a prison "for the punishment of minor [offenses] of negro slaves." Slaves of both sexes were tied to "a sort of crane" and "drawn up, while the feet [were] bound tight to a plank. The body [was] stretched out as much as possible, and thus the miserable creature" received her lashes. In 1816 a city visitor relocated from one boardinghouse to another to escape the "disagreeable sounds" emanating from the Sugar House. Charleston slaves also dreaded the treadmill, upon which they walked almost constantly for eight hours while guarded by a jailer armed with a cowhide lash. Once city officials installed a second treadmill, up to twenty-four slaves could pace simultaneously. With insidious efficiency, these treadmills operated mills that ground corn to feed the prisoners being punished on the treadmills. Whenever slave women were "uppity" or failed to complete their tasks satisfactorily, and certainly when they ran away (if their owners captured them), they were whipped, "every other week for a number of months." Likewise, if they were caught "with pencil an' paper, that was a major crime" and also provoked harsh corporal punishment. The unique pain derived from such retribution comprised a part of who and what slave women were, and who their mistresses (and other white women) were not.[30]

Debilitating disease and injury (whether inflicted by owners or not) endangered slave women in other ways as well as imposing physical discomfort. In Charleston, as in any slave society, a slave woman's value to the slave owner turned on her ability to perform required tasks; her identity as laborer largely determined her place in the city and differentiated her from the leisured lady. From an owner's perspective, illness fundamentally impaired the worker and, hence, undermined who and what that slave woman was. Thus, the master-class woman reinforced her identity as a fragile lady when she duly submitted to health problems, but the slave woman, when struck by disease, confronted an enemy that threatened (not confirmed) her position in Charleston's social order as well as endangering her physical well-being. Unlike white women and free women of color, slave women risked separation from their families if they became ill. In February 1837, a Charleston auctioneer declared one unnamed mother "valueless and offensive [because] she could not retain her water." However, the woman had two sons, aged four and five, and an auctioneer estimated that the boys might go for $600 on the block. He sold this ailing mother's sons away from her rather than jeopardizing a sale by keeping the family together. Just three years later, the owner of another slave, Hannah, sold her to a man in north Georgia. Although Hannah was "a good washer and ironer," and a skilled "house servant," her owner replaced her with "a younger woman some time before" because she "occasionally . . . had slight rheumatism in her arm and shoulder." Hannah's new owner subsequently contested the sale when doctors discovered that she "was seriously diseased in the ovaria and uterus." Hannah had inoperable cancer, which not only threatened her life, but also triggered her sale out-of-state and away from family and friends. Unlike their mistresses and other free women in the city, slave women were doubly vulnerable when they fell ill: sickness weakened their bodies and troubled their minds as it did to all people, but physical problems also endangered family ties and bonds of friendship precisely when those connections were so crucial.[31]

Even when slave women and their family members enjoyed perfect health, sickness still destroyed slave families. The death of slave owners frequently resulted in estate sales. In the years following the end of the American Revolution, many war widows sold slaves to pay off debts or to generate the cash necessary to begin a new life. Estate sales and auction announcements persisted as prominent fixtures in Charleston newspapers throughout the antebellum period. Just as illness habitually presaged death, death produced ripples of upheaval, reorganization, and slave sales. Regardless of who was ill—slave or mistress—illness sharply outlined their entwined social identities and personal experiences.[32]

Sick slave women were also vulnerable in an insidious way that Charleston ladies would never endure. Slaves feared landing in an infirmary affiliated with the city's medical schools. They dreaded the thought of becoming "interesting case[s] . . . for the benefit and instruction of . . . pupils." The Medical College of the State of South Carolina actively recruited black patients by exempting slave owners from physician charges; an owner had only to pay for the ill slave's food and nursing. In 1831 the medical school readily admitted that it sought and obtained "subjects . . . for every purpose" from the black population to continue "proper dissections . . . without offending any individuals."[33]

Medical students in Charleston were not just probing cadavers. From 1845 to 1849, one James Marion Sims experimented on at least a half-dozen slave women while trying to cure a common but painful and debilitating ailment called vesico-vaginal fistula. This condition—a break in the wall separating the bladder from the vagina—resulted from trauma during childbirth, and allowed urine to pass through the vagina rather than the urethra. The constant flow of urine produced "fetid odors, irritated skin, and frequent infections of the reproductive organs." Each woman endured up to thirty painful operations before Dr. Sims claimed to have cured the slaves and, by 1855, he also boasted improvement on the sutures used in correcting this condition. James tested his procedure on seven additional slaves, and later extolled "the indomitable courage of these long-suffering women" who enabled him to find a surgical solution to the intractable debility.[34]

By 1841 trustees of the medical college established a year-round hospital and candidly boasted that "the slave population of the city, and neighboring plantations, [was] capable of furnishing ample materials for clinical instruction." The school recruited new students by vaunting its ready supply of teaching "material," which provided an opportunity to view "all the common diseases of the climate" as well as a variety of "surgical diseases requiring operations for their relief" to which, school officials claimed, slaves were "peculiarly liable." In a similar vein, those announcing Charleston's new "negro hospital" in 1860 noted that this facility would provide ample "material" for study by those attending the nearby medical college. Individuals as well as institutions viewed slaves in this same light. In 1838 physician T. Stillman sought fifty "negroes" considered incurable. He advertised that he would pay "[t]he highest cash price" to owners "wishing to dispose of them."[35]

Neither women of the master class nor free women of the brown elite could fully comprehend, much less experience, slave women's terror of the city's clinics and hospitals, but Charleston's free, impoverished women of color as well as indigent white women shared this distrust of city infirmaries. Medical school advertisements did not proclaim it, but these poor women of all colors also constituted teaching fodder: the hospital of the Medical College of the State of South Carolina admitted poor white people as well as slaves and free people of African descent. The pain of these women was another woman's gain; like the doctor at mid-century who claimed success in surgically curing vesico-vaginal fistula, others also experimented on slave women (and poor white, black, and brown free women) in order to perfect procedures that later benefited women of the master class. Who they were determined the type and location of treatment they received, and that treatment, in turn, distinguished slave women and poor free women from Charleston ladies.[36]

The misery of destitute women contrasted starkly with the privileged lives of master-class women, even when those wealthy ladies fell ill and endured their own tragedies. The city's free and poor white, black, and brown women possessed few resources to draw on when they succumbed to illness. If Charleston's public institutions deemed them worthy, destitute white women secured assistance from that quarter. During the five years after Charleston Orphan House opened its doors in autumn 1790, approximately one hundred white women beseeched that institution's board of commissioners to admit their children. Often these mothers were ill or disabled, which exacerbated their poverty and inability to support themselves and their children. These impoverished supplicants represented only a fraction of the city's penniless white women, some of whom resided in the Poor House. Constructed in 1768, this facility mirrored the decrepit "inmates," and its wretched conditions rendered the Charleston Poor House a place of last resort. Throughout the antebellum period, an average of one hundred people inhabited the poor house at any given time. Although this institution's records provide only random information about the sex of inmates and out-relief recipients, data indicate that more than half of the inmates were men. Women dominated the out-relief rolls, avoiding this house of no return until extremity forced them in.[37]

The city's destitute women wound up shattered and crushed by their poverty, many of them ultimately succumbing to the illnesses that had driven them deeper into penury. This was partly because of their resort to prostitution, a sure avenue to disease. Too many languished, not only in the Poor House hospital but also in that hospital's "maniac department," an infamous unit that thrust women into a downward spiral from which few recovered. In 1795 state legislators authorized city commissioners of the poor to confine white "lunatics" in a special ward within the Poor House. Any white person "laboring under insanity or other mental malady [and] found wandering or strolling about the streets" was locked in this "maniac department." A quarter-century later, Charleston's city council declared that all "Insane Persons of Color," who were at large and creating a "public nuisance," would also be confined in the Poor House's maniac ward. If that person was a slave, her owner was responsible for all costs incurred. Until 1820 slaves hired to work at the Poor House had been the only people of color who crossed its threshold, but rising suspicions and fears of "unruly negroes" drove this new municipal policy. Thereafter, the "cell keeper for the insane" guarded "deranged" inmates of all colors in the specially "fitted up" lunatic department of the Charleston Poor House. Many city residents agreed with the mayor, who, in 1838, declared it "repugnant to [his] feelings" to house deranged colored people in "an institution whose benefits were specifically intended for destitute whites." But white Charlestonians also concurred that this policy was preferable to letting them "go at large at the imminent hazard of [them committing] murder, arson, or any other crime." Consequently, while physically ill poor women of color were refused even the most basic care at the Poor House hospital, their mentally ill counterparts shared with poor white women the dubious distinction of confinement in that hospital's lunatic department.[38]

Unlike other Poor House inmates, women outnumbered men in the maniac department of the Poor House hospital. Throughout the antebellum period, between twenty and forty mental patients could be found here at any given time, and visiting doctors made scanty efforts to treat these women. Neither resources nor interest inclined toward active care. Periodic economic depression and attendant reductions in state allocations to that institution aggravated dreadful living conditions. In 1832, the Poor House's commissioners reported that they could provide "neither security for the safety of the persons confined" in the lunatic department "nor comforts for their accommodation." This situation worsened over the next twenty years, as Poor House buildings fell into disrepair while the number of admissions climbed. And as early as 1832, the lunatic department was overflowing and in desperate need of repairs; by 1850, one doctor reported that most of the inmates suffered from scurvy. Four years later, a physician at the state asylum in Columbia complained that recent transfers from the Charleston Poor House arrived filthy and verminous. Such was the lot of poor women with real or alleged mental disorders. They languished under circumstances no elite lady would ever know, and worse than what most of the city's slave women endured.[39]

The laboring poor, unlike women of the master class, possessed few options if diagnosed with a "disorder in [the] head," as was Georgina Izard Smith in 1815. But this wealthy young woman did not land in the "maniac department" of the Poor House. Instead her mother journeyed with Georgina to Niagara Falls, elsewhere in New York, and to New Jersey in order to restore her health. Instead of taking a curative trip like Georgina Izard Smith's, a "Negro Wench" named Beck, the (white) sisters Angelica and Louisa Bunuel, as well as Mary Hanahan and Sarah Waters, and another slave named Agnes, were all quartered in the maniac department. Admitted in 1819 by her owner, Beck was rational and healthy enough to be "of great use to the Institution in washing the Clothes of the Maniacs." Her owner left her in the Poor House long after she was declared "well" to work off the debt he had incurred in admitting her.[40]

The case of Angelica and Louisa Bunuel hints at the terror some women may have experienced in this special section of the Poor House, where no Charleston lady ever ventured and where the sane and insane poor routinely intermingled. In 1832 the Poor House's commissioners declared Angelica a "confirmed lunatic," but they maintained that her previously "insane" sister, Louisa, had recovered. Nevertheless, the commissioners retained both women in the lunatic ward and subsequently transferred them to the state asylum in Columbia. This practice created a situation in which lucid women like Louisa were trapped and lived in fear of truly disturbed and violent inmates. In 1844 an attending doctor physically restrained Mary Hanahan, a "poor and nearly friendless young woman," because staff could not otherwise control her. Sarah Waters was similarly uncontrollable. Neighbors carried Sarah into the poor house after she collapsed, overcome by grief, when her husband abandoned her in 1850. Her depression turned violent as Sarah periodically "kick[ed] at the privates of men" in the maniac ward. After a thwarted suicide attempt, she developed the habit of smearing her feces on the walls. Commissioners intoned that Sarah "exhibited venereal propensities, throwing herself on a female lunatic who is similarly disposed." Living in this same ward was a perfectly sane woman named Agnes. Her owner rid himself of this unproductive slave by lodging her in the maniac department. Her only flaws were that she was badly disfigured and ran away frequently. Nevertheless, her owner claimed she "presented a public nuisance" and threatened citizens of Charleston because of her "uncontrollable fondness for the streets." Quartered in a ramshackle facility with no distinctions made for the severity and type of their symptoms, all women in the maniac department were subjected to violent attacks and "unearthly whoopings and halooings" from the more troubled residents. Mentally disturbed master-class ladies endured their own torments, but what distinguished them from these poor maniac ward inmates was that ladies did so in private or surrounded by loved ones rather than by shrieking fellow sufferers.[41]

Death visited the homes of the rich as well as the poor, but Charleston ladies also escaped demise in a dilapidated public institution. Women who staggered or were dragged in to the Poor House's hospital and its infamous lunatic department frequently did not depart under their own steam. In July 1820, a Poor House commissioner toured the hospital area and found twenty-nine patients in a room "so badly ventilated that [he] breathed with difficulty." Heat exacerbated the combined odors of sores, ulcers, scurvy, scrofula, syphilis, and the vomit of patients suffering from "mania à potu," the "brain disease of drunkards." Childbirth—a risky proposition under the best conditions—usually ended in death for Poor House inmates. City officials recommended establishing a maternity ward in the Poor House, but neither the city nor the state provided funds to implement this idea. Just five days before Christmas in 1850, Mrs. Fayan delivered her first child, a girl, in the Poor House hospital. She labored over eighteen hours and then slipped in and out of a coma for nine days. Emaciated, Mrs. Fayan had little milk for her infant, so nurses fed the baby sugar water. Mrs. Fayan and the child survived until January 4. Two of five other white patients on the ward with Mrs. Fayan when she gave birth died as well. One of them, a Mrs. Gough, was hastened along this path by treatments of strychnine and chloroform. The women who died in the Poor House were placed into coffins "before the eyes of all" and carted off to potter's field. And even in death, these white women entwined women's lives by reinforcing white Charlestonians' perceptions that women of African descent were more robust than the lowest white women.[42]

Increasingly after 1839, Irish and German immigrant women predominated among those who died within the walls of the city's Poor House. During the thirty years immediately preceding the Civil War, Charleston (and other coastal cities like Savannah, Mobile, and New Orleans) absorbed waves of immigrants from the North. In 1836 alone, over 32,500 passengers purchased one-way tickets to Charleston from New York; steerage passenger figures for 1845, 1849, and 1855 indicate a substantial southern flow of poor immigrants. Just before mid-century, nearly 13 percent of the white laboring population in Charleston comprised women, many of whom were recent arrivals. Once they arrived, poor white women, especially those with children to support, faced few paid work options aside from domestic service, piecework (on which they could not survive) or prostitution. Louise Tesky was widowed when her son was eight years old. She moved from one job to another, sinking further into poverty each year. Desperate, she placed her son in the Orphan House and began working as a cook in one of the city's boardinghouses for sailors. She likely prostituted herself to supplement meager wages. In 1845 Frances Rychbosch, a despairing widow with four children, sold her furniture and her clothes piecemeal trying to survive. Physically and mentally overwhelmed by unrelenting poverty, Frances became "deranged in mind and wholly incapable of affording her children the smallest assistance." In the same year, another widow "thrice within the last two months" teetered on "the borders of the grave through excessive labour striving to work for the bread of her children." She and others vainly struggled to support themselves and their children with needlework, for which they earned twenty-five or thirty cents per day.[43]

Charleston was not a place for destitute white women, immigrant or native, because it was a city built upon slave labor, not free labor, and it was dominated by affluent, frolicking members of the ruling class. Charleston was a city for elite ladies. It was they who could thrive in slave society. In glaring contrast, if immigrant women survived anguish, starvation, the deaths of their children, alcoholic husbands, and a dearth of jobs to secure a competency, they fell victim to the city's periodic epidemics. Although infectious diseases afflicted all residents, yellow fever hit these immigrants hard; over 100 died in 1849 and hundreds more in 1854, 1856, and 1858. Ladies fled Charleston when illness struck, but poor women had no money to run and no place to go. Roper Hospital, a paupers' clinic that opened in the 1850s, treated fever victims as well as the casualties of chronic poverty. In 1856, the commissioners of Charleston Poor House (now renamed the Alms House) convinced city councilmen to contract with Roper to relieve the Alms House of its responsibility to the "insane, the sick, and the vicious" poor. From that time until the end of the Civil War, poor women who were ill sought medical help at the new outpatient Roper Clinic, where they continued to receive inadequate medical treatment. A young Irish immigrant named Cathy Kenny washed clothes in the Orphan House by day and slept under houses and on the street at night. She developed a chronic (unspecified) health condition. Unable to afford proper medical care, she resorted to Roper. Cathy Kenny's homelessness and encounters with illness defined her as a certain kind of woman and, by pointed contrast, also highlighted how far her situation diverged from the experiences of the city's wealthiest ladies. Most women shared ongoing battles with debility and ill health, but it was the details of their struggles that simultaneously entwined them while distinguishing one type of woman from another.[44]

Cathy Kenny's plight also typifies how Charleston's poor white women cobbled together a meager and insufficient existence for themselves and their children from multiple sources, like the Poor House and Orphan House, the Shirras paupers' dispensary, and, in the 1850s, Roper Clinic and Hospital. Unlike poor women of color, white women could also resort to institutionalization at the city's two major public facilities (the Poor House and the Orphan House), but they avoided admittance whenever possible, preferring out-relief instead. In 1826 the city expended approximately $4,400 to provide outdoor relief to 163 adults and 192 children and to institutionalize 390 people. The out-relief rolls comprised mostly women and children.[45]

Destitute white women also beseeched private charitable organizations for assistance, as did women of color, and both turned to the Ladies Benevolent Society (LBS), founded in 1813. However keenly the LBS Visiting Committee's members encountered the chronic distress of Charleston's poor women of all colors, LBS ladies could not truly know the depth of that affliction. Poor women's pain, hunger, and illness were, thus, diminished to a quarterly recitation of numbers aided and dollars expended. The lives of the city's poorest women, inscribed in the pages of LBS meeting minutes, constituted a "dull record of the sad and stern realities of everyday life—a record of misery and want and woe, made doubly wretched by sickness and its attendant ills."[46]

Here was a symbiotic relationship: poor women needed basic necessities and rich women needed to be benevolent. Once validated by the elite LBS ladies as sick, impoverished, and worthy of Christian charity, women and children received periodic visits from two or three ladies of the master class, who ventured into the "abodes of wretchedness to relieve the sufferers within." Women of the LBS volunteered for Visiting Committee duty, which obligated them to visit the sick poor in one of the city's districts. They "carefully investigated" the "character and circumstances" of each person requesting aid, and "inquired . . . whether they [had] availed themselves of the bounty of the public institutions," such as churches or the Poor House. Once accepted by the LBS, a sick person received specified allotments of food and fuel and, if necessary, the society paid for nursing services. Only in extreme circumstances did the LBS pay for a physician; they expected patients to use the (dreaded) Poor House hospital, Shirras dispensary, or Roper Clinic. The Society did not limit its aid to women, but most of their "patients" were, in fact, destitute women. In a June 1825 meeting, the LBS determined to continue helping "old Mrs. Cowie," a "pitiable object" who "greatly suffered" from leprosy, whose "eyes [were] in a high state of inflammation, and her body a perfect skeleton." A white woman, Mrs. Cowie had "supported herself and two Children by the Labour of her own hands" in her younger days. Her offspring could not afford to repay Mrs. Cowie in kind, as they barely supported their own young families.[47]

Free women of color also relied on the LBS for food, fuel, and occasional nursing assistance. In their reports, LBS ladies distinguished between them and the white supplicants by recording only their given names, thus according them less respect. In this way, benevolent ladies linked all women's lives (theirs included) in the act of providing charity, but they positioned themselves above all other women and differentiated among poor women by color. In June 1825, three LBS Visiting Committee members called on a free black woman named Mary McNeile at her home on Pinckney Street, not far from the wharves of East Bay. The ladies subsequently reported that Mary—not Mrs. McNeile—had "the Leprosy," that "only a pittance of church money [was] allowed her," and that she had "no other support." The ladies recommended against dropping Mary, and their other two "colored pensioners" who had "grown old upon [the Society's] hands." They justified their endorsement by reminding other LBS members that neither Mary nor the other two women (also referred to by first name only) could "be received into the Poor House, not being insane."[48]

Society members also segregated poor white women and poor women of color by adopting the Poor House procedure of requiring "certificates signed by some respectable white persons, as to the character and necessities" of free women of color requesting out-relief. After 1835 the LBS had extended its services to the city's upper wards, called the Charleston Neck, where "the number of Patients render[ed] the task a most arduous one." Slaves and free poor black and brown people, as well as white people of the laboring classes (including Irish and German immigrants), numerically dominated the Neck, and LBS ladies decided their new policy would "guard [the Society] against imposition." Their white "patients" in the Neck and in the lower wards were not subject to this rule.[49]

Just as thousands of destitute women relied upon the Ladies Benevolent Society to subsist, a small and dedicated core of the LBS prided themselves on their faithful service to these unfortunate women. It was a relationship of mutual dependency. "When on her own sick-bed," LBS member Mrs. North "call[ed] her Domestics to her, and direct[ed] them what particular supplies to carry to each of [the LBS] Patients." Mrs. North was "not forgetful even then, of her duty toward the sick poor under her care," and she sent her slave women to minister to free but poor white, brown, and black women when illness rendered her incapable of doing it herself. Mrs. North needed the poor women to fulfill her role in Charleston nearly as much as the poor women needed Mrs. North's help. And in the end, she directed her slave woman to carry on the benevolent work, on her behalf, toward the city's destitute free women of all colors.[50]

Health was a cherished and evanescent condition and its antithesis was the norm. Disease, infirmity, and death frequently attended Charleston women. While the persistence of these dire companions typified all of life in the late eighteenth and nineteenth centuries, women confronted illness and death uniquely because maternity's shadow loomed over them and medical training inculcated the conviction that "the peculiarities of the Female, independent of sexual organization" compelled unique therapies.[51]

Conclusion

It is impossible wholly to understand slavery and slave society without fully illuminating women's experiences, and a true portrait of women's lives emerges only when all the players—slave women, free women of African descent, white women of the laboring classes, and master-class women—are analyzed in juxtaposition.

The American Revolution profoundly altered every woman's life and affected all groups of women. First, on a personal level, the sheer mayhem in South Carolina—economic dislocation, rampaging soldiers (on both sides), guerilla warfare, and British siege and occupation—created physical and emotional scars from which some women never recovered. It is, perhaps, old news to point out the viciousness of the Revolution in the South or the transformative effects of any military conflict, but what has been overlooked thus far is the way that the war, and its aftermath, magnified and entangled women's interdependent lives and relationships, roles, and self-perceptions. The misfortune of one individual rippled across the social landscape and swelled into life-altering events for many women and their families. When a wealthy woman ran short of liquid assets, female shopkeepers and artisans had lighter pockets, and the city's poorest women went begging for lack of charitable contributions; and when a patriot artisan lost business to a loyalist counterpart, that family's slaves might flee to freedom or, conversely, be appropriated and sold by British officers. Likewise, when a slave woman ran, her mistress's life changed. It is common knowledge that one of the war's greatest effects was the mass exodus of thousands of slaves from the low country. This enormous loss of laborers hardened slave owners' resolve to shore up the institution of slavery and steeled slaves' determination to remain free. The revolutionary era marked a turning point in the growth of Charleston's free black and brown populations. However, what has not been underscored is the way that these extraordinary demographic transformations affected women's perceptions of one another. Harried mistresses eyed slave women with greater suspicion. Slave women, who had tasted small liberties and observed the ruling class being ruled by occupation forces, braced themselves for future confrontations, confident of their ability to negotiate the convoluted relations of power in slave society. In public and private speech, women and men of the master class drew upon their wartime struggles with slaves, refined and reiterated diametric images of women, and deployed those embellished stereotypes to rationalize the supremacy not only of elite ladies over all other women but also of the master class over all other social groups. Post-Revolution social reconstruction became distinctly gendered work.

On a more positive note, many women gleaned from the war a sense of their own political identities and strength. Affluent ladies seized upon opportunities presented by the experiment of nation building and proved that the recreational was political. They suffused with political meaning their customary role as Charleston's social arbiters and deftly transformed the social and cultural into the political and civic: they created a public and political role—the civic host—in a world that excluded women from politics. In this respect a thread of continuity joined wealthy southern and northern women, many of whom also experienced the politicizing effects of the American Revolution. Although freedom was race-specific and nation building in the Deep South was all about reinvigorating slavery, slaves also realized a new sense of empowerment. If they had chosen to remain in South Carolina, they negotiated for greater concessions, like the liberty to choose a different owner; if they had opted to leave, they declared with confidence to Crown officials that they had been born free. In petitions to the new state government, free laboring women also revealed an awareness of their entitlement. They vowed that confiscated property should be returned to them because they had earned it through their own "toil, frugality and attention." In these and similar efforts to re-forge their lives amid, and in the wake of, physical and emotional turmoil, the city's women alternately clashed and cooperated. But in so doing they highlighted the shared dependency of southern women's lives in this formative era. Their experiences provide a southern perspective—a panorama complicated by slavery—on women's transition from the eighteenth to the nineteenth centuries.[1]

Protocols and customs surrounding marriage and sex defined who was black and white, slave and free. Members of the master class created the ruling paradigm, replete with its potent constellation of character traits and behavioral dictates. This archetype was one part colonial "Goodwife" and one part Victorian-era passionless lady, and the model bore far-reaching implications for what a young belle could and could not do with her life. The elite paragon simultaneously privileged and constrained her; she derived contractual benefits, yet she was bound by the agreement and beholden to both her lord and her "lessors." Slave women approached unions with men differently and, ironically, in the act of forging a new way of connection with men, they unwittingly strengthened the predominant model. Elite ladies and the master-class way of marriage were all that slave women and slave marriage could not be. These two marital patterns emerged and drew strength from daily examples of their difference, and yet a third strand—laboring women's experiences—sprouted in juxtaposition to both. Black, brown, and white women of the laboring classes could not live the ideal because they were rarely given the option to trade protection and leisure for maintenance and dependence. Nevertheless, authors of the aristocratic ideal compared them negatively to the prototype even if (and because) those laboring women had already consciously rejected it by their words and actions. Women as well as men perpetuated their narrow marital ideal, but it was men of the master class—slave-owning chancellors at law—who enforced it legally. They sustained their high position, in part, by comparing all women to a model whose tenets sustained their own deeply rooted dominion.

While much about this ruling paradigm resonates with the experiences of women throughout mainland North America during the same eras, South Carolina's uniqueness becomes quickly apparent in case reports concerning domestic abuse. White married women who went to court—whether they were of the laboring classes or the master class—publicly unmasked the ideal and exhibited a savvy understanding of their own legal and economic disabilities and of the judicial compulsion to uphold the ideal of paternalism. Many had clearly breached the prevailing marital standard by failing to "exhibit" themselves as models of "conjugal propriety," yet they successfully exploited the law to force their husbands' compliance with the very paradigm they (and their husbands) had violated. All wronged wives played the trump card when they challenged courts to make the ideal real. And all of these "unruly women" fundamentally threatened the social order by divulging the fact—occasionally in gruesome detail—that some men fell far short of the benevolent and protective patriarch. A fascinating irony was at work in the adjudication of abuse cases. In the act of publicly petitioning courts for assistance, women actually reinforced the multiple and overlapping hierarchies on which slave society was built. As part of this legal process, they described their own submissive status, rehearsed their husbands' dominance and marital obligations, and elaborated a class- and race-specific image of womanhood. Whether intentionally or unwittingly, women (as well as men) used these courtrooms to reiterate their places in society and enforce compliance with the perquisites and obligations inherent in their positions. And as judges elaborated their rationales for rejecting or supporting these claims, women obliquely participated in the process by which depositions and court testimony were transformed into tools wielded by the master class to construct and maintain their social dominance. While there is no disputing the fact that South Carolina's legal system alleviated gross neglect and cruelty suffered by many women, it is also likely that more than one of those women walked away from the courtrooms wondering if the "fair sex" would ever achieve full social justice.[2]

Charleston residents constructed race in the process of reproducing and demarcating it, and that construction enterprise bore multiple meanings. Urban propinquity fostered daily and multilayered mingling, including sexual relations, between people of African and European descent. The forms of sexual mixing and their precipitating motives varied immensely, because social relations among people of different colors in Charleston ranged from genuine affection to smoldering animosity. Few would dispute the fact of slave women's sexual abuse. Certainly sexual mixing occurred, in part, because many southern white men understood forced sex as a "ritualistic re-enactment of the daily pattern of social dominance" upon which their world and their personal power rested. Sexual exploitation of slave women extended naturally from the overweening power of the master, that frontline of control over slaves. However, mixing also ensued because there was money to be made from sex, people available for exploitation, and an established, legitimate slave-hiring system that expedited the sex trade in Charleston. Slave women were sexually violated by their owners, and some were likely forced by greedy owners into selling sex. But some women of color also exploited their exploiters. They wielded sex as a tool of survival; they ameliorated their condition by providing sex in return for some material advantage. That behavior did not transform them into prostitutes or concubines. Rather, many women of African descent resisted enslavement or accommodated to their oppression in slave society by acting as their own sexual agents. Whatever its forms, and apart from the myriad purposes it served, mixing bore seeds that the master class found disruptive. Herein lay a great irony, for sexual mixing buttressed white men's power but produced "admixture[s] of negro blood" in a society that grounded "the presumption of freedom or slavery" in color. Sexual mixing simultaneously characterized and dichotomized Charleston just as it both defined and separated the city's women.[3]

Examining the varieties of sexual mingling in the slave South—for example, analyzing that blurry line between housekeeper and concubine, or investigating the interface between prostitution and slavery—also reveals a need to rethink traditional definitions of sexual practices. The fixed designations of concubine and prostitute bear little meaning in the slave South, where custom and law conspired to give white men property rights in the sexuality of enslaved women. In addition, analysis of sex in slave societies demonstrates that sex and gender functioned both to maintain and to contest power. At times in Charleston, slave women acted in ways that reframed abusive sexual practice as a means of empowerment. The realities of sexual practice and, in particular, sex between women of color and white men, demand reconceptualization of the power relations in slave society. Scholars have already established that slave owners did not wield absolute control over their slaves. They could not hold all the cards all the time. Sex and sexual practices were essential to the continuous negotiations of domination and resistance between slaves and slave owners as they manipulated each other. Slavery transformed sexual practices and sexual practices transformed slavery. This reality complicates portraits of the social and economic institution of slavery on which the Old South was built.

The experiences of everyday life reveal the ways in which different groups of women encountered distinct prospects, practices, and realities in both work and leisure, and how those differences, in turn, defined them and reinforced social chasms. In the face of an ideology that equated "laborer" with "slave" and exempted white people (especially white women) from physical labor, most women worked in this urban slave society. This reality tangled neat categories of white and black, leisured lady and working wench. The city's *feme sole* traders, other businesswomen, female artisans, educators, health professionals, benevolent ladies, and domestic workers served visible, active, fundamental economic roles. Women figured prominently in all capacities of that defining feature of urban labor relations, the slave-hiring system. Slave women and free women of color dominated Charleston markets, establishing a nexus between plantation garden economies and urban slave and free family economies. They forged economic and social links that reached to the city wharves, slave blocks, and beyond with purchases of goods and family members alike.

Women also performed perhaps the most crucial labor of all when they reproduced slave society in the act of rearing their children in the ways of southern urban society. Women of the master class donned the mantle of benevolence and taught younger kinswomen to follow in their footsteps. Slave women schooled their children in strategies of survival, honing the next generation's mastery of that delicate balance between compliance and resistance. Free women of color taught their daughters how to negotiate on the shifting and sometimes hostile terrain between slavery and freedom. The city's laboring white women tutored their daughters in a variety of skilled trades to provide their families a competency, while destitute poor women demonstrated to their children how to subsist in the city, or they died trying. Women were defined and differentiated through different attitudes toward work, where they worked and under whose supervision, the tasks they accomplished, whether or not they received wages, and whether they were permitted to keep those earnings. The distinctions braided their lives together but the strands remained discrete.

In this city renowned for its spirited social life, play was work, work was play, and all women maximized the utilitarian functions of leisure. When white ladies and brown elite women played, they socialized their children and strengthened Charleston's social divides. Each time young belles whirled on the dance floor or traversed city streets in grand style, they reinforced the dominion of their class. But their recreation concurrently presaged work for slave women, a fact that rendered the identities of frolicking ladies and laboring wenches mutually dependent. Slave women had the least time for amusements precisely because their hard work made possible the leisure of their mistresses. Often slave women worked even when playing. A Sunday after-dinner diversion or a rendezvous on Sullivan's Island was fun, but these leisure forms also functioned as resistance, and these lessons did not fall on deaf ears when slave children were near. Girls and boys learned how to navigate urban slave society and expand or establish their own boundaries, in part, by watching their mothers at play. In addition, ritualized leisure forms like weddings and funerals perpetuated African American folkways: the work of social reproduction. Slave women also played while working. They visited friends and family while transacting business at market and appropriated extra time away from owners while on walks with children, delivering messages for mistresses and performing other routine tasks. Free women of the brown elite, free laboring women of color, and white women of the working classes also played, and their experiences fell at disparate points on a continuum ranging from the leisured lady to the laboring slave woman. Leisure was didactic, discriminating, defining. It provided opportunities to rest, revitalize, and resist. How women chose to socialize, their opportunities for recreation, and the nature and frequency of those activities differed from woman to woman, for leisure represented much more than amusement in Charleston. It demarcated and differentiated the lady, the woman, and the wench.

Hierarchy began at home and flourished under South Carolina law. Women who came to court confronted a political culture that celebrated localism and the independence of individual white men. Those white men dominated the southern household, a microcosm of slave society. Nineteenth-century industrialization, with its reorganization of work away from home and the growth of a distinct middle-class, bypassed Charleston. Unlike in the North, no bourgeois model of domesticity empowered southern ladies by emphasizing their dominance in the private sphere. This rhetoric lost its bite as it traveled south. Reliance on slave labor and the law of slavery buttressed Charleston's twin ideologies of paternalism and patriarchy. Therefore, the law intervened only when a patriarch publicly and flagrantly violated his duties as protector and provider. In disputes involving violence against slaves, the courts interceded not to diminish a master's power but (as in domestic disputes) to maintain a balance between that domination and outside restraint. Female victims of crime, as well as criminals, thus confronted dubious justice in courts predisposed to upholding the patriarchal power and the authority of the master class. Entangled private and public hierarchies of power sprouted and drew strength from the male-dominated southern household.[4]

From the 1780s through the antebellum era, low-country legislators and judges affixed their control over the social order by exploiting tightly entwined notions of gender and race. Creation and enforcement of South Carolina law relied heavily upon diametric notions of black and white women. Courts did not merely uphold civil law (which naturally discriminated against slaves, women of color, and white women), judges also infused their decisions with powerful words and images of these avowed inferiors. Statute and case law consistently functioned as forums for elaborating stereotypical traits of slave women and free women of color, which implicitly and explicitly differentiated them from white ladies. In addition, South Carolina law manifested the tenacity of the master class in discriminating between the sexuality of white women and slave women. The courts also rationalized and neutralized the potential disorder created by women who violated behavioral expectations, as when they dismissed white prostitutes and female ruffians as unfortunate oddities, or when they metaphorically blackened these white unruly women. In these ways, the interdependent legal status of women was essential to the maintenance of the larger social organization and daily social interaction. Statute and case law emerged from and buttressed a volatile ideological concoction centered on notions of sex and gender, race and race relations, class and class distinctions.

While pregnancy, childbirth, and categorization as uterus-driven beings united all women, they experienced illness and death distinctively because disease models and treatments varied according to wealth and race as well as sex. Generalities about female peculiarities were refracted by other realities, notably race, condition, and class. The experiences of impoverished white women and brown elite women were simultaneously similar yet strikingly distinct, for both gave birth, but wealthy brown women did not do so in an alley or in the Poor House hospital. Likewise, destitute women of all colors struggled against insuperable odds to feed, clothe, and house themselves and their families, but only white women could lodge their children in the Orphan House or seek shelter at the Charleston Poor House when they were too ill to care for them. And the city's poorest women of all colors feared what might befall them in paupers' clinics and hospitals affiliated with Charleston medical schools, but women of color singularly endured the double jeopardy of sex and race: white medical men espoused particular treatments for people of African descent, a strategy derived "naturally" from "the very great difference . . . between the blacks and whites."[5]

As manifest in this medical practitioner's notions of "blacks and whites," women's lives entwined, in part, because of their similar and disparate experiences of illness and health. Treatments prescribed for women of color were influenced by those administered to white women, and poor women's care (or lack thereof), in part, derived from their failure to measure up to that Charleston paragon, the delicate and genteel lady. Furthermore, the wealthiest white women and most destitute women of all colors were tightly entwined in acts of charity. Full validation of master-class women as benevolent ladies and "directresses" of Charleston society hinged on the sickness and poverty of other city women. As in every aspect of women's lives, who they were and who they were not governed their struggles with pregnancy, childbirth, and a host of maladies. Treatment was likewise interdependent. The care that women received (or its absence), from whom, and where they received it depended on what sort of women they were and were not.[6]

Charleston women lived their lives and forged their identities in a volcanic confluence of social categories (race, color, condition, wealth, and gender), where female subordination was imperative to the social order. The common experiences born of being female in a fervently patriarchal slave society knit women together, but urban slave society did not give rise to consistent coalitions. White women did not share one set of attitudes and values. The same held true of affluent brown elite women and poor black and brown women. Neither did the southern ideology of domesticity lend itself to cross-race or cross-class gender bonds. Social chasms of color, bondage, and wealth separated women and fomented a volatile familiarity. Ironically, the more women and men strove to maintain distinctions among different groups or categories of women, the more tightly they entwined them. What one woman was not, another woman was; the act of differentiating among women emphasized the reciprocal nature of women's images, their identities, their realities. The differences bred interdependence—for their lives converged in mutual definition—and that dependence underscored distinctions. The dynamic was circular as well as reciprocal. Consequently, women were who they were not only because they were physically different from men, or because they were dominated by men, but also because they adopted (and were assigned) different and contrasting roles. Charleston women were defined, constrained, and empowered by this mutuality of their lives.

Examining the urban South through the prism of women's experiences not only accentuates the rich diversity and mutual dependency of women's lives in the late eighteenth and nineteenth centuries, but also highlights how slavery affected women of all colors and social positions. In addition, illuminating the detail of women's daily lives, scrutinizing Charleston's complex and cross-hatched social boundaries and positioning women, together with urban slavery, at the center of analysis, emphasizes the vital roles of both gender and the women themselves in building, maintaining, and contesting urban slave society. Women participated in the daily task of weaving a world of patriarchy, paternalism, racism, and classism. They were not passive victims of gendered dictates.

Similar subjects and players have, admittedly, been examined elsewhere in varied contexts of American women's history and the history of slavery. However, by zeroing in on the city, by including women of African and European descent, by incorporating slave women and free women of color, by embracing white laboring women as well as the destitute poor, and by drawing evidence from a broad period of time, I am suggesting a new way to examine the intricacies and interrelatedness of southern women's lives. By integrating these themes and different groups of women, a simple but profound reality can be distilled from that complexity: while subjection to patriarchal domination largely defined the category of woman, individual Charleston women learned who they were and what roles were expected of them through daily interaction with each other. They gained their identities by playing off of the different roles ascribed to them (and those they shaped) in day-to-day social intercourse. To understand women's co-dependent roles and realities is to attain a more textured portrait of the urban South and of what it meant to be a woman in a world where race, color, and condition as well as gender and class determined destiny. Slavery enmeshed women's lives, and diametric images of women in urban slave society wielded the power to define, entwine, and divide.

Appendix 1

Revolutionary War Pension and
Bounty-Land-Warrant Applications

The Records

The American Revolution Pension Records comprise approximately 80,000 files on over 2,600 rolls of microfilm arranged in alphabetical order solely by last name of the applicant.[1] The first congressional legislation authorizing payment of pensions for Revolutionary War service was dated 26 August 1776, but the first legislation for widows was a Continental Congress resolution four years later. That measure offered half-pay for seven years to widows and orphans of officers who met certain service criteria. Only in June 1832 did the federal government legislate service pensions for all Revolutionary soldiers and sailors, continental and state. Every man who had served at least two years in the Continental Line, state troops, volunteers, or militia was eligible for full pay for life. Those who had served at least six months (but short of two years) could apply for pensions of less than full pay. The law also stipulated that widows and orphans were entitled to the balance due a pensioner upon his death. The law narrowly defined "balance" to mean only the money due from the last payment until the date of death of a pensioner. Usually this amounted to one partial monthly payment. The widow or children did not continue to receive the pension. The majority of applications were filed following this 1832 legislation. Although requests were made to the United States government, they were initiated in the county or town in which the veteran or widow lived. Applicants appeared before a court of record and described under oath the service for which a pension was being claimed. Widows had to show proof of the date and place of their marriages and of their husbands' type and length of military service. Hundreds could not provide this necessary evidence and the Pension Board refused their claims.

The Universe of Applicants

I first compiled a list of South Carolina applicants using an indispensable finding aid, the *Index of Revolutionary War Pension Applications in the National Archives* (Washington, D.C.: National Genealogical Society, 1976). I included in this sample every single entry from the state that included a woman's name as well as the veteran's name, evidence that the widow had filed claim. I excluded records listing South Carolina as the secondary state (indicating the petitioners who no longer resided in Carolina), as well as five applications in which the petitioners were clearly from the back country. This yielded a sample of over 400 names.

I next reviewed all 404 (microfilm) applications searching for clues as to where, in South Carolina, the veterans and their wives lived, a necessary step to eliminate all who did not reside in or near the city of Charleston. I was left with only twenty-six women. All others were either unquestionably not from the Charleston area or they could not be verified as Charleston residents.

Among these twenty-six, the typical pension applicant (widow) was born between 1752 and 1770, thereby growing up during the years leading to the American Revolution. The average age at marriage was eighteen, although 26 percent married younger, between the ages of fourteen and sixteen. Most of the women (65 percent) were wed at the close of the Revolution and enjoyed a long married life; they lived with their husbands eleven to twenty-five years before becoming widows (65 percent of the applicants were married eleven to forty years), and four women actually reached their golden wedding anniversaries. Once widowed, the majority remained so, although the seven youngest widows (27 percent) did remarry.

In 1790 at the time of the first federal census, most (future) pensioners lived with their husbands in households of twelve persons, five or six of whom were slaves. White women and girls outnumbered the men in most of these homes, so these women lived with other female kin (sisters, cousins, aunts, mothers, or mothers-in-law) as well as their husbands, children, and slaves.

Over forty years later, when most (65 percent) of the twenty-six women applied for American Revolution pension benefits, friends and family gave depositions on their behalf as these widows attempted to prove their eligibility. This testimony reveals that distinct networks of four or five women testified for each other, and at least two of these groups divided along ethnic lines. Members of Charleston's Jewish community, Judith DeLyon Abrahams, Rebecca Sarzedas Cohen, Rachel Lazarus, and Cecilia Solomons, supported each other. Likewise, Mary Johnson Anthony, Elizabeth Henley Gabeau, Massey Phillips Graves, Margaret B. Gruber, and Elizabeth Phillips Mitchell provided testimony for one another; their husbands had all labored as Charleston artisans, and case depositions reflected this common ground.

List of Charleston Pension Applicants

Name	DOB	Name	DOB
Judith DeLyon Abrahams	1763	Mary Elizabeth Kennedy	1786
Mary Johnson Anthony	1762	Sarah Daniels Lawrence	1760
Mary Baker	1770	Rachel Lazarus	1762
Susannah Tenant Brown	1766	Mary Wilkinson Legare	1764
Lydia Ball Bryan	1757	Mary G. Mathews	1762
Ann Cobia	1765	Mary Young Mazyck	1764
Rebecca Sarzedas Cohen	1762	Elizabeth P. Mitchell	1752
Elizabeth Henley Gabeau	1755	Mary Broughton Motte	1752
Elizabeth R. George	1755	Elizabeth F. Righton	1769
Massey Phillips Graves	1756	Catharine T. Smith	1772
Margaret B. Gruber	1760	Cecilia Solomons	1767
Ann Wilson Hall	1763	Ann B. Taylor	1769
Elizabeth W. Jeffords	1762	Sarah Tucker	1761

Appendix 2

South Carolina Court System and the Case Universe

The Court System

Unlike the organization of northern courts that celebrated egalitarianism and state activism as the essence of republicanism, the evolution of Carolina's legal system tacked differently. After the American Revolution, Charleston-style republicanism underscored the necessity of remaining free from the control of others and avoiding the threat of centralized power. This fundamental commitment derived largely from slavery and the mandate of a master's dominion, as well as from the notion of honor, that "constellation of ideas and values in which a man's sense of self-worth rested on the degree of respect commanded from others." Individual autonomy ranked high within this ideological cluster and undergirded low-country legal culture throughout the closing decades of the eighteenth century and into the next century. This persistence of individualism thwarted periodic efforts by a few legislators to reorganize the state's multiple, decentralized, and overlapping courts.[1]

A woman with legal grievances (or a woman on the other side of the dock) faced tangled and confusing legal jurisdictions. She first encountered a local official such as a justice of the peace, mayor, or other magistrate, appointed by state legislators. These men depended on court fees as well as the goodwill of the state legislature, and some of them were "greedy . . . incompetent [and] notoriously untrained in the law" because South Carolina law did not require that all justices and magistrates have legal training. They administered "irregular and unequal" justice in jury-less summary trials, or summary proceedings. In 1785 Charleston jurists refused to participate in a newly reorganized county court system that diminished this highly localized authority. State legislators acquiesced to the noncompliance, and local low-country officials maintained their power.[2]

Cases presented to grand juries and, if brought to trial, heard before petit juries, represented the next level of judicial jurisdiction, but a high rate of summary acquittals against white people and informal settlements precluded many cases from advancing to this stage. Nevertheless, if a woman's case proceeded further, she found herself in a district circuit court, conducted biannually by peripatetic appellate judges, and subsequently in one of several overlapping appeals courts. In 1824 state legislators streamlined this legal maze by establishing one central appeals court, consisting of three men who exercised final jurisdiction in both law and equity. However, in 1835 state legislators dissolved this consolidated court of appeals, a decision that bespoke opposition of the master class to centralized power and any encroachment on "informal systems of authority" or "plantation justice." It also revealed legislators' irritation at what they deemed overly liberal rulings on "negro rights" by, particularly, Justice John Belton O'Neall. They restored the pre-1824 system of two separate appellate systems—one in law and one in equity—each of which comprised several circuit judges and chancellors who heard cases in Columbia and Charleston. After 1836, split decisions by these courts could be appealed to a combined (law/equity) conference court, creating an astonishingly convoluted configuration in which one judge might hear a case three times. A separate state "court of ordinary" (later the probate court) authenticated wills, administered estates, appointed guardians, and issued marriage licenses. Not until 1859 did the legislature restore the 1824 structure.[3]

In Charleston a separate city court—in the 1780s known as the Court of Wardens, in 1801 renamed the Court of Inferior Jurisdiction, and in 1820 designated the City Court of Charleston—was empowered by the state legislature to try all misdemeanors occurring within the city. The court's jurisdiction expanded several times during the nineteenth century and, in 1836, a separate Police Court was added to the city's judicial system. The Police Court wielded the power to inflict corporal punishment and to incarcerate those charged of crimes within the city. Thus, throughout the eighteenth and nineteenth centuries, Charleston women who came to court braved not only judges bent on safeguarding patriarchal power, but also a confusing institutional morass.[4]

Mining legislative and court records to assess women's status and to appraise the use of criminality by the master class in wielding social control presents several challenges. Not all criminal acts found their way into the courts. The Magistrates and Freeholders courts established under South Carolina's black code were not required to keep written records of court proceedings until 1839; lower court records are incomplete for the eighteenth and nineteenth centuries; and not all cases rose to the Appeals Court level, the records of which are more consistent. Given these limitations, quantitative analyses of the frequency of crime, the profile of those who commit crimes, and conviction rates by race, status, and gender are skewed and inconclusive.[5]

Moreover, eighteenth- and nineteenth-century experimentation with different judicial systems confounds any study of crime in the United States, South Carolina not excepted. The records of summary trials, or summary proceedings, are not extant and many cases never advanced to a documented stage in the legal process. Finally, at the district circuit court level within South Carolina, six district assemblies divided into courts of General Sessions (criminal cases) and Common Pleas (civil cases), with frequent overlap between the two sometimes thwarting their apparent distinctions. Common Pleas courts, in turn, held separate sessions for law and equity cases—parallel courts within the duality of the General Sessions and Common Pleas courts. In equity, the state's five chancellors presided over four circuits, and met corporately at term's end to decide appeals from their respective circuits. But, as mentioned earlier, this legal structure varied because state legislators repealed then reinstated and revised the law/equity appeals system several times during the period covered. At least seventeen different magistrates compiled court reports for proceedings at law and equity (and appeals in both) during the period studied, some of them serving as reporters for cases of both types.

The Cases

Of necessity, my study of court cases focused on white courts because the law did not require South Carolina's Magistrates and Freeholders courts (the black courts) to keep records. But enslaved and free African Americans appeared in these court records precisely because their lives entwined with European Americans in matters ranging from property disputes to assault and murder. None of these (white) courts, however, deemed "Negroes" competent witnesses. To compile a sample including women of African as well as European descent as either plaintiffs or defendants, I first reviewed the topical index in the South Carolina volume of Helen Tunnicliff Catterall's *Judicial Cases Concerning American Slavery and the Negro,* and flagged likely subjects, such as cohabitation, free negroes, fugitive slaves, marriage, miscegenation, poll tax, property rights, slave prices, and slave hire. After reviewing the case summaries in Catterall, I targeted those cases I wanted to read in their entirety in the actual court reports. However, in browsing through the indices of these volumes, it quickly became apparent that my search terms had not captured other cases—on women's property issues or domestic abuse to name just two— pertinent to my study. Consequently, I revamped my search strategy: I read the index of each volume of case reports using an expanded list of eighty-four search terms (e.g., administratrix, bastardy, bawdy house, cohabitation, concubinage, dower, illegitimacy, inheritance, manumission, marriage, slaves, sole trader). Still not satisfied that I was hitting all the cases of interest, I then scanned each volume, case by case, in chronological order, beginning with Bay's and DeSaussure's reports and continuing through Richardson's reports at law and equity.

Widening my search by reviewing nearly fifty volumes of reports at law and over thirty volumes of reports at equity during the period 1783–1868 yielded a total sample of well over 300 court cases. These either involved African American and European American women directly or the testimony and judicial decisions revealed perceptions, dictates, or proscriptions about women's roles and status.

Abbreviations

CCA	City of Charleston Archives
CCL	Charleston County Library
CG	*Carolina Gazette*
City Gazette	*Charleston City Gazette & Daily Advertiser*
CLS	Charleston Library Society
CMJR	*Charleston Medical Journal and Review*
COC	Robert Scott Smalls Library, Special Collections, College of Charleston, South Carolina
DU	William R. Perkins Library, Duke University, Durham, North Carolina
FCA	Female Charitable Association
Free Negro Tax Books	State Free Negro Capitation Tax Books, Charleston, South Carolina, SCDAH
GPA	*Gazette and Public Advertiser*
GSSC	*Gazette of the State of South Carolina*
HHR	Harriott Horry Rutledge Papers, DU
JBG Diary	John Berkely Grimball Diary, SHC #970
JCHA	*Journal of the Commons House of Assembly*
JGAHR	*The State Records of South Carolina: Journals of the General Assembly and House of Representatives, 1776–1780*
LBS	Ladies Benevolent Society
LC	Manuscript Division, Library of Congress, Washington, D.C.
LFS	Ladies Fuel Society
MR	Miscellaneous Records, SCDAH
Rawick	George P. Rawick, ed., *The American Slave: A Composite Autobiography*
Rawick, ser. 1, vol. 2	Series 1, Volume 2, South Carolina, Parts 1 and 2
Rawick, ser. 1, vol. 3	Series 1, Volume 3, South Carolina, Parts 3 and 4
Rawick, ser. 1, vol. 12	Series 1, Volume 12, Georgia, Part 1
RSCG	*Royal South Carolina Gazette*
RWP	Revolutionary War Pension and Bounty-Land-Warrant Application Files
SCAGG	*South Carolina and American General Gazette* (formerly *South Carolina Weekly Gazette*)
SCDAH	South Carolina Department of Archives and History, Columbia, South Carolina
SCG	*South Carolina Gazette*
SCGCJ	*South Carolina Gazette and Country Journal*
SCGGA	*South Carolina Gazette and General Advertiser*
SCHGM	*South Carolina Historical and Genealogical Magazine* (continued as SCHM)

SCHM	*South Carolina Historical Magazine* (formerly *South Carolina Historical and Genealogical Magazine*)
SCHS	South Carolina Historical Society, Charleston, South Carolina
SCL	South Caroliniana Library, University of South Carolina, Columbia, South Carolina
SCSG	*South Carolina State Gazette*
SCWG	*South Carolina Weekly Gazette* (continued as *South Carolina and America General Gazette*)
SGSC	*State Gazette of South Carolina*
SHC	Southern Historical Collection, Wilson Library, University of North Carolina at Chapel Hill
SLJ	*Southern Literary Journal and Monthly Magazine*
SLSC	*The Statutes at Large of South Carolina*, comps. Thomas Cooper and David J. McCord
USDJ	Law Library, United States Department of Justice, Washington, D.C.
WHL	Waring Historical Library, Medical University of South Carolina, Charleston, South Carolina

Notes

Introduction

1. Undated newspaper clipping, "Message to Hell," in 30/23, folder 1, South Carolina File, SCHS.

2. Quoted in Brown, *Good Wives, Nasty Wenches*, 1.

3. The legal term is "sole trader" (or *feme sole* trader), derived from English Common Law, denoting a woman who possessed an economic and legal identity. A married woman could attain this status only with the permission of her husband. Otherwise she was a *feme covert*, literally a "woman covered," or a person whose legal and economic identities were subsumed beneath those of her husband.

4. Surveyor general quoted in Petty, *Growth and Distribution of Population*, 49–50. Bridenbaugh, *Cities in Revolt*, 216. On the wealth of Charleston residents see the 1830 through 1860 censuses. See also Johnson, "Wealth and Class in Charleston in 1860," 66–67.

5. See Kerber, *Women of the Republic*, 11–12; Norton, *Liberty's Daughters*. Joan Hoff-Wilson triggered a firestorm of debate with her essay, "The Illusion of Change: Women and the American Revolution." Kerber and Norton rebutted this work. See also Kerber, "'History Can Do It No Justice,'" and "'The Paradox of Women's Citizenship in the Early Republic'"; Norton, "'What an Alarming Crisis Is This'"; Kierner, *Beyond the Household*; Brown, "Antiauthoritarianism and Freedom in Early America," and other essays in the round table discussion, "Deference or Defiance in Eighteenth-Century America?" *Journal of American History* 85 (June 1998): 77–85, 13–97. One thread ties together these disparate analyses: the American Revolution emerges as "deeply radical" (its shock waves jarred all human relations) yet "deeply conservative" (its leaders retreated from its potentially destabilizing effects on, particularly, gender and race relations). Quoted in Kerber, "'History Can Do It No Justice,'" 41.

6. U.S. Bureau of the Census, *Heads of Families, First Census*. The first three federal censuses (1790 to 1810) did not distinguish between men and women when enumerating free people of color and slaves, but by extrapolating from population distribution averages of four census years beginning in 1820, it is possible to estimate the earlier percentages women represented in Charleston's population. Women composed over 3,700 or 46 percent of the total white population at the time of the first U.S. census in 1790. From 1820, when the census first enumerated slave women and men separately, until 1850, female slaves represented an average of 27 percent of the total city population and nearly 56 percent of the slaves. During that same period, free women of color made up approximately 4 percent of Charleston resi-

dents and over 60 percent of the city's free people of color. Applying these percentages to the 1790 Charleston population yields 4,360 slave women and 503 free women of color. Adding these estimates to the actual white female population of 3,700 produces a total of nearly 8,600 Charleston women, or almost 53 percent of city residents. Contemporary comments on the surfeit of white women and women of color corroborate these rough estimates. From 1820 to 1860, female slaves outnumbered male slaves. In 1840 and 1850 there were over 2,000 more slave women than slave men in the city. U.S. Bureau of the Census, fourth through eighth (1820–1860) censuses.

7. For examples of the better literature on women in slave societies, see Clinton, *Plantation Mistress;* White, *"Ar'n't I a Woman";* Fox Genovese, *Within the Plantation Household;* Graham, *House and Street;* Beckles, *Natural Rebels;* Shepherd et al., eds., *Engendering History;* McCurry, *Masters of Small Worlds;* Schwalm, *A Hard Fight for We;* Weiner, *Mistresses and Slaves;* Schwartz, *Born in Bondage;* Fett, *Working Cures.*

8. I am indebted to Kathleen Brown's lucid distillations of the categories in her introduction to *Good Wives, Nasty Wenches, and Anxious Patriarchs,* 4.

1. The Place and the People

1. Kovacik and Winberry, *South Carolina: A Geography,* 15, 23–24, 26–27. See also Silver, *A New Face on the Countryside.*

2. Quoted in Martineau, *Retrospect of Western Travel,* 2:227 (hereafter *Retrospect*); Olmsted, *The Cotton Kingdom,* 499.

3. Brewster, *Summer Migrations,* v.

4. Quoted in Miranda, *The New Democracy in America,* 25. See also Savitt and Young, eds., *Disease and Distinctiveness in the American South.*

5. Captain Martin quoted in Merrens, ed., *The Colonial South Carolina Scene,* 230–31.

6. Hodgson, *Remarks during a Journey through North America,* 114–15; Hall, *Travels in North America;* and Stuart, *Three Years in North America,* the latter two sources excerpted in *South Carolina, The Grand Tour,* ed. Clark, 122–23, 99 (hereafter Clark, *The Grand Tour*).

7. Quoted in Michaux, *Travels to the West of the Alleghany Mountains,* in Clark, *The Grand Tour,* 35; Martineau, *Retrospect,* 2:224. On the buzzards, see Martineau, *Retrospect,* 2:228; Bremer, *Charleston One Hundred Years Ago,* 8; Bernhard, *Travels through North America,* in Clark, *The Grand Tour,* 105. Municipal law protected the birds that fed on refuse and offal, thus providing a service to the city. On slaves, see *SCG,* 1, 8 June 1769. See also Higgins, "Charleston: Terminus and Entrepot of the Colonial Slave Trade," 118; Olwell, *Masters, Slaves, and Subjects,* 223.

8. Quoted in *Courier* (Charleston), 30 May 1857; Miranda, *The New Democracy in America,* 14, 25, 29.

9. Quoted in Bremer, *Charleston One Hundred Years Ago,* 7; Martineau, *Retrospect,* 2:227; Mackay, *The Western World,* in Clark, *The Grand Tour,* 239. On

slave punishment and sale, see Hall, *Travels in North America,* in Clark, *The Grand Tour,* 123; Herz, *My Travels in America,* 78; Clark, *The Grand Tour,* 106–107, 124–27, 140, 204, 255–57, 279–80; Hodgson, *Remarks during a Journey,* 125–26; Martineau, *Retrospect,* 2:236; Murray, *Letters from the United States,* 198.

10. While slave women made up roughly half the slave populations of these other four locations, they composed a much smaller percentage of those cities' total residents than did Charleston's slave women (2.2 percent in Baltimore, 14.9 percent in New Orleans, 17.4 percent in Richmond, and 21.9 percent in Savannah). 1820 through 1860 Census, Population Schedules of Charleston, New Orleans, Savannah, Richmond and Baltimore.

11. In the years 1790, 1794, 1796, 1801, and 1802, women constituted 4.5 percent, 4.1 percent, 3.5 percent, 5.2 percent, and 9.2 percent, respectively, of all those listed in the annual directories, or an average of 5.3 percent of the listings. Hagy, *People and Professions,* 9, 35, 49, 73, 91; Hagy, *City Directories for Charleston;* Hagy, *Charleston, South Carolina City Directories;* Hagy, *Directories for the City of Charleston.*

12. Gray, *History of Agriculture,* 723, 730, 735–38, 1026–31; Fraser, *Charleston,* 197–98.

13. Bellows, *Benevolence among Slaveholders,* 81–84, 105; Silver, "A New Look at Old South Urbanization," 150, 154–55; Smith and Courtenay, "Sketch of the History of Charleston," 304–306; Fraser, *Charleston,* 212, 235.

14. The 1820 census was the first to enumerate slaves and free people of color by sex and age, but enumerators grouped people of color in different and fewer age categories than they did white people. Over 4,100 slaves and in excess of 560 free people of color were younger than fourteen; over 4,200 white people were under sixteen. Thus, nearly 9,000 (35 percent) of the city's total population of 25,356 were under sixteen. 1820 and 1840 censuses.

15. Quoted in Martineau, *Retrospect,* 2:238–40; Kemble, *Journal of a Residence,* 36–38; Gaillard Hunt, *Life in America One Hundred Years Ago,* 71. Hall, *Travels in Canada, and the United States;* Tasistro, *Random Shots and Southern Breezes . . . ;* and Hall, *The Aristocratic Journey,* all in Clark, *The Grand Tour,* 55–56, 186, 145. See also Arfwedson, *The United States and Canada;* Lyell, *A Second Visit to the United States of North America,* in Clark, *The Grand Tour,* 175, 218; Johnson, "Wealth and Class in Charleston in 1860," 66–67, 73.

16. Quoted in Wood, *Black Majority,* 234; Fraser, *Charleston,* 54–55; *SCG,* 18 March 1732, 31 July 1736.

17. Ebenezer Hazard and Josiah Quincy, quoted in Fraser, *Charleston,* 130, 199–200. See also Wikramanayake, *A World in Shadow,* 76, 82; Johnson and Roark, *No Chariot Let Down,* 3–15.

18. Wallace, *South Carolina,* 24–25, 27, 32, 92, 102–103; Mills, *Statistics of South Carolina,* 390–91; Johnson and Sloan, *South Carolina: A Documentary Profile,* 33, 101.

19. French migration accelerated when religious persecution of Protestants increased after Louis XIV revoked the Edict of Nantes in 1685. The Edict,

issued in 1598, had established uneasy but peaceful coexistence between Catholics and Protestants. Hirsch, *Huguenots of Colonial South Carolina*, 3–5, 14–53, 90–91, 96, 100–101, 239–40, 261–62; *SCG*, 24 December 1772; Silver, "A New Look at Old South Urbanization," 148–49; Hagy, *This Happy Land*, 1, 6–7, 11, 13, 15; Ramsay, *Ramsay's History of South Carolina*, 1:5–6, 8–9; Wallace, *South Carolina*, 24–26, 37; Simms, *The History of South Carolina*, 52–53; Tobler, *South Carolina and Georgia Almanack*. In Anglicizing names, De la Motte became Motte, for example, and Lewis Timothée changed his name to Louis Timothy.

20. Kovacik and Winberry, *South Carolina: A Geography*, 69–73; Bridenbaugh, *Cities in the Wilderness*, 8, 177, 204, 332; Bridenbaugh, *The South in the Building of the Nation*, 8, 15, 23; Fraser, *Charleston*, 15, 26, 42, 47–48, 145, 219; Wood, *Black Majority*, 36–40, 43–45, 55–56, 58, 61–62, 79, 88–91, 131–33.

21. Wood, *Black Majority*, 219; Fraser, *Charleston*, 45–49, 63; Wallace, *South Carolina*, 48–49; Kovacik and Winberry, *South Carolina: A Geography*, 73; Clifton, *Life and Labor on Argyle Island*, x–xi; Menard, "Slavery, Economic Growth, and Revolutionary Ideology in the South Carolina Lowcountry," 244–77 (esp. 259–60). See also Carney, *Black Rice;* Wright, *South Carolina: A Bicentennial History*, 104–106.

22. Governor Nathaniel Johnson, 1708, quoted in Wood, *Black Majority*, 144. Menard, "Slave Demography in the Lowcountry," 280–303. Contemporaries and historians alike have used the misnomer, "black majority," to connote numerical dominance of people whose skin color actually ranged from black to nearly white. Olwell, *Masters, Slaves, and Subjects*, 21–26; *SLSC*, 4:397–417; Minchinton, "A Comment on 'The Slave Trade to Colonial South Carolina: A Profile,'" 47–57.

23. Quoted in "The Humble Petition and Representation of the [Charleston] Council and Assembly of Your Majesty's Province of South Carolina to the King's Most Excellent Majesty," 26 July 1740, reprinted in Fraser, *Charleston*, 67–69.

24. In 1708, Carolina's total black population (4,100) for the first time outnumbered white inhabitants (4,080), and of those 4,080 white people, 120 women and men were servants. The remaining 1,400 inhabitants were enslaved Indians. In 1760, approximately 4,300 (54 percent) of Charleston's 8,000 residents were slaves. Fifteen years later, slaves still composed over one-half of Charleston's 12,000 inhabitants. "South Carolina Population as Reported by the Governor and Council, September 17, 1708," reprinted in Wood, *Black Majority*, 144; Bridenbaugh, *Cities in Revolt*, 333–34; Wallace, *South Carolina*, 197; Fraser, *Charleston*, 28, 102, 135. I have applied South Carolina Governor William Bull's 1770 population percentages to the total city population of ten years earlier to obtain a rough estimate of the population composition in 1760.

25. Wells, "Household Size and Composition," 546–47.

26. Governor William Bull, "A Representation of the Present State . . . of South Carolina," 30 November 1770; William Pollard, 1 February 1774; "Charleston, S.C., in 1774 as Described by an English Traveller," all quoted in Merrens,

The Colonial South Carolina Scene, 268, 277, 283; *SCGCJ,* 19 May, 3 November 1772. See also *SCG,* 8 August 1771; 10 March 1772; 27 September, 6 December 1773; 31 October 1774; *SCAGG,* 20 January 1775; 12 January 1776; Donnan, "The Slave Trade into South Carolina," 822–23, 826–27; Morgan, "Black Life in Eighteenth-Century Charleston," 188–90; Gomez, *Exchanging Our Country Marks.* In his 1751 estimation of "the value of South Carolina," the province's governor reported that "the people in Charles Town [were] a little more than a 6th part of the inhabitants of the providence," and that there were "about 25,000 white people and 40,000 Negroes in the province." Accordingly, 4,167 white people and 6,667 "Negroes" lived in Charleston at that time. James Glen, Esq., Governor, quoted in Merrens, *The Colonial South Carolina Scene,* 180, 182.

27. Quoted in *SCGCJ,* 19 May 1772; *SCG,* 5 December 1771; Schweninger, "Slave Independence and Enterprise in South Carolina," 107; *SCG,* 22 October 1763; 24 September, 26 November 1772. See also *SCG,* 8 June 1765; Esterby et al., *JCHA,* 21 May 1741, 18. One historian has estimated that approximately "several hundred slave women were regularly engaged in selling" goods in city markets. Olwell, *Masters, Slaves, and Subjects,* 178.

28. Quoted in *SCG,* 31 May 1770. See deeds of manumission: Alexander Hewat's to Diana, 16 April 1777; John Speid's to Betty, 29 September 1778; Mathew Daniels' to [his wife] Betty and their three children, 12 July 1757; Benjamin Smith's to Ruth and their two children, 5 May 1763, MR vols. SS 49–50, RR 572, LL 254–55, 603–604.

29. Quoted in Seeber, *On the Threshold of Liberty,* 14–15; "Presentments of the Grand Jury of Charlestown," *SCG,* 24 May 1773; 3 June 1774; Thomas Farr, *SCAGG,* 4 November 1780; *SCG,* 24 September 1772. See also *SCG,* 17 September 1772; 27 March, 7 November 1775; *SCGCJ,* 8 November 1768; 9 June 1772.

30. On runaways, see *SCG,* 31 May, 5 July, 4 October 1760; 25 April 1761. The sample included a total of 1,279 ads in the *SCG, SCWG,* and *SCGCJ,* reprinted in Windley, *Runaway Slave Advertisements,* 179–347, 412–79, 599–703.

31. Quoted in *SCG,* 11 January 1768; 14 November, 5 July 1771; *SCAGG,* 30 March 1772; 14 November 1769.

32. Quoted in *SCG,* 22 November, 30 December 1760; *SCGCJ,* 27 January 1767; *SCG,* 1 December 1766; *SCAGG,* 12, 25 February 1772. See also *SCG* 6 September 1760; 14 November 1766; 13 January, 17 December 1772; 30 August 1773; *SCAGG,* 12, 25 February 1772; 23 December 1774; *SCGCJ,* 27 January 1767.

33. Quoted in *SCG,* 7 August 1762; 5 September 1771; 11 July 1761; *SCAGG,* 21 September 1772; *SCG* 11 July 1761. See also *SCG,* 14 March, 27 June, 12 December 1761.

34. Quoted in *SCG,* 3 September 1763; *SCGCJ,* 11 July 1775. One historian has suggested that creoles "born into slavery may well have had different 'notion[s] of liberty' . . . than those who had memories of Africa and of freedom." Olwell, *Masters, Slaves, and Subjects,* 47.

35. Quoted in *SCG,* 29 November 1773; 27 June 1774; *SCAGG,* 9 December

1774; *SCG,* 24 September 1772; 20 June 1768; "Presentments of the Grand Jury," *SCG,* 25 January 1772. See also *SCG,* 5 December 1771; 17 December 1772; *SCAGG,* 17 April 1771; 21 September 1772.

36. Quoted in Morgan, "Black Life," 216. In winter 1765, groups of slaves paraded through the streets reenacting recent (white) public demonstrations against the Stamp Act. City resident Henry Laurens deemed these "domestic broils . . . more awful and distressing than Fire, Pestilence, or Foreign Wars." Quoted in Olwell, *Masters, Slaves, and Subjects,* 225. See also Morgan, "Black Life," 220; Morgan, "Black Society in the Lowcountry," 108–109.

37. Quoted in "Journal of the Court of General Sessions, 1769–1776," 8–328, SCDAH; *SCG,* 26 October 1769; 19 April, 3 May 1770; Fraser, *Charleston,* 104. Eckhard, *Digest of the Ordinances,* 81; "Presentments of the Grand Jury," *SCG,* 15 April 1745; 29 October 1772. On dram shop licensees see *SCG,* 29 April 1763; 9 May 1768; 15 November 1770; 22 February; 16, 19 April, 24 May 1773. See also Morgan, "Black Life," 206–208.

38. Quoted in Fraser, *Charleston,* 104, 117; *SCG,* 29 June 1767; Bellows, *Benevolence among Slaveholders,* 8. See also Hamer, "The Fate of the Exiled Acadians in South Carolina," 199–208; Nash, *The Urban Crucible,* 159–63; Easterby, "Public Poor Relief in Colonial Charleston," 83–86; Weir, *Colonial South Carolina: A History,* 214.

39. Quoted in *SCG,* 7 August 1762. See also *SCG* 11 July 1761; 4 September 1771; Coclanis, *The Shadow of a Dream,* 115, table 4-4; Schweninger, "Prosperous Blacks in the South, 1790–1990," 35; Schweninger, "Property-Owning Free African-American Women in the South," 17.

40. Quoted in Fraser, *Charleston,* 120, 112. See also Rosengarten, *Between the Tracks,* 10–12, 21–22; "Charleston, S.C., in 1774 as Described by an English Traveller," in Merrens, *The Colonial South Carolina Scene,* 281.

41. Governor Glen, 1749, quoted in Rogers, *Charleston in the Age of the Pincknkeys,* 72–75. See also Fraser, *Charleston,* 118, 121, 127–30.

42. Quoted in Fraser, *Charleston,* 131, 134; *SGC,* 1 March 1773; Cohen, *The South Carolina Gazette, 1732–1775,* 92–106, 146–69; Bagdon, "Musical Life in Charleston," 146–54.

43. Quoted in Fraser, *Charleston,* 137.

44. Quoted in Fraser, *Charleston,* 139; "Charleston, S.C., in 1774," in Merrens, *The Colonial South Carolina Scene,* 285; *SCGCJ,* 2, 16 August 1774.

45. Quoted in Tobias, "Charles Town 1764," 67–68.

46. Eliza Pinckney, quoted in Ravenel, *Eliza Pinckney,* 267.

2. Disorder and Chaos of War

1. Quoted in Olwell, *Masters, Slaves, and Subjects,* 6.

2. Continental Army General Nathanael Greene quoted in Hoffman, "The 'Disaffected' in the Revolutionary South," 294; General Greene's aide, William Pierce, quoted in Royster, *A Revolutionary People at War,* 278. Ferocity continued: in 1780 nearly 66 percent of 1,000 American battlefield deaths and

90 percent of 2,000 wounded occurred in South Carolina. Nadelhaft, *The Disorders of War,* 61; Lambert, *South Carolina Loyalists in the American Revolution,* 186, 189, 306–307 (hereafter Lambert, *South Carolina Loyalists*); SLSC 4:479–80; Hemphill, *JGAHR,* 186.

3. *Centennial of Incorporation,* 97; Stoesen, "The British Occupation of Charleston, 1780–1782," 80; Ramsay, *Ramsay's History of South Carolina,* 1:271–72; Lambert, *South Carolina Loyalists,* 255–56; Quarles, *The Negro in the American Revolution,* 167–72.

4. Quoted in Olwell, *Masters, Slaves, and Subjects,* 231; Drayton, *Memoirs of the American Revolution,* 179–80; James Habersham to Robert Keen, 11 May 1775, quoted in Olwell, *Masters, Slaves, and Subjects,* 233.

5. On work restrictions, see "Proclamation" printed in the *Royal Gazette,* 7–11 April 1781.

6. Bridenbaugh, *Cities in Revolt,* 333; Ramsay, *Ramsay's History of South Carolina,* 1:271–72; Hodges, *The Black Loyalist Directory;* Moultrie, *Memoirs of the American Revolution,* 2:356; Frey, *Water from the Rock,* 179.

7. Quoted in *SCAGG,* 19 January, 7, 28 October, 4 November 1780. On others who ran from their owners but lived and worked in the city during occupation, see *SCAGG,* 22 November, 6 December 1780; 3, 20 January 1781; *Royal Gazette,* 28 April–2 May, 16–19 May, 25–29 August, 8–12 and 19–22 September, 22–26 December 1781; 16–19 January, 20–23 February 1782.

8. "Extract of a Letter to a Gentleman in Philadelphia," 7 February 1776, quoted in Olwell, *Masters, Slaves, and Subjects,* 239; Henry Laurens to Richard Richardson, 19 December 1775, in Hamer, *Papers of Henry Laurens,* 10:576.

9. Moultrie, *Memoirs of the American Revolution,* 1:113; Henry Laurens to Richard Richardson, 19 December 1775, in Hamer, *Papers of Henry Laurens,* 10:576. On "Negroe Dragoons," see William Matthews, 26 April 1782; Lieutenant Bell Tilden, n.d.; Colonel Charles Cotesworth Pinckney, 13 August 1782; Francis Marion, 30 August 1782; Thomas Bee, 9 December 1782, quoted in Olwell, *Masters, Slaves, and Subjects,* 258–59.

10. "Inspection Roll of Negroes," Book Nos. 1, 2, and 3, New York City, April–November 1783, in Hodges, *Black Loyalist Directory.* Hodges has transcribed a list, originally compiled by British officials in New York City, of several thousand people of color who embarked from that port over seven months in 1783. While not exhaustive, the list documents the fact that at least these 110 Charleston slave women secured freedom via British ships. On Lucia, see Hodges, *Black Loyalist Directory,* Book 1.

11. David Ramsay quoted in Stoesen, "The British Occupation of Charleston, 1780–1782," 80–81. Ramsay has maintained that "between the years 1775 and 1783" the state "lost twenty-five thousand negroes." No distinction was made in this account between slaves and free people, women and men. Ramsay, *Ramsay's History of South Carolina,* 1:271–72; quoted in Olwell, *Masters, Slaves, and Subjects,* 268–69. On the evacuation, see *The Centennial of Incorporation,* 97; Lambert, *South Carolina Loyalists,* 255–56; Quarles, *The Negro in the American Revolution,* 167–72; Return of the People from South Carolina,

Charlestown, 13th December 1782," quoted in Barnwell, "The Evacuation of Charleston by the British in 1782," 26.

12. Testimony of James Alexander on behalf of Leonard Askew, 28 April 1787; Memorial of John Chambers, 19 October 1787, Commission of Enquiry into the Losses and Services of the American Loyalists, reel 56, 150–51, 497, SCDAH.

13. Wilkinson, *Letters of Eliza Wilkinson*, 26–31 (hereafter Wilkinson, *Letters*). On accusations of slaves stealing from their owners during British raids, see Eliza Pinckney to Mrs. R. E. [unreadable], 25 September 1780, Charles Cotesworth Pinckney Family Papers, series 1, box 5, LC (hereafter Pinckney Family Papers).

14. Quoted in Wilkinson, *Letters*, 53–55; Archibald Campbell to (unknown), 9 January 1779, quoted in Morgan, "Black Society in the Lowcountry, 1760–1810," 109.

15. Wilkinson, *Letters*, 28–29.

16. On Bettina, see Charles Pinckney Account Book, quoted in Olwell, *Masters, Slaves, and Subjects*, 159, note 76. Quoted in Eliza Pinckney to Mrs. R. E. [unreadable], 25 September 1780, Pinckney Family Papers, series 1, box 5, LC; Ravenel, *Eliza Pinckney*, 304; Henry Laurens to James Laurens, 2 July, 20 August 1775; 7 June 1777; Henry Laurens to John L. Gervais, 5 September 1777, quoted in Olwell, *Masters, Slaves, and Subjects*, 159–60, 163, 165.

17. Quoted in Webber, "Extracts from the Journal of Mrs. Ann Manigault, 1754–1781," 128–41; Fraser, *Charleston*, 157.

18. Quoted in *SCAGG*, 19 February 1778. Rogers, *Charleston in the Age of the Pinckneys*, 58; Bridenbaugh, *Cities in the Wilderness*, 193, 351–52.

19. On resales of slaves by the British in the West Indies, see Quarles, *The Negro in the American Revolution*, 177. On Betty, see Fraser, *Charleston*, 158.

20. Quoted in Baurmeister, *Revolution in America*, 350; *Royal Gazette*, 14 March 1781; "An Account of the Life of Mr. David George," quoted in Olwell, *Masters, Slaves, and Subjects*, 255; Testimony of John Pearson, 11 November 1783; Elizabeth Thompson, 11 November 1783; and Journal of Samuel Mathis, 3 April 1781, quoted in Olwell, *Masters, Slaves, and Subjects*, 255.

21. Henry Clinton to Charles Cornwallis, 20 May 1780, quoted in Frey, *Water from the Rock*, 119; General James Patterson to the Board of Police, 13 June 1780, Proceedings of the Board of Police, British Public Record Office records, microfilm copy, SCDAH, C05, 520, 2; Eliza Lucas Pinckney to [unknown], 25 September 1780, Pinckney Family Papers, LC. See also Fraser, *Charleston*, 164.

22. Eliza Lucas Pinckney to Thomas Pinckney, 13 September 1780, Pinckney Family Papers, SCHS.

23. *Royal Gazette*, 28 March 1782; Ravenel, *Eliza Pinckney*, 282–83. Quoted in David Stephens to John Wendell, 20 February 1782, in "Boyd-Stephens Letters," *Proceedings* (Massachusetts Historical Society) 48 (1915): 342–43.

24. Depositions of Mrs. Elizabeth [Samways] Mitchell and Mrs. Massey Graves, 16 July 1838, Pension Application of Elizabeth Mitchell [Microfilm] Roll

2114, RWP. Fraser, *Charleston,* 120–21, 127–29; Sellers, *Charleston Business on the Eve of the American Revolution,* 9, 11, 134, 209–16, 220.

25. See examples of economic hardship in the following depositions in pension applications: Joseph Righton, 14 May 1838, Pension Application of George Mathews, Roll 1651; Sarah Johnson, 13 July 1843, Pension Application of Joseph Baker, Roll 118; Job Palmer, 5 July 1838, Pension Application of James Graves, Roll 1111; Elizabeth [Samways] Mitchell, 16 July 1838, and Joseph Righton, 15 July 1838, Pension Application of Elizabeth Mitchell, Roll 2114, RWP.

26. Proclamation printed in *Royal Gazette,* 7–11 April 1781; Nadelhaft, *The Disorders of War,* 94.

27. Depositions of Mrs. Elizabeth [Samways] Mitchell, Mrs. Massey Graves, Joseph Righton, and Mary Anthony, 15 and 16 July 1838, Pension Application of Elizabeth Mitchell, Roll 2114, RWP. Neither Elizabeth Samways, nor anyone with that last name, appeared in the city directories of 1785, 1790, 1794, 1796, 1801, and 1802, or in the 1790 and 1800 censuses. She may have remarried, relocated, or died shortly after her husband's death. Hagy, *People and Professions of Charleston.*

28. Eleanor Lestor (22 May 1786) and Elizabeth Thompson claims testimony, Audit Office Papers, series 12, vols. 48 and 46, 360–61 and 77–79 and series 13, vol. 134, 5 and vol. 136, 7, quoted in Norton, "'What an Alarming Crisis Is This,'" 217.

29. Petition of fifty-one women, 4 February 1780, in Hemphill, *JGAHR,* 274–75.

30. Petitions of Mary Inglis Junior, 8 December 1791, and Eleanor Mackey, 5 February 1784, Legislative Petitions, SCDAH, quoted in Kierner, *Southern Women in Revolution,* 116–18, 176–77.

31. Deposition of: Elizabeth [Samways] Mitchell, 16 July 1838, Pension Application of Elizabeth Mitchell, Roll 2114; Massey Graves, 6 July 1838, Job Palmer, 5 July 1838, and John Cart, 16 July 1838, Pension Application of James Graves, Roll 1111, RWP. Moore, *Abstracts of the Wills of the State of South Carolina,* 117. Petitions of Florence Cooke and Elizabeth Beard, quoted in Kierner, *Southern Women in Revolution,* 172, 188–90. See also Stoesen, "The British Occupation of Charleston," 72–73.

32. Mary Cape subsequently petitioned successfully for the return of her husband and recovery of part of their holdings. Mary Cape, quoted in Kierner, *Southern Women in Revolution,* 129–32. See also the petition of Jane Villepontoux, another merchant wife, in Kierner, *Southern Women in Revolution,* 134–35.

33. Petition of Mary Pratt, quoted in Kierner, *Southern Women in Revolution,* 63.

34. Petition of Ann Timothy, "Printer to the State," quoted in Kierner, *Southern Women in Revolution,* 182–85.

35. Quoted in Vestry Books, 1780, St. Philip's Church, vol. 3, April 1775–April 1795, Charleston, South Carolina.

36. *SGSC,* 2 September 1778; Petition of Mary Sansum, quoted in Kierner, *Southern Women in Revolution,* 39–40; *SCG,* 11 April 1771, 24 September

1772; Bridenbaugh, *Cities in Revolt,* 227, 358; Weir, *Colonial South Carolina,* 123, 170; Lambert, *South Carolina Loyalists,* 254–56.

37. Ramsay, *Ramsay's History of South Carolina,* 1:195.

38. Quoted in *Royal Gazette,* 23 June 1781; Webber, "Josiah Smith's Diary 1780–1781" (January 1932): 71; Webber, "Smith's Diary" (October 1933): 206–207.

39. On the lists, see Fraser, *Charleston,* 167; Salley, *Journal of the House of Representatives,* 3, 12–13; Salley, *Journal of the Senate,* 54, 72, 73–80. In 1783 and 1785, state legislators amended the Confiscation Acts, allowing listed loyalists to maintain some personal property and, specifically, providing maintenance to "widows and orphans" of loyalists. *SLSC,* 4:516–26, 555–57, 666–67; 6:629–33, 634–35.

40. Quoted in Fraser, *Patriots, Pistols, and Petticoats,* 148.

41. *Centennial of Incorporation,* 97; Stoesen, "The British Occupation of Charleston," 80–81; Ramsay, *Ramsay's History of South Carolina,* 1:271–72; Lambert, *South Carolina Loyalists,* 250–56; Quarles, *The Negro in the American Revolution,* 167–72; "Return of the People from South Carolina, Charlestown, 13th December 1782," quoted in Barnwell, "The Evacuation of Charleston," 7–8, 12, 26.

42. Miranda, *The New Democracy in America,* 24.

43. Printer Peter Timothy to William Henry Drayton, 22 August 1775, quoted in Barnwell, "Correspondence of Hon. Arthur Middleton, Signer of the Declaration of Independence," 131; Levett, "Loyalism in Charleston, 1761–1784," 3–4, 8, 10.

44. Henry Laurens quoted in Fraser, *Charleston,* 148.

45. Quoted in Wilkinson, *Letters,* 28–31. See also Ravenel, *Eliza Pinckney,* 240–41, 247, 250, 274–78, 280, 308–10. William Taggart died in 1783 without receiving compensation for the lost property. Mary Taggart petitioned the state legislature four times (and also the federal government) before Carolina lawmakers satisfied her claim in 1801. Petitions of Mary Taggart, 2 December 1794, 9 December 1796, 25 November 1800, Legislative Petitions, SCDAH.

46. Quoted in Eliza Pinckney to Mrs. R. E. [unreadable], 25 September 1780, Pinckney Family Papers, series 1, box 5, LC; Ravenel, *Eliza Pinckney,* 267, 276–77, 301–304, 308–10.

47. For examples, see Porter v. Dunn, 1 Bay 53 (S.C. 1787); Lambert, *South Carolina Loyalists,* 241.

48. SLSC, 4:487–90; Margaret and her heirs subsequently lost the estate to public auction in 1783. Coker, "Absentees as Loyalists in Revolutionary War South Carolina," 120–21.

49. Quoted in Stoesen, "The British Occupation of Charleston," 72, 74, 76. Depositions of: Mary Anthony, 30 May 1838, Pension Application of Mary Anthony, Roll 68; Mary Baker, 5 August 1844, Pension Application of Mary Baker, Roll 118; Sarah Lawrence, 20 November 1838, Pension Application of Sarah Lawrence, Roll 1532; Elizabeth [Hamilton] George, 15 December 1837, Pension Application of Elizabeth George, Roll 1170, RWP; Ramsay, *Ramsay's History of South Carolina,* 1:263.

50. Captain Goodin and Eliza Wilkinson quoted in Wilkinson, *Letters*, 2, 6, 79. Waring, *A History of Medicine in South Carolina*, 2:100–103; Davidson, *Friend of the People*, 42–44.

51. Wilkinson, *Letters*, 99–103.

52. Quoted in Ramsay, *Ramsay's History of South Carolina*, 1:253–54; Wilkinson, *Letters*, 94–97; Stoesen, "The British Occupation of Charleston," 74.

53. Wilkinson, *Letters*, 86.

54. Quoted in Wilkinson, *Letters*, 86; Miss Trapier to Harriott Pinckney Horry, August 1775, in Ravenel, *Eliza Pinckney*, 264–65.

55. Wilkinson, *Letters*, 53, 18–19, 61.

56. Quoted in [Charles Cotesworth Pinckney], Fourth of July Oration, Charleston, 1789, Pinckney Family Papers, LC. On women of color, see *SCGGA*, 26 March 1783; "Memorial of Sundry Inhabitants of Charleston on the Improper Importation of Negroes," 11 December 1797, General Assembly Petitions, 1797, #87, Records of the General Assembly, SCDAH. On white women, see the 1789 Pinckney Fourth of July Oration in its entirety, Pinckney Family Papers, LC; Wilkinson, *Letters*, 79; Alice Izard (Charleston) to Margaret Izard Manigault, 29 May 1801, Manigault Papers, SCL, Simms, *History of South Carolina*, 393; Ramsay, *Ramsay's History of South Carolina*, 1:197–98. On heroic actions by ladies, see C. C. Pinckney, Sr. (grandson of Rebecca Motte), Flat Rock, to Mr. Editor, 27 September 1855, Rebecca Motte Collection, P/4208, SCL; Deposition of Harriott P. Rutledge, 9 October 1855, Rebecca Motte Collection, SCL. Ravenel, *Eliza Pinckney*, 283–86.

57. On this paradigm of "true women"—made problematic by the Charleston evidence—see Welter, "The Cult of True Womanhood, 1820–1860," 151–74; Cott, "Passionless," 219–36; and Berg, *The Remembered Gate*.

3. Rebuilding and Resisting

1. Quoted in Barnwell, "The Evacuation of Charleston by the British in 1782," 20–21. Fraser, *Patriots, Pistols, and Petticoats*, 151–52.

2. Wilkinson, *Letters of Eliza Wilkinson*, 61.

3. *City Gazette*, 14 May 1791.

4. Quoted in *City Gazette*, 14 May 1791. Thirty-two years later, Charleston's civic hosts figured just as centrally in preparations for and during the visit of revolutionary hero, the Marquis de Lafayette. Robert Molloy, *Charleston, A Gracious Heritage*, 83.

5. Quoted in Kerber, *Women of the Republic*, 11–12. Eliza Pinckney and Miss Trapier quoted in Ravenel, *Eliza Pinckney*, 308, 264–65. Williams, *A Founding Family*, 10–13.

6. Mongin and Wife, late Pendarvis v. Baker and Stevens, 1 Bay 73, 76 (S.C. 1789).

7. Ann Legge quoted in 17 January 1783, General Assembly Petitions, SCDAH. See also Margaret Brisbane, 22 February 1783; Mary Inglis, 25 January 1783; Sarah Jones, 25 January 1783; Sarah Glen, 24 January 1783; Eleanor Mackie,

5 February 1784; Ann Legge, 17 January 1783, General Assembly Petitions, SCDAH; "An Act to Enable Mary Cumming to Sell and Convey Certain Lands . . . ," Records of the General Assembly, [S.C.] House of Representatives, 7 March 1789, microfilm, USDJ; Kierner, *Southern Women in Revolution, 1776–1800,* 211–13.

8.   Margaret Brisbane quoted in 22 February 1783, General Assembly Petitions, SCDAH. *Feme sole* was a legal, economic, and social classification which differentiated unmarried from married women and allowed women to own and operate businesses, execute binding contracts, and sue and be sued on their own accounts. Blackstone, *Commentaries on the Laws of England,* 1:430; 2:213–16, 497–99; Rice, *Digested Index of the Statute Law,* 357; *SLSC,* 2:593; 3:616–21; 6:212–13, 236–37.

9.   City resident quoted in *Charleston Times,* 28 October 1818; 12 June 1821. Rogers, *Charleston in the Age of the Pinckneys,* 52; Nash, "Urbanization in the Colonial South," 3–29; Fraser, *Charleston,* 81–82, 182; Hunt, *Life in America One Hundred Years Ago,* 71–72; Trenholm, "Centennial Address before the Charleston Chamber of Commerce," 11 February 1844.

10.   Quoted in *SCG,* 1 March 1783; *GPA,* 16 August; 3, 6 September 1785. Margaret Izard Manigault quoted in letter to Gabriel Manigault, 20 November 1792, Manigault Family Papers, SCL. The Marine Anti-Britannic Society verbally, and occasionally physically, assaulted individual members of the master class, set fires, and rioted in the streets. Their print attack relentlessly likened low-country "Nabobs" to the British aristocracy. Fraser, *Charleston,* 171–72.

11.   Kemble, *Journal of a Residence,* 36–38; Hunt, *Life in America,* 71; Lyell, *A Second Visit to the United States,* in Clark, *The Grand Tour,* 218.

12.   *SLSC,* 4:540; "Act of the South Carolina General Assembly, 12 March, 1783," in *SCGGA,* 25 March 1783. See also "A Proclamation," in *SCWG,* 29 March 1783 and in *SCGGA,* 25 March 1783.

13.   Mary Russel quoted in *GSSC,* 15 January 1784, in Windley, *Runaway Slave Advertisements,* 382. On Jenny, Dido, and Tissey, see *SGSC,* 11 August 1785, in Windley, *Runaway Slave Advertisements,* 391. See also *GSSC,* 21 February 1785; and *SGSC,* 29 September 1785; 13, 20 February, 25 May, 14 August, 2 October 1786; 23 August 1787; 11 February, 21 April, 1 May, 18 September 1788; 16 April 1789, in Windley, *Runaway Slave Advertisements,* 389, 392, 395–96, 399–401, 405–408. On Nancy and Tinah, see *SGSC,* 14 August 1786; 16 April 1789, in Windley, *Runaway Slave Advertisements,* 400–401, 408. See also *GSSC,* 1, 29 April, 6 May, 17 July, 2 August, 1, 18 November, 16 December 1784; *SGSC,* 18 February 1790, in Windley, *Runaway Slave Advertisements,* 382–88, 410; *GSSC,* 18 November 1784; "Charleston News" in *Columbian Herald* (Columbia), 18 May 1786; and *City Gazette,* 13 June 1788; 21 August 1797.

14.   For additional examples of slave women "harbored" in Charleston, see Windley, *Runaway Slave Advertisements,* 382, 387, 391, 395, 401, 408, 570–75. Dias, *Power and Everyday Life,* 5; *Heads of Families, First Census;* 1800 Census.

15.　On "ladies in distress," see *SCGGA*, 26–30 August, 30 August–2 September 1783. See also widows publicly announcing their need/desire to settle their husbands' estates in *SCGGA*, 21 June, 22, 29 March, 1, 5, 26 April, 24, 28 June, 1, 5, 8, 12, 15, 19, 22, 26, 29, 30 July, 2, 5, 9, 12, 16 August, 16–19 August, 19–23 August, 23–26 August, 26–30 August, 30 August–2 September 1783. For examples of postwar sales, see *SCGGA*, 7 June, 8, 12, 15, 19, 22, 26, 29 July, 2, 5, 9, 12, 16, 16–19, 23–26 August, 30 August–2 September 1783. On prewar sales, see extant issues of the *SCAGG* from 3 August 1779 to 4 February 4 1780. I chose these two periods of the *Gazette* (which changed names several times) because I could obtain access to nearly complete, uninterrupted runs of what was one of the city's principal newspapers.

16.　In 1785 a nationwide depression spread to Charleston, the price of African slaves dropped, and planters and city merchants were deeply in debt to British creditors. Economics drove the 1787 decision to ban slave importations, a prohibition the legislature successively renewed for sixteen years. Higgins, "Charleston: Terminus and Entrepot of the Colonial Slave Trade," 118. Jordan, *The White Man's Burden*, 126; Jordan, *White over Black*, 318. See also Nadelhaft, *The Disorders of War*, 148–49; Rogers, *Evolution of a Federalist*, 101. On the 1784 figure, see George Abbott Hall quoted in Drayton, *A View of South-Carolina*, 166–67. See also Berlin, *Many Thousands Gone*, 308–309; Kulikoff, "Uprooted Peoples," 149–50; Morgan, "Black Society in the Lowcountry, 1760–1810," 129–31. Sources on African importations do not specify the number of slaves remaining in Charleston. At best the data differentiate among yearly imports from Africa, the West Indies, and U.S. locations (interstate trade). Michael Tadman has estimated that 6,500 "new Africans were settled" in South Carolina in the 1790s, and 14,000 for the period 1800 to 1809. By then the low country was already a "net exporter of her own slaves (in the 1790s net exportations of some 2,000 slaves and from 1800–1809 of some 11,000 slaves)." By 1820 the entire state exported more slaves than it imported. Tadman, *Speculators and Slaves*, appendix 1, 226–27, 12. See also Nadelhaft, *Disorders of War*, 258, notes 24, 26.

17.　William Whittaker quoted in 1795, in Rae, *Turtle at Mr. Humble's*, 95. Quoted in "Memorial of Sundry Inhabitants of Charleston on the Improper Importation of Negroes," 11 December 1797, General Assembly Petitions, 1797, #87, SCDAH. In 1792 the state extended its 1787 ban on the African slave trade to include slaves from "the West India Islands, or any other place beyond the sea." *SLSC*, 7:430–31, 433, 435, 436, 450; Fraser, *Charleston*, 184–85; Molloy, *Charleston: A Gracious Heritage*, 83–84; Rogers, *Charleston in the Age of the Pinckneys*, 111; Berlin, *Many Thousands Gone*, 319.

18.　Order Book, 30th Regiment 7th Brigade, South Carolina Militia, 1793–1814, 26 August 1793, SCHS; Eckhard, *A Digest of the Ordinances*, 180; 1790 through 1810 censuses; Wikramanayake, *A World in Shadow*, 65–66.

19.　On the Daniel Cannan incident, see *SCGGA*, 10 May 1783. For additional examples see *SCGGA*, 8, 18, 24, 26 April, 3, 10, 24 May 1783. On refusing to name owners, see *SCWG*, 17 May, 14 June 1783. See also *SCWG*, 15 March 1783.

20.　Koger, *Black Slaveowners*, 88.

21. On Hannah Norman, see Koger, *Black Slaveowners,* 88; South Carolina Marriage Settlements, vol. 1: 1785–1792, 365; vol. 14: 1838–1841, 249–53, 323–24, SCDAH. On white widows selling slaves to achieve stability, see *SCGGA,* 3, 10, 24, 27 May 1783. In 1775 approximately one-half of Charleston's 12,000 residents were slaves, and by 1810, nearly 12,000 slaves lived in this city of over 25,000 people. Bridenbaugh, *Cities in Revolt,* 333–34; Wallace, *South Carolina,* 197; Fraser, *Charleston,* 28, 135; Berlin, *Many Thousands Gone,* 317; 1830 Census; "Recapitulation," in 1830 Census. On slave trading, see Tadman, *Speculators and Slaves,* 118–21; Russell, "Sale Day in Antebellum South Carolina" (Ph.D. diss.). See also *SCGGA,* 17 September 1783.

22. Quoted in *SGSC,* 20 February 1786; Presentments of the Charleston Grand Jury, in *SCSG,* 7 February 1799. For additional evidence of women hawking baked goods, milk, fruits, vegetables, and sand, see *State Gazette,* 13 February 1786; *City Gazette,* 18 July 1788; 8 July 1789; *SCSG,* 10 February, 22 December 1796; 14 September 1798; Charleston *Courier,* 10 February 1803; 30 September 1806. See also Presentments of the Grand Jury, in *State Gazette,* 23 February 1786; 20 June 1791. On 1839 complaints and laws, see also *SLSC,* 7:22.

23. On Judy, see *SCGGA,* 26 April 1783. For additional examples, see *Royal Gazette,* 22 September 1781, in Windley, *Runaway Slave Advertisements,* 589; "List of Slaves to be Sold at Auction," 12 September 1798, Alexander Ingles Papers, #1001, SCL; and *City Gazette,* 2 June 1797. On the historian's study of runaway ads, see Morgan, "Black Society in the Lowcountry," 100, 114.

24. Quoted in Olwell, *Masters, Slaves, and Subjects,* 282–83. See also Berlin, *Many Thousands Gone,* 290; Berlin, "The Revolution in Black Life," 363; Morgan, "Black Society in the Lowcountry," 113. On the Yates family, see Anna Yates to Elizabeth Ann Yates, 17 July 1822, Yates Family Papers, 11–478, folder 2, SCHS. On wills, see White et al., Executors of Margaret White v. Vaughan, Guardian of M. E. Harper, 1 Hill Eq. 253 (S.C. 1835). See also Huger v. Huger, 9 Richardson Eq. 217, 238 (S.C. 1857); Hodges v. Chick, 10 Richardson Eq. 178 (S.C. 1858); Cureton v. Massey, 13 Richardson Eq. 104, 106 (S.C. 1866). The will in *Cureton* was drafted before 1858 (when the testator died), but the appeals process continued for at least eight years. On Barbara (or Barbary) Bampfield, see Koger, *Black Slaveowners,* 89.

25. Morgan, "Black Society in the Lowcountry," 115–16; Olwell, "Becoming Free," 4–6. Olwell's more abbreviated search through Carolina manumissions has confirmed Morgan's findings. Olwell has discovered that 53 percent (199) of all South Carolina manumissions between 1737 and 1785 (379) were recorded in the ten years after 1775; a total of 394 were recorded from 1750 to 1790. On Hagar and Antigua, see "An Ordinance for Enfranchising a Negro-Woman, and Her Child, Late the Property of Mr. John Smyth," Records of the General Assembly, 12 March 1783, USDJ. In 1790 enumerators counted 7,700 slaves and nearly 590 free people of color in the city. Slaves made up 47 percent of the total city population, followed by white men, who numbered nearly 4,400 (27 percent of the city total), white women who numbered just over 3,700 (23 percent), and 586 free people of color (4 percent). *Heads of Families, First Census;* Ramsay, *Ramsay's History of South Carolina,*

1:271–72; 1790 through 1810 censuses. On the 1770 population, see South Carolina Governor William Bull in 1770, in Bridenbaugh, *Cities in Revolt,* 333–34; Wallace, *South Carolina,* 197.

26. Olwell, "Becoming Free," 5–7; Morgan, "Black Society in the Lowcountry," 116.

27. Emphasis added. *SLSC,* 4:540, 7:397, 402, 407.

28. SLSC, 7:440, 443.

29. Koger, *Black Slaveowners,* 38–39, 168; *Heads of Families, First Census;* City directories, 1816, 1819, 1822, in Hagy, *Charleston, South Carolina, City Directories,* 24, 61, 98.

30. In 1763 "free Mulatto man" Thomas Cole paid £86 sterling for his wife, Ruth, and two children, Barbary and Tom. MR, 5 May 1763, vol. LL603, SCDAH, in Olwell, "Becoming Free," 16. For examples of women, see MR, 21 November 1782, 3 July 1784, UU142; 10 May 1784, UU115, SCDAH, in Olwell, "Becoming Free," 12.

31. On Jane see MR, 13 July 1782, TT165, SCDAH, in Olwell, "Becoming Free," 12. Forty-five of the seventy-six self-purchases (59 percent) between 1737 and 1785, in which adult slaves' sex was clearly identified, were transacted by slave women, and only thirty-one (41 percent) by slave men. Sixty-two of the total 105 self-purchases were recorded between 1775 and 1785. Olwell, "Becoming Free," 10–12.

32. The petitioners did not clearly state their native kingdom or country. "Petition of Francis, Daniel, Hammond and Samuel (Free Moors) . . . and Fatima, Flora, Sarah, and Clarinda," 28 December 1789, in Kierner, *Southern Women in Revolution,* 213–14.

33. Eckhard, *Digest of the Ordinances,* 180; "Petition of the People of Colour," n.d., General Assembly Petitions, 1794, #216, SCDAH; Wikramanayake, *World in Shadow,* 65–66.

34. "Rules and Regulations," November 1, 1790, Brown Fellowship Society microfilm, COC.

35. Brown Fellowship Society microfilm, COC.

36. Koger, *Black Slaveowners,* 167; Harris, "Charleston's Free Afro-American Elite," 295.

37. Harris, "Charleston's Free Afro-American Elite," 296; Fitchett, "The Free Negro in Charleston, South Carolina" (Ph.D. diss.), 122, 301.

38. Kierner, *Southern Women in Revolution,* xxi, xxv.

39. Quoted in Florence Cooke, 21 January 1783, General Assembly Petitions, SCDAH; Elizabeth Beard, 16 November 1797, in Kierner, *Southern Women in Revolution,* 190; Catherine Read to Elizabeth Read Ludlow, n.d. [1806], Read Family Papers, SCL. See also Eleanor Mackey, 5 February 1784, in Kierner, *Southern Women in Revolution,* 176–77. Both Florence Cooke and Eleanor Mackey's language manifested an ideal dubbed by historians as republican motherhood, heretofore ascribed almost exclusively to wealthier women. Kerber, *Women of the Republic,* 11. On domestic, dependent pleas, see excerpts of Mary Fraser petition, 30 November 1796; Elizabeth Atkins, 1 Febru-

ary 1783; Elizabeth Willoughby, 19 January 1791; Mary Elliott, 4 December 1798, reprinted in Kierner, *Southern Women in Revolution,* 97, 111–12, 141, 221–23. Mary Beth Norton has concluded that home and family rather than political views or the Revolution were the primary concern of petitioners. Kathy Roe Coker has agreed and referred to the women as "apolitical." While some women focused on their domestic role and needs, evidence from South Carolina does not support this conclusion. Norton, *Liberty's Daughters,* 176–77; Coker, "The Calamities of War," 52. Thompson and Lumpkin, *Journals of the House of Representatives 1783–1784,* 15, 613.

40. Ann Timothy, 12 February 1785; 21 January, 30 October 1788; 21 February 1789; 18 January, 3 December 1791, General Assembly Petitions, SCDAH. See also Elizabeth Mitchell, 10 February 1783, General Assembly Petitions, SCDAH; Ann Timothy, 16 January 1790, in Kierner, *Southern Women in Revolution,* 182–85.

41. The law mandated that all goods exposed for sale in the markets or streets of the town, by slaves, "from and after the 10th day of April next, [would] be seized, and disposed of, agreeable to the directions of the act of the General Assembly." *SCGGA,* 26 March 1783. Petitioners included Emelia Meurset, Mary Seagood, Lena Callaghan, Elizabeth Purse, Sarah Yates, Catherine Duvall, Elizabeth Gilbert, Martha Wiggins, and Maria Litunk. Most were not of the master class, and likely owned but one slave each. One or two may have hailed from wealthy families, but the war had depleted their resources. "The Petition of Sundry Widows of Charles Town," General Assembly Petitions, 5 August 1783, #160, SCDAH.

42. Smith, *A Charlestonian's Recollections,* 65.

43. This 1796 legislation was equally ineffective, as evidenced by the redundant measures passed in 1817, 1825, 1834, and 1835. *SLSC,* 7:434–35, 454–55, 465–66, 516–17, 529. On colonial and post-Revolution custom, see Eliza Johnson, *SCGCJ,* 30 September 1766; "The Stranger," *SCG,* 24 September 1772; Presentments of the Grand Jury of Charlestown, in *SCG,* 24 May 1773; Ichabod Attwell, *SGSC,* 13 February 1786; Frederick Smith, *Royal Gazette,* 26 December 1781; Claudius Gaillard, *City Gazette,* 16 August 1790.

44. Petition of the bakers of Charleston, 19 February 1784, General Assembly Petitions, SCDAH. In 1788 seamstresses petitioned the state's Senate, and the following winter sent the same entreaty to the House. Petition of Sundry Seamstresses, 25 February 1788 and 26 January 1789, General Assembly Petitions, SCDAH. For comments of seamstresses and legislators, see Petition of Sundry Seamstresses, 25 February 1788. For exchange between "Julia" and "Cornelia," see *Charleston Morning Post and Daily Advertiser,* 11 April 1786, quoted in Nadelhaft, *Disorders of War,* 117.

45. Jackson, *Privateers in Charleston, 1793–1796,* 11–17, 24, 48, 63, 91.

46. Quoted in Alms House Minutes, 29 December 1800; 8 January 1801; 19 October 1803, CCA; Bellows, *Benevolence among Slaveholders,* 6, 74. Alms House Minutes, 24 February, 20 January, 7 August, 17 August, 27 December 1801, CCA.

47. Quoted in German Friendly Society Meeting Minutes, 1766–1787, 4 June,

27 August 1783; 21 January, 27 October 1784; 18 January, 27 December 1786, SCL. For multiple examples of women petitioning for and receiving aid, see 1783 and 1784 German Friendly Society Minutes, SCL.

48. Quoted in "Memorial of Intendant," n.d., General Assembly Petitions 1793, #9, SCDAH; "Memorial of Intendant and Wardens of Charleston," n.d., General Assembly Petitions, 1795, #21, SCDAH.

49. Petitions of Sarah Glen, 23 January 1783; Hannah Ash and Margaret Ash, 21 November 1795, in Kierner, *Southern Women in Revolution,* 34, 88–91.

4. Marriage and Cohabitation within the Aristocratic Paradigm

1. Quoted in Devall v. Devall, 4 DeSaussure Eq. 79, 83 (S.C. 1809). On the role of marriage, see Schwalm, "*A Hard Fight for We.*" Rogers, *Charleston in the Age of the Pinckneys,* 23; Hagy, *This Happy Land,* 162.

2. Slaves (over 7,600) and free people of African descent (586) composed the largest segment (over half) of Charleston's population, and census enumerators did not differentiate them by sex. Free women of color headed sixty-one households, free men of color headed only thirty-seven households, and five couples were listed together as a household head. All data in this paragraph is based on *U.S. Heads of Families, First Census,* 9, 38–44.

3. The 1848 census, like most censuses of this period, is flawed. It omitted the city's slaves and free people of color and contains errors. Nevertheless, it provides additional information on work and city demography and can be used in conjunction with the U.S. census. Widowers numbered only 180 compared to 877 widows. Women outlived men if they survived their childbearing years, and they also declined to remarry. This pattern was not unique to Charleston, but the city did have a higher percentage of widows than Boston and five European cities. Profiling marriage patterns is complicated by the nature of other extant demographic data. Until 1850, the U.S. census named only household heads and recorded just numbers of others by age categories (divided by sex). Until 1820, census takers did not differentiate between female and male slaves or free people of color. Also, city officials never systematically recorded antebellum marriages of white people or people of color. Chapman, "Inadequacies of the 1848 Charleston Census"; Dawson and DeSaussure, *Census of the City of Charleston,* 25–28.

4. Pease and Pease, *Ladies, Women, and Wenches,* 11. Dawson and DeSaussure, *Census of the City of Charleston,* 26–27. While no similar statistics exist for the late eighteenth century, contemporary accounts indicate that this 1848 marriage pattern likely held true in previous decades. Elizabeth Ann Saylor Yates married a cooper named Joseph in 1802 when she was fourteen years old. Elizabeth outlived Joseph. Young daughter of the prominent Izard family, Georgina, was only two years older than Elizabeth when she married in 1809. Elizabeth A. Yates to Harrison Gray Otis, U.S. Senator from Massachusetts, 30 September 1820, typescript copy, Yates Family Papers, 11–478, folder 1, SCHS; *Charleston City Funds and Taxpayers,* SCHS; Alice Izard to Margaret Izard Manigault, 5 March 1809, Manigault Family Papers, SCL. See also JBG Diary, 18 April 1856, 2:60.

5. English case law quoted in Anonymous, 2 DeSaussure Eq. 198, 202 (S.C. 1803); Blackstone, *Commentaries,* 1:430.

6. Salmon, *Women and the Law of Property,* 14–18.

7. Quoted in Vaigneur v. Kirk, 2 DeSaussure Eq. 640, 646 (S.C. 1808). On the marriage to a niece, see Bowers v. Bowers, 10 Richardson Eq. 551, 556 (S.C. 1858). On divorce, see Mattison v. Mattison, 1 Strobhart Eq. 387, 392 (S.C. 1847). On South Carolina Distinctiveness, see Basch, *Framing American Divorce,* 23, 49, 59–60; Bardaglio, *Reconstructing the Household,* 33.

8. Quoted in Cusack v. White, 2 Mill 368, 370, 376 (S.C. 1818). On the 1795 law, see Denton and Wife v. English, 3 Brevard 281 (S.C. 1814); Farr v. Thompson, Cheves 37 (S.C. 1839); Bowers v. Newman, 2 McMullan 647 (S.C. 1842); Fable v. Brown, 1 Hill Eq. 290 (S.C. 1835).

9. Quoted in Cusack v. White, 2 Mill 368, 372, 375; Denton and Wife v. English, 3 Brevard 281; Bell v. Nealy, 1 Bailey 312 (S.C. 1829); Judge John Belton O'Neall, 1833 and 1847, quoted in McCurry, *Masters of Small Worlds,* 87.

10. Quoted in Carroll, "Woman," in *The Charleston Book,* 134, 137–38. "C.R.C." originally published his poem in the *Southern Literary Journal* 3 (November 1836): 182–83. See also "Woman and Her Needs," *De Bow's Review,* 272–74, 286–89.

11. Quoted in Weiner, *Mistresses and Slaves,* 64–65, 71.

12. Quoted in Carson, *Life, Letters, and Speeches,* 75–76. Ulrich, *Good Wives,* xiii–xiv; Brown, *Good Wives, Nasty Wenches, and Anxious Patriarchs,* 24–27, 100–104.

13. JBG Diary, 10 April 1834, 3:26. Meta Morris Grimball's father, Colonel Lewis Morris (then a widower) married Amarantha Lowndes, eldest daughter of James Lowndes, during the winter of 1834 in Charleston.

14. Quoted in Cockrill v. Calhoun, 1 Nott and McCord 285, 287 (S.C. 1818); Commonplace Book of Maria H. Drayton Gibbes, Gibbes-Gilchrist Papers, folder 22, n.p., n.d., SCHS; Carroll, "Woman," in *The Charleston Book,* 137–38; Carson, *Life, Letters, and Speeches,* 75–76. On women's amiability, see JBG Diary, 1:111; Alice Izard to Henry Izard, Esq., 27 April 1808, Ralph Izard Papers, Box II, folder 20, SCL; Elizabeth M. Izard [E. M. I.] to Mrs. Alice Izard, 14 March 1809, Ralph Izard Papers, II, 23, SCL.

15. Quoted in [Anon.], "Marrying for Money," 229–33.

16. Alice Izard to Margaret Izard Manigault, 5 March 1809, Manigault Papers, SCL; Alice Izard to Henry Izard, Esq., 9 May 1809, II, 24; Alice Izard, to "The Hon[ora]ble Ralph Izard, Senator in Congress, 4 November 1794, 1:5; and Alice Izard to Ralph Izard, 9 November 1794, 1: 4, Ralph Izard Papers, SCL.

17. On marriage and death notices, see *GSSC,* 23 July, 27 August, 10 September 1783.

18. Quoted in Robert F. W. Allston, to Adele Petigru Allston, 1 March 1852, Robert F. W. Allston Family Letters, vol. 2, 1843–1858, SCL; Alice Izard to Henry Izard, Esq., 9 May 1809, Ralph Izard Papers, vol. 2, 24, SCL.

19. Alice Izard to Margaret Izard Manigault, 29 May 1801, Manigault Papers, SCL.

20. Margaret Izard Manigault to Alice Izard, 17 January 1812, Manigault Papers, SCL; Margaret Izard Manigault to Mary [Mrs. Charles Cotesworth] Pinckney, 2 April 1809, Manigault Papers, SCL.

21. "Records of the Taylor Family," typewritten reminiscences of Mrs. [Sally Elmore] Thomas Taylor, series 3, folder 4, 12, Franklin Harper Elmore Papers, #814, SHC; King, *Gerald Gray's Wife and Lily*, 72, 161.

22. Alice Izard (quoting Georgina Izard) to Margaret Izard Manigault, 5 March 1809; Alice Izard to Margaret Izard Manigault, 23 December 1807; 5 March 1809; Margaret Izard Manigault to Mary [Mrs. Charles Cotesworth] Pinckney, 2 April 1809; Alice Izard to Margaret Izard Manigault, 4 May 1809; Joseph Smith quoted in Alice Izard to Margaret Izard Manigault, 5 March 1809, in Manigault Papers, SCL. Quoted in *The Gazette* (Charleston), 24 September 1783.

23. Quoted in Boyce v. Owens, 1 Hill 8, 10 (S.C. 1833); Basch, *Framing American Divorce*, 49. See also Mattison v. Mattison, Strobhart Eq. 387, 392 (S.C. 1847).

24. Quoted in Jelineau v. Jelineau, 2 DeSaussure Eq. 45, 50 (S.C. 1801).

25. Quoted in Boyd v. Boyd, 1 Harper Eq. 144, 145 (S.C. 1824). See also Hair v. Hair, 10 Richardson Eq. 163 (S.C. 1858); Rhame v. Rhame, 1 McCord Eq. 197, 202 (S.C. 1826). Basch, *Framing American Divorce*, 47–49. On adultery and "ill usage," see State v. Brunson and Miller, 2 Bailey 149 (S.C. 1831); Taylor v. Taylor, 4 DeSaussure Eq. 165 (S.C. 1811); Hair v. Hair, 10 Richardson Eq. 163. On Judith Williams and the requirement of "double mistreatment," see Williams v. Williams, 4 DeSaussure Eq. 188 (S.C. 1811); Threewits v. Threewits, 4 DeSaussure Eq. 560 (S.C. 1815); Thompson v. Thompson, 10 S.C. Eq. 416 (S.C. 1859). Judges repeatedly used the term "alimony" in referring to an allowance paid by the husband to his wife for support. Unlike twentieth-century usage, the term did not imply legal divorce.

26. Jelineau v. Jelineau, 2 DeSaussure Eq. 48, 45, 46, 51. Emphasis added.

27. On the marital bargain or the expected rights married women acquired in return for legal and economic disabilities, see Prather v. Prather, 4 DeSaussure Eq. 33, 38 (S.C. 1809); Anonymous, 2 DeSaussure Eq. 198, 202.

28. Quoted in Anonymous, 4 DeSaussure Eq. 94, 95, 96, 97, 98, 99, 101 (S.C. 1810).

29. Quoted in Anonymous, 4 DeSaussure Eq. 94, 96, 97, 98, 99, 100.

30. Taylor v. Taylor, 4 DeSaussure Eq. 165; Threewits v. Threewits, 4 DeSaussure Eq. 560; quoted in Converse v. Converse, 9 Richardson Eq. 538 (S.C. 1856).

31. Quoted in Taylor v. Taylor, 4 DeSaussure Eq. 175; Bell and Wife v. Nealy, 1 Bailey 312, 313 (S.C. 1829); and Anonymous, 2 DeSaussure Eq. 204.

32. Threewits v. Threewits, 4 DeSaussure Eq. 561, 565, quoted on 575; Taylor v. Taylor, 4 DeSaussure Eq. 169, 170, quoted on 175; Converse v. Converse, 9 Richardson 537, 539, 542, 549, quoted on 569, 558. On abused women refused the property they brought into the marriage, see also Rhame v. Rhame, 1 McCord Eq. 197, 204, 209; Anonymous, 4 DeSaussure Eq. 94, 101, 102.

33. Jacob and Mary Kougley to "Dear Sir," 19 March 1832, The Holloway Scrap

Book, COC, quoted in Fitchett, "The Traditions of the Free Negro in Charleston, South Carolina," 149.

34.　"JMJ" [James M. Johnson] to "Dear Henry" [Henry Ellison], 23 December 1859, Ellison Family Papers, P/8799, SCL. Eliza Ann was the daughter of Matilda and William (April) Ellison of Sumter District, South Carolina, and for most of her life she lived at her family's home near Stateburg. Eliza Ann died at age fifty-nine on 4 March 1870. She left one son from her first marriage. Johnson and Roark, *Black Masters*, 3–4, 83–86, 109–10, 122–23, 208–209, 330.

35.　"A Slaveholder to Editor," *Mercury* (Charleston), 25 October 1859.

36.　Quoted in Johnson and Roark, *Black Masters*, 213–15. See also 202–203, 208, 216–17, 223, 225, 380; and *Charleston Directory . . . 1840 . . .*; Ford, "Westons," in *Census of the City of Charleston*, 173.

37.　Quoted in Crane, "Two Women, White and Brown," 212. Thomas Bonneau's will quoted in Fitchett, "Traditions of the Free Negro," 146. On Jennet and Thomas Bonneau, see Johnson and Roark, *Black Masters*, 108–109, 208, 222, 223. On mothers bequeathing slaves and other property to daughters, see Koger, *Black Slaveowners*, 24–25, 94–95. On Barbara Tunno, see Kennedy-Haflett, " 'Moral Marriage,' " 210–11; Woodson, *Free Negro Heads of Families*, 156; *Charleston Directory . . . 1840 . . .*; *Free Negro Tax Books*, 1841, SCDAH. On Maria and Anthony's slave origins, see Johnson and Roark, *Black Masters*, 243–44. On Maria Weston and other wealthy or comfortable women of color, see *List of Taxpayers, 1860*, SCHS.

38.　Michael Eggart, "Anniversary Address," Minutes of the Friendly Moralist Society, 11 June 1848, and New York *Tribune*, 10 November 1860, quoted in Johnson and Roark, *Black Masters*, 215, 225. In 1795, state legislators enacted the first tax of "two dollars per head, on all free negroes, mulattoes, and mistizoes, between the ages of sixteen and fifty years." The legislature amended the act in 1822, 1845, 1847, 1856, and 1858, when legislators assessed all free people between fifteen and fifty at $2.75. The Charleston City Council enacted a separate and higher tax for its free people of color that superseded the state assessment. Acts of the Assembly, South Carolina, 1795, SCDAH; *SLSC*, 4:461, 540; Eckhard, *Digest of the Ordinances*, 287.

5. Marriage and Cohabitation outside the Aristocratic Paradigm

1.　Quoted in Rawick, ser. 1, vol. 3, 152, 247. See also a 1792 court dispute over the ownership of a slave girl given as a wedding present: Johnston and Henderson v. Dilliard, 1 Bay 232 (S.C. 1792). While state statute law did not explicitly state this prohibition, case law specified that slaves could not "legally contract marriage," that the "marriage of such an one [slave] [was] morally good, but in point of law, the union of slave and slave or slave and free negro [was] concubinage merely." *SLSC*, 7:397–417; O'Neall, *Negro Law*, 22–23.

2.　Quoted in Rawick, ser. 1, vol. 2, 233–36, 226–32. See also Higgins, "Charleston: Terminus and Entrepot of the Colonial Slave Trade," 118; Tadman, *Speculators and Slaves*, 33, 91–92.

3.   Quoted in Carroll, "Woman," in *The Charleston Book*, 134, 137–38; "Woman and Her Needs," 272–74, 286–89; Commonplace Book of Maria H. Drayton Gibbes, Gibbes-Gilchrist Papers, folder 22, SCHS; *GSSC*, 16 July 1783.

4.   Quoted in *SCGGA* (Charleston), 27 May 1783; Bill of Sale and List of Slaves to be Sold at Auction, 12 September 1798, Alexander Ingles Papers, SCL; Rawick, ser. 1, vol. 3, 152.

5.   On these images, see Jelineau v. Jelineau, 2 DeSaussure Eq. 45 (S.C. 1801); State v. Scott, 1 Bailey 270 (S.C. 1829); Farr v. Thompson, Cheves 37 (S.C. 1839); O'Neall & Chambers v. The South Carolina Railroad Company, 9 S.C. 465 (S.C. 1856); *SCGGA*, 20 May 1783; Rawick, ser. 1, vol. 3, 10.

6.   If two different people had owned Kettura and Isaac, Kettura's owner would have been compensated monetarily for this lost property. "The State v. Isaac, the Slave of Edward Carew—Petition, Charleston," General Assembly Petitions, 3 July 1834, folder 247, SCDAH.

7.   "Recapitulation" [1790–1830] in *1830 Census;* 1820 through 1860 censuses.

8.   Quoted in *GSSC*, 16 July 1783. See also *SCGGA*, 8 April, 13 May 1783. On judges referring to slave wives and husbands, see Porter v. Dunn, 1 Bay 53 (S.C. 1787). On slaves without husbands/fathers, see *GSSC*, 10 September 1783; *SCGGA* 12 April 1783; Petition of William Rouse, 21 February 1800, Charleston County Court of Equity Bills, 1800, SCDAH; Rawick, ser. 1, vol. 3, 271; Herz, *My Travels in America*, 78.

9.   James Louis Petigru to Susan Dupont Petigru [King], 5 September 1859, in Carson, *Life, Letters, and Speeches.*

10.   On slave owner complaints about slaves cohabiting without permission, see *SCAGG*, 19 January 1776; *City Gazette*, 25 July 1797. The expression coined here, "separated union," sounds like an oxymoron, but captures reality: a couple committed to each other but forced, by slavery, to live apart. Municipal officials registered marriages of neither white people nor free people of color until 1853. State laws passed in 1856 and 1858 required registration of births, marriages, and deaths, but were repealed in 1861. Officials never systematically recorded this data until well after the Civil War. *SLSC*, Act Nos. 4264, 4410, and 4516.

11.   Quoted in *SCGGA*, 2 May 1783. Michael Tadman has estimated that over 1.1 million slaves, 30 percent of whom lived in South Carolina and Maryland, entered the South's interregional slave trade. Fully 70 percent of those 1.1 million slaves were "sold by planters to traders based at cities, such as Richmond and Charleston." Tadman, *Speculators and Slaves*, 12, 21, 31–41, 225–27.

12.   Quoted in Rawick, ser. 1, vol. 3, 309.

13.   Quoted in Lyles v. Bass, Cheves 85, 86 (S.C. 1840). On other men freeing enslaved spouses, see Koger, *Black Slaveowners*, 63–64, 74, 83, 91. As early as 1800, state legislators began restricting manumission, and in 1820 prohibited manumission of any slave except by special petition to the legislature. Its

members ignored most petitions. A state law enacted on 19 December 1835 made it unlawful "for any Free Negro or Person of Color to migrate into this State" including residents "who may hereafter leave the State" and subsequently try "to return again into the same." Violators were liable to imprisonment, corporal punishment, and sale as slaves. Brevard, *Alphabetical Digest of the Public Statute Law*, 2:255; *SLSC*, 6:245; 7:442–43, 459–60, 461, 463, 466, 470; Flagg, *Digested Index of the Statute Law*, 195; *Ordinances of the City of Charleston*, 378–79, 380.

14.   Cline v. Caldwell, 1 Hill 423, 424, 425, 427 (S.C. 1833). The force of custom is evident in Justice O'Neall's reference to Elizabeth and John as "married," impossible under South Carolina law.

15.   See also, Miller v. Reigne, 2 Hill 592 (S.C. 1835); Lyles v. Bass, Cheves 85, 86; Mathews v. Mathews Executrix, 1 McMullan Eq. 410 (S.C. 1842).

16.   Quoted in *Courier*, 14 August 1804. On Nanny, see Morgan, "Black Life in Eighteenth-Century Charleston," 215.

17.   On women who rejected the white ideal, see Rawick, ser. 2, vol. 2, 226–32, 233–36. The eight classes at Trinity Methodist included 265 women and 125 men. The church expelled 15 slave women for adultery and 1 for drunkenness. Four men were dismissed for adultery (3 percent of slave men), one for non-attendance, and one for fighting. Trinity Methodist Episcopal Church Roll, 1821–1868, folder 3, SCHS.

18.   Rawick, ser. 2, vol. 2, 226–32, 233–36. The notion of consensual sex between slaves and owners is much debated and problematic because of the uneven power relations of slavery. This woman's sexual relationship with her owner may have been coerced after her decision to leave Edisto. Their child became a Charleston bricklayer.

19.   Quoted in Boyd v. Boyd, 1 Harper Eq. 144 (S.C. 1824); Prince v. Prince, 1 Richardson Eq. 282 (S.C. 1845).

20.   Quoted in O'Neall, *Negro Law*, sec. 47, 13. On criticism of mixed marriages, see State v. Harden quoted in Powers v. McEachern, 7 Richardson 290, 293, 294 (S.C. 1876). In 1865 southerners coined the term "miscegenation" as a racist condemnation of mixing. *SLSC*, 7:397.

21.   "Franz Zebedaeus Schmelizle, or The Vigil of the Bridegroom," 25–26; "White Lily," and "How Gertrude Was Married," *Russell's Magazine* 3 (June 1858): 267, 245, 248; "Marrying for Money," 229–33.

22.   Charleston County Court of General Sessions, Bills of Indictment, No. 1786/1A through No. 1808/27A and No. 1807/29A Oversize, Box 44, 12 January 1801, SCDAH (hereafter Bills of Indictment, SCDAH); Bills of Indictment, 5A, January 1801; and 41A, 17 April 1807, SCDAH.

23.   Quoted in Rawick, ser. 1, vol. 3, 211; Hagy, *This Happy Land*, 166. On the tale of Thiennette, see "Franz Zebedaeus Schmelizle, or The Vigil of the Bridegroom," 23–30. *Hazans*, later called cantors, sang or chanted liturgical music and led congregations in prayer.

24.   City resident Daniel Elliot Huger Smith quoted in Smith, *A Charlestonian's Recollections*, 64–65. George Bedon quoted in Fitchett, "Traditions of the

Free Negro," 148. On poor white girls, see Minutes of the Charleston Orphan House, 25 November, 2 December 1790, CCA (hereafter Orphan House minutes); Orphan House "Rules and Regulations," adopted July 1791, Orphan House minutes; Elzas, *The Jews of South Carolina*, 285–86. On city belles, see quote in Robert F. W. Allston to Adele Petigru Allston, 1 March 1852, Allston Family Letters, SCL.

25. Quoted in Hargroves v. Meray, 2 Hill Eq. 174, 175 (S.C. 1835). In this case, Thomas Hargroves and his wife, the former Susan Wheeler (now administratrix of her first husband's estate), disputed William Wheeler's conveyance of "a family of negroes" to Mary Evans Meray.

26. It is nearly impossible to document numbers of free women who wed slaves. In 1860 only 4 percent of free women of color who headed households "had a coresiding spouse . . . [but] most of them did . . . have children." Many of these women likely were married to slave men who may or may not have lived with them; if the husbands did live in the households, census enumerators would have listed them as slaves, not husbands. Quoted in Johnson and Roark, *Black Masters*, 208–12, 225, 378; Koger, *Black Slaveowners*, 168, 169, note 24. See also *Heads of Families, First Census;* 1820 through 1860 censuses. Census enumerators (inconsistently) differentiated between "black" and "mulatto" people. In 1860, approximately one-quarter of Charleston's free women of color were dark-skinned. Of the 143 "black" women who headed households, 97 were mothers, and only 5 of them lived with a spouse. Fully 92 percent of "mulatto" male household heads with coresiding spouses in 1860 had married "mulatto" rather than "black" women. Average wealth of "mulatto" women exceeded that of "black" women by three times. On color consciousness, see *Rules and Regulations of the Brown Fellowship Society Established at Charleston, S.C., 1st November 1790* (Charleston, S.C.: J. B. Nixon, 1844), COC; *Rules and Regulations of the Friendly Moralist Society*, COC. See also Johnson and Roark's analysis of the 1860 census in *Black Masters*, 208–12, 378–79.

27. Quoted in Stansell, *City of Women*, xiii, 217, 221. See also Peiss, *Cheap Amusements*. On the Lyons, Princes, and Jewish ecclesiastical divorce, see Hagy, *This Happy Land*, 178–79.

28. Quoted in Torre v. Summers, 2 Nott & McCord 267, 268 (S.C. 1820). See also Bell and Wife v. Nealy, 1 Bailey 312 (S.C. 1829).

29. Quoted in Barnwell, *The Character of Eve*, 21–22. William preached his sermon in St. Peter's Church, and it was published "for the benefit of the Ladies Benevolent Society of Charleston." On Elizabeth Dillon's, Catherine Doyle's, and other women's criminal activities, see State v. Arden, 1 Bay 487 (S.C. 1795); 28 June, 17 September 1806, Bills of Indictment, 36A-2, 36A-3, 16A-2, Box 44, SCDAH; State v. Parkerson and Mary Parkerson, his wife, 1 Strobhart 169 (S.C. 1847). On "worthless" women, see quote in Thompson v. Thompson, 10 S.C. Eq. 416, 418 (S.C. 1859). The presiding judge in this case uttered these words in discounting testimony of two "unworthy" women. He deemed plaintiff Jane Thompson several notches up from her friends, but pointedly accused her of being "very far from" the expected standard of "conjugal propriety."

30. Quoted in *SCGGA*, 31 May 1783; Bell v. Nealy, 1 Bailey 312 (S.C. 1829).

31. See Johnson v. Johnson, 1 DeSaussure Eq. 595 (S.C. 1800); Vaigneur v. Kirk, 2 DeSaussure Eq. 640 (S.C. 1808); Cockrill v. Calhoun, 1 Nott & McCord 285 (S.C. 1818); Fryer v. Fryer 9 S.C. Eq., 85, 92 (S.C. 1832); State v. Hilton, 3 Richardson 434 (S.C. 1832); Rutledge v. Tunno et al., 41 S.E. 308 (S.C. 1904). Despite its 1904 date, the Tunno case debated a nineteenth-century relationship.

32. Quoted in North v. Valk et al., Dudley Eq. 212, 221, 222, 223 (S.C. 1837). The plaintiff, North, initiated this action to secure a portion of Wightman's estate for Elizabeth and her children. Defendants "Valk et al." represented Wightman's other heirs who disputed Elizabeth's claim.

33. North v. Valk, Dudley Eq. 212, 221, 222.

34. Quoted in State v. Brunson and Miller, 2 Bailey 149, 150, 151 (S.C. 1831); Boyd v. Boyd, 1 Harper 144, 145. Emphasis added. See also Williams v. Prince, 3 Strobhart 490 (S.C. 1849); Thompson v. Thompson, 10 S.C. Eq. 416.

35. Prince v. Prince, 1 Richardson 282, 284, 285, 286. Beth Elohim's *bet din,* or (Jewish) ecclesiastical court, had sanctioned the Princes' divorce in 1840, the second of only two recorded in Charleston. As true of the first one in 1788, the state neither interfered with nor recognized its legality, possibly because "the 'peculiar institution' of Judaism so baffled the authorities that they allowed the Jews to do things according to their own laws." During Sarah's 1845 petition for alimony, the secular (state) court made no mention of the 1840 proceeding. Quoted in Hagy, *This Happy Land,* 178–79.

36. Quoted in Prince v. Prince, 1 Richardson 282, 286, 287, 288, 290.

37. Prince v. Prince, 1 Richardson 282, 286, 287, 288, 289, 290. See also Thompson v. Thompson, 10 S.C. Eq. 416, 419.

38. Quoted in Anonymous, 2 DeSaussure Eq. 198, 205 (S.C. 1803); Converse v. Converse, 9 Richardson Eq. 565–66 (S.C. 1856). See also Threewits v. Threewits, 4 DeSaussure Eq. 560, 576 (S.C. 1815).

6. Mixing and Admixtures

1. *SCG,* 18 March 1732; 31 July 1736; Martineau, *Society in America,* 2:328; Davis, *Travels of Four Years and a Half in the United States of America* (1803), quoted in Morgan, "Black Life in Eighteenth-Century Charleston," 211.

2. On sexual exploitation, see White, *Ar'n't I a Woman?;* Painter, "Of *Lily,* Linda Brent, and Freud," 93–109; Beckles, "Property Rights in Pleasure," 692–701; Jacobs, *Autobiography of a Slave Girl;* Herz, *My Travels in America,* 78; Rawick, ser. 1, vol. 2.

3. Brown, *Good Wives, Nasty Wenches, and Anxious Patriarchs,* 181. See also McCurry, *Masters of Small Worlds.*

4. On "consensual" sex, see Merrens, "A View of Coastal South Carolina in 1778: The Journal of Ebenezer Hazard," 190; Will of Joseph Roper in Moore, *Abstracts of Wills,* 417; Vose v. Hannahan, 10 S.C. 465 (S.C. 1857). See also contemporaries quoted in Morgan, "Black Life in Eighteenth-Century Charleston," 210–11. On emancipation, see in Thorne v. Fordham, 4 Richardson Eq.

222, 223 (S.C. 1852); Bowers et al. v. Newman, 2 McMullan Eq. 647 (S.C. 1842). On the population increase, see Coclanis, *The Shadow of a Dream*, 115, table 4-4; Morgan, "Black Life," 194–96, 212; Berlin, *Many Thousands Gone*, 232, 234–36, 239, 319–20, 331–32. On the prevalence of women, see Olwell, "Becoming Free, 5–6.

5.   On Sylvia, see Fraser, *Charleston*, 130. On Rebecca Kelly, see Somers v. Smyth, 2 DeSaussure Eq. 214, 217 (S.C. 1803). Administrators of the estate of plaintiff Somers contested deeds of property and bills of sale executed on 18 August 1794, in which Samuel Adams conveyed nearly all his property to Rebecca Kelly. The defendant, John Smyth, served as Samuel Adams's administrator and represented Rebecca Kelly's interests. On Jenny and Rebecca Thorne, see Hagy, *This Happy Land*, 100; Thorne v. Fordham, 4 Richardson Eq. 222, 223; Koger, *Black Slaveowners*, 33. See also Moore, *Abstracts of Wills*, 131; Miller v. Mitchell, Bailey Eq. 428 (S.C. 1831); Fable and Franks v. Brown, 1 Hill Eq. 290 (S.C. 1835); Carmille v. Administrator of Carmille, et al, 2 McMullan Eq. 635 (S.C. 1842); Monk v. Pinckney, 9 Richardson Eq. 279 (S.C. 1857). On manumission law, see Brevard, *Alphabetical Digest of the Public Statute Law*, 2:255 (hereafter Brevard, *Digest*); SLSC, 6:245, 7:442–43, 459–60, 461, 463, 466, 470; Flagg, *Digested Index of the Statute Law*, 195; *Courier*, 1, 12 December 1821. On Celestine, see *Free Negro Tax Books*. See also Ford, *Census of the City of Charleston*, 117; Koger, *Black Slaveowners*, 75; Powers, *Black Charlestonians*, 37.

6.   Quoted in Conveyance of Property, 12 October 1813, Hagar Richardson Estate Papers, 12/194–276, SCHS. Vanderhorst Biography and Genealogy, and Confirmation of manumission, 10 May 18[unreadable], Vanderhorst Papers, 30/04, SCHS; Tax receipts, 25 May 1819; 6 May 1820, Richardson Estate Papers, SCHS.

7.   Quoted in Ford, Escheator v. Dangerfield, 8 Richardson Eq. 96, 97 (S.C. 1856); Fable and Franks v. Brown, 1 Hill Eq. 290, 299.

8.   Quoted in Dougherty v. Executors of Dougherty, 2 Strobhart Eq. 63, 64, 67 (S.C. 1848). See also the case of Daphne, her owner, George Broad, and their eleven children. George's trusted friend and estate executor, John Dangerfield, sold three of Daphne and George's children. Ford, Escheator v. Dangerfield, 8 Richardson Eq. 95, 96, 97, 98.

9.   On white men bequeathing property, see Carmille v. Carmille et al , 2 McMullan Eq. 635, 639, 645 (S.C. 1842); Thorne v. Fordham, 4 Richardson Eq. 222; Broughton v. Telfer, 3 Richardson Eq. 431 (S.C. 1851). On white men who acknowledged paternity in their wills, see Farr et al. v. Thompson, Cheves 37 (S.C. 1839); Vose v. Hannahan, 10 S.C. 465; *Record of Wills of Charleston County*, vol. 40, Will Book A, 1834–39, 203, CCL. On bastardy law, see Brevard, *Digest*, 1:66–68; SLSC, 5:270–71; State v. Clark, 2 Brevard 385 (S.C. 1810); State v. Clements, 1 Speers 48 (S.C. 1842).

10.   Quoted in Simms, "The Morals of Slavery," 228; Fuller, *Chaplain to the Confederacy*, 72–73. On other cases of likely sexual exploitation, see runaway ads: GSSC, 1 September 1784; 21 February 1785; 14 August 1786;1 May 1788; 7 October 1790; SCAGG; 29 November 1780; *Royal Gazette*, 20–23 February 1782.

11. Quoted in Manigault, "Autobiography," 78, SHC; Lyell, *Second Visit to the United States,* 1:271 (hereafter Lyell, *Second Visit*); Herz, *My Travels in America,* 78. See also Margaret Izard Manigault to Gabriel Henry Manigault, 6 December 1808, Louis Manigault Papers, DU; Margaret Izard Manigault to Charles Manigault, 3 January 1813, Manigault Family Papers, SCL; Charles Manigault to R. Habersham & Co., 1 November 1846, Manigault Letter Book, typescript copy, 8, Manigault Papers, SCL; Louis Manigault to Charles Manigault, 22 November 1852, Louis Manigault Papers, DU; Mellon, *Bullwhip Days,* 297. In late 1806, a Monsieur Sannite Ferret highlighted twenty-five-year-old Arsinete's "big breasts" in his runaway ad, an atypical detail to include in newspaper announcements of missing slaves. His sexual advances likely contributed to Arsinete's decision to run. *L'Oracle* (Charleston), 5 January 1807. See also 11 July 1807 on runaway, Désirée. On urban compounds, see Rosengarten, *Between the Tracks,* 31, 34, 55; Porter, *Lead On! Step by Step,* 217; personal visit by the author to the Aiken-Rhett compound, Charleston, South Carolina, 13 June 1997.

12. Quoted in Morgan, "Black Life in Charleston," 211; Martineau, *Society in America,* 2:328; Kemble, *Journal of a Residence,* 14; Lyell, *Second Visit,* 1:271. See also Gilman, *Recollections of a Southern Matron,* 116; Grimké, *Letters on the Equality of the Sexes,* 53–54. On the impact of mixing on white people, see Simms, "The Morals of Slavery," 228–29. The slave who revealed the Vesey plan to his owner reaped substantial rewards (including his freedom and a life annuity) from municipal officials. Over 125 slaves and free people of color were arrested; 35 were hung; others were banished from the state. Pearson, *Designs Against Charleston,* 1, 144; Lofton, *Insurrection in South Carolina.*

13. Ebenezer Hazard quoted in Merrens, "A View of Coastal South Carolina," 190.

14. Quoted in *Mercury,* 29 October 1823. On Maria, Elsey, and Catharine Maria, see Hagy, *This Happy Land,* 100. On other white men's bequests to African American women, see Thomas Hanscome Will, 3 January 1832, quoted in Pease and Pease, *Ladies, Women, and Wenches,* 107; Koger, *Black Slaveowners,* 41, 170; Harris, "Charleston's Free Afro-American Elite," 297.

15. Quoted in Thomas N. Holmes testimony, 3 February 1903, submitted to Charleston County Court of Common Pleas, "Case and Exceptions for Appeal, The State of South Carolina in the Supreme Court, November Term 1901," Langdon Cheves III Legal Papers, SCHS 12–107, folder 5, 43 (hereafter Holmes testimony, Cheves Papers, 5, SCHS); Theodore E. Mitchell testimony, 3 February 1903, Cheves Papers, 5, 45, SCHS; Farr v. Thompson, Cheves 37. Evidence on Margaret and Adam derives from testimony and other court documents from an 1891 estate dispute that slogged through state courts over thirteen years. Depositions by elderly former slaves related their experiences in the Tunno household; Margaret and Adam's brown and white heirs battled over conflicting claims. Rutledge v. Tunno et al., 41 S.E. 308 (S.C. 1902); Rutledge v. Tunno et al., 48 S.E. 297 (S.C. 1904); Rutledge v. Tunno 69 S.C. 400 (S.C. 1904); "Case and Exceptions for Appeal, The State of South Carolina in the Supreme Court, November Term 1901," Cheves Papers, 5 (hereafter "Case and Exceptions," Cheves Papers, SCHS). On the lawsuit, see Kennedy-Haflett, " 'Moral Marriage,' " 206–26. At trial, Liston W. Barguet testified that Adam

Tunno educated and treated him "properly as [a] Grandparent should." Liston's grandfather died when he was twelve, and his mother, "was at [Adam's] bedside when he died." Margaret died in late 1839 or early 1840, eight years after Adam died. Liston W. Barguet deposition, 29 December 1902, Cheves Papers, 5, 37; Will of Adam Tunno, 16 June 1831, Will Book G, 1826–1834, 651, 733; and Will of Margaret Bettingall, 16 May 1838, Will Book I and J, 1839–1845, 32, WPA Typescripts, CCL (hereafter Tunno will and Bettingall will); *Courier,* 28 December 1832. Holmes testimony, 40; Mitchell testimony, 45, Cheves Papers, 5, SCHS.

16. Quoted in Beckles, *Natural Rebels,* 142–44, 146; Karasch, *Slave Life in Rio de Janeiro,* 89–90, 185–86. On Virginia and North Carolina, see Hodes, *White Women, Black Men.*

17. Quoted in Mackay, *The Western World,* excerpted in Clark, *The Grand Tour,* 239. On the ubiquity of slave women in Charleston, their work, and their labor relations, including hiring and self-hire, see chapter 7. From September 1844 to August 1848, an average of two to three people per month paid for hiring advertisements in one city newspaper. *Courier,* "Advertisements," 34–604, "Cash Received" ledger, SCHS. See also *GSSC,* 15 January 1784; Rawick, ser. 1, vol. 2, 226–32, 233–36, Charles Manigault to Louis Manigault, 17 January 1860, reprinted in Clifton, *Life and Labor on Argyle Island,* 291; Singleton, "The Slave Tag," 45–53.

18. On jumping the fence, see *City Gazette,* 24 July 1800. On Silvia, see *SCGGA,* 7 June 1783. On Nanny and dances, see Morgan, "Black Life," 215, 211. On hiring, see *RSCG,* 21 December 1780; *CG,* 16 April 1801; 24 March 1810; 12 June 1816; 11 June 1817; *Courier,* 4 April 1807; 24 March 1810; 27 June 1811; 19 November 1821; 3 December 1824. See also David S. Yates to Mrs. Yates, 30 July 1824, Yates Family Papers, 11 478, folder 7, SCHS; *SGSC,* 20 February 1786; *SCSG,* 21 July 1798; Anna Yates to Elizabeth Ann Yates, 17 July 1822, Yates Family Papers, folder 2, SCHS; Anne [or Anna] Yates to "My Dear Sister" [not identified], 20 August 1824, Yates Family Papers, folder 6, SCHS; Hodgson, *Remarks during a Journey,* 142–43; Koger, *Black Slaveowners,* 158.

19. Quoted in *SCAGG,* 29 November 1790; *Royal Gazette,* 20 February 1782; *Charlestown Gazette,* 11 January 1780; *SCGGA,* 23 September 1783, reprinted in Windley, *Runaway Slave Advertisements,* 573, 595, 706. On the valet and slave, see Herz, *My Travels in America,* 72–74. See also Foster, *Written by Herself,* 102, 105. On "market wenches," see *SCGGA,* 1 April 1784; Gilman, *Recollections of a Southern,* 135.

20. Quoted in Beckles, *Natural Rebels,* 142–44, 146; Smith and Courtenay, "Sketch of the History of Charleston," 304–305. See also Leland, "Early Taverns in Charleston," n.p.; Charles Fraser Commonplace Book, 123, COC; *Mercury,* 16, 21 September 1837; 20 June 1839. On "bawds," see Pressley, *Law of Magistrates and Constables,* 77–78; *SLSC,* 6:236. On the "Big Brick," see Smith and Courtenay, "Sketch of the History of Charleston," 304–305; Fraser, *Charleston,* 212, 235; Leland, "Early Taverns"; *List of the Taxpayers of Charleston, 1860,* 218.

21. On Dietrick Olandt, quoted in *Mercury,* 16, 21 September 1837; 20 June 1839. See also City Directory of 1835–1836; On Cornel June, see *Morning Post* (Bos-

ton), 7 November 1835; City Directory of 1835, reprinted in Hagy, *Directories for the City of Charleston*, 47. On Mrs. Street, quoted in Stuart, *Three Years in North America*, 2:101. On hiring arrangements, see Paul Cross Papers, folder 12, 24 January 1789, SCL; Receipt, 1 April 1815, P/9095, SCL; Receipt Book, 1829–1889, Mary Aldret Papers, SCHS; JBG Diary, 10 October 1832; 7 April, 14 August 1833; 7 May 1834, SHC.

22.   *SCGGA*, 27 May 1783; Hagy, *People and Professions of Charleston;* Dawson and DeSaussure, *Census of the City of Charleston*, 29–35.

23.   On "brutal" and "barbarous" treatment in urban areas, see Rawick, ser. 1, vol. 2, 233–36; Stuart, *Three Years in North America* (1833), 107; Angelina Grimké quoted in Lerner, *The Grimké Sisters from South Carolina*, 264–65. On urban life and the sex market, see Smith and Courtenay, "Sketch of the History of Charleston," 304–306; Fraser, *Charleston*, 212, 235. See also Karasch, *Slave Life in Rio de Janeiro*, 89–90, 185–86, 205; Beckles, *Natural Rebels*, 142–44.

24.   In a sample of over two hundred South Carolina court cases, only three referenced the possibility of "mulattoes" having a white mother; none of the three commented directly on the sexual relations between white women and men of color. See also Hodes, *White Women, Black Men;* Fox-Genovese, *Within the Household*, 241.

25.   Henri Herz witnessed Zampo's purchase and heard the account of subsequent events several months later from a Charleston "Creole." Herz, *My Travels in America*, 79–82.

26.   Quoted in Peases, *Ladies, Women, and Wenches*, 157. Meeting Minutes, Commissioners of the Poor House, 25 February 1830; 20 June, 29 August, 11 November, 23 December 1840, CCA (hereafter Poor House Minutes). See also Morgan, "Black Life," 221; State v. Elizabeth Mills, 9 May 1835, Records of Indictments and Subpoenas, Charleston County Court of General Sessions, SCDAH.

27.   Quoted in State v. Scott, 1 Bailey 270 (S.C. 1829). On the white mother and "negro" father, see State v. [Mary] Hayes, 1 Bailey 275 (S.C. 1829). On white wives and black or mixed-race men, see Cline v. Caldwell, 1 Hill 423 (S.C. 1833); and State v. Cantey, 2 Hill 614 (S.C. 1835). On the notion of sexual power subjugating women, see Somers v. Smyth, 2 DeSaussure Eq. 214; Simms, "The Morals of Slavery," 228. See also Brown, *Good Wives, Nasty Wenches*, 332, 334.

28.   Quoted in State v. Motley and Blackledge, 7 Richardson 324, 334, 335 (S.C. 1854). See also State v. Harden, 2 Speer 155 (S.C. 1844). African Americans as a "curse" quoted in Morton v. Thompson, 6 Richardson Eq. 370, 372 (S.C. 1854) and Olmsted, *The Cotton Kingdom*, 1:307–308. Following the Vesey insurrection in 1822, state legislators ordered "a minute and particular account of the actual condition of [the free brown and black] population" and passed new, more restrictive laws against slaves and free people of color, but neutralized extremist legislative proposals to banish all free people of African descent from the state. While they concluded that people of mixed race did not pose a threat, lawmakers advocated strong measures to safeguard slavery and the

legal and social disabilities of free people of color. Johnston, *Race Relations in Virginia and Miscegenation in the South*, 84–85; Pearson, *Designs Against Charleston*, 147–62. See also Johnson and Roark's *Black Masters*, chap. 5, "Freedom Besieged."

29. Quoted in State v. Davis, 2 Bailey 558, 559 (S.C. 1831); State v. Cantey, 2 Hill 614, 615; State v. Davis, 2 Bailey 558; Monk v. Jenkins, 1 Hill Eq. 13, 14 (S.C. 1834); A South-Carolinian, *A Refutation of the Calumnies*, 84–85. See also *SLSC*, 7:398. "Admixtures" quoted in State v. Cantey, 2 Hill 614, 615.

30. Quoted in State v. Cantey, 2 Hill 614, 615, 616; King, ads [at the suit of] James Wood, and Mary, his wife, 1 Nott & McCord 184, 185 (S.C. 1818). The term "mulatto" denoted not merely an admixture, but also "one gotten between . . . different species of animals . . . as a mule," and connoted social and legal degradation. For this reason, in 1818, Mary Wood filed suit (through her husband) against another Charleston resident who had called her a mulatto. The court ruled the term "actionable," and upheld Mary's "action of slander" stating that she had incurred "the greatest injury . . . to [her] reputation and feelings." State v. Scott, 1 Bailey 270, 273. See also [Narcissa] Smith v. [Samuel] Hamilton, 10 S.C. 44 (S.C. 1856).

31. Elizabeth was born on the Banana Islands (now Sierre Leone) around 1741. Quoted in Porcher, "Upper Beat of St. John's, Berkeley: A Memoir," 34–36. See also George, *The Rise of British West Africa*, 66.

32. Quoted in Merrens, "Journal of Ebenezer Hazard," 190; Stuart, *Three Years in North America*, 111.

33. Quoted in Painter, "Of *Lily*, Linda Brent, and Freud," 98–99, 103–104, 106. King, *Gerald Gray's Wife and Lily*, xiv, 43–44, 109, 200–202. Because he was his white master's son, Isiah Jefferies's white mistress considered him a "bone of contention" between her and her husband. Quoted in State v. Scott, 1 Bailey 270, 273. See also Jelineau v. Jelineau, 2 DeSaussure Eq. 45, 51 (S.C. 1801); Rawick, ser. 1, vol. 3, 17–19.

7. Work and Workers

1. Quoted in State v. Cantey, 2 Hill 614, 615 (S.C. 1835).

2. Heads of Families, First Census; Dawson and DeSaussure, *Census of the City of Charleston*, 29. In 1860, over 600 free women of color (50 percent of all free workers of color) labored as dressmakers, tailoresses, and mantua makers (220), seamstresses (158), laundresses and washers (150), house servants (46), cooks (14), nurses (21), and milliners (4). Johnson and Roark, *Black Masters*, 344; Rosengarten *Between the Tracks*, 81.

3. Fox-Genovese and Weiner have emphasized the ambivalent interactions of mistresses and slaves, but Weiner, unlike Fox-Genovese, has concluded that white women on large plantations "recognized common experiences" with slave women. Fox-Genovese, *Within the Plantation Household*, 142, 164; Weiner, *Mistresses and Slaves*, 2, 75.

4. Quoted in Pease and Pease, *Ladies, Women, & Wenches*, 148, 159.

5. Quoted in Rawick, ser. 1, vol. 3, 51–53. See also Martineau, *Retrospect,* 1:214; Johnson and Roark, *Black Masters,* 157.

6. Quoted in Ewart v. Nagel, 1 McMullan 32, 34 (S.C. 1840). Although women's reproductive labor constituted a tangible, economic quantity, that work was not calculated into the larger economy. On this topic, see Robertson and Klein, *Women and Slavery in Africa;* Boydston, *Home and Work.*

7. Quoted in Bellows, *Benevolence among Slaveholders,* xiv.

8. Quoted in Preamble, "Rules and Regulations of the Female Charitable Association for Relief of the Sick Poor of Charleston Neck," 21 July 1824, Female Charitable Association records, 50–260 (hereafter FCA, SCHS). Ladies Benevolent Society Journal 2, 1823–1871 (original, oversize, handwritten volume), 15 December 1826, SCHS (hereafter LBS Journal, SCHS); "A List of Members for Life and Annual Subscribers to the Ladies Benevolent Society," Constitution of the Ladies Benevolent Society, SCL (hereafter LBS, SCL).

9. Quoted in "Act of Incorporation and Constitution of the Ladies Benevolent Society," 15 September 1813, typescript copy, LBS, SCL; Article IX, LBS Constitution, SCL; Annual Report of the Board of Managers to the Ladies' Benevolent Society, LBS Journal, 15 September 1824, SCHS.

10. LBS Journal 2, 15 June 1825, SCHS.

11. Quoted in Rule 1, FCA Rules and Regulations, FCA, SCHS. Not until 1849 did municipal officials extend city limits to incorporate the Neck.

12. FCA minutes, Annual Meeting, 21 July 1825; 28 July, 21 October 1824; 21 January, 21 July, 21 October 1825; 21 January 1826, FCA, SCHS. Emphasis added.

13. LBS Minutes, 15 December 1835; 2 February 1836; 15 September 1839, LBS, SCL; FCA minutes, 14, 20 January 1835; 25 May 1859 (quoted in 20 January 1835 meeting), FCA, SCHS. See also Murray, "Charity within the Bounds of Race and Class," 60–61.

14. Fuel Society minutes, 6 September 1833; 6 October 1839, Ladies Fuel Society Records, SCHS (hereafter LFS minutes); "A Communication on the Subject of the Fuel Society Prepared for Publication by the Rev. D. Cobia," 19 May 1834, LFS, SCHS; "An Appeal to the Pious and Charitable, on Behalf of the Ladies Fuel Society, by the Rev. P. Trapier 1835," LFS, SCHS. See also News Clipping, *News and Courier,* 21 February 1983, LFS, SCHS; handwritten public appeal, n.d. [c. 1859], LFS, SCHS.

15. Quoted in Annual Meeting, 21 July 1827, FCA, SCHS. "First Annual Report of the Ladies' Auxiliary Christian Association of Charleston, South Carolina," 8 May 1858, SCHS pamphlets; List of "incorporations and religious societies," Comprehensive Index, SCDAH; "Life Members of the Charleston Bible Society," 12–14, SCHS pamphlets; Goodbody, *A Goodly Heritage;* Dues receipts, 1831–1835, Gregorie Society of St. Philip's Church, Daniel Huger business papers, Bacot-Huger papers, SCHS; William H. Gilliland Account Book, 1860–1861, n.p., DU; Elzas, *The Jews of South Carolina,* 283–86; Minutes of the Charleston Alms House, 29 June 1801, microfilm copy, CCA (hereafter Alms House minutes); "Letter to the Commissioners from the Lady Commis-

sioners," 1851, Charleston Orphan House Papers, CCA; Minutes of the Charleston Orphan House, 20 June 1844, microfilm copy, CCA (hereafter Orphan House minutes).

16.   Rawick, ser. 1, vol. 3: 9, 10, 19, 25, 76, 110, 112, 121–23, 126, 129, 153, 213; *Southern Patriot,* 14 August 1817; Rawick, ser. 1, vol. 3, 35–37; Rawick, ser. 1, vol. 2, 10–11, 62–63, 212, 234; Rawick, ser. 1, vol. 2, 177, 179, 183–84, 279, 327–28.

17.   Quoted in Rawick, ser. 1, vol. 3, 35–37. See also Rawick, ser. 1, vol. 3, 126, 129, 260–65.

18.   Quoted in Rawick, ser. 1, vol. 2, 10–11, 177–79, 183–84.

19.   Quoted in Rogers, *The History of Georgetown County, South Carolina,* 320; Rawick, ser. 1, vol. 3, 35–37; ser. 1, vol. 3: 10, 213. Smith, *A Charlestonian's Recollections* (hereafter Smith, *Recollections*). On Cynthia, see Grace Brown Elmore Reminiscences, 13 November 1860, SCL.

20.   Quoted in Rawick, ser. 1, vol. 3, 218–25. Genia Woodbury lived on a plantation just outside the city. Because her experience is like that of slave girls in the city, I have taken the liberty of using her narrative. On sales that separated mothers and children, see Stuart, *Three Years in North America,* 2:110–11; Martineau, *Retrospect,* 2:236.

21.   Rawick, ser. 1, vol. 3, 35–36, 184–86, 257–58.

22.   On testing slaves, see the case of Delia Thompson and her mistress in Rawick, ser. 1, vol. 3, 160–61. On the Charleston Work House and its facilities, see *The Southern Patriot,* 29 August 1817.

23.   Quoted in Sophia Watson to Henry Watson, 2 May, 3, 15 June 1848, Henry Watson Jr. Papers, DU. On urban and rural slaves, see Rawick, ser. 1, vol. 3, 1–2, 147–50, 242–44; Rawick, ser. 1, vol. 2, 224–25; Rawick, ser. 1, vol. 12, 19–20; Blassingame, *Slave Testimony,* 374.

24.   Quoted in Martineau, *Retrospect,* 2:214. See also Wright and Tinling, *Being the Travel Diary and Observations of Robert Hunter, Jr.,* 290, 292, 294; City Directories of 1790, 1807, 1819, 1840, in Hagy, *People and Professions;* Dawson and DeSaussure, *Census of the City of Charleston,* 31–35. See also tables 6 and 7.

25.   On the descriptor, "swarm[s]," see Mackay, *The Western World,* excerpted in Clark, *The Grand Tour;* Bremer, *Charleston One Hundred Years Ago.* On huckstering women, see Martineau, *Retrospect,* 2:237, 2:239–40; Smith, *Recollections,* 65; Anonymous Travel Journal, 27 November 1850; Marianne (Bull) Cozens Diary, 1830, December 1830, 1–10, SHC.

26.   Quoted in Presentments of the Grand Jury of Charlestown District, reprinted in *SCAGG,* 3 December 1779; "The Stranger," *SCG,* 24 September 1772, reprinted in Morgan, "Black Life in Eighteenth-Century Charleston," 202–203; "Sketches of South Carolina," *The Knickerbocker* 21 (May 1843): 446–48; *The Knickerbocker* 22 (July 1843): 1–6, reprinted in Clark, *The Grand Tour,* 205; Martineau, *Retrospect,* 2:239–40; Bremer, *Homes,* 2:499. See also *SLSC,* 9:692, 696; City Council v. Goldsmith, 2 Speers 428 (S.C. 1844). On slave women purveying goods for their mistresses, see "The Petition of Sundry

Widows of Charles Town," General Assembly Petitions, 1783, 5 August 1783, SCDAH. On slaves and free women of color marketing goods on their own behalf, see Martineau, *Retrospect,* 2:227, 239; Smith, *Recollections,* 65.

27. There are no extant records from Charleston manufactories. Wallace, *South Carolina,* 378–79. On Nancy Williams, see Rawick, ser. 1, vol. 3, 188–90.

28. Quoted in Diary of Lucy Ruggles, volume 2, 28 July 1846, n.p., Daniel Ruggles Papers, DU; Hindus, "Black Justice under White Law," 589. Hindus has found that "many prosecutions in this category [crimes against the person] were brought against female house slaves for crimes allegedly committed against the master's children." The average punishment was just over forty lashes, but over 8 percent of those convicted received 100 or more. See also James Louis Petigru to Jane Petigru, 13 September 1826, reprinted in Carson, *Life and Letters and Speeches,* 73–75; Charlotte Trezevant Gignilliat, "Reminiscences," 2 typescript volumes, c. 1905–1906, n.p., SCL; Rawick, ser. 1, vol. 2, 233–36.

29. Quoted in City Council of Charleston v. Cohen, 2 Speer 408 (S.C. 1843); Rawick, ser. 1, vol. 3, 158. See also, W. S. Smith, "A Dissertation on the Detection of Arsenic" (Inaugural Thesis, Medical College of the State of South Carolina, 1838), WHL; Rawick, ser. 1, vol. 2, 195–98; Rogers, *Charleston in the Age of the Pinckneys,* 23. On arson, see R. Howard to Elizabeth A. Yates, 18 June 1826, Yates Family Papers, SCHS; Morgan, "Black Life," 216–17; *City Gazette,* 22 November 1797, 10 July 1798; *SCSG,* 6 July 1798.

30. See Boyd v. Boyd, Harper Eq. 144 (S.C. 1824), in which the presiding judge declared one Nancy Boyd, "as able to work as the husband." Courts clearly distinguished laboring women from ladies, and held the former responsible for directly contributing to the family economy.

31. Quoted in Orphan House minutes, 18 October 1790, Charleston Orphan House Commissioners Minutes, microfilm copy, CCA; and Rules and Regulations of the Charleston Orphan House, July 1791, Orphan House minutes. Orphan House minutes, July 1791; 9 August 1792; 3 January 1793; 2, 9 June 1796. See also Belcher ads. Commissioners of the Orphan House of Charleston, 2 McCord 23 (S.C. 1822); King, *History and Records of the Charleston Orphan House,* 17.

32. On abusive treatment and lack of food, see Orphan House minutes, 13 October 1791; 19 January, 12 July 1792; 18 August 1793; 4 December 1794; 17 May, 23 August 1795. See also the 22 November 1810 "Petition of the Intendant and Wardens of the City of Charleston," in which city officials requested extra funding from the state legislature, in part, because municipal funds could not maintain, feed, clothe, and educate "upwards of one hundred and thirty orphans (which, if neglected would be outcasts in Society)." General Assembly Petitions 1810, SCDAH. On Elizabeth Margaret Somers and Jane Fleming, see Orphan House minutes 24 January 1793; 20 August 1795.

33. Mrs. Milligan may have been one of the city's many tavern or innkeepers, or married to James Milligan, the city jailer. Orphan House minutes, 19 Septem-

ber 1793; 12 April 1792; City directories of 1790, 1794, in Hagy, *People and Professions.* On Theresa Harrigan, see Orphan House minutes, 19 June 1796.

34. On children taken from and returned to the Orphan House by parents, see Orphan House minutes, 14, 28 November 1793; 7 September 1794.

35. In her study of midwestern businesswomen, Lucy Eldersveld Murphy has (as I have) categorized as artisans women who worked as: bakers, confectioners, pastry chefs, basket makers, jewelers, milliners, mantua makers, needleworkers, painters, seamstresses, silversmiths, tailoresses, and upholsterers. Murphy, "Business Ladies," 65–89; Dawson and DeSaussure, *Census of the City of Charleston,* 29–35. Scholars have used slaveholding as an indication of wealth or "index of prosperity." In 1820 slightly over 72 percent of households among free people of color reported owning at least one slave. The 1860 tax list included 151 free women of color, among whom 63 (42 percent) owned one or more slaves, and 81 percent (122) possessed real estate worth $1,000 or more and/or owned slaves. Forty women (27 percent) owned real estate valued at over $2,000. "List of the Taxpayers," 315–34, SCHS; Rosengarten, *Between the Tracks,* 79, 81.

36. Walsh, *Charleston's Sons of Liberty,* 17; *SCWG,* 15 March 1783; *GSSC,* 6 May 1784. On Heloise Boudo and Elizabeth Dumoutet, see Burton, *South Carolina Silversmiths,* 23, 26–27, 49–50.

37. Burton, *South Carolina Silversmiths,* 13, 29, 141. On Anna Miller, see Campbell v. Kinlock, 9 S.C. 300 (S.C. 1856); on Isabel Peace, see D. L. Wardlaw ("your affectionate father") to "Miss Sally M. Wardlaw at Madame Tognos's Tradd Street," 24 January 1855, David Lewis Wardlaw Papers, P/8847, SCL.

38. Mrs. Ramadge quoted in *SCGGA,* 2, 6, 13, 27 May 1783. "City Treasurer's Office, Charleston" (receipt for Ann Cross's tavern license, £500 sterling), 15 April 1787, Paul Cross Papers, folder 6, SCL; "Corporation Tax, 1788," n.d., Paul Cross Papers, folder 9 (Ann Cross paid taxes on land, seven slaves, and £50 "Stock in trade"); 14 December 1782 receipt for "four Prime or Grown Negroes" received of Louis Pissoa from Paul Cross, "River Riopongoe on the Windward Coast of Africa," Paul Cross Papers, folder 7, SCL.

39. Contemporaries referred to Catherine Coates's husband, Thomas, as a "sea captain"; evidence points to his involvement in the slave trade. Typed and handwritten notes on "Taverns, Inns, Hotels, Coffee Houses in Charleston," Miscellaneous File Folder, 30–23/1, SCHS. On Mrs. Calder, see *Courier,* 18 October 1806; 31 January, 30 March 1809.

40. Quoted in JBG Diary, SHC #970 (typed transcript), vol. 10, 37–38, 18 May 1851, SHC. See also JBG Diary, 1:109, 13 October 1833; 6:53, 28 April 1840; 7:47, 28 July 1844; 8:47, 11 October 1846; 10:12, 20 December 1848, SHC. In 1802, the city was home to two female physicians. Hagy, *People and Professions,* 91; Dawson and DeSaussure, *Census of the City of Charleston,* 29–35.

41. JBG Diary, 1:46, 85, 98; 4:3, 52; 6:2, SHC.

42. "Jones: Times of Crisis, Time of Change," 1–2, SCDAH. Jones had purchased his hotel at public auction in 1815 for $13,000. Mesne Conveyances, Book M8, 399–402, Register of the Mesne Conveyance Office, Charleston, South Caro-

lina. Dawson and DeSaussure, *Census of the City of Charleston,* 29–35; City Directory of 1801, in Hagy, *People and Professions,* 73. On teachers and boarding school mistresses, see Hagy, *People and Professions,* 9, 35, 73, 91; Dawson and DeSaussure, *Census of the City of Charleston,* 29–35; *SCGGA,* 26 April, 2, 6 May 1783; JBG Diary, 11:35, 29 May 1854; 11:61, 16 May 1856; 11:76, 14 May 1857, SHC; Angie to "Much loved Sister," 3 January 1854, Augustus F. Edwards Papers, DU; Biographical data, Mary Stanley Bunce Palmer Dana, Shindler Papers, SCL; Mary to "My own dear Husband," 1, 6 January 1857, Shindler Papers, SCL. On tuition costs, see handwritten Broadside for Ladies Seminary, 30 November 1845, Pierre Teller Babbit Papers, P/8956, SCL; Jeremiah A. Yates to "Dear Madam," 7 September 1822, Yates Family Papers 11–478/folder 2, SCHS; JBG Diary, 10:25, 5 May 1850; 10:31, 20 May 1850; 11:35, 29 May 1854; 11:49, 4 August 1855, SHC. Farnham, *The Education of the Southern Belle,* 57, 84, 116, 182. "Your own loving sister Cad" to "Dear George," 22 September 1851, George A. Gordon Papers, DU.

43. Schenck, *Directory and Stranger's Guide for the City of Charleston;* Rosengarten, *Between the Tracks,* 92.

44. Charleston Ordinance, 28 October 1806, *Digest of the Ordinances of the City,* 170–71; "Bill to Amend the Act for Better Government of Slaves and Free Persons of Color," 8 December 1845, Records of the South Carolina Legislature, SCDAH; "Report of the South Carolina Committee on Colored People," 7 December 1858, SCDAH; *SCGGA,* 31 March, 13 May 1783.

45. Quoted in Mackay, *The Western World,* in Clark, *The Grand Tour,* 239. On hiring ads, see "Advertisements," *Courier,* 34–604, "Cash Received" ledger, SCHS; "Statement of Receipts and Expenditures by the City Council of Charleston, 1849–1850," 95, 102, 107, 157, SCHS; Rosengarten, *Between the Tracks,* 70; Singleton, "The Slave Tag," 41–65.

46. On Ann Cross, see Receipt, 24 January 1789, Paul Cross Papers, folder 12, SCL. On Frances Pinckney and Mary Aldret, see Receipt, 1 April 1815, P/9095, SCL; Receipt Book, 1829–1889, Mary Aldret Papers, SCHS. JBG Diary, 10 October 1832; 7 April, 14 August 1833; 7 May 1834, SHC.

47. Quoted in *SCGGA,* 31 March, 12 April 1783. On Harriet Eddington's mother, see Rawick, ser. 1, vol. 2, 1.

48. JBG Diary, 13 May 1835, SHC.

49. The 1835–1836 city directory listed Camilla's residence and work place as Hempstead, a section of the Charleston Neck. City Directory of 1835–36, in Hagy, *Directories for the City of Charleston.* JBG Diary, 13 May 1835, SHC; Koger, *Black Slaveowners,* 91. Koger has incorrectly transcribed Camilla's last name as "Johnson" rather than "Dunstan."

50. At least 25 percent of Charleston's free women of African descent labored as skilled artisans. City Directory of 1822, in Hagy, *Charleston, South Carolina City Directories;* City Directory of 1830–31, in Hagy, *Directories for the City of Charleston;* Purse, *Charleston City Directory and Strangers Guide for 1856;* Koger, *Black Slaveowners,* 150, 158.

51. Quoted in Wikramanayake, *A World in Shadow,* 105. Koger, *Black Slaveowners,* 141, 159; Schweninger, *Black Property Owners in the South,* 24. On Clarinda

and Caroline Laurens Read, see Maffitt v. Read, 11 Richardson Eq. 285, 286, 291 (S.C. 1860). On carters, draymen, and street cleaning, see Eckhard, *Digest of Ordinances,* 21–23, 32–38, 254, 256–57; Rosengarten, *Between the Tracks,* 108–18. *SCGGA,* 12 April 1783; "Charleston City Funds and Taxpayers, 1850–51," 5, 13, 15, 27, 41, 53, 69, 83, 95, 109, 121, 149, SCHS.

52. The "negro wench" remained nameless in court documents. Guardian of Sally, a Negro v. Beaty, 1 Bay 260, 262 (S.C. 1792). Neither the attorneys nor the judge referred to Sally as the woman's daughter. The court called her the "wench's . . . young favourite [*sic*]."

53. Quoted in Guardian of Sally v. Beaty, 1 Bay 260, 261, 262. On the case that overturned precedent, see Gist v. Toohey, 2 Richardson 424, 425 (S.C. 1846).

54. Quoted in Anna [or Anne] Yates to Elizabeth Ann Yates, 17 July 1822, Yates Family Papers, folder 2, SCHS; "M. Mitchell" to "Dear Sister," 26 October 1822; Anna Yates to Elizabeth Ann Yates, 13 November 1822; John R. Rogers [executor] to Mrs. Elizabeth Ann Yates, 31 July 1823; and David Yates to Mrs. Elizabeth Ann Yates, 30 July 1824, Yates Family Papers, SCHS. After 1820, state law forbade manumission except by special petition to the state legislature. *SLSC,* 6:245, 7:459; *Courier,* 1, 12 December 1821.

55. Quoted in *SCSG,* 21 July 1798; *Royal Gazette,* 21 January 1782; Vinyard v. Passalaigue, 2 Strobhart 536 (S.C. 1847); Lyell, *A Second Visit to the United States,* 1:224.

56. Quoted in Gaillard v. Le Seigneur and Le Roy, 1 McMullan 146 (S.C. 1841); *SLSC,* 6:213. See also Newbiggin v. Pillans and Wife, 2 Bay 161, 162, 163, 164 (S.C. 1798); Wallace v. Rippon, 2 Bay 112 (S.C. 1797); City Directories of 1796, 1801, 1806, 1807; 1800 Census, 131, in Hagy, *People and Professions.* On abandoned wives, see Wright v. Wright, 2 DeSaussure Eq. 241 (S.C. 1804); Cusack v. White, 2 Mill 368 (S.C. 1818). On the law of *feme sole* and *feme covert,* see Blackstone, *Commentaries,* 1:430; 2:213–16, 2:497–99; Reeve, *The Laws Respecting Women,* 117–36; Reeve, *The Law of Baron and Feme,* 3, 8, 160, 192–93. On South Carolina law, see Rice, *Digested Index of the Statute Law,* 357; *SLSC,* 2:593; 3:616–21; 6:212–13, 6:236–37; Parramore, "Feme Sole Traders in South Carolina" (M.A. thesis); Salmon, *Women and the Law of Property,* 46–49.

57. Quoted in M'Daniel v. Cornwell, 1 Hill 431 (S.C. 1833); Surtell ads. Brailsford, 2 Bay 333, 335, 338 (S.C. 1801); Samuel and Catherine Caroline Smith, Marriage bonds, Misc. Docs., 3S (1803), SCDAH; Megrath v. Robertson, 1 DeSaussure Eq. 445, 446 (S.C., 1794). From 1790 to at least 1794, Susannah Tennant headed a Charleston household at 81 Tradd Street that included her daughter and ten slaves. Heads of Families, First Census, 42; City Directories of 1790, 1794, in Hagy, *People and Professions.* See also Dr. John and Anne Mackie (1786), Misc. Docs., 2W, 408; Julian and Elizabeth Marion (1794), Misc. Docs., 3E, 445; Jacob and Judith Saures (1799), Misc. Docs., 3M, 218, SCDAH; Miller v. Tolleson, 1 Harper Eq. 145 (S.C. 1824); *SLSC,* 2:593. Sole trader Ann Pillans also attempted unsuccessfully to hide behind coverture. Newbiggin v. Pillans and Wife, 2 Bay 162.

58. Quoted in Vinyard v. Passalaigue, 2 Strobhart 536, 542 (S.C. 1847). Catharine

Sasportas's husband, Sherry Sasportas, executed a deed to grant his wife sole trader status. Like most *feme sole* trader deeds, Sherry's document did not specify Catharine's trade or intended enterprise. Likewise, we do not know in what business Dye Waring engaged, only that she lent money to fellow city resident, Abraham Moise. However, sole trader deeds often record the occupations of the husbands or trustees executing the documents. Secretary of State, Miscellaneous Records, vol. 30, 165–66; vol. 3Y, 258–60, SCDAH.

59. M'Dowall v. Woods, 2 Nott and McCord, 242, 247 (S.C. 1820). Justice Richardson expressed similar misgivings in Gaillard v. LeSeigneur and LeRoy, 1 McMullan 146, 151 (S.C. 1841).

60. Quoted in Cleland v. Taylor, 4 McCord 413, 417 (S.C. 1828); M'Dowall v. Woods, 2 Nott and McCord 242, 245, 247; Covington v. Bussey, 4 McCord 413, 414 (S.C. 1828).

61. Quoted in M'Daniel v. Cornwell, 1 Hill 428, 429; M'Dowall v. Woods, 2 Nott and McCord 242, 244, 245.

62. Quoted in M'Daniel v. Cornwell, 1 Hill 428, 431; Ewart v. Nagel, 1 McMullan 32, 34. In this case, the court ruled against one Mrs. M. G. Nagel, who engaged in the shipping trade.

8. Leisure and Recreation

1. Gilman, *The Living of Charlotte Perkins Gilman,* 116.

2. Bridenbaugh, *Myths and Realities,* 80–82, 116–17; Bridenbaugh, *Cities in the Wilderness,* 464; Bridenbaugh, *Cities in Revolt,* 402; Bowes, *The Culture of Early Charleston,* 106–20; Crawford, *Romantic Days in the Early Republic,* 307–12.

3. Quoted in *American Literature and Charleston Society* (Charleston, S.C.: Walker and James, 1853), 30. On the predominance of young girls, see Montlezun, "Charleston in 1817," in Johnson and Sloan, *South Carolina,* 262; Hall, *The Aristocratic Journey,* in Clark, *The Grand Tour;* Bowes, *The Culture of Early Charleston,* 115; Ravenel, *Charleston,* 385, 428; JBG Diary, 30 January, 9 February 1850, SHC.

4. Quoted in Ralph Izard to Alice Izard, 4 March 1809, Ralph Izard Papers, Box 2, folder 23, SCL; R. M. Rutledge to Lieutenant Rutledge [*U.S. Ship St. Louis,* Pensacola, West Florida], 10 April 1833, Rutledge Family Papers, folder 2, SCL. See also Ravenel, *Charleston the Place and the People,* 385, 428 (hereafter Ravenel, *Charleston*); Hall, *The Aristocratic Journey,* in Clark, *The Grand Tour,* 140, 148; Kemble, *Journal of a Residence,* 39–40; Joseph Manigault to Gabriel Manigault, December 1786, quoted in Hash, "A Lowcountry Christmas," 11.

5. See Alice Izard to Henry Izard, 23 January, 12 April 1807, Ralph Izard Papers, Box 1, folders 15, 16, SCL; Alice Izard to Margaret Izard Manigault, 6 March 1816, Manigault Family Papers, SCL; Hall, *The Aristocratic Journey,* in Clark, *The Grand Tour,* 143–44; Ravenel, *Charleston,* 385, 428.

6. Wilkinson, *Letters of Eliza Wilkinson,* 105, 281–83; Fraser, *Patriots, Pistols, and Petticoats,* 145.

7. Quoted in Miranda, *The New Democracy in America*, 25–26.

8. See above, chapter 3, "Rebuilding and Resisting."

9. Quoted in Ravenel, *Charleston*, 446–49; Frazier, *Charleston*, 205.

10. Quoted in King, *Gerald Gray's Wife and Lily*; and Gilman, *Recollections of a Southern Matron*, 116 (hereafter Gilman, *Recollections*). See also *L'Oracle*, 27 August 1807. The *Oracle* was a short-lived, French-language newspaper printed twice weekly from January to December, 1807.

11. JBG Diary, 19 February 1850, series 2, folder 20, vol. 10, 23, SHC.

12. Gilman, *Recollections*, 118–20.

13. Quoted in King, *Gerald Gray's Wife and Lily*, 167. The quadrille is a French dance, usually in 6/8 or 2/4 time (from which the American square dance derives), which was popular in the eighteenth and nineteenth centuries.

14. Quoted in Hall, *Travels in North*, 149–52; Gilman, *Recollections*, 117. On Charleston's great hospitality, see Martineau, *Retrospect of Western Travel*, 1:225 (hereafter Martineau, *Retrospect*); Hall, *The Aristocratic Journey*, in Clark, *The Grand Tour*, 145.

15. Quoted in Ravenel, *Life and Times of William Lowndes*, 54–55; Drayton, *A View of South-Carolina*, in Clark, *The Grand Tour*, 29; Stuart, *Three Years in North America*, 2:98–100. The all-male Jockey Club, founded in 1735, derived from Carolinians' love of the British aristocracy and its passion for the hunt. On the "display of beautiful women," see John Randolph (1796), in Frasei, *Charleston*, 181; Ravenel, *Life and Times of William Lowndes*, 40; Smith, *A Charlestonian's Recollections*. See also Crawford, *Romantic Days*, 307–12; Mohl, "The Grand Fabric of Republicanism," 179; Taylor, "The Gentry of Antebellum South Carolina," 116–17.

16. Quoted in Ralph Izard, Jr. to [his mother] Alice Izard, 4 March 1809, Ralph Izard Papers, Box 2, folder 23, SCL; Alice DeLancey Izard to Margaret Izard Manigault, 9 March 1809, Manigault Family Papers, SCL; Margaret Izard Manigault to Alice DeLancey Izard, 3, 12 March 1809, Izard Family Papers, LC; Margaret Izard Manigault to Mary Stead Pinckney [Mrs. Charles Cotesworth Pinckney], 20 March 1809, Manigault Family Papers, SCHS. On the Grimball dinner, see John Grimball quoted in JBG Diary, 29 January 1847, SHC. See also JBG Diary, 26 February 1856, SHC; Charles Manigault to [his brother] Louis Manigault, 28 February 1856, quoted in Clifton, *Life and Labor*, 211–12.

17. Quoted in Kemble, *Journal of a Residence*, 40. The city assessed a $20 or $30 (depending on the carriage) annual tax on each carriage. "List of the Taxpayers of Charleston, 1860" (Charleston, 1861), SCHS.

18. Quoted in Louisa Minot to William Minot (Boston), 9, 19 February 1838, Louisa Minot Papers, SCL. See also excerpted travel accounts of Francis Hall, Auguste Lavasseur, and Margaret Hunter Hall, in Clark, *The Grand Tour*, 54–55, 86, 102, 145–46. See Louisa Minot to Mary Minot, 8 February 1838; Louisa Minot to William Minot, 19 February 1838, Louisa Minot Papers, SCL. See also Hall, *Travels in Canada and the United States*; and Bernhard, *Travels through North America*, in Clark, *The Grand Tour*, 54–55, 88, 101.

19. Quoted in Alice Izard to Henry Izard, 23 January 1807, Ralph Izard Papers, Box 1, folder 15, SCL. On fears of "vapors rising from the rice-fields and swamps" during the summer months, which brought "certain death to white" people, see Arfwedson, *The United States and Canada*, in Clark, *The Grand Tour*, 176; Bremer, *Charleston One Hundred Years Ago*, 15–16; Stuart, *Three Years in North America*, 2:105; Miranda, *The New Democracy in America*, 33; Rebecca Middleton Rutledge to Lieutenant Edward Cotesworth Rutledge, 24 October 1839, Rutledge Family Papers, folder 5, SCL; JBG Diary, 12 November 1839, SHC. On the high cost of travel, see Alice Izard to Ralph Cotesworth Izard, 2, 4, 9, 17, 22 November 1794, Ralph Izard Papers, SCL. On the Grimballs' trip, see JBG Diary, May–October 1835, 2–50, 56–70, SHC. See also Brewster, "Planters from the Low-Country and their Summer Travels," 35–41.

20. Rebecca Motte [Lowndes] Rutledge to Lieutenant Edward Cotesworth Rutledge, 13 September 1839, Rutledge Family Papers, folder 5, SCL.

21. Harriott's mother, Rebecca, summered in Boston to escape Charleston's heat and facilitate her health. Harrie (Harriott) remained in Charleston in her Aunt Holbrook's care. Quoted in Harriott Horry Rutledge (and her aunt, Harriott Pinckney Rutledge Holbrook) to Mrs. (Rebecca Motte Lowndes) Edward Cotesworth Rutledge, 7, 18, 24 June, 17 July, 26 August, 17 September 1841, Harriott Horry Rutledge Papers (hereafter HHR Papers, DU). See also Margaret Izard Manigault to Alice Izard, 6 September, 8 October 1802; Alice Izard to Margaret Izard Manigault, 27 September 1802, Manigault Family Papers, SCL; JBG Diary, 1 May 1834; 10 May 1839; 8 May 1850, SHC; King, *Gerald Gray and Lily*, 64.

22. Quoted in Harriott Horry Rutledge to Mrs. (Rebecca Motte Lowndes) Edward Cotesworth Rutledge, 18 June, 17 July 1841, HHR Papers, DU; Harriott Pinckney Holbrook to Mrs. (Rebecca Motte Lowndes) Edward Cotesworth Rutledge, 26 August 1841, HHR Papers, DU.

23. Quoted in Harriott Horry Rutledge to Mrs. [Rebecca Motte Lowndes] Edward Cotesworth Rutledge, 17 September 1841, HHR Papers, DU.

24. Quoted in Rawick, ser. 1, vol. 2, 91–96. State courts ruled that "a planter who spends, as a guest and at the house of a friend, four months every summer in the City of Charleston, is a resident of the city." Bartlett v. Brisbane, 2 Richardson 489 (S.C. Court of Law, 1846). On slave family separations and reunions, see "Taxable Property of Gabriel Manigault," 1 October 1804 (separation of his 26 Charleston slaves and 256 plantation slaves); Alice Izard to Margaret Izard Manigault, 9 December 1815, Manigault Family Papers, SCL; JBG Diary, 13, 27 May 1835, SHC.

25. Quoted in Gilman, *Recollections*, 118.

26. Quoted in Gilman, *Recollections*, 114, 116.

27. Quoted in *City Gazette and Daily Advertiser*, 26 December 1798; Hash, "A Lowcountry Christmas," 12–13. Residents expended anywhere from less than one-fifth of a day's wages up to a full day's wages to gain entrance. Male wage laborers earned from 50 cents to a dollar per day in 1828; a skilled mason's average daily wage was $1.26. In contrast, one white woman earned a monthly salary of $16.70 as a church organist, or from $3.34 to $4.18 per

Sunday (54 cents daily). U.S. Dept. of Labor, *History of Wages in the United States,* 58; Record Book and Minutes, 1825–1850, 30–31, Independent or Congregational Church Charleston, SCL.

28.   *L'Oracle,* 29 January 1807.

29.   Morgan, "Black Life in Eighteenth-Century Charleston," 194–95, 202–203. Martineau, *Retrospect,* 1:239–40; Bremer, *The Homes of the New World,* 2:499.

30.   Quoted in Gilman, *Recollections,* 206–207, 271–72. See also Lyell, *Travels in North,* 146.

31.   Quoted in Eckhard, *Digest of the Ordinances,* 170 (emphasis added); Whilden, "Reminiscences of Old Charleston," 404–406.

32.   Quoted in Montlezun, "Charleston in 1817," in Johnson and Sloan, *South Carolina,* 262; Morgan, "Black Life," 227; Charleston *Courier,* 14 August 1804. On the number of "tippling houses," see Bridenbaugh, *Cities in Revolt,* 227, 358. On the city's mixed reputation, see Hunt, *Life in America One Hundred Years,* 36, 71–72.

33.   Quoted in Hodgson, *Remarks during a Journey,* 130–31; Herz, *My Travels in America,* 75.

34.   McCord, "Recollections of Louisa Rebecca Hayne McCord," 11, SCL.

35.   Quoted in James M. Johnson (Charleston) to Henry Ellison, 23 December 1859, Ellison Family Papers, SCL. The Ellison family seat was upcountry, in Sumter District, but two sons married Charleston women in the 1840s. Johnson and Roark, *Black Masters,* 107–109, 112, 113, 120.

36.   Quoted in *SLSC,* 4:459, 470. Moses Levy, quoted in James M. Johnson to Henry Ellison, 3 September 1860, Ellison Family Papers, SCL. See also Johnson and Roark, *Black Masters,* 250.

37.   Quoted in "A Resident and Native to the Editor," *Mercury,* 25 October 1859, quoted in Johnson and Roark, *Black Masters,* 189. See also 376, n. 122, for citations to similar comments throughout October and November 1859.

38.   "An Ordinance for the Government of Negroes and Other Persons of Color within the City of Charleston," 28 October 1806, quoted in Eckhard, *Digest of the Ordinances,* 170.

39.   The 1826 *Christian Almanac* enumerated over 4,000 Charleston free and slave communicants, a likely underestimation of the true number of churchgoers. In 1820, slaves and free people of color numbered just over 14,000. Gilman, *Recollections,* 270; 1820 Census. Trinity Methodist Episcopal Church Roll, 1821–1868, Class lists, 1822, n.p., SCHS. Johnson and Roark, *Black Masters,* 227–32; Mood, *Methodism in Charleston,* 132. Pearson, *Designs Against Charleston,* 49–51; Durden, "The Establishment of Calvary Protestant Episcopal Church for Negroes in Charleston," 63–84; Fraser, *Charleston,* 228.

40.   James M. Johnson to Henry Ellison, 14 May 1860, Ellison Family Papers, SCL

41.   In 1809, citywide economic decline forced Vaux Hall owner Alexander Placide to curtail his grand designs. Whilden, "Reminiscences of Old Charleston," in *Year Book, City of Charleston,* 402–12; Fraser, *Charleston,* 183–84, 186;

Montlezun, "Charleston in 1817," in Johnson and Sloan, *South Carolina: A Documentary Profile*, 260–62.

9. Women and the Law

1. Peter W. Bardaglio has emphasized the corporatist impulses of slavery as the driving force behind legal rulings involving family and sexual practices. Michael Stephen Hindus has also demonstrated how slavery contoured legal strategies and the evolution of social control. Although both works accurately portray the close links among race, sex, and social order, neither Bardaglio nor Hindus has discussed the influence of class distinctions in southern construction and interpretation of law. Bardaglio, *Reconstructing the Household;* Hindus, *Prison and Plantation.*

2. Quoted in Records of Charleston District Court of General Sessions, Bills of Indictment, 1801–2A, 3A, and 5A, SCDAH. On "thieving negro," see newspaper runaway ads, travel accounts, and Equity Court cases. See also Petition of William Rouse, 21 February 1800, CH 162, 163, Charleston County Court of Equity, Bills of Indictment, SCDAH. All but four of the forty-four indictments during this time involving women (accused criminals or victims) were for assault. Bills of Indictment, 1801–2A, 3A, 5A, 12 January 1801, No. 1786–1A through 1808–27A, SCDAH.

3. The law of 1740 totally revised and combined earlier laws, including the 1712 slave code. On "negro courts," see *SLSC,* 7:343–47, 400–403. Sections 15–17, 24 enumerated at least eight crimes, in addition to all felonies specified under (white) Carolina law, as capital offenses when committed by slaves and free people of color. Judges reiterated that "all crimes and offenses 'committed by free negroes, Indians . . . mulattoes, or mestizoes shall be' [tried] in the same manner as is provided for the trial of crimes and offen[s]es committed by slaves." State v. Belmont, 4 Strobhart 445, 446 (S.C. 1850). On white intervention, see Lenoir v. Sylvester, 1 Bailey 632 (S.C. 1830); Linam v. Johnson, 2 Bailey 137 (S.C. 1831); Cline v. Caldwell, 1 Hill 423 (S.C. 1833); Frazier v. Executors of Frazier, 2 Hill Eq. 304, 306 (S.C. 1835). On upholding appeals of African Americans, see Nash, "Negro Rights, Unionism, and Greatness on the South Carolina Court of Appeals," 167–69. Historian Linda Gordon has defined the term "politics" as "ordered systems of reproducing and/or changing power relations." This functional understanding moves beyond a narrow application (political parties and electoral politics) of the term and describes social relations of power in the slave South. Gordon, "Killing in Self-Defense," 27.

4. Quoted in *SLSC,* 7:426. See also 7:343–47, 397–417, 435, 440, 448, 454, and 4:540. Michael Hindus and Bertram Wyatt-Brown (*Southern Honor*) are among those who have elaborated the South's tolerance and encouragement of informal authority and justice. "[T]here was an extralegal counterpart to nearly every major element of the legal and criminal justice system . . . [and] plantation justice handled much slave crime." Hindus, *Prison and Plantation,* 35–37.

5. Bills of Indictment, 1801-5-A, 12 January 1801, SCDAH.

6.　Quoted in *SLSC*, 4:411, 11:169. On "accidental murder" of slaves, see *SLSC*, 11:169 (1841/#2837); 11:738 (1858/#4422); State v. Andrew Montgomery and Wife, Cheves 120 (S.C. 1840). Rev. Thornwell quoted in *The Rights and the Duties of the Masters*. State legislators did not mandate written records of the (black code's) Magistrate and Freeholders courts until 1839, which has shrouded in secrecy and oblivion proceedings of the local bodies that tried capital and non-capital crimes charged against people of color. O'Neall, *Negro Law*, 34.

7.　Quoted in Helton v. Caston, 2 Bailey 95, 97, 98 (S.C. 1831). In this and other cases, the law also specified that any person who "unlawfully" whipped or beat a slave "*not* under his or her charge, without sufficient provocation, by word or act," would be fined. See also White v. Chambers, 2 Bay 70 (S.C. 1796); and State v. Wilson, Chevis 163 (S.C. 1840).

8.　On cruel punishment, see the 1740 black code as applied in State v. Wilson, Cheves 163. On whipping, see *SLSC*, 4:400–402, 463. By May 1846, Carolina legislators also forbade public whipping of white men, fearing "the crowd of our colored population usually attendant upon such exhibitions [would] be actuated" by "self-[con]gratulation in the degradation of the white by the same punishment to their own level." Grand Jury Presentments, Charleston District, May term 1846, General Assembly Loose Legislative Papers, 1831–1859, SCDAH (hereafter Presentments).

9.　Quoted in *SLSC*, 7:615. See also 7:431–37, 440–43, 461–68; J[ames] M. Johnson to Henry Ellison, 20 August 1860, Ellison Family Papers, folder 3, SCL; Huger and Sarah, her child per prochein ami McCready v. Barnwell, 5 S.C. 273 (S.C. 1852); State Ex Relatione Fanning & Lord v. The Mayor of Charleston, 12 Richardson 480, 481 (S.C. 1860); Presentments, May Term 1846, SCDAH.

10.　Quoted in Memorial of Sundry Inhabitants of Christ Church Parish, Slavery Petitions, 8 December 1821, Loose Legislative Papers 1800–1830, SCDAH, Petition, October Term 1854, Presentments, SCDAH. On severe beatings of slaves, see Rawick, ser. 1, vol. 2, 10–11, 183–84, 209, 233–36; Rogers, *Charleston in the Age of the Pinckneys*, 146–48; Stuart, *Three Years in North America*, 2:168–69.

11.　Quoted in Ex parte R. B. Boylston, 2 Strobhart 41, 42, 43, 44 (S.C. 1847).

12.　M'Vaughters v. Elder, 2 Brevard 7, 12 (S.C. 1809).

13.　Quoted in Harley v. Platts, 6 S.C. 310, 312, 313 (S.C. 1853). South Carolina slaves could "acquire property," but not legally own or bequeath it; the property "inure[d] [accrued] to the master." Bowers et al. v. Newman, 2 McMullan 647 (S.C. 1842).

14.　Pepoon, Guardian of Phebe v. Clarke, 1 Mill 65, 66, 68 (S.C. 1817). A second justice, one Yancey, voted against Johnson's decision, but was overruled.

15.　Quoted in Huger and Sarah, her child per prochein ami McCready v. Barnwell, 5 S.C. 274; Susan, a Free Woman of Color v. Wells, 2 Brevard 177 (S.C. 1811); State v. Hill, 2 Speers 150, 157, 161 (S.C. 1843). On the 1800 act and its consequences, see Linam v. Johnson, 2 Bailey 137 (S.C. 1831); *SLSC*, 4:436–46, 451–54, 459–60, 470–74. See also *SLSC*, 7:431–37, 440–43, 461–68; Governor Seabrook's message to the South Carolina legislature, *Journal of the House of Representatives*, 23.

16. Quoted in State v. Hill, 2 Speers 150 (emphasis added). On Patience McKenzie Marshall, see Ex Parte, Adam Tunno, Bailey Eq. 387, 388 (S.C. 1831). Joseph Morton left in excess of $2,000 in real estate, which was sold, and the proceeds were invested in 1823 by Adam Tunno at the request of Martha and her granddaughter, Patience. Martha and Joseph's relationship to Adam is unclear; they may have been relatives of Adam's longtime partner, Margaret Bettingall, a free woman of color. On the ban against free African Americans, see *SLSC*, 7:436, 444, 447, 459, 463, 466, 470. State legislators passed the first prohibition in 1800, and successive bans or amendments to the restriction in 1801, 1802, 1820, 1823, 1825, 1835, 1848, and 1856.

17. *City Gazette*, 11 December 1788 quoted in Hall, "'Nefarious Wretches, Insidious Villains, and Evil-Minded Persons,'" 152, 168; Martineau, *Retrospect of Western Travel*, 1:238–39. On the unnamed white victim, see *City Gazette*, 3 March 1788. On Mary Buffin, see *City Gazette*, 7 October 1788.

18. Quoted in Stoney, "The Footpad's Memorial," in Ravenel, *Charleston Murders*; *City Gazette*, 29 March 1788.

19. Quoted in State v. Simmons and Kitchen, 1 Brevard 5, 6 (S.C. 1794); State v. Arden, 1 Bay 487, 488 (S.C. 1795). On "thieving" and "conniving negroes" see Bills of Indictment, 1801–2A, 3A, 5A, 12 January 1801, SCDAH.

20. State v. Arden, 1 Bay 487, 488.

21. Undated newspaper clipping, "Message To Hell," in South Carolina File, SCHS. See also Ravenel, *Charleston Murders*, 59. A review of over three hundred eighteenth- and nineteenth-century South Carolina legal cases uncovered only three trials in which women stood convicted of murder.

22. Amended in 1795, the 1703 "Act against Bastardy" remained in force throughout the nineteenth century. *SLSC*, 2:224. On northern versus southern bastardy law, see D'Emilio and Freedman, *Intimate Matters*, xvii, 32–34, 49, 94; Bardaglio, *Reconstructing the Household*, 90–92; Laslett et al., *Bastardy and Its Comparative History*.

23. Quoted in Brevard, *Alphabetical Digest of the Public Statute Law*, 1:66–68; *SLSC*, 5:270–71. See also O'Neall, *The Negro Law*, 23. For case law examples see State v. Clark, 2 Brevard 385 (S.C. 1810); State v. Clements, 1 Speers 48 (S.C. 1842). Although local officials retained the power to fine, imprison, and coerce white unmarried mothers into naming the fathers of their children, this amendment also deleted an earlier provision allowing white women to be whipped publicly for failure to pay the bastardy fine. On the inheritance provision, see Barwick v. Miller, 4 DeSaussure Eq. 434 (S.C. 1815); Jones v. Burden et al., 4 DeSaussure Eq. 439 (S.C. 1814); Shearman v. Angel, Bailey Eq. 351 (S.C. 1831); Breithaupt v. Bauskett, 1 Richardson Eq. (S.C. 1838); Ford v. McElray, 1 Richardson Eq. (S.C. 1844).

24. Quoted in Bills of Indictment, 1805–7A, 21 March 1805; 1806–36A-2/3, 28 June 1806; 1806–16A-2, 17 September 1806, SCDAH; State v. Hart, July 1813, Court of General Sessions, SCDAH. See also State v. Harris, May 1818,

Court of General Sessions, SCDAH; Bills of Indictment, 1805–3A, 18 May 1805; 1806–13A, 31 March 1806; 1806–25A, 1 April 1806; 1808–12A, 8–10A, 31 March, 1 April 1808; Bills of Indictment March, May, June 1805; January–April 1806; July, September–December 1806; January, April, August 1807; January, April, July, October, November 1808; and 1808–21A, 22–A, SCDAH; State v. Parkerson and Mary Parkerson, his Wife, 1 Strobhart 169 (S.C. 1847); Hagy, *This Happy Land*, 52, 122–24. The 1806 city directory lists Benjamin Duprey, livery stable, and Benjamin Duprey, carpenter; both resided on Church Street. The 1809 city directory lists a John Mattuce, butcher. City directories, in Hagy, *City Directories for Charleston*, 32, 37, 119.

25.   Michael Hindus has found that over 48 percent of Charleston criminal prosecutions were assaults, compared to just over 5 percent for murders, during the eight years prior to the American Revolution. During six decades beginning in 1800, nearly 56 percent of state prosecutions were for assault; only 2 percent were for murder. These data on the latter period include thirteen counties and encompass a four-year sample (1857–1860) of Charleston County criminal prosecutions. Charleston city indictments and settlements from 1786 to 1835 support Hindus's assessment that assaults dominated in Charleston as for the state. Hindus, *Prison and Plantation*, 63–65; Bills of Indictment, 1786–1808, SCDAH; John Wroughton Mitchell Receipt Book, 1817–1835, SCL. Christine Stansell has found these networks to be signs of community strength and cooperation rather than indications of "pathologies" among the urban poor. Stansell, *City of Women*, chap. 3.

26.   Quoted in State v. Solomon, May Session, 1818, Bills of Indictment, Court of General Sessions, SCDAH; Hagy, *This Happy Land*, 1, 16–18.

27.   Quoted in City Council v. Van Roven, 2 McCord 465, 466, 468 (S.C. 1823). See also City Council v. King, 4 McCord 487 (S.C. 1828).

28.   Quoted in State v. Parkerson, 1 Strobhart 169, 170 (S.C. 1847).

29.   Quoted in Boyd v. Boyd, 1 Harper Eq. 144, 145 (S.C. 1824). See also Hair v. Hair, 10 Richardson Eq. 163, 173 (S.C. 1858); State v. Brunson and Miller, 2 Bailey 149 (S.C. 1831); Jelineau v. Jelineau, 2 DeSaussure Eq. 45, 49 (S.C. 1801).

30.   See examples in Cusack v. White, 2 Mill 368, 371–73, 375 (S.C. 1818); Bell v. Nealy, 1 Bailey 312, 315 (S.C. 1829).

31.   Quoted in Bills of Indictment, 1786–1808, 23 January 1806, 10A-2, Box 44, SCDAH; *Mercury*, 16, 20, 21 September 1837; 20 June 1839; 12 November 1840. See also *Rules and Regulations for the General Government of the Police*, section 118. On the "negroe dance," see 17 November 1795, Deposition of William Johnson and James Allison, quoted in 1795 Governor's Message to the Senate, and 7 November 1795 testimony by Peter S. Ryan before City Intendant, John Edward, in Miscellaneous Documents, SCDAH.

32.   On sexual freedom for white men, see Cusack v. White, 2 Mill 368, 370, 371, 372; Denton v. English, 3 Brevard 281 (S.C. 1814). On white "whores," see *SLSC*, 6:22–23. In case law, see Shecut v. McDowell, 1 Treadway 35 (S.C. 1812); Boyd v. Brent, 3 Brevard 353 (S.C. 1812); Freeman v. Price, 2 Bailey

115 (S.C. 1831); Anonymous, 1 Hill 251 (S.C. 1833). On the 1835 story, see Pease and Pease, *Ladies, Women and Wenches,* 149.

10. Illness and Death

1.   Quoted in DuPont, "On the Peculiarities of the Female" (inaugural thesis, The Medical College of the State of South Carolina, 1858), 29, WHL (hereafter medical thesis, WHL); Jones, "On The Peculiarities of the Female," medical thesis, 1829, 8–9, WHL. Of nearly 1,900 "inaugural theses" written between 1824 (when the state's first school of medicine was founded) and 1860, almost 1,200 cover topics chosen by students ten or more times, among which are women's catamenia (menstruation), puerperal (childbed) fever, pregnancy, and amenorrhea. Others wrote about abortion, accoucheurs, breast-feeding, ovarian dropsy, influence of imagination upon a "foetus in utero," uterine hemorrhage, ovarian cysts, and "prolapsus uteri." Roberta O. Burkett et al., comps., *A Bibliography of Inaugural Theses of Graduating Students of The Medical College of South Carolina* (Charleston, S.C.: Waring Historical Library, Medical University of South Carolina, typescript document, n.d.), i, vii–ix, table I.

2.   Quoted in Leavitt, *Brought to Bed,* 14, 20. See also Ball, "On the Origin of the Different Human Species," medical thesis, 1837, WHL; McLoud, "Hints on the Medical Treatment of Negroes," medical thesis, 1850, WHL.

3.   Quoted in Fraser, *Charleston,* 131; Mills, *Statistics of South Carolina,* 462–64. See also "Virginia in 1785," 411.

4.   Quoted in 8 December 1798, Petition of Sundry Inhabitants of the City of Charleston . . . against Butchers," General Assembly Petitions, 1798, #90, SCDAH; William Hume to Henry L. Pinckney, 18 December 1838, in Henry Laurens Pinckney, "Remarks . . . on the Subject of Interments and the Policy of Establishing a Public Cemetery, Beyond the Precincts of the City," in Pease and Pease, *The Web of Progress,* 196. See also untitled list of grievances of "Respectable Inhabitants on Charleston Neck" concerning butcher pens and other matters, General Assembly Grand Jury Presentments, 1821, #1, n.d., Charleston District, October Term 1821, SCDAH (hereafter Presentments); [Unprinted grievance against butcher pens], Presentments, 1824–1844, #4, n.d., May Term, 1824; Rosengarten, *Between the Tracks,* 102–105; Mills, *Statistics,* 393–95, 402, 440, 461.

5.   Quoted in Alice Izard to Margaret Izard Manigault, 28 March 1808, Manigault Family Papers, SCL. See also Alice Izard to Margaret Izard Manigault, 24 March 1811, Manigault Family Papers, SCL. Dengue fever (also called "breakbone" and "broken bone" fever) caused severe pains, fever, and rash. It could kill but was not dreaded like yellow fever, typhoid, and malaria. A survey of Charleston's health, published over fifty years after Mills's 1826 *Statistics,* decried "reports . . . indicating the ratio of mortality in Charleston as being extremely high, and [declared them] . . . prejudicial to the good name of the city." This 1883 report declared New York's death rate higher in all but one of six years between 1830 and 1880. This tally excluded slaves and free people of color, which skewed the figures in Charleston's favor. Mills, *Statis-*

tics, 450–51; *Charleston: The Centennial of Incorporation*, 136; Waring, *A History of Medicine in South Carolina*, 1:107, 113, 130, 140, 148, 152, 158; 2:30–32, 35, 38, 40, 44–46, 47, 52–54; Fraser, *Charleston*, 189.

6.   Cassedy, *Medicine in America*, 11–12; Fett, *Working Cures*.

7.   Frost quoted in Waring, *A History of Medicine*, 2:231.

8.   A study of the nature and distribution of diseases (epidemiology) among people of African descent was not wholly specious; fewer African Americans contracted certain strains of malaria and yellow fever than did people of European descent. Cassedy, *Medicine*, 29, 35, 37, 42–43, 51. See also Fett, *Working Cures*, chap. 6.

9.   Quoted in Johnson, *Oration Delivered before the Medical Society of South Carolina*. On causes of death and high infant mortality, see Waring, *A History of Medicine*, 2:44–46, 60, 62–63; "Record of Interments for 1821," CLS; Dawson, "Report of Interments in the City of Charleston . . . from 1828 to 1846"; Ramsay, *The Charleston Medical Register for the Year 1802* (Charleston, S.C.: W. P. Young, 1802). See also Mills, *Statistics*, 450; Cassedy, *Medicine*, 46–47.

10.   Quoted in Leavitt, *Brought to Bed*, 14, 20. See also Gordon, *Woman's Body, Woman's Right*, 48–49. On American demographic trends, see Grabill et al., "Demographic Trends," 375, 379, 390–91; Reed, *From Private Vice to Public Virtue*; Smith, "Family Limitation, Sexual Control and Domestic Feminism in Victorian America," 5–6, 44; Wells, *Revolutions in Americans' Lives*. Charleston did not mandate systematic birth, marriage, or death records until nearly 1860; impressionistic data before that time derives from correspondence, journals, periodic reports, and church registers.

11.   Information on Alice DeLancey Izard and her family derives from reading nearly 100 letters from 1794 to 1812 in the Ralph Izard Papers, SCL, and over 210 letters from 1791 to 1823 in the Manigault Family Papers, SCL. Samples include Margaret Izard Manigault to Gabriel Manigault, 23 November 1792, Manigault Papers, SCL; Alice Izard to Margaret Izard Manigault, 29 May, 10, 24, 29 June, 9, 22, 27 July, 1 October 1801; 22 April, 22 August 1802; 27 November 1808; 18 April 1816; 20 May 1817; 1 January, 19 February 1819, Manigault Family Papers, SCL. See also Margaret Izard Manigault to Alice Izard, 17 June 1801; 20 August, 19 September, 3 December 1802; Manigault Family Papers, SCL; Margaret Izard Manigault to [her cousin and "dear friend," Mary] Mrs. [Charles Cotesworth] Pinckney, 5 February 1809, Manigault Family Papers, SCL; Margaret Izard Manigault to [her sister, Georgina] Mrs. Allen Smith, 1 September, 20 October 1816, Manigault Family Papers, SCL.

12.   Alice Izard to Margaret Izard Manigault, 7 June 1807, Manigault Family Papers, SCL; Clifton, *Life and Labor*, xviii–xxi.

13.   Quoted in A. I.[Nancy] Deas to Mrs. [Margaret Izard] Manigault, 30 June 1814, and Margaret Izard Manigault to "My dear Brother" [her brother-in-law, Joseph Manigault], 6 December 1809, Manigault Family Papers, SCL. See also Alice Izard to Henry Izard, Esq., 14 August 1807; 15 October 1806; Alice Izard to Margaret Izard Manigault, 21 July 1814; Henry Izard to [his sister] Margaret Izard Manigault, 28 February 1813; Margaret Izard Manigault to

[her sister, Georgina] Mrs. Allen Smith, 20 October 1816; Alice Izard to Margaret Izard Manigault, 19 January, 9 March 1815; 20 May 1817; 1 January, 19 February 1819; M. C. Darby [a family friend] to Margaret Izard Manigault, 9 November 1822, Manigault Family Papers, SCL. On childbearing, see Alice Izard to Margaret Izard Manigault, 27 July 1801; 10 March 1811; 18 April 1816, Manigault Family Papers, SCL. Saint Anthony's fire includes "any of several inflammations or gangrenous conditions . . . of the skin." *Webster's Ninth New Collegiate Dictionary* (1985), s.v. "Saint Anthony's fire."

14.   Quoted in Alice Izard to Henry Izard, Esq., 22 July 1807, Ralph Izard Papers, SCL; Alice Izard to Margaret Izard Manigault, 26 August 1802, Manigault Family Papers, SCL. See also Alice Izard to Henry Izard, 12 June 1808; Alice Izard to Margaret Izard Manigault, 26 August 1802; 3, 17 March 1811; 22 February, 9 March 1815; 19 February 1819; A. I. [Nancy] Deas to Margaret Izard Manigault, 8 September 1814; 14 September 1815, Manigault Family Papers, SCL; Louisa C. Lord to "My dear Anna," 12 May, 23 July 1851; Louisa C. Lord to "Dear Martha," July [no date] 1852; Louisa C. Lord to "Mr. Noble," 28 January 1853, Louisa C. Lord Papers, 11/271, folders 1, 2, SCHS.

15.   Quoted in A. I. [Nancy] Deas to Margaret Izard Manigault, 23 July 1813, Manigault Family Papers, SCL. For other examples of this approach to illness and adversity, see R[ebecca] M. Rutledge to Lieut[enant] Rutledge, 15 May, 3 June 1833, Rutledge Family Papers, folder 2, SCL; Gilman, *Recollections of a Southern Matron*, 267.

16.   For statistics on Charleston's female slave population, see 1800 through 1860 censuses. On childbearing and mortality rates, see Gibbes, Jr., *Annual Report of the Registrar of Births, Deaths and Marriages*, 8, tables 1A, 1B, 106–109, 158–59. See also White, "Female Slaves: Sex Roles and Status in the Antebellum Plantation South," in *Half Sisters of History*, ed. Clinton.

17.   Quoted in Alice Izard to Ralph Izard, 1 January 1795, Ralph Izard Papers, SCL; David Yates to Elizabeth Ann Yates, 30 July 1824, Yates Family Papers, SCHS. See also Alice Izard to Henry Izard, 3 December 1807, Ralph Izard Papers, SCL. On mortality rates, see Dawson and DeSaussure, *Census of the City of Charleston*.

18.   Quoted in Alice Izard to Margaret Izard Manigault, 18 April, 3 May 1816, Manigault Family Papers, SCL. See also Alice Izard to Margaret Izard Manigault, 16 April 1809, Manigault Family Papers, SCL.

19.   Quoted in Rawick, ser. 1, vol. 2, 145–47. On ads for wet nurses, see *SCGGA*, 31 March, 12 April 1783; *Courier*, 1 March 1805. See also *Courier*, advertisement accounts, "Cash received," SCHS.

20.   Quoted in JBG Diary, SHC #970, series 2, folder 18, 4, 13 October 1833, SHC. Millie Barber quoted in Rawick, ser. 1, vol. 2, 39–40. See also quote in Rawick, ser. 1, vol. 2, 233–36. On other related perceptions of slave women, see Pope, "On the Professional Management of Negro Slaves," medical thesis, 1837, 14–15, WHL; Ball, "On the Origin of the Different Human Species," medical thesis, WHL; McLoud, "Hints on the Medical Treatment of Negroes," medical thesis, WHL; Haller, "The Negro and the Southern Physician," 238–53.

21.   Quoted in Cartwright, "The Diseases and Physical Peculiarities of the Negro

Race," *Charleston Medical Journal and Review* 6 (1851): 645–46. See also Cartwright, "The Diseases and Physical Peculiarities of the Negro Race," *New Orleans Medical and Surgical Journal* 8 (1851): 187, 189; "Review of Cartwright on the Diseases of the Negro Race," *Charleston Medical Journal and Review* 6 (1851): 830; A. P. Merrill, "An Essay on the Distinctive Peculiarities of the Negro Race," *Memphis Medical Record* 4 (1855): 134; Collins, "On Menstruation," medical thesis, 37, WHL; McMillen, *Motherhood in the Old South,* 87–88.

22.   Quoted in Rawick, ser. 1, vol. 3, 71–73, 127–29, 156, 160, 168, 172, 175, 214, 271–76. Francis Peyre Porcher quoted in Fett, *Working Cures,* 65. See also Porcher, "Sketch of the Medical Botany of South Carolina," 677–862; Porcher, "A Medico-Botanical Catalogue of the Plants and Ferns of St. John's Berkeley," medical thesis, 1847, WHL; Goodson, "Medical-Botanical Contributions of African Slave Women to American Medicine," 200–201; Geggus, "Slave and Free Colored Women in Saint Domingue," in *More Than Chattel,* ed. Gaspar and Hine, 263; Bush, "Hard Labor: Women, Childbirth, and Resistance in British Caribbean Slave Societies," in *More Than Chattel,* 204–206. On Charleston fears of poison, see Martineau, *Society in America,* 2:120–21; Rawick, ser. 1, vol. 2, 195–98; ser. 1, vol. 3, 158.

23.   Quoted in Rawick, ser. 1, vol. 3: 249, 252. On "Maum Katie," see Towne, *Letters and Diary of Laura M. Towne,* 144–45.

24.   Quoted in Alice Izard to Margaret Izard Manigault, 3 February 1816, Manigault Family Papers, SCL. For her part, Alice planned to hire out the entire family to supplement her income. Three years later "Poor Beck" died. At least one of her daughters had predeceased her. Alice noted Beck's death as an addendum in a letter. Alice Izard to Margaret Izard Manigault, 19 February 1819, Manigault Family Papers, SCL.

25.   Quoted in David Yates to Mrs. Yates, 30 July 1824, Yates Family Papers, 11–478, folder 7, SCHS; Jesse T. Cooper to Charles Manigault, 30 July, 14 August 1849; and "List of Slaves," 27 April 1851, in Clifton, *Life and Labor,* 69–70, 77. See also Anne Yates to Elizabeth Ann Yates, 20 August 1824, Yates Family Papers, SCHS; SCSG, 21 July 1798.

26.   Quoted in Young ads. Plumeau, Harper 543 (S.C. 1827); Parkerson v. Dinkins, 1 Rice 185, 186 (S.C. 1839); Boinest v. Leignez, 2 Richardson 464, 465 (S.C. 1846); McLoud, "Hints on the Medical Treatment of Negroes," medical thesis, 2–4, 8–11, 13, 19, WHL. See also Farr v. Gist, 1 Richardson 68 (S.C. 1844).

27.   Quoted in Anne Yates to "My dear Sister" (unnamed), 20 August 1824, Yates Family Papers, folder 6, SCHS; *Southern Patriot,* 14 August 1817; Lloyd v. Monpoey, 2 Nott & McCord 446 (S.C. 1820). See also Fairchild v. Bell, 1 Brevard 538 (S.C. 1807); Rodrigues ads. Habersham, 1 Speer 314 (S.C. 1843); Toomer v. Gadsden, 4 Strobhart 193 (S.C. 1850). In *Fairchild,* the owner of an unnamed female slave beat her, drove her from his house, and left her to die from exposure and the bruises he inflicted. A physician took the woman in and administered medical care, after finding her "in the road, in a miserable condition, almost naked, shockingly beaten, and having an iron on her leg of fifteen pounds weight." The doctor subsequently sued the woman's owner for reimbursement of his costs, and eventually won his case when the Constitu-

tional Court overturned a lower court (jury) ruling for the defendant, the woman's owner.

28. Quoted in Alice Izard to Margaret Izard Manigault, 26 September, 20 August, 11, 20 September 1805; 9 December 1815, Manigault Family Papers, SCL.

29. Quoted in Alice Izard to Margaret Izard Manigault, 5 February 1802; Alice Izard (Black Point, N.J.) to Margaret Izard Manigault, 12 August 1817, Manigault Family Papers, SCL; Gilman, *Recollections,* 235.

30. Quoted in Rawick, ser. 1, vol. 2, 195–98, 233–36; Bernhard, *Travels through North America,* in Clark, *The Grand Tour;* Alice Izard to Margaret Izard Manigault, 28 February 1816, Manigault Family Papers, SCL. See also Rawick, ser. 1, vol. 3, 161; ser. 1, vol. 2, 10–11, 122–23, 209; Angelina Grimké, "American Slavery as It Is: Testimony of a Thousand Witnesses," in *Voices of the Old South: Eyewitness Accounts, 1528–1861,* ed. Alan Gallay, excerpted from Theodore Weld, ed., *American Slavery as It Is* (1839; reprint, Athens: University of Georgia Press, 1994), 380–86. Tryon, *A Mirror for Americans,* 2:288–89. On laws regarding whipping, see *SLSC,* 4:400–402, 463; 7:397–417; Desprang v. Davis, 3 McCord 16, 17 (S.C. 1825); Jarvis (Assignee of the Sheriff of Charleston) v. Alexander, Chevis 143 (S.C. 1840).

31. Quoted in Bennet ads. Carter, Riley 287 (S.C. 1837); Rodrigues ads. Habersham, 1 Spears 314. On additional disputes over ill or injured slaves, see Timrod v. Shoolbred, 1 Bay 324 (S.C. 1793); Limehouse v. Gray, 1 Treadway 73 (S.C. 1812); F. Y. Porcher ads. Richard Caldwell, 2 McMullan 558 (Charleston City Court, 1841).

32. Executrixes of their husbands' estates, like Elizabeth Froget, Sarah Parmenter, Mary Samwayes (or Samways), Mary Brack, and Ann Hrabouski, sold slaves and other property at public auction. *SCGGA,* 8 April, 3, 10, 24, 27 May 1783. See also *SGSC,* 28 March, 4 April 1785; "Sale at John's Island on the Plantation of the late John Holmes," 5 February 1824, Estate Book of John Holmes, SCHS; two broadsides advertising estate sales of 235 and 102 slaves each, 1 November 1859, 24 January 1860, Hutson Lee Papers, SCHS.

33. Quoted in *Courier,* 14, 16 November 1837; Medical College of South Carolina Circular of 1831, in Fry, *Night Riders in Black Folk History,* 173–74.

34. Quoted in Savitt, "The Use of Blacks for Medical Experimentation and Demonstration in the Old South," 344–45. James Marion Sims quoted in Savitt, "The Use of Blacks for Medical Experimentation," 344–45.

35. Quoted in "Annual Circular of the Trustees and Faculty of the Medical College of the State of South Carolina . . . Session of 1840–41," (Charleston, 1840); "Negro Hospital," *CMJR* 15 (1860): 850; Charleston *Mercury,* 12 October 1838. See also Savitt, "The Use of Blacks for Medical Experimentation," 331–48; Savitt, *Medicine and Slavery,* 245; David C. Humphrey, "Dissection and Discrimination: The Social Origins of Cadavers in America, 1760–1915," New York Academy of Medicine, *Bulletin* (September 1973): 819–27; Waring, *A History of Medicine,* 2:75–76, 79.

36. Savitt, "The Use of Blacks for Medical Experimentation," 334.

37.   On 18 October 1790, Charleston's Intendant, Arnoldus Vanderhorst, and the city council ratified "An Ordinance for the Establishment of an Orphan House in the City of Charleston for the purpose of supporting and educating poor orphan children and those of poor distressed and disabled parents who are unable to support and maintain them." Minutes of the Orphan House, 18 October 1790 to 15 August 1796, CCA. From 1830 to 1848, a total of over 7,300 men, women, and children resorted to living at the Poor House; only 100 resided there at any given time. Bellows, *Benevolence among Slaveholders*, 74, 77–78; Dawson and DeSaussure, *Census of the City of Charleston*, 48–49; Haber and Gratton, "Old Age, Public Welfare and Race," 265–66; Mills, *Statistics of South Carolina*, 396, 432, 528, 628, 648, 733.

38.   Quoted in Eckhard, *Digest of the Ordinances*, 203–206; McCandless, *Moonlight, Magnolias, and Madness*, 23–24; City Council v. Cohen, 2 Speer 408, 416 (S.C. 1843); Letter from the Charleston City Council, inserted in Charleston Commissioners of the Poor, Meeting Minutes, 1800–1856, 6 March 1820, CCA; Poor House Minutes, 20 September 1801; 29 September 1806; 9 January 1809; 19 March 1810; Pinckney, *Report Containing a Review of the Proceedings of the City Authorities*, 39–40. See also Poor House Minutes, 29 December 1800; 21 September, 14 December 1801; Waring, *A History of Medicine*, 1:134.

39.   Quoted in Poor House Minutes, 26 January 1832. See also Mills, *Statistics of South Carolina*, 431–32; McCandless, *Moonlight, Magnolias, and Madness*, 33, 74–75, 164, 172. On conditions in the Poor House, see Poor House Minutes, 28 February, 10, 24 April, 8 May 1828; 24, 28 June, 30 November 1832; 7, 21 February 1833. Although Charleston began sending some "insane" inmates to the State Lunatic Asylum (in Columbia) after 1833, the transfers were periodic and idiosyncratic. Until the state assumed financial responsibility for the poor insane in 1871, Charleston taxpayers paid less to keep the insane in their own community than to transfer them to Columbia. Some inmates proved useful in performing chores in the Charleston Poor House. Poor House Minutes, 26 January 1832; 9 January, 16 March, 28 September, 12, 15 October 1853.

40.   Quoted in Alice Izard to Margaret Izard Manigault, 11 May, 1 June 1815; 11 May 1817, Manigault Family Papers, SCL; Waring, *A History of Medicine*, 134. In the same year of Beck's admission, the city council employed nurses, women of African descent, to care for those in the Poor House labeled insane.

41.   Quoted in Poor House Minutes, 7 February 1833; 3 January 1844; 18 September, 18, 25, 26 November 1850; 10 May, 12 November 1853. See also Poor House Minutes, March 1831; 29 January 1845. On the municipal ordinance regarding insane people, see Poor House Minutes, 6 March 1820; Eckhard, *Digest of the Ordinances*, 203–206.

42.   Quoted in Waring, *History of Medicine*, 2:134; Poor House Minutes, November 1852. Alcoholism was a leading cause of institutionalization in the mid-nineteenth century. Finley, "On Mania à Potu," medical thesis, 1829, 1, WHL. See also Orphan House Minutes, 18 August 1793; Poor House Minutes, 21 February 1822; 20 August 1828; 15 January, 16 July, 24 September 1829; 4 Febru-

ary, 5 August 1840; 5 February 1841; 26 February 1846; Bellows, *Benevolence among Shareholders,* 82. Poor House Minutes, 16 November 1824; 8 May 1828; 16 July 1829; Mills, *Statistics of South Carolina,* 431–32. On Mrs. Fayan, see Casebook of [Dr.] E. B. Flagg, 21, 22, 29 December 1850; 4 January 1851, Flagg Papers, folder 5, SCHS (hereafter Flagg Casebook). On Mrs. Gough, see Flagg Casebook, 6 December 1850, SCHS. See also Flagg Casebook, 4, 11, 12, 15, 16, 19, 22 November, 1, 6, 11, 14, 16, 17, 21, 22, 29 December 1850; 4, 18, 29 January, 2, 6, 18 February 1851, SCHS.

43. Quoted in Orphan House Minutes, 25 March 1845. On immigrants, see Mills, *Statistics of South Carolina,* 431–32; Waring, *A History of Medicine,* 1:134–36; Silver, "A New Look at Old South Urbanization," 149; Dawson and DeSaussure, *Census of the City of Charleston;* Bellows, *Benevolence among Shareholders,* 89–90, 92–96. On Francis Ruchbosch, see quotes in Orphan House Minutes, 30 January 1856. See also Orphan House Minutes, 16 January 1857.

44. Quoted in McCandless, *Moonlight, Magnolias, and Madness,* 176. On alcoholic husbands causing destitution among Charleston's poor women, see Bellows, *Benevolence among Shareholders,* 84–85. On disease, see Waring, *History of Medicine,* 35; Roper Hospital Casebook No. 2, 26 May 1859; 14 March, 29 May 1860, WHL (hereafter Roper Casebook, 2). On Cathy Kenny, see Roper Casebook 2, 29 May 1860.

45. Mills, *Statistics of South Carolina,* 396, 432, 528, 628, 648, 733; Haber and Gratton, "Old Age, Public Welfare and Race," 265–66; Bellows, *Benevolence among Shareholders,* 74, 77–78.

46. Quoted in Meeting Minutes, 15 September 1841, Ladies Benevolent Society Journal 2, 1823–1871, SCHS (hereafter LBS Minutes). From its founding in September 1813 to its annual meeting eleven years later, Society members had visited and provided material assistance to over 2,900 "destitute sick poor." From 1823 to 1834, the Society expended an annual average of nearly $1,900 on 254 people, or just under $7.50 per person per year. *Constitution of the Ladies' Benevolent Society of Charleston and Regulations for the Visiting Committee* (Charleston, S.C.: A. E. Miller, 1852), 4–5 (hereafter LBS Constitution); Meeting Minutes of Annual Meetings, September 1823 through September 1834, LBS Minutes.

47. Quoted in LBS Minutes, 15 September 1825; LBS Constitution, 4–5; LBS Minutes, 15 September 1825. See also LBS Minutes, Annual Meetings, September 1823 through September 1834; Waring, *History of Medicine,* 24.

48. LBS Minutes, 15 June 1825.

49. Quoted in LBS Minutes, 15 December 1835; 15 June 1825; 2 February 1836; 15 September 1839; 15 September 1840.

50. Quoted in LBS Minutes, 15 September 1825. Mrs. North died in 1825. LBS minutes constantly mentioned "the unsparing hand of death" upon its own. The death toll reached five to seven per year. See also 15 September, 1 December 1826; 15 September 1831; 15 June 1832; 15 September 1839; 15 Septem-

ber 1843; 15 September 1846; 25 October 1852; 25 October 1856; 26 October 1857.

51. Jones, "On the Peculiarities of the Female," medical thesis, 5, WHL.

Conclusion

1. Quoted in Florence Cooke, 21 January 1783, General Assembly Petitions, SCDAH.

2. Quoted in Thompson v. Thompson, 10 S.C. Eq. 416, 419 (S.C. 1859); Bynum, *Unruly Women*, 14. See also Kathleen M. Brown's analysis of how the juxtaposition of "good wives" and "nasty wenches" was "crucial to the foundations of social order" in colonial Virginia. Brown, *Good Wives, Nasty Wenches*, 104.

3. Quoted in Jordan, *The White Man's Burden*, 72; State v. Davis, 2 Bailey 558, 559 (S.C. 1831); State v. Motley and Blackledge, 7 Richardson 334 (S.C. 1854).

4. On the ideology of separate spheres, true womanhood, and transformed domesticity, see Welter, "Cult of True Womanhood: 1820–1860," 151–74; Smith-Rosenberg, *Disorderly Conduct*; Ryan, *Cradle of the Middle Class*; Cott, *The Bonds of Womanhood*; Sklar, *Catharine Beecher*; Boydston, et al., *The Limits of Sisterhood*. On the distinctive nature of the southern household and its impact on domestic law, see Bardaglio, *Reconstructing the Household*, 23–36.

5. Quoted in McLoud, "Hints on the Medical Treatment of Negroes," medical thesis, 14, WHL.

6. Quoted in Ewart v. Nagel, 1 McMullan 32, 34 (S.C. 1840).

Appendix 1

1. Congress authorized Bounty Land Warrants in 1776 to substitute for wages it could not pay its soldiers. The number of acres of land promised—ranging from 100 to 1,100 acres—was based on the soldier's rank. The warrants were granted until 1855. When the soldier died, his heirs took claim to the land. The number of applicants for bounty lands exceeded the number of applicants for pensions; the two types of claims have been microfilmed together. Revolutionary War Pension and Bounty Land Warrant Application Files, Record Group 360, National Archives, Washington, D.C.

Appendix 2

1. Quoted in Bardaglio, *Reconstructing the Household*, 5. See also Wyatt-Brown, *Southern Honor*; Shalhope, "Thomas Jefferson's Republicanism and Antebellum Southern Thought," 529–56; "The Doctrine of the 'Higher Law,'" *Southern Literary Messenger* 17 (March 1851): 136–37.

2. Quoted in "Report of the Judiciary Committee (1846)," filed with Marion Grand Jury Presentments, 1850, General Assembly Loose Legislative Papers, 1831–1859, SCDAH; Brevard, *Alphabetical Digest of the Public Statute Law*, 1:xvi. See also Hindus, *Prison and Plantation*, 30.

3.   Quoted in Hindus, *Prison and Plantation,* 26, 36 (see also 61–63). See also Alexia J. Helsley and Michael E. Stauffer, *South Carolina Court Records: An Introduction for Genealogists* (Columbia, S.C.: South Carolina Department of Archives and History, 1993), 1–3, 9, 12, 17–18; Catterall, *Judicial Cases Concerning American Slavery and the Negro,* vol. 2, 269–70; Cooper and McCord, *SLSC,* 7:163–342 (esp. 325, 334, 339–41, 647); Nash, "Negro Rights, Unionism, and Greatness on the South Carolina Court of Appeals," 141.

4.   Unpublished inventory of the Charleston city court records, CCA.

5.   V. A. C. Gatrell and T. B. Hadden, "Criminal Statistics and Their Interpretation," in *Nineteenth-Century Society: Essays in the Use of Quantitative Methods for the Study of Social Data,* ed. E. A. Wrigley (Cambridge, U.K.: University Press, 1972), 336–96; Hindus, *Prison and Plantation,* 59–84. On the record-keeping requirement, see *SLSC,* 7:22.

Bibliography

Unpublished Sources

Charleston County Library, Charleston, South Carolina
    Record of Wills of Charleston Country
Charleston Library Society, Charleston, South Carolina
    Charleston City Yearbooks
    Charleston Newspapers
    Charleston Municipal Reports
City Of Charleston Archives, Charleston, South Carolina
    Charleston Alms House Records
    Charleston City Council Journals
    Charleston Orphan House, Commissioners Minutes
    Charleston Poor House Journals, Minutes
College of Charleston, Charleston, South Carolina
    Brown Fellowship Society Records
    Charles Fraser Commonplace Book
    Friendly Moralist Society Records
    German Friendly Society Minutes
    South Carolina Society Minutes
    St. John's German Lutheran Church Records
Duke University, William R. Perkins Library, Special Collections, Durham, North
    Carolina
    Augustus F. Edwards Papers
    William H. Gilliland Account Book, 1860–1861
    George A. Gordon Papers
    Louis Manigault Papers
    Lucy Ruggles Diary, 1845–1848
    Harriott Horry Rutledge Papers, 1841
    Shindler Family Papers
    Henry Watson Jr. Papers
Library of Congress, Washington, D.C.
    Izard Family Papers
    Charles Cotesworth Pinckney Family Papers
Museum of Early Southern Decorative Arts (MESDA), Winston-Salem, North Carolina
    Index of Early Southern Artists and Artisans
National Archives, Washington, D.C.
    RG 29 Records of the Bureau of the Census, Federal Manuscript Census, South
    Carolina
    RG 360 Revolutionary War Pension and Bounty-Land-Warrant Application Files
South Carolina Department of Archives and History, Columbia, South Carolina
    Acts of the Assembly of South Carolina (microfilm)

Charleston County, Court of General Sessions, Records of Indictments and Sub-
poenas
Commission of Enquiry into Losses and Services of American Loyalists (micro-
film)
Court of Appeals, Decrees in Equity Cases
General Assembly Loose Legislative Papers, 1831–1859
General Assembly Petitions, 1783–1860
Grand Jury Presentments, 1783–1860
Miscellaneous Records: Manumissions, Deeds, Marriage Settlements, Inventories
Proceedings of the Board of Police (microfilm)
Records of St. Philip's Episcopal Church
Records of Wills—Charleston County, Vols. 1, 51
State Free Negro Capitation Tax Books, Charleston, South Carolina, 1811–1860
(microfilm)
South Carolina Historical Society, Charleston, South Carolina
Mary Aldret Papers
Bacot-Huger Papers
Charleston Records of the Orphan House
Charleston Records of the Poor House
Langdon Cheves III Legal Papers
Female Charitable Association Papers and Minutes
Flagg Papers (Casebook of Dr. E. B. Flagg)
Gibbes-Gilchrist Papers
Harriott Pinckney Horry Journal
John Holmes Estate Book
Ladies Benevolent Society Papers and Minutes
Ladies Fuel Society Papers and Minutes
Hutson Lee Papers
Louisa C. Lord Papers
Manigault Family Papers
Methodist Charitable Society Minute Book
Methodist Church Society Records
Order Book, South Carolina Militia, 1793–1814
Pinckney Family Papers
Poor House Hospital Prescription and Record Books
Dr. Francis Peyre Porcher Prescription Book
Register of the Transient Sick and Poor of the Charleston Alms House, 1807–1850
Hagar Richardson Estate Papers
South Carolina File, "Inns, taverns, hotels and coffee houses"
Lists of Taxpayers
Trinity Methodist Church Records
Arnoldus V. Vanderhorst Papers
Yates Family Papers
South Caroliniana Library, University of South Carolina, Columbia, South Carolina
Robert F. W. Allston Family Papers
Pierre Teller Babbit Papers
Brown Fellowship Society Papers
Paul Cross Papers
Ellison Family Papers

Grace Brown Elmore Reminiscences
Fuel Society Papers
German Friendly Society Minutes (typed transcripts)
Charlotte Trezevant Gignilliat Reminiscences
Independent or Congregational Church Records, Charleston
Alexander Ingles Papers
Ralph Izard Papers
Ladies Benevolent Society Journals
Manigault Family Papers (microfiche)
Recollections of Louisa Rebecca Hayne McCord
Louisa Minot Papers
John Wroughton Mitchell Receipt Book, 1817
Rebecca Motte Collection
Read Family Papers
Rutledge Family Papers
Shindler Family Papers
David Lewis Wardlaw Papers
Southern Historical Collection, Wilson Library, University of North Carolina, Chapel
Hill, North Carolina
Marianne (Bull) Cozens Diary, 1830
Franklin Harper Elmore Papers, 1819–1910
John Berkely Grimball Diary (typed transcripts)
Gabriel Edward Manigault Autobiography (mss)
Lucy E. McIver Papers
Trapier Family Papers, 1752–1887
Waring Historical Library, Medical University of South Carolina, Charleston, South
Carolina
Inaugural Theses of Graduating Students, 1825–1860
Roper Hospital Casebook

Newspapers

Carolina Gazette
Charleston City Gazette & Daily Advertiser, 1789–1832
Charleston Times
Courier (after 1830, *News and Courier*)
De Bow's Review
The Gazette
Gazette and Public Advertiser
Gazette of the State of South Carolina
The Magnolia
Mercury
L'Oracle
Royal Gazette
Royal South Carolina Gazette
South Carolina Gazette
South Carolina Weekly Gazette (continued as *South Carolina and America General Ga-zette*)
South Carolina Gazette and Country Journal

South Carolina Gazette and General Advertiser
Southern Patriot
State Gazette
State Gazette of South Carolina

Published Primary Sources

Achates [Thomas Pinckney]. *Reflections Occasioned by the Late Disturbances in Charleston, by Achates.* Charleston, S.C.: A. E. Miller, 1822.

American Literature and Charleston Society. Charleston, S.C.: Walker and James, 1853.

Bargar, B. D., ed. "Charlestown Loyalism in 1775: The Secret Reports of Alexander Innes." *South Carolina Historical Magazine* 63 (July 1962): 125–36.

Barnwell, Robert W., ed. "Correspondence of Hon. Arthur Middleton, Signer of the Declaration of Independence." *South Carolina Historical and Genealogical Magazine* 27 (1926): 183–213.

Barnwell, William H. *The Character of Eve: A Sermon, Addressed to Young Ladies.* Charleston, S.C.: John Russell, 1847.

Bartram, William. *Travels through North and South Carolina, Georgia, East and West Florida.* Philadelphia: N.p., 1791.

Baurmeister, Carl Leopold. *Revolution in America, Confidential Letters and Journals, 1776–1784, of Adjutant General Major Baurmeister of the Hessian Forces.* Translated and annotated by Bernhard Alexander Uhlendorf. New Brunswick, N.J.: Rutgers University Press, 1957.

Blackstone, William. *Commentaries on the Laws of England.* 5 vols. 1765–69. Reprint. New York: Oceana Publications, 1967.

———. *The Laws Respecting Women.* With a foreword by Shirley Raissi. 1777. Reprint. Dobbs Ferry, N.Y.: Oceana Publications, 1974.

Blassingame, John W., ed. *Slave Testimony: Two Centuries of Letters, Speeches, Interviews, and Autobiographies.* Baton Rouge: Louisiana State University Press, 1977.

Bremer, Fredrika. *Charleston One Hundred Years Ago: Being Extracts from the Letters of Fredrika Bremer during Her Visit to Charleston in 1850.* 1856. Reprint. Charleston, S.C.: St. Albans Press, 1951.

———. *Homes of the New World: Impressions of America.* Trans. Mary Howitt. 2 vols. New York: Harper and Brothers, 1856.

Carroll, Charles R. "Woman." In *The Charleston Book: A Miscellany in Prose and Verse,* ed. William Gilmore Simms, 134–40. 1845. Reprint. Spartanburg, S.C.: Reprint Co., 1983.

Carson, James Petigru. *Life, Letters and Speeches of James Louis Petigru, The Union Man of South Carolina.* Washington, D.C.: W. D. Lowdermilk and Co., 1920.

Cartwright, Samuel A. "The Diseases and Physical Peculiarities of the Negro Race." *Charleston Medical Journal and Review* 6 (1851): 645–46.

Charleston: The Centennial of Incorporation, 1783–1883. Charleston, S.C.: News and Courier Book Presses, 1884.

Charleston Directory and Strangers' Guide for 1840 and 1841. Charleston, S.C.: T. C. Fay, 1840.

Clark, Thomas D., ed. *South Carolina: The Grand Tour, 1780–1865.* Columbia: University of South Carolina Press, 1973.

Clifton, James M., ed. *Life and Labor on Argyle Island: Letters and Documents of a Savannah River Rice Plantation, 1833–1867.* Savannah, Ga.: Beehive Press, 1978.

Davis, John. *Travels of Four and One-Half Years in the United States of America; during 1798, 1799, 1800, 1801, and 1802.* London: N.p., 1803.

Dawson, John L. "Report of Interments in the City of Charleston . . . from 1828 to 1846." Charleston, S.C.: Miller and Browne, 1846.

Dew, Thomas R. "On the Characteristic Differences between the Sexes, and on the Position and Influence of Woman in Society." *Southern Literary Messenger* 1 (May, July, August 1835): 493–512, 621–32, 672–91.

Drago, Edmund L., ed. *Broke by the War: Letters of a Slave Trader.* Columbia: University of South Carolina Press, 1991.

Drayton, John. *Memoirs of the American Revolution as Relating to the State of South Carolina.* 2 vols. Charleston, S.C.: A. E. Miller, 1821.

———. *A View of South-Carolina, as Respects Her Natural and Civil Liberties.* Charleston, S.C.: John A. Dacqueny, 1802.

Easterby, J. H., ed. "Public Poor Relief in Colonial Charleston: A Report to the Commons House of Assembly About the Year 1767." *South Carolina Historical and Genealogical Magazine* 17 (April 1941): 83–86.

———. *The South Carolina Rice Plantation as Revealed in the Papers of Robert F. W. Allston.* Chicago: University of Chicago Press, 1945.

Easterby, J. H., et al., eds. *Journal of the Commons House of Assembly.* Columbia: University of South Carolina Press, 1951–1989.

Ellet, Elizabeth F. *The Women of the American Revolution.* 3 vols. New York: Baker and Scribner, 1848, 1850.

Foster, Frances Smith. *Written by Herself: Literary Production by African American Women, 1746–1892.* Bloomington: Indiana University Press, 1993.

"Franz Zebedaeus Schmelizle, or The Vigil of the Bridegroom." *Southern Literary Journal and Monthly Magazine* (September 1835): 23–30.

Fraser, Charles. *Reminiscences of Charleston.* Charleston, S.C.: John Russell, 1854.

Gibbes, Robert W., Jr., M.D. *Annual Report of the Registrar of Births, Deaths, and Marriages for the Legislature of South Carolina, for the Year Ending December 31, 1856.* Columbia, S.C.: N.p., 1865.

Gilman, Caroline Howard. *Recollections of a Southern Matron.* New York: Harper and Brothers, 1850.

Gilman, Charlotte Perkins. *The Living of Charlotte Perkins Gilman: An Autobiography.* 1935. Reprint. New York: Arno Press, 1972.

Grimké, Sarah M. *Letters on the Equality of the Sexes, and the Condition of Women.* 1838. Reprint. New York: Source Book Press, 1970.

Hagy, James W., ed. *Charleston, South Carolina, City Directories for the Years 1816, 1819, 1822, 1825, and 1829.* Baltimore, Md.: Clearfield Co., 1996.

———. *City Directories for Charleston, South Carolina, for the Years 1803, 1806, 1807, 1809, and 1813.* Baltimore, Md.: Clearfield Co., 1995.

———. *Directories For the City of Charleston, South Carolina, For the Years 1830–31, 1835–36, 1837–38, and 1840–41.* Baltimore, Md.: Clearfield Co., 1997.

———. *People and Professions of Charleston, South Carolina, 1782–1802.* Baltimore, Md.: Clearfield Co., 1992.

Hall, Captain Basil. *Travels in North America, in the Years 1827 and 1828.* 3 vols. Edinburgh, Scotland: Cadell and Co., 1829.

Hamer, Philip M., et al., eds. *The Papers of Henry Laurens.* 14 vols. to date. Columbia: University of South Carolina Press, 1968–2003.

Herz, Henri. *My Travels in America*. Trans. Henry Bertram Hill. 1847. Reprint. Ann Arbor, Mich.: Edwards Brothers, 1963.

Hodges, Graham Russell, ed. *The Black Loyalist Directory: African Americans in Exile after the Revolution*. New York: Garland Publishing, 1996.

Hodgson, Adam. *Remarks during a Journey through North America in the Years 1819, 1820, and 1821 in a Series of Letters*. 1823. Reprint. Westport, Conn.: Negro Universities Press, 1970.

Howe, Mark A. DeWolfe, ed. "Journal of Josiah Quincy, Junior, 1773." *Proceedings of the Massachusetts Historical Society* 49 (June 1916): 424–81.

Hunt, Gaillard. *Life in America One Hundred Years Ago*. 1814. Reprint. New York: Harper and Brothers, 1914.

Jacobs, Harriet. *Autobiography of a Slave Girl, Written by Herself*. Boston: Harvard University Press, 2000.

Johnson, Elmer D., and Kathleen Lewis Sloan, comps. and eds. *South Carolina: A Documentary Profile of the Palmetto State*. Columbia: University of South Carolina Press, 1971.

Johnson, Joseph. *Oration Delivered before the Medical Society of South Carolina, at Their Anniversary Meeting, December 24, 1807*. Charleston, S.C.: Marchant, Willington and Co., 1808.

Johnson, Michael P., and James L. Roark, eds. *No Chariot Let Down: Charleston's Free People of Color on the Eve of the Civil War*. Chapel Hill: University of North Carolina Press, 1984.

Johnson, William. *Sketches of the Life and Correspondence of Nathanael Greene, Major General of the Armies of the United States, in the War of the Revolution*. 2 vols. Charleston, S.C.: A. E. Miller, 1822.

Kemble, Frances Anne. *Journal of a Residence on a Georgian Plantation in 1838–1839*. 1863. Reprint. Athens: University of Georgia Press, 1984.

Kierner, Cynthia A. *Southern Women in Revolution, 1776–1800: Personal and Political Narratives*. Columbia: University of South Carolina Press, 1998.

King, Susan Petigru. *Gerald Gray's Wife and Lily: A Novel*. With an introduction by Jane H. Pease and William H. Pease. 1855, 1864. Reprint. Durham, N.C.: Duke University Press, 1993.

Lyell, Sir Charles. *Travels in North America in the Years 1841–42*. 2 vols. 1845. Reprint. New York: Arno Press, 1978.

———. *A Second Visit to the United States of North America*. 2 vols. New York: Harper and Brothers, 1849.

"Marrying for Money." *Russell's Magazine* 3 (June 1858): 229–33.

Martineau, Harriet. *Retrospect of Western Travel*. 2 vols. 1838. Reprint. New York: Haskell House, 1969.

———. *Society in America*. 2 vols. 3d ed. New York: Saunders and Otley, 1837.

Mellon, James, ed. *Bullwhip Days: The Slaves Remember*. New York: Weidenfeld and Nicolson, 1988.

Merrens, H. Roy, ed. *The Colonial South Carolina Scene: Contemporary Views, 1697–1774*. Columbia: University of South Carolina Press, 1977.

———. "A View of Coastal South Carolina in 1778: The Journal of Ebenezer Hazard." *South Carolina Historical Magazine* 73 (October 1972): 177–93.

Merrill, A. P. "An Essay on the Distinctive Peculiarities of the Negro Race." *Memphis Medical Record* 4 (1855): 134–40.

Mills, Robert. *Statistics of South Carolina, Including a View of Its Natural, Civil, and Military History, General and Particular.* 1826. Reprint. Spartanburg, S.C.: Reprint Co., 1972.

Miranda, Francisco de. *The New Democracy in America: Travels of Francisco de Miranda in the United States, 1783–84.* Trans. Judson P. Wood. Ed. John S. Ezell. Norman: University of Oklahoma Press, 1963.

Mohl, Raymond A. "The Grand Fabric of Republicanism: A Scotsman Describes South Carolina, 1810–1811." *South Carolina Historical Magazine* 71 (July 1970): 170–88.

Montlezun, Baron de. "Voyage fait dans les annees 1816 et 1817, de New York a la Nouvelles Orleans." In *South Carolina: A Documentary Profile of the Palmetto State,* ed. Elmer D. Johnson and Kathleen Lewis Sloan, 260–62. Columbia: University of South Carolina Press, 1971.

Mood, F. A. *Methodism in Charleston: A Narrative of the Chief Events Relating to the Rise and Progress of the Methodist Episcopal Church in Charleston.* Nashville, Tenn.: Southern Methodist Publishing House, 1856.

Moore, Caroline, comp. and ed. *Abstracts of the Wills of the State of South Carolina, 1760–1784.* Columbia, S.C.: R. L. Bryan Co., 1959.

Motes, Margaret Peckham, ed. *Free Blacks and Mulattos in South Carolina: 1850 Census.* Baltimore, Md.: Clearfield Co., 2000.

Moultrie, William. *Memoirs of the American Revolution So Far As It Related to the States of North and South-Carolina, and Georgia.* 2 vols. New York: D. Longworth, 1802.

Murray, Amelia M. *Letters from the United States, Cuba and Canada.* 2 vols. New York: G. P. Putnam and Co., 1856.

Olmsted, Frederick Law. *The Cotton Kingdom: A Traveller's Observations on Cotton and Slavery in the American States.* 1953. Reprint. New York: Random House, 1984.

——. *A Journey in the Seaboard Slave States, with Remarks on Their Economy.* New York: Dix and Edwards, 1856.

Payne, Daniel A. *The History of the African Methodist Episcopal Church.* 1891. Reprint. New York: Arno Press, 1969.

Pearson, Edward A., ed. *Designs against Charleston: The Trial Record of the Denmark Vesey Slave Conspiracy of 1822.* Chapel Hill: University of North Carolina Press, 1999.

Pinckney, Elise, ed. *The Letterbook of Eliza Lucas Pinckney.* 1972. Reprint. Columbia: University of South Carolina Press, 1997.

Pinckney, Henry Laurens. *Remarks . . . on the Subject of Interments and the Policy of Establishing a Public Cemetery Beyond the Precincts of the City.* Charleston, S.C.: Walker, Evans, and Co., 1858.

——. *A Report Containing a Review of the Proceedings of the City Authorities from First September 1838, to First August 1839.* Charleston, S.C.: W. Riley, 1839.

Porcher, Francis. "Sketch of the Medical Botany of South Carolina." *Transactions of the American Medical Association* 2 (1849): 677–862.

Porcher, Frederick A. "Upper Beat of St. John's, Berkeley: A Memoir." *Transactions of the Huguenot Society of South Carolina* (November 1906): 31–78.

Porter, A. Toomer. *Lead On! Step by Step: Scenes from Clerical, Military, Educational and Plantation Life in the South, 1828–1898.* New York: G. Putnam's Sons, 1898.

Purse, R. S., comp. *Charleston City Directory and Strangers Guide for 1856.* New York: J. F. Trow, 1856.

Ramsay, David. *Ramsay's History of South Carolina from Its First Settlement in 1670 to the Year 1808.* 2 vols. Newberry, S.C.: W. J. Duffie, 1858.

Ravenel, Harriott Horry. *Charleston: The Place and the People.* New York: MacMillan Co., 1906.

——. *Eliza Pinckney.* New York: Charles Scribner's Sons, 1896.

——. *Life and Times of William Lowndes of South Carolina, 1782–1822.* Boston: Houghton, Mifflin and Co., 1901.

Rawick, George P., ed. *The American Slave: A Composite Autobiography.* Series 1, Vol. 2, *South Carolina, Parts 1 and 2.* Westport, Conn.: Greenwood Publishing Co., 1972.

——. *The American Slave: A Composite Autobiography.* Series 1, Vol. 3, *South Carolina, Parts 3 and 4.* Westport, Conn.: Greenwood Publishing Co., 1972.

——. *The American Slave: A Composite Autobiography.* Series 1, Vol. 12, *Georgia, Part 1.* Westport, Conn.: Greenwood Publishing Co., 1972.

Reeve, Tapping. *The Law of Baron and Feme, of Parent and Child, of Guardian and Ward, of Master and Servant, and of the Powers of Court of Chancery.* 1816. Reprint. New York: Source Book Press, 1970.

——. *The Laws Respecting Women.* 1777. Reprint. Dobbs Ferry, N.Y.: Oceana Publications, 1974.

Rules and Regulations for the General Government of the Police Department of the City of Charleston. Charleston, S.C.: Walker and Evans, 1856.

Schenck, James R. *The Directory and Stranger's Guide for the City of Charleston.* Charleston, S.C.: Archibald E. Miller, 1822.

Seeber, Edward D., ed. and trans. *On the Threshold of Liberty: Journal of a Frenchman's Tour of the American Colonies in 1777.* Bloomington: Indiana University Press, 1959.

Shecut, J. L. E. W. *Medical and Philosophical Essays: Containing Topographical, Historical, and Other Sketches of the City of Charleston from Its First Settlement to the Present Period.* Charleston, S.C.: A. E. Miller, 1819.

Simms, William Gilmore. *The History of South Carolina from Its First European Discovery to Its Erection into a Republic.* New York: Richardson and Co., 1866.

——. "The Morals of Slavery (1837)." In *Pro-Slavery Argument, as Maintained by the Most Distinguished Writers of the Southern States.* 1852. Reprint. New York: Negro Universities Press, 1968.

Smith, Daniel Huger Elliot. *A Charlestonian's Recollections, 1846–1913.* Charleston, S.C.: Carolina Art Association, 1950.

Smith, Daniel Huger Elliot, and A. S. Salley, Jr., eds. *Register of St. Philip's Parish, 1754–1810.* 1927. Reprint. Columbia: University of South Carolina Press, 1971.

Smith, J. J. Pringle. "Some Accounts of the Government of the City of Charleston before and after the Revolution of 1776." In *Year Book City of Charleston, 1881.* Charleston, S.C.: News and Courier Book Presses, 1881.

Smith, J. J. Pringle, and William A. Courtenay. "Sketch of the History of Charleston." In *Year Book City of Charleston, 1880.* Charleston, S.C.: Walker, Evans, and Cogswell, 1880.

A South-Carolinian. *A Refutation of the Calumnies Circulated against the Southern and Western States, Respecting the Institution and Existence of Slavery Among Them.* Charleston, S.C.: A. E. Miller, 1822.

Southern Business Directory and General Commercial Advertiser. Charleston, S.C.: Walker and James, 1854.

Stuart, James. *Three Years in North America.* 2 vols. 3d ed. Edinburgh, Scotland: Robert Cadell, 1833.

Thornwell, Rev. Dr. [James Henley]. *The Rights and the Duties of the Masters: A Sermon*

Preached at the Dedication of a Church Erected in Charleston, S.C., for the Benefit and Instruction of the Coloured Population. Charleston, S.C.: Walker and James, 1850.

Tobias, Thomas J., ed. "Charles Town 1764." *South Carolina Historical Magazine* 68 (April 1966): 67–68.

Tobler, John. *South Carolina and Georgia Almanack for 1785.* Charleston, S.C.: N.p., 1785.

Towne, Laura M. *Letters and Diary of Laura M. Towne Written from the Sea Islands of South Carolina 1862–1884.* Ed. Rupert Sargent Holland. New York: Negro Universities Press, 1969.

Trenholm, W. L. *Centennial Address before the Charleston Chamber of Commerce, February 11, 1844.* Charleston, S.C.: News and Courier Book Presses, 1844.

Trollope, Frances. *Domestic Manners of the Americans.* Ed. Donald Smalley. Gloucester, Mass.: Peter Smith, 1968.

Tryon, Warren S., comp. *A Mirror for Americans: Life and Manners in the United States, 1790–1870 as Recorded by American Travelers.* 2 vols. Chicago: University of Chicago Press, 1952.

Tustin, Joseph P., ed. *Diary of the American War: A Hessian Journal.* New Haven, Conn.: Yale University Press, 1979.

Uhlendorf, Bernhard Alexander, ed. and trans. *The Siege of Charleston with an Account of the Province of South Carolina: Diaries and Letters of Hessian Officers from the von Jungkenn Papers in the William L. Clements Library.* Ann Arbor: University of Michigan Press, 1938.

Webber, Mabel L., ed. "Extracts from the Journal of Mrs. Ann Manigault, 1754–1781." *South Carolina Historical and Genealogical Magazine* 20 (April 1919): 128–41.

———. "Josiah Smith's Diary, 1780–1781." *South Carolina Historical and Genealogical Magazine* 33 (January 1932): 1–28.

———. "Josiah Smith's Diary, 1780–1781." *South Carolina Historical and Genealogical Magazine* 34 (October 1933): 194–210.

Whilden, William G. "Reminiscences of Old Charleston." In *Year Book City of Charleston, 1896.* Charleston, S.C.: N.p., 1896.

Wilkinson, Eliza. *Letters of Eliza Wilkinson, During the Invasion and Possession of Charlestown, S.C., by the British in the Revolutionary War.* Ed. Caroline Gilman. New York: Samuel Colman, 1839.

Windley, Lathan A., ed. *Runaway Slave Advertisements: A Documentary History from the 1730s to 1790.* Vol. 3, *South Carolina.* Westport, Conn.: Greenwood Press, 1983.

"Woman and Her Needs," *De Bow's Review* 13 (September 1852): 272–89.

Wright, Louis B., and Marion Tinling, eds. *Being the Travel Diary and Observations of Robert Hunter, Jr., A Young Merchant of London.* San Marino, Calif.: Huntington Library, 1943.

Government Documents

Brevard, Joseph, comp. *An Alphabetical Digest of the Public Statute Law of South Carolina.* 3 vols. Charleston, S.C.: John Hoff, 1814.

Catterall, Helen Tunnicliff, ed. *Judicial Cases Concerning American Slavery and the Negro.* Vol. 2, *Cases from the Courts of North Carolina, South Carolina, and Tennessee.* 1926. Reprint. New York: Octagon Books, Inc., 1968.

Charleston City Funds and Taxpayers, 1850–51. Charleston, S.C.: A. E. Miller, 1851.

Chisolm, J. Bachman, and Simeon Hyde. *An Index-Digest of the Reports of the Supreme Court of South Carolina*. Charleston, S.C.: Walker, Evans and Cogswell, 1882.

A Collection of Ordinances of the City Council of Charleston 1818–1823. Charleston, S.C.: A. E. Miller, 1823.

Cooper, Thomas, and David J. McCord, comps. *The Statutes at Large of South Carolina*. 13 vols. Columbia, S.C.: A. S. Johnston, 1836–1875.

Dawson, J. L., and H. W. DeSaussure. *Census of the City of Charleston, South Carolina, for the Year 1848*. Charleston, S.C.: J. B. Nixon, 1849.

De Bow, J. D. B., ed. *The Industrial Resources, Statistics, etc., of the United States and More Particularly of the Southern and Western States*. 3 vols. 1852. Reprint. New Orleans, La.: Office of De Bow's Review, 1853.

———. *Statistical View of the United States . . . Being a Compendium of the Seventh Census of the United States*. Washington, D.C.: Beverley Tucker, 1854.

Digest of the Ordinances of the City Council of the City of Charleston from the Year 1783 to October 1818. Charleston, S.C.: Archibald E. Miller, 1818.

Eckhard, George B., comp. *A Digest of the Ordinances of the City Council of Charleston, from the Year 1783 to October 1844*. Charleston, S.C.: Walker and Burke, 1844.

Flagg, Charles E. B., comp. *A Digested Index of the Statute Law of South Carolina, 1837–1857*. Charleston, S.C.: Courtenay and Co., 1858.

Ford, Frederick A. *Census of the City of Charleston, South Carolina for the Year 1861*. Charleston, S.C.: Evans and Cogswell, 1861.

Grimke, John F., ed. *Public Laws of the State of South Carolina from Its First Establishment as a British Province Down to the Year 1790*. Philadelphia: N.p., 1790.

Hemphill, William Edwin, et al., eds. *The State Records of South Carolina: Journals of the General Assembly and House of Representatives, 1776–1780*. Columbia: University of South Carolina Press, 1970.

Journal of the House of Representatives of the State of South Carolina. Columbia, S.C.: I. C. Morgan, 1850.

List of the Taxpayers of the City of Charleston for 1859. Charleston, S.C.: Evans and Cogswell, 1860.

List of Taxpayers of the City of Charleston for 1860. Charleston, S.C.: Evans and Cogswell, 1861.

The Militia and Patrol Laws of South Carolina December 1844 Published by Order of the General Assembly. Columbia, S.C.: A. S. Johnston, 1845.

O'Neall, John Belton, comp. *The Negro Law of South Carolina, Collected and Digested by John Belton O'Neall, One of the Judges of the Courts of Law and Errors of the Said State*. Columbia, S.C.: John G. Bowman, 1848.

Ordinances of the City of Charleston from the 19th of August 1844, to the 14th of September 1854. Charleston, S.C.: A. E. Miller, 1854.

Pressley, B.C. *The Law of Magistrates and Constables in the State of South Carolina*. Charleston, S.C.: Walker and Burke, 1848.

Rice, William. *A Digested Index of the Statute Law of South Carolina from the Earliest Period to the Year 1836, Inclusive*. 2 vols. Charleston, S.C.: J. S. Burges, 1838.

Salley, A. S., ed. *Journal of the House of Representatives of South Carolina, January 8, 1782–February 26, 1782*. Columbia: University of South Carolina Press, 1916.

———. *Journal of the Senate of South Carolina, January 8, 1782–February 26, 1782*. Columbia: University of South Carolina Press, 1941.

Thompson, Theodora, and Rosa Lumpkin, eds. *Journals of the House of Representatives, 1783–1784*. Columbia: University of South Carolina Press, 1977.
United States Bureau of the Census. *Aggregate Returns for the United States, Census for 1820*. Washington, D.C.: Gales and Seaton, 1821.
———. *Compendium of the Enumeration of the Inhabitants and Statistics of the United States . . . From the Returns of the Sixth Census*. Washington, D.C.: Thomas Allen, 1841.
———. *Fifth Census; or Enumeration of the Inhabitants and Statistics of the United States, 1830*. Washington, D.C.: Duff Green, 1832.
———. *Heads of Families at the First Census of the United States Taken in the Year 1790: South Carolina*. 1908. Reprint. Baltimore, Md.: Genealogical Publishing Co., 1966.
———. *Historical Statistics of the United States, Colonial Times to 1970*. Washington, D.C.: Government Printing Office, 1976.
———. *Population of the United States in 1860*. Washington, D.C.: Government Printing Office, 1864.
———. "Recapitulation: 1810." In *Fifth Census*. Washington, D.C.: Gales and Seaton, 1821.
———. *Return of the Whole Number of Persons within the Several Districts of the United States*. Washington, D.C.: Duane, 1801.
———. *The Seventh Census of the United States: 1850*. Washington, D.C.: Robert Armstrong, 1853.
———. *Statistical View of the United States*. Washington, D.C.: Government Printing Office, 1850.
———. *Twelfth Census of the United States, 1900, Statistical Atlas*. Washington, D.C.: Government Printing Office, 1903.
United States Department of Labor, Bureau of Labor Statistics. *History of Wages in the United States from Colonial Times to 1928*. 1934. Reprint. Detroit, Mich.: Gale Research Co., 1966.

Case Reports

Bailey's Equity & Law Reports, 1828–1832 (3 vols.)
Bay's Law Reports, 1783–1804 (2 vols.)
Brevard's Law Reports, 1793–1816 (3 vols.)
Cheves's Equity & Law Reports, 1839–1840 (2 vols.)
DeSaussure's Equity Reports, 1784–1816 (4 vols.)
Dudley's Equity & Law Reports, 1837–1838 (2 vols.)
Harper's Equity & Law Reports, 1823–1824 (2 vols.)
Hill's Equity & Law Reports, 1833–1837 (5 vols.)
McCord's Equity & Law Reports, 1821–1828 (6 vols.)
McMullan's Equity & Law Reports, 1840–1842 (3 vols.)
Mill's Law Reports, 1817–1818 (2 vols.)
Nott and McCord's Law Reports, 1817–1820 (2 vols.)
Rice's Equity & Law Reports, 1838–1839 (2 vols.)
Richardson's Equity & Law Reports, 1831–1832, 1844–1846, 1850–1868 (30 vols.)
Riley's Equity & Law Reports, 1836–1837 (1 vol.)
Speers's Equity & Law Reports, 1842–1844 (3 vols.)

Strobhart's Equity & Law Reports, 1846–1850 (9 vols.)
Treadway's Law Reports, 1812–1816 (2 vols.)

Secondary Sources

Allgor, Catherine. *Parlor Politics: In Which the Ladies of Washington Help Build a City and a Government.* Charlottesville: University Press of Virginia, 2000.

Anderson, J. P. "Public Education in Ante-Bellum South Carolina." *South Carolina Historical Association Proceedings* (1933): 3–11.

Anzilotti, Cara. *In the Affairs of the World: Women, Patriarchy, and Power in Colonial South Carolina.* Westport, Conn.: Greenwood Press, 2002.

Bagdon, Robert J. "Musical Life in Charleston, South Carolina, from 1732 to 1776 as Recorded in Colonial Sources." Ph.D. diss., University of Miami, 1978.

Bardaglio, Peter W. *Reconstructing the Household: Families, Sex, and the Law in the Nineteenth-Century South.* Chapel Hill: University of North Carolina Press, 1995.

Barnwell, Joseph W. "The Evacuation of Charleston by the British in 1782." *South Carolina Historical Magazine* 11 (January 1910): 1–26.

Basch, Norma. *Framing American Divorce: From the Revolutionary Generation to the Victorians.* Berkeley: University of California Press, 1999.

———. *In the Eyes of the Law: Women, Marriage, and Property in Nineteenth-Century New York.* Ithaca, N.Y.: Cornell University Press, 1982.

Beckles, Hilary McD. *Natural Rebels: A Social History of Enslaved Black Women in Barbados.* New Brunswick, N.J.: Rutgers University Press, 1989.

———. "Property Rights in Pleasure: The Marketing of Enslaved Women's Sexuality." In *Caribbean Slavery in the Atlantic World,* ed. Verene Shepherd and Hilary McD. Beckles, 692–701. Princeton, N.J.: Markus Wiener Publishers, 2000.

Bellows, Barbara L. *Benevolence among Slaveholders: Assisting the Poor in Charleston, 1670–1860.* Baton Rouge: Louisiana State University Press, 1993.

Berg, Barbara J. *The Remembered Gate: Origins of American Feminism—The Woman and the City, 1800–1860.* New York: Oxford University Press, 1978.

Berlin, Ira. *Generations of Captivity: A History of African-American Slaves.* Cambridge, Mass.: Belknap Press of Harvard University Press, 2003.

———. *Many Thousands Gone: The First Two Centuries of Slavery in North America.* Cambridge, Mass.: Belknap Press of Harvard University Press, 1998.

———. "The Revolution in Black Life." In *The American Revolution: Explorations in the History of American Radicalism,* ed. Alfred F. Young, 349–82. DeKalb: Northern Illinois University Press, 1976.

———. *Slaves without Masters: The Free Negro in the Antebellum South.* New York: Oxford University Press, 1974.

Bowes, Frederick P. *The Culture of Early Charleston.* Chapel Hill: University of North Carolina Press, 1942.

Boydston, Jeanne. *Home and Work: Housework, Wages, and the Ideology of Labor in the Early Republic.* New York: Oxford University Press, 1990.

Boydston, Jeanne, Anne Margolis, and Mary Kelley, eds. *The Limits of Sisterhood: The Beecher Sisters on Women's Rights and Women's Sphere.* Chapel Hill: University of North Carolina Press, 1988.

Brewster, Lawrence F. "Planters from the Low-Country and Their Summer Travels." *Proceedings of the South Carolina Historical Association* (1943): 35–41.

———. *Summer Migrations and Resorts of South Carolina Low-Country Planters.* Durham, N.C.: Duke University Press, 1947.

Bridenbaugh, Carl. *Cities in Revolt: Urban Life in America, 1743–1776.* 1955. Reprint. New York: Capricorn, 1964.

———. *Cities in the Wilderness: The First Century of Urban Life in America, 1625–1742.* 1938. Reprint. New York: Alfred A. Knopf, 1964.

———. *Myths and Realities: Societies of the Colonial South.* 1952. Reprint. New York: Atheneum, 1971.

Brown, Kathleen M. "Antiauthoritarianism and Freedom in Early America." *Journal of American History* 85 (June 1998): 77–85.

———. *Good Wives, Nasty Wenches, and Anxious Patriarchs: Gender, Race, and Power in Colonial Virginia.* Chapel Hill: University of North Carolina Press, 1996.

Buckley, Thomas E. *The Great Catastrophe of My Life: Divorce in the Old Dominion.* Chapel Hill: University of North Carolina Press, 2002.

Burton, E. Milby. *South Carolina Silversmiths, 1690–1860.* Charleston, S.C.: Charleston Museum, 1942.

Bynum, Victoria E. *Unruly Women: The Politics of Social and Sexual Control in the Old South.* Chapel Hill: University of North Carolina Press, 1992.

Carney, Judith. *Black Rice: The African Origins of Rice Cultivation in the Americas.* Cambridge, Mass.: Harvard University Press, 2001.

Cassedy, James H. *Medicine in America: A Short History.* Baltimore, Md.: Johns Hopkins University Press, 1991.

Censer, Jane Turner. "'Smiling through Her Tears': Ante-Bellum Southern Women and Divorce." *American Journal of Legal History* 25 (January 1981): 24–47.

Chapman, Ann. "Inadequacies of the 1848 Charleston Census." *South Carolina Historical Magazine* 68 (1967): 130–53.

Clinton, Catherine, ed. *Half Sisters of History: Southern Women and the American Past.* Durham, N.C.: Duke University Press, 1994.

———. *The Plantation Mistress: Woman's World in the Old South.* New York: Pantheon, 1982.

Coclanis, Peter A. *The Shadow of a Dream: Economic Life and Death in the South Carolina Low Country, 1670–1920.* 1989. Reprint. New York: Oxford University Press, 1991.

Cohen, Henning, ed. *The South Carolina Gazette, 1732–1775.* Columbia: University of South Carolina Press, 1953.

Coker, Katherine Roe. "Absentees as Loyalists in Revolutionary War South Carolina." *South Carolina Historical Magazine* 96 (April 1995): 119–34.

Coker, Kathy Roe. "The Calamities of War: Loyalism and Women in South Carolina." In *Southern Women: Histories and Identities,* ed. Virginia Bernhard et al., 47–70. Columbia: University of Missouri Press, 1992.

Cott, Nancy F. *The Bonds of Womanhood: "Woman's Sphere" in New England, 1780–1835.* 1977. 2nd ed. New Haven, Conn.: Yale University Press, 1997.

———. "Passionlessness: An Interpretation of Victorian Sexual Ideology, 1790–1850." *Signs* 4 (winter 1978): 219–36.

Crane, Virginia Glenn. "Two Women, White and Brown, in the South Carolina Court of Equity, 1842–1845." *South Carolina Historical Magazine* 96 (July 1995): 198–220.

Crawford, Mary Caroline. *Romantic Days in the Early Republic.* London: Gay and Hancock, 1913.

Davidson, Chalmers G. *Friend of the People: the Life of Dr. Peter Fayssoux of Charleston, South Carolina.* Columbia: South Carolina Medical Association, 1950.

D'Emilio, John, and Estelle B. Freedman. *Intimate Matters: A History of Sexuality in America.* New York: Harper and Row, 1988.

Dias, Maria Odila Silva. *Power and Everyday Life: The Lives of Working Women in Nineteenth-Century Brazil.* Trans. Ann Frost. New Brunswick, N.J.: Rutgers University Press, 1995.

Donnan, Elizabeth. "The Slave Trade into South Carolina before the Revolution." *American Historical Review* 33 (July 1928): 804–28.

Durden, Robert F. "The Establishment of Calvary Protestant Episcopal Church for Negroes in Charleston." *South Carolina Historical Magazine* 65 (1964): 63–84.

Elzas, Barnett A. *The Jews of South Carolina: From the Earliest Times to the Present Day.* Philadelphia: J. B. Lippincott, 1905.

Fett, Sharla M. *Working Cures: Healing, Health, and Power on Southern Slave Plantations.* Chapel Hill: University of North Carolina Press, 2002.

Fitchett, E. Horace. "Charleston's Free Afro-American Elite." Ph.D. diss., University of Chicago, 1950.

———. "The Origin and Growth of the Free Negro Population of Charleston, South Carolina." *Journal of Negro History* 26 (1941): 421–37.

———. "Traditions of the Free Negroes in Charleston, South Carolina." *Journal of Negro History* 25 (April 1940): 140–52.

Fox-Genovese, Elizabeth. *Within the Plantation Household: Black and White Women of the Old South.* Chapel Hill: University of North Carolina Press, 1988.

Fraser, Walter J., Jr. *Charleston! Charleston! The History of a Southern City.* Columbia: University of South Carolina Press, 1989.

———. *Patriots, Pistols, and Petticoats: "Poor Sinful Charles Town" during the American Revolution.* 1945. 2d ed. Columbia, S.C.: R. L. Bryan Co., 1993.

Frey, Sylvia R. *Water from the Rock: Black Resistance in a Revolutionary Age.* Princeton, N.J.: Princeton University Press, 1991.

Fry, Gladys-Marie, *Night Riders in Black Folk History.* 1975. Reprint. Athens: University of Georgia Press, 1991.

Fuller, A. James. *Chaplain to the Confederacy: Basil Manly and Baptist Life in the Old South.* Baton Rouge: Louisiana State University Press, 2000.

Gaspar, David Barry, and Darlene Clark Hines, eds. *More than Chattel: Black Women and Slavery in the Americas.* Bloomington: Indiana University Press, 1996.

Gayle, Charles Joseph. "Nature and Volume of Exports from Charleston, 1724–1774." *South Carolina Historical Society Proceedings* (1937): 25–33.

George, Claude. *The Rise of British West Africa.* 1904. Reprint. London: Frank Cass and Co., 1968.

Gillespie, Joanna Bowen. *The Life and Times of Martha Laurens Ramsay, 1751–1811.* Columbia: University of South Carolina Press, 2001.

Ginzberg, Lori D. *Women and the Work of Benevolence: Morality, Politics, and Class in the Nineteenth-Century United States.* New Haven, Conn.: Yale University Press, 1990.

Gomez, Michael A. *Exchanging Our Country Marks: The Transformation of African Identities in the Colonial and Antebellum South.* Chapel Hill: University of North Carolina Press, 1998)

Goodbody, Harriet Linen. *A Goodly Heritage: A History of Episcopal Churchwomen in the Diocese of South Carolina.* Charleston, S.C.: Nelson Printing, 1984.

Goodson, Martia Graham. "Medical-Botanical Contributions of African Slave Women to American Medicine." *Western Journal of Black Studies* 11 (1987): 198–203.

Gordon, Linda. "Killing in Self-Defense." Review of *More than Victims: Battered Women, the Syndrome, Society, and the Law,* by Donald Alexander Downs. In *The Nation,* 24 March 1997, 27.

———. *Woman's Body, Woman's Right: A Social History of Birth Control in America.* 1974. Reprint. New York: Penguin Books, 1977.

Grabill, Wilson H., Clyde V. Kiser, and Pascal K. Whelpton. "Demographic Trends: Marriage, Birth, and Death." In *The American Family in Social-Historical Perspective,* ed. Michael Gordon, 375–91. New York: St. Martin's Press, 1973.

Graham, Sandra Lauderdale. *House and Street: The Domestic World of Servants and Masters in Nineteenth-Century Rio de Janeiro.* Austin: University of Texas Press, 1988.

Gray, Lewis C. *History of Agriculture in the Southern United States to 1860.* 2 vols. 1933. Reprint. Gloucester, Mass.: Peter Smith, 1958.

Greenberg, Kenneth S. *Masters and Statesmen: The Political Culture of Slavery.* Baltimore, Md.: Johns Hopkins University Press, 1985.

Haber, Carole, and Brian Gratton. "Old Age, Public Welfare and Race: The Case of Charleston, South Carolina 1800–1949." *Journal of Social History* 21 (winter 1987): 263–79.

Hagy, James W. "Her 'Scandalous Behavior': A Jewish Divorce in Charleston, South Carolina, 1788." *American Jewish Archives* 41 (fall/winter 1989): 394–403.

———. *This Happy Land: The Jews of Colonial and Antebellum Charleston.* Tuscaloosa: University of Alabama Press, 1993.

Hall, John A. "'Nefarious Wretches, Insidious Villains, and Evil-Minded Persons': Urban Crime Reported in Charleston's *City Gazette,* in 1788." *South Carolina Historical Magazine* (July 1987): 151–68.

Haller, John S., Jr. "The Negro and the Southern Physician: A Study of Medical and Racial Attitudes 1800–1860." *Medical History* (1972): 238–53.

Hamer, Marguerite B. "The Fate of the Exiled Acadians in South Carolina." *Journal of Southern History* 4 (February 1938): 199–208.

Hanger, Kimberly S. *Bounded Lives, Bounded Places: Free Black Society in Colonial New Orleans, 1769–1803.* Durham, N.C.: Duke University Press, 1997.

Harris, Robert L., Jr. "Charleston's Free Afro-American Elite: The Brown Fellowship Society and Humane Brotherhood." *South Carolina Historical Magazine* 82 (October 1981): 289–310.

Hash, C. Patton. "A Lowcountry Christmas." *Carologue* (winter 1993): 8–25.

Henry, H. M. *Police Control of the Slave in South Carolina.* 1914. Reprint. New York: Negro Universities Press, 1968.

Higgins, W. Robert. "Charleston: Terminus and Entrepot of the Colonial Slave Trade." In *The African Diaspora: Interpretive Essays,* ed. Martin L. Kilson and Robert I. Rotberg. Cambridge, Mass.: Harvard University Press, 1976.

Hilliard, Sam Bowers. *Atlas of Antebellum Southern Agriculture.* Baton Rouge: Louisiana State University Press, 1984.

Hindus, Michael Stephen. "Black Justice under White Law: Criminal Prosecutions of Blacks in Antebellum South Carolina." *Journal of American History* 63 (December 1976): 575–99.

———. *Prison and Plantation: Crime, Justice, and Authority in Massachusetts and South Carolina, 1767–1878.* Chapel Hill: University of North Carolina Press, 1980.

Hirsch, Arthur Henry. *The Huguenots of Colonial South Carolina.* 1928. Reprint. Hamden, Conn.: Archon Books, 1962.

Hodes, Martha. *White Women, Black Men: Illicit Sex in the Nineteenth-Century South.* New Haven, Conn.: Yale University Press, 1997.

Hoffman, Ronald. "The 'Disaffected' in the Revolutionary South." In *The American Revolution: Explorations in the History of American Radicalism,* ed. Alfred F. Young, 273–316. Dekalb: Northern Illinois University Press, 1976.

Hoff-Wilson, Joan. "The Illusion of Change: Women and the American Revolution." In *The American Revolution: Explorations in the History of American Radicalism,* ed. Alfred F. Young, 383–445. Dekalb: Northern Illinois University Press, 1976.

Jackson, Melvin H. *Privateers in Charleston, 1793–1796: An Account of a French Palatinate in South Carolina.* Washington, D.C.: Smithsonian Institution Press, 1969.

Johnson, Michael P. "Wealth and Class in Charleston in 1860." In *From The Old South to the New: Essays on the Transitional South,* ed. Walter J. Fraser, Jr., and Winfred R. Moore, Jr. Westport, Conn.: Greenwood Press, 1981.

Johnson, Michael P., and James L. Roark. *Black Masters: A Free Family of Color in the Old South.* New York: W. W. Norton and Co., 1984.

Johnson, Whittington B. *Black Savannah, 1788–1864.* Fayetteville: University of Arkansas Press, 1996.

Johnston, James Hugo. *Race Relations in Virginia and Miscegenation in the South, 1776–1860.* Amherst: University of Massachusetts Press, 1970.

Jones, Anne Goodwyn. "Southern Literary Women as Chroniclers of Southern Life." In *Sex, Race, and the Role of Women in the South,* ed. Joanne V. Hawks and Sheila L. Skemp. Jackson: University Press of Mississippi, 1983.

Jordan, Winthrop D. *The White Man's Burden: Historical Origins of Racism in the United States.* New York: Oxford University Press, 1974.

———. *White over Black: American Attitudes toward the Negro, 1550–1812.* Chapel Hill: University of North Carolina Press, 1968.

Kennedy, Cynthia M. " 'Nocturnal Adventures in Mulatto Alley': Sex in Charleston, South Carolina." In *Searching for Their Places: Women in the South Across Four Centuries,* ed. Thomas H. Appleton, Jr. and Angela Boswell, 37–56. Columbia: University of Missouri Press, 2003.

Kennedy-Haflett, Cynthia. " 'Moral Marriage': A Mixed-Race Relationship in Nineteenth-Century Charleston, South Carolina." *South Carolina Historical Magazine* 97 (July 1996): 206–26.

Kerber, Linda K. *Women of the Republic: Intellect and Ideology in Revolutionary America.* 1980. Reprint. New York: W. W. Norton and Co., 1986.

———. " 'History Can Do It No Justice': Women and the Reinterpretation of the American Revolution." In *Women in the Age of the American Revolution,* ed. Ronald Hoffman and Peter J. Albert, 3–42. Charlottesville: University Press of Virginia, 1989.

———. "The Paradox of Women's Citizenship in the Early Republic." *American Historical Review* 97 (April 1992): 349–78.

Kierner, Cynthia. *Beyond the Household: Women's Place in the Early South, 1700–1835.* Ithaca, N.Y.: Cornell University Press, 1998.

King, Susan L., comp., *History and Records of the Charleston Orphan House, 1790–1860.* Easley, S.C.: Southern Historical Press, 1984.

Koger, Larry. *Black Slaveowners: Free Black Slave Masters in South Carolina, 1790–1860.* Jefferson, N.C.: McFarland & Co., 1985.

Kovacik, Charles F., and John J. Winberry. *South Carolina, A Geography.* Boulder, Col.: Westview Press, 1987.

Kulikoff, Allan. "Uprooted Peoples: Black Migrants in the Age of the American Revolution, 1790–1820." In *Slavery and Freedom in the Age of the American Revolution,* ed. Ira Berlin and Ronald Hoffman, 143–71. 1983. Reprint. Urbana: University of Illinois Press, 1986.

Lambert, Robert Stansbury. *South Carolina Loyalists in the American Revolution.* Columbia: University of South Carolina Press, 1987.

Laslett, Peter, Karla Oosterveen, and Richard M. Smith, eds. *Bastardy and Its Comparative History.* Cambridge, Mass.: Harvard University Press, 1980.

Leavitt, Judith Walzer. *Brought to Bed: Childbearing in America, 1750–1950.* New York: Oxford University Press, 1986.

Lebsock, Suzanne. *The Free Women of Petersburg: Status and Culture in a Southern Town, 1784–1860.* New York: W. W. Norton, 1985.

Leland, John G. "Early Taverns in Charleston." *Preservation Progress* 16 (May 1971): n.p.

Lerner, Gerda. *The Grimké Sisters from South Carolina: Pioneers for Woman's Rights and Abolition.* 1967. Reprint. New York: Schocken Books, 1971.

Levett, Ella Pettit. "Loyalism in Charleston, 1761–1784." *Proceedings of the South Carolina Historical Association* (April 1936): 3–17.

Lofton, John. *Insurrection in South Carolina: The Turbulent World of Denmark Vesey.* 1964. Reprint. *Denmark Vesey's Revolt: The Slave Plot That Lit the Fuse to Fort Sumter.* Kent, Ohio: Kent State University Press, 1983.

McCandless, Peter. *Moonlight, Magnolias, and Madness: Insanity in South Carolina from the Colonial Period to the Progressive Era.* Chapel Hill: University of North Carolina Press, 1996.

McCurry, Stephanie. *Masters of Small Worlds: Yeoman Households, Gender Relations, and the Political Culture of the Antebellum South Carolina Low Country.* 1995. Reprint. New York: Oxford University Press, 1997.

McMillen, Sally G. *Motherhood in the Old South: Pregnancy, Childbirth, and Infant Rearing.* Baton Rouge: Louisiana State University Press, 1990.

Menard, Russell R. "Slave Demography in the Lowcountry, 1670–1740: From Frontier Society to Plantation Regime." *South Carolina Historical Magazine* 96 (October 1995): 280–303.

———. "Slavery, Economic Growth, and Revolutionary Ideology in the South Carolina Lowcountry." In *The Economy of Early America: The Revolutionary Period, 1763–1790,* ed. Ronald Hoffman and John J. McCusker, 244–77. Charlottesville: University of Virginia Press, 1988.

Minchinton, Walter. "A Comment on 'The Slave Trade to Colonial South Carolina: A Profile.'" *South Carolina Historical Magazine* 95 (January 1994): 47–57.

Mohl, Raymond A. "The Grand Fabric of Republicanism: A Scotsman Describes South Carolina, 1810–1811." *South Carolina Historical Magazine* 71 (July 1970): 170–88.

Molloy, Robert. *Charleston: A Gracious Heritage.* New York: D. Appleton-Century, 1947.

Morgan, Philip D. "Black Life in Eighteenth-Century Charleston." *Perspectives in American History,* new ser. 1, vol. 1 (1984): 187–232.

———. "Black Society in the Lowcountry, 1760–1810." In *Slavery and Freedom in the Age of the American Revolution,* ed. Ira Berlin and Ronald Hoffman, 83–141. 1983. Reprint. Urbana: University of Illinois Press, 1986.

Murphy, Lucy Eldersveld. "Business Ladies: Midwestern Women and Enterprise, 1850–1880." *Journal of Women's History* 3 (spring 1991): 65–89.

Murray, Gail S. "Charity within the Bounds of Race and Class: Female Benevolence in the Old South." *South Carolina Historical Magazine* 96 (January 1995): 54–70.

Nadelhaft, Jerome J. *The Disorders of War: The Revolution in South Carolina.* Orono: University of Maine at Orono Press, 1981.

Nash, A. E. Keir. "Negro Rights, Unionism, and Greatness on the South Carolina Court of Appeals: The Extraordinary Chief Justice John Belton O'Neall." *South Carolina Law Review* 21 (1969): 141–90.

Nash, Gary. *The Urban Crucible: Social Change, Political Consciousness, and the Origins of the American Revolution.* 1979. Abridged ed. Cambridge, Mass.: Harvard University Press, 1986.

Nash, R. C. "Urbanization in the Colonial South: Charleston, South Carolina, as a Case Study." *Journal of Urban History* 19 (1992): 3–29.

Norton, Mary Beth. *Liberty's Daughters: The Revolutionary Experience of American Women, 1750–1800.* Glenview, Ill.: Scott Foresman and Co., 1980.

———. "'What an Alarming Crisis Is This': Southern Women and the American Revolution." In *The Southern Experience in the American Revolution,* ed. Jeffrey J. Crow and Larry Tice, 203–34. Chapel Hill: University of North Carolina Press, 1978.

Olwell, Robert. "Becoming Free: Manumission and the Genesis of a Free Black Community in South Carolina, 1740–90." In *Against the Odds: Free Blacks in the Slave Societies of the Americas,* ed. Jane G. Landers, 1–19. London: Frank Cass and Co., 1996.

———. *Masters, Slaves, and Subjects: The Culture of Power in the South Carolina Low Country, 1740–1790.* Ithaca, N.Y.: Cornell University Press, 1998.

Painter, Nell Irvin. "Of *Lily,* Linda Brent, and Freud: A Non-Exceptionalist Approach to Race, Class, and Gender in the Slave South." In *Half Sisters of History: Southern Women and the American Past,* ed. Catherine Clinton, 94–106. Durham, N.C.: Duke University Press, 1994.

Parramore, Mary R. "Feme Sole Traders in South Carolina." M.A. Thesis, University of South Carolina, 1991.

Pease, Jane H., and William H. Pease. *A Family of Women: The Carolina Petigrus in Peace and War.* Chapel Hill: University of North Carolina Press, 1999.

———. *Ladies, Women, and Wenches: Choice and Constraint in Antebellum Charleston and Boston.* Chapel Hill: University of North Carolina Press, 1990.

———. *The Web of Progress: Private Values and Public Styles in Boston and Charleston, 1828–1843.* New York: Oxford University Press, 1985.

Peiss, Kathy. *Cheap Amusements: Working Women and Leisure in Turn-of-the Century New York.* Philadelphia: Temple University Press, 1986.

Petty, Julian J. *The Growth and Distribution of Population in South Carolina.* 1943. Reprint. Spartanburg, S.C.: Reprint Co., 1975.

Powers, Bernard E. *Black Charlestonians: A Social History, 1822–1885.* Fayetteville: University of Arkansas Press, 1994.

Quarles, Benjamin. *The Negro in the American Revolution.* New York: W. W. Norton and Co., 1961.

Rae, Pamela. *Turtle at Mr. Humble's: The Fortunes of a Mercantile Family, England and America, 1758–1837.* Otley, W. Yorkshire: Smith Settle, 1992.

Ravenel, Beatrice St. Julien, ed. *Charleston Murders.* New York: Duell, Sloan and Pearce, 1947.

Reed, James. *From Private Vice to Public Virtue: Birth Control in America.* New York: Basic Books, 1978.

Robertson, Claire C., and Martin A. Klein, eds. *Women and Slavery in Africa.* Madison: University of Wisconsin Press, 1983.

Rogers, George C., Jr. *Charleston in the Age of the Pinckneys*. 1969. Reprint. Columbia: University of South Carolina Press, 1995.

——. *Evolution of a Federalist: William Loughton Smith of Charleston, 1758–1812*. Columbia: University of South Carolina Press, 1962.

——. *The History of Georgetown County, South Carolina*. Columbia: University of South Carolina Press, 1970.

Rosengarten, Dale, et al. *Between the Tracks: Charleston's East Side during the Nineteenth Century*. Charleston, S.C.: Charleston Museum, 1987.

Royster, Charles. *A Revolutionary People at War: The Continental Army and American Character, 1775–1783*. Chapel Hill: University of North Carolina Press, 1979.

Russell, Thomas David. "Sale Day in Antebellum South Carolina: Slavery, Law, Economy, and Court-Supervised Sales." Ph.D. diss., Stanford University, 1993.

Ryan, Mary P. *Cradle of the Middle Class: The Family in Oneida County, New York, 1790–1865*. 1981. Reprint. New York: Cambridge University Press, 1987.

Salmon, Marylynn. *Women and the Law of Property in Early America*. Chapel Hill: University of North Carolina Press, 1986.

Savitt, Todd L. "The Use of Blacks for Medical Experimentation and Demonstration in the Old South." *Journal of Southern History* 48 (August 1982): 331–48.

Savitt, Todd L., and James Harvey Young, eds. *Disease and Distinctiveness in the American South*. Knoxville: University of Tennessee Press, 1988.

Schwalm, Leslie A. *"A Hard Fight for We": Women's Transition from Slavery to Freedom in South Carolina*. Urbana: University of Illinois Press, 1997.

Schwartz, Marie Jenkins. *Born in Bondage: Growing up Enslaved in the Antebellum South*. Cambridge, Mass.: Harvard University Press, 2000.

Schweninger, Loren. *Black Property Owners in the South, 1790–1915*. Urbana: University of Illinois Press, 1990.

——. "Property Owning Free African-American Women in the South, 1800–1870." *Journal of Women's History* 1 (winter 1990): 13–44.

——. "Prosperous Blacks in the South, 1790–1880." *American Historical Review* 95 (February 1990): 31–56.

——. "Slave Independence and Enterprise in South Carolina, 1780–1865." *South Carolina Historical Magazine* 93 (April 1992): 101 25.

Scott, Anne Firor. *The Southern Lady: From Pedestal to Politics, 1830–1930*. 1970. Reprint. Charlottesville: University of Virginia Press, 1995.

Sellers, Leila. *Charleston Business on the Eve of the American Revolution*. Chapel Hill: University of North Carolina Press, 1934.

Senese, Donald J. "Building the Pyramid: The Growth and Development of the State Court System in Antebellum South Carolina, 1800–1860." *South Carolina Law Review* 24 (1972): 352–79.

——. "The Free Negro and the South Carolina Courts, 1790–1860." *South Carolina Historical Magazine* 68 (1967): 140–53.

Shalhope, Robert E. "Thomas Jefferson's Republicanism and Antebellum Southern Thought." *Journal of Southern History* 42 (November 1976): 529–56.

Shepherd, Verene, Bridget Brereton, and Barbara Bailey, eds. *Engendering History: Caribbean Women in Historical Perspective*. New York: St. Martin's Press, 1995.

Silver, Christopher. "A New Look at Old South Urbanization: The Irish Worker in Charleston, South Carolina, 1840–1860." *South Atlantic Urban Studies* 3 (1979): 141–72.

Silver, Timothy. *A New Face on the Countryside: Indians, Colonists, and Slaves in South Atlantic Forests, 1500–1800*. New York: Cambridge University Press, 1990.

Singleton, Theresa A. *"I, Too, Am America": Archaeological Studies of African-American Life.* Charlottesville: University Press of Virginia, 1999.

———. "The Slave Tag: An Artifact of Urban Slavery." *South Carolina Antiquities* 16 (1984): 45–53.

Sklar, Kathryn Kish. *Catharine Beecher: A Study in American Domesticity.* New York: W. W. Norton and Co., 1976.

Smith, Daniel Scott. "Family Limitation, Sexual Control and Domestic Feminism in Victorian America." *Feminist Studies* 1 (winter–spring 1973): 40–57.

Smith-Rosenberg, Carroll. *Disorderly Conduct: Visions of Gender in Victorian America.* 1985. Reprint. New York: Oxford University Press, 1985.

The South in the Building of the Nation. Vol. 2, *Political History of the Southern States.* Richmond, Va.: Southern Historical Publication Society, 1909.

Souvenir Program of the One-Hundredth Anniversary of the Founding of the A.M.E. Church in the South held at Emmanuel A.M.E. Church. Charleston, S.C.: N.p., 1963.

Stansell, Christine. *City of Women: Sex and Class in New York, 1789–1860.* 1982. Reprint. Urbana: University of Illinois Press, 1987.

Stoesen, Alexander R. "The British Occupation of Charleston, 1780–1782." *South Carolina Historical Magazine* 63 (April 1962): 71–82.

Stowe, Steven M. *Intimacy and Power in the Old South: Ritual in the Lives of the Planters.* Baltimore, Md.: Johns Hopkins University Press, 1987.

Tadman, Michael. *Speculators and Slaves: Masters, Traders, and Slaves in the Old South.* Madison: University of Wisconsin Press, 1989.

Taylor, Rosser H. "The Gentry of Antebellum South Carolina," *North Carolina Historical Review* 17 (April 1940): 116–17.

Terry, George D. "A Study of the Impact of the French Revolution and the Insurrections in Saint Dominque upon South Carolina, 1790–1805." M.A. thesis, University of South Carolina, 1975.

Ulrich, Laurel Thatcher. *Good Wives: Image and Reality in the Lives of Women in Northern New England, 1650–1750.* 1982. Reprint. New York: Oxford University Press, 1983.

"Virginia in 1785." *Virginia Magazine of History and Biography* 23 (1915): 411.

Wade, Richard C. *Slavery in the Cities: The South, 1820–1860.* New York: Oxford University Press, 1964.

Wallace, David Duncan. *South Carolina: A Short History: 1520–1948.* Chapel Hill: University of North Carolina Press, 1951.

Walsh, Richard. *Charleston's Sons of Liberty: A Study of the Artisans, 1763–1789.* Columbia: University of South Carolina Press, 1959.

Waring, Joseph I. "Charleston Medicine, 1800–1860." *Journal of the History of Medicine* 31 (July 1976): 320–42.

———. *A History of Medicine in South Carolina, 1670–1900.* 2 vols. Columbia, S.C.: R. L. Bryan Co., 1964, 1967.

Weiner, Marli F. *Mistresses and Slaves: Plantation Women in South Carolina, 1830–80.* Urbana: University of Illinois Press, 1998.

Weir, Robert M. *Colonial South Carolina: A History.* New York: KTO Press, 1983.

Wells, Robert V. "Household Size and Composition in the British Colonies in America, 1675–1775." *Journal of Interdisciplinary History* 4 (spring 1974): 546–47.

———. *Revolutions in Americans' Lives: A Demographic Perspective of the History of Americans, Their Families, and Their Society.* Westport, Conn.: Greenwood Press, 1982.

Welter, Barbara. "The Cult of True Womanhood 1820–1860." *American Quarterly* 18 (1966): 151–74.

White, Deborah Gray. *Ar'n't I a Woman? Female Slaves in the Plantation South.* New York: W. W. Norton, 1985.

Whitman, Stephen T. *The Price of Freedom: Slavery and Manumission in Baltimore and Early National Maryland.* Lexington: University of Kentucky Press, 1997.

Whitten, David O. "The Medical Care of Slaves on South Carolina Rice Plantations." M.A. thesis, University of South Carolina, 1963.

Wikramanayake, Marina. *A World in Shadow: The Free Black in Antebellum South Carolina.* Columbia: University of South Carolina Press, 1973.

Williams, Frances Leigh. *A Founding Family: The Pinckneys of South Carolina.* New York: Harcourt, Brace, Jovanovich, 1978.

Wood, Peter H. *Black Majority: Negroes in Colonial South Carolina from 1670 through the Stono Rebellion.* 1974. Reprint. New York: W. W. Norton and Co., 1975.

Woodson, Carter G. *Free Negro Heads of Families in the United States in 1830.* Washington, D.C.: Association for the Study of Negro Life and History, 1925.

——. *Free Negro Owners of Slaves in the United States in 1830.* Washington, D.C.: Association for the Study of Negro Life and History, 1925.

Wright, Louis B. *South Carolina: A Bicentennial History.* New York: W. W. Norton and Co., 1976.

Wyatt-Brown, Bertram. *Southern Honor: Ethics and Behavior in the Old South.* New York: Oxford University Press, 1982.

Zierden, Martha. "A Trans-Atlantic Merchant's House in Charleston: Archaeological Exploration of Refinement and Subsistence in an Urban Setting." *Historical Archaeology* 33, no. 3 (1999): 32–47.

——. "The Urban Landscape, the Work Yard, and Archaeological Site Formation Processes in Charleston, South Carolina." In *Historical Archaeology and the Study of American Culture,* ed. Lu Ann De Cunzo and Bernard L. Herman, 285–317. Knoxville: University of Tennessee Press, 1996.

Index

Page numbers in italics refer to tables.

Mishaw, Elizabeth, 135; Noisette, Margaret, 27; Raper, Susanna Cole, 150; Sasportas, Catharine Maria, 118, 155; Waring, Dye, 155; Weston, Maria, 93. *See also* Free people of color

Brown Fellowship Society: formation of, 67; mentioned, 92, 93

Capitation tax. *See* Free Negro Capitation Tax

Charity: and class relations, 48, 73, 132–34; and enforcement of patriarchy, 72–73; home visits, 133, 209–10; as public policy, 154, 184, 205–206, 208–209, 277nn37,39; and race relations, 133–34; women's work, 48, 49–50, 67–68, 131, 132–35, 210, 218. *See also* Brown Fellowship Society; Female Charitable Association; German Friendly Society; Ladies Benevolent Society; Ladies Fuel Society; Orphan House; Poor House; Women, master-class

Charleston, S.C.: characteristics of work in, 127–31 (*see also* Work); difficulty of travel in, 13, 181–82; diseases and deaths in, 190–95 (*see also* Illness and death); economic development, 19–20, 22, 23 (*see also* Rice; Work); epidemics in, *see* Epidemics; expansion of city boundaries, 20, 29; founding of, 18–19, 175; geography, topography, and climate of, 11–12, 19, 191; high social season in, 28, 130, 157, 158, 160–63, 166, 169–70, 183; urban estates in, 12, 116, 130–31; visitors comments about, 12–14, 16, 57, 158, 159, 162, 181 (*see also individual travelers' names*)

Charleston Orphan House. *See* Orphan House

Childbirth, 190, 195, 196, 197–99, 201, 207–208, 217. *See also* Children

Children: in Charleston, 15, 16, 107, 131, 158, 160, 164–66; infant mortality, 195, 196, 197, 207; laboring free, 104, 141–42, slaves, 96, 135–37, 138, 178. *See also* Leisure; Orphan House; Population, Charleston; Women, *by social group;* Work

Civic hosts, 53–54, 160, 213. *See also* Master class, importance of leisure and pageantry to

Class: defined, 7

Clinton, General Sir Henry, 39, 45

Clothing: and class and race distinctions, 21–22, 24. *See also* Women

Concubinage. *See* Sexual behavior; Sexual regulation

Confiscation Acts, 31, 42, 44, 46, 49, 55–56, 69, 238n39

Courts: as construction sites of class, gender, and race, 8 (*see also* Laws); S.C. Court System, 8, 223–24

Crime: assault, 174, 176–77, 180, 181–82, 185–87, 268n2, 271n26 (*see also* Domestic abuse); bastardy, 115, 183, 184; in Charleston, 1, 68, 72; "crimes against the person," 140, 260n28; murder, 1, 87, 97, 176, 181, 182, 183, 270n21; rape, 38, 116, 117, 123, 181 (*see also* Sexual exploitation); theft, 174, 175–76. *See also* Laws;

Culture of illness of death, 195–97

Death. *See* American Revolution; Children; Epidemics; Illness and death

Disease. *See* American Revolution; Epidemics; Illness and death

Divorce: regulation under Jewish law, 105, 108–109; regulation under S.C. law, 80, 81, 86

Domestic abuse, 86–91, 97, 101, 107–108, 109, 187, 214. *See also* Marriage

Dower, 55, 105, 106

Dyssli, Samuel, 18

Edisto Island, 33, 101

Emancipation. *See* Manumission

Epidemics, 190, 192, *193–94,* 208. *See also* American Revolution; Illness and death

Female Charitable Association, 132, 133–34. *See also* Charity; Ladies Benevolent Society; Ladies Fuel Society

Feme covert: defined, 56, 79, 153, 187

Feme sole: defined, 56, 153, 240n8. *See also* Sole traders

Feme sole traders. *See* Sole traders

Fisher, Lavinia and John, 1. *See also* Law

Free blacks. *See* Brown elite; Free people of color; Women

Free brown elite. *See* Brown elite

Free Negro Capitation Tax, 67, 93, 114, 248n38

Free people of color: and the first reconstruction, 64–68; church activities of, 171, 267n39; during the American Revolution, 35, 39–40; formation of urban population, 18, 64–68, 243n30; forms and functions of leisure, 171–72; guardians of, 180; kidnapping of, 179–80; mentioned, 33, 40; politicization and self-perceptions of, 66–67; public comment on, 14, 18, 117, 118, 124, 126, 180; relations with slaves, 24, 62, 78, 97, 99–100, 104, 138, 171; relations with white people, 64–65, 133, 134, 171–72; resistance, petitions, and protests of, 66–67, 99, 100; restrictions on, 53, 61, 65, 67, 125, 147, 168, 170, 171, 172, 179, 180, 256n28 (see also Laws); as slave owners, 62, 65, 93, 114, 261n35; in the urban economy, 14, 65, 67, 104, 172; use of the term, 8. See also Brown elite; Laws; Manumission; Market women; Marriage; Population, Charleston; Sexual relationships, interracial; Women, free brown or black; Work

Free people of color, surnames known: Bampfield, Barbara Maria Cole, 63, 150; Barquet, Barbara Tunno and John Pierre, 93, 118; Bass, Robert, 99; Bedon, George, 104; Bettingall, Margaret, 93, 118–19; Bonneau, Jennet (or Jeanette) and Thomas, 93, 135; Borduck, Emma, 147; Chapman, Maria, 118; Cline, Elizabeth and John, 100; Cole, Ruth, 150; Cole, Thomas, 66; Deas, Ann, 27, 146–47; Dereef, Joanna, 92; Dereef, Richard E., 93; Dunstan, Camilla, 149, 150; Eggart, Michael J., 92; Fraser, Mary, 39; Fuller, Nat, 92; Gallman, Cato, 100; Holloway, Elizabeth, 150; Ives, Sophia, 147; Johnson, Eliza Ann and James, 91, 248n34; Jones, Jehu, 147; Kougley, Mary and Jacob, 91; Marshall, Patience McKenzie, 180–81; McNeile, 210; Michael, Maria, 147; Miller, Gabriella, 135; Mishaw, Elizabeth, 135; Mitchell, Harriott and John, 175; Morton, Martha Patience, 181; Nell, Maria, 147; Noisette, Margaret, 27; Norman, Hannah, 62; Peace, Isabel, 143; Pinckney, Izabella, 39; Raper, Susanna Cole, 150; Richardson, Hagar, Sarah, Eliza and Peter, 114; Roussell, Hagar, 39; Sasportas, Catharine Maria, 118, 155; Seymour, Charlotte, 65; Seymour, Elizabeth (or Eliza), 65; Seymour, Sally, 65–66; Seymour, William, 65–66; Vanderhorst, Martha, 150; Waring, Dye, 155; Warren, Mary, 66; Weston, Maria, 93

Free people of color, surnames unknown: Amy, 27; Elsey, 118; Fatima, Flora, Sarah, and Clarinda, 66; Hagar, 66; Judah, Malinda, Tabitha, and Lizzy, 180; Mildred, Genelazier, and Catharine, 67; Phebe, 179–80; Susan, 180

Friendly Moralist Society, 93

Gender: defined, 7, 112; and the law, 1, 3, 100–102, 107, 115, 174–78, 217; and race, 1, 2, 83, 93, 96, 97, 103, 115, 117, 135, 137, 174, 210, 217; representations of, 1, 7, 51, 77, 81, 83, 96, 103–104, 105, 107, 117, 132, 196–97,

217; as a tool in constructing and perpetuating power, 1, 30, 81, 82, 83, 97, 102, 107, 108–109, 112, 115, 117, 132–35, 174, 177, 179, 188–89, 217, 218–19 (see also Laws); and work, 129–30, 135–36. See also Womanhood

German Friendly Society, 72

Good wives: representations of (and their antitheses) in S.C. case law, 81, 105, 107–109, 251n29; representations of in correspondence and literature, 82, 84, 96; role of in the household, 81, 82, 83, 156, 213 (see also Marriage; Women, master-class)

Goose Creek Parish (alleged) conspiracy, 21

Grace Episcopal Church, 135

Greene, General Nathanael, 53

Guardian of Sally v. Beaty, 151–52, 262n52

Hazard, Ebenezer, 18

Head tax. See Free Negro Capitation Tax

Health and health care. See Illness and death

Hiring. See Slave hiring

Hodgson, Adam, 13

Hucksters. See Market women

Identity: effects of the American Revolution on, 49, 51, 212–13; formation of in social juxtaposition, 2, 4, 7, 8, 29, 30, 40, 50, 51, 67, 68, 73, 77–78, 95, 105, 110, 111–12, 115, 131, 133, 135, 136, 137, 140, 142, 149, 153, 156, 157, 158, 166, 170, 172–73, 174, 191, 199, 201, 203, 205, 209, 210, 212–19. See also American Revolution, women's politicization; Marriage; Women, by social group

Illness and death: in Charleston, 12, 85, 190–95, 272n5; culture of illness and death, 195–97; among free women of color, 205–206, 210, 217–18; among master-class women, 195–97, 217; medical experimentation on people of color, 204–205, 218; medical professionals' perceptions of people of color, 190–91, 194, 198–99, 201, 204, 218; medical professionals' perceptions of women, 190, 217, 272n1; among slave women, 197–205, 206, 217–18; among white laboring women, 205–11, 217–18. See also American Revolution; Epidemics; Poor House; Women; Women, by social groups

Immigrants, 2, 15, 18, 19, 26, 56, 60, 72, 108–109, 113, 114, 133, 135, 139, 143, 186, 208–209, 231n19. See also Women, Irish; Women, Jewish; Women, white laboring

Interracial sex. See Sexual relationships, interracial

Sole traders, 3, 131, 153–56, 186, 215, 229n3
Stono Rebellion (1739), 20–21
St. Cecilia Society, 158
St. Luke's Protestant Episcopal Church, 92
St. Michael's Church, 135
St. Philip's Episcopal Church, 67, 91, 93, 135
Sullivan's Island, 12, 31, 33, 41, 101, 169, 170

Tarleton, Colonel Banastre, 44
Taverns and tippling houses: women as
    owners/operators, 26, 42, 45, 121, 143,
    144–45, *145*, 148, 186
Tories. *See* American Revolution, loyalists
    during
Trinity Methodist Episcopal Church, 101,
    250n17
True Womanhood. *See* Gender; Womanhood

Vesey, Denmark insurrection, 160, 171, 186

Washington, President George, 54, 160
Whigs. *See* American Revolution, patriots
White laboring people. *See* Laboring white
    people
Womanhood: class-specific ideals of, 102, 103–
    104, 107–109, 174, 182, 184, 186, 187, 189,
    197; contingent definitions of, 2, 7, 51, 77,
    83, 137, 174, 187, 189, 197; race-specific
    ideals of, 1, 51, 83, 93, 94, 96, 97, 103, 130,
    133, 137, 176, 177, 179, 189, 210. *See also*
    Gender; Laws
Women: in Charleston on the eve of the
    American Revolution, 22–29; and construc-
    tion and perpetuation of social boundaries,
    2, 4, 21, 29, 56–57, 59, 72, 83, 91, 210, 213–
    14, 216, 218–19 (*see also* Women, *by social
    group*); experiences with illness, 190–211; as
    healers, 192 (*see also* Women, slaves); medi-
    cal views of, 190, 272n1; as a percentage
    of Charleston population, *see* Population,
    Charleston; prominence in urban slave so-
    ciety, 2–7, 13, 14, 23–26, 37–38, 57, 127–56,
    128–29, 215, 233n27, 257n2 (*see also* Work);
    and uneven justice by S.C. courts, 174–89,
    214. *See also* Gender; Sexual relationships,
    interracial; Womanhood; Women, *by social
    group;* Work
Women, brown elite: benevolent work of, 135;
    experiences with illness and death, 204,
    217, 218; formation and growth of, 26–27,
    64–66 (*see also* Manumission; Sexual rela-
    tionships, interracial); forms and functions
    of leisure and social activities, 41, 170–71,

216; marriage, 65–66, 91–93, 170; mother-
    hood and childrearing, 150, 216; as prop-
    erty owners and *rentiers,* 27, 65–66, 114,
    150–51; skilled work of, 65–66, 142–43.
    See also Brown elite; Free people of color;
    Identity; *Rentiers*
Women, free brown or black: appearance and
    clothing of, 14, 39–40; church activities of,
    171, 267n39; competition with white labor-
    ing women, 25, 69, *128–29*, 142–44, 146–
    47; experiences with illness and death, 190,
    194, 197, 199, 205–206, 209–10, 217–18;
    and the first reconstruction, 64–68; forms
    and functions of leisure, 171–72, 216; har-
    boring runaway slaves, 24; as housekeepers,
    113, 118; as property owners, 114; mar-
    riage, 102–104, 106, 110, 213; politicization
    of, 67; relations with slaves, 172 (*see also*
    Marriage); relations with white people, 103,
    133, 134, 139, 171, 172; restrictions on, *see*
    Free people of color; sexual protocols of,
    117–19; as skilled artisans, 142–43, 261n35;
    skilled and unskilled work of, 15, 65, 102,
    104, 113, 127–29, *128–29*, 138, 139, 141,
    142–43, 144, *145*, 146–48, 150, 154, 155,
    257n2; as slave owners and hirers, 62, 65,
    93, 114, 143, 144, 148–49, 150, 261n35 (*see
    also Rentiers*); treatment under S.C. law,
    174–80. *See also* Brown elite; Free people of
    color; Identity; Market women; Sexual rela-
    tionships, interracial; Women, brown elite
Women, Irish, 15–16, 26, 135, 208, 209. *See
    also* Immigrants; Women, white laboring
Women, Jewish, 103–104, 105, 108–109, 135,
    186. *See also* Immigrants; Women, white
    laboring
Women, master-class: during the American
    Revolution, 32, 36, 39, 40, 47–52; appear-
    ance, clothing, and public comment on, 21–
    22, 54, 57, 160, 162, 163; aristocratic model
    of marriage, 77–86, 95, 96–97, 100, 101,
    102, 213–14 (*see also* Good wives; Mar-
    riage); benevolent work of, 49, 131–34, 209–
    10, 218; central role of in construction and
    perpetuation of social boundaries, 21, 56–
    57, 59, 73, 131–32, 133, 134, 158, 160, 162–
    63, 210, 214, 216; domestic abuse, *see* Do-
    mestic abuse; enforcement of patriarchy,
    55, 214; on the eve of the American Revolu-
    tion, 27–28; experiences with illness and
    death, 195–97; and the first reconstruction,
    53–59, 159–60; importance of in leisure and
    pageantry, 4, 28, 53–54, 157, 158–66, 216

(*see also* Civic hosts); motherhood, child-rearing, and domestic work, 82, 131–32, 137, 145–46, 159, 161, 164–65, 216 (*see also* Good wives); resistance, 51, 84–85, 91; self-perceptions of, 54, 57, 69 (*see also* American Revolution, women's politicization); treatment under S.C. law, 79–81, 86–91; work, 131–35, 131n6 *See also* Identity; Master class, *individuals' names; Rentiers*

Women, slaves: during the American Revolution, 32–39; appearance, clothing, and public comment on, 14, 23, 24, 153, 198 (*see also* Market women); experiences with illness and death, 197–205, 275n27; family formation, 33, 37, 61, 78, 95–102, 138; forms and functions of leisure, 101, 157, 166–69, 216; as healers, 192, 199–200; as housekeepers, 113–14, 118; marriage, 78, 95–102, 213 (*see also* Sexual relationships); motherhood and childrearing, 96, 135–36, 137, 140, 153, 198, 216; relations with free people of color, 97, 99–100, 138, 171; relations with white people, 66, 70, 71, 135, 136, 138, 151–52, 168, 172 (*see also* Sexual exploitation; Sexual relationships, interracial); role in funerals, 168; skilled and unskilled work of, 24–25, 33, 36–37, 38, 39, 58, 65, 71, 98, 113, 119, 127–29, *128–29*, 130, 135–40, 143, 146, 147, 148, 149–50, 198–99, 200, 201, 203, 206 (*see also* Market women); treatment under S.C. law, 174–80; in the urban economy, 23, 25, 38, 62–64, 70, 71, 138–39, 156, 215, 233n27 (*see also* Market women). *See also* Identity; Laws; Manumission; Runaway slaves; Sexual behavior; Slave hiring; Slaves, punishments and restrictions on; Slaves, resistance of; Slaves, sale of

Women, white laboring: during the American Revolution, 40–47; competition with women of color, 25, 69, *128–29*, 142–44, 146–47, 148; different treatment under the law, 102, 107–109, 156; experiences with illness and death, 205–11; and the first reconstruction, 68–73; forms and functions of leisure, 157–58, 167, 171–73; indigent, 26, 44, 68, 72, 73, 123, 133, 205, 206–11 (*see also* Charity; Orphan House; Poor House; Prostitutes and prostitution); marriage, 102–10, 213; motherhood and childrearing, 141, 142, 154–55, 216; politicization and self-perceptions of, 69–71; protest and resistance of, 69, 70–71, 104–106, 154–55; relations with people of color, 26, 71, 103, 123, 141, 143; skilled and unskilled work of, 15, 26, 28, 42, 44, 45, 69–70, 71, 102, 104, 121, 127–29, *128–29*, 140–47, *145*, 154, 208–209; as skilled artisans, 142–43, 261n35; as slave owners and hirers, 70, 71, 121, 143, 144, 148–49 (*see also Rentiers*); treatment under S.C. law, 181–89, 214, 217; in the urban economy, 3, 69–71, 102, 215. *See also* Identity; Laboring free people; Laws; Prostitutes and prostitution; Sole traders

Work: characteristics of in Charleston, 127–31, 139–40; childrearing, 16, 216 (*see also* Women, *by social group*); of children, 96, 104; as defining class, race, and caste distinctions, 127, 203, 215–16 (*see also* Charity); manufacturing, 139–40; wages, 146, 149, 266n27; of women, 14–16, 57, 102, 127–56, 215 (*see also* Women, *by social group*). *See also* Charity; Free people of color; Slave hiring; Sole traders; Women, *by social group*

Working out. *See* Slave hiring

CYNTHIA M. KENNEDY earned her Ph.D. from the University of Maryland at College Park. She is currently Associate Professor of History at Clarion University of Pennsylvania, specializing in the history of slavery and U.S. women's history.